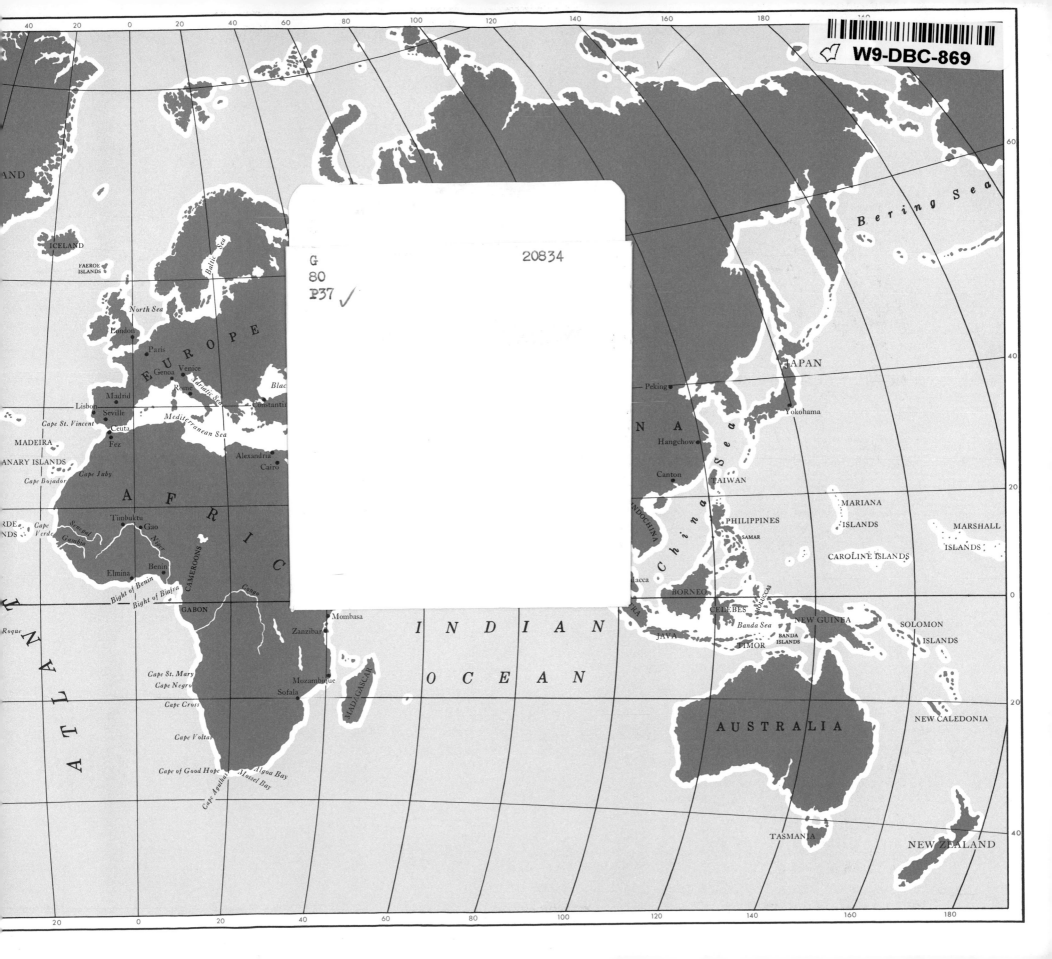

The
Discovery
of the
Sea

OTHER BOOKS BY J. H. PARRY

The Spanish Theory of Empire in the Sixteenth Century

The Audiencia of New Galicia in the Sixteenth Century

Europe and a Wider World, 1415–1715

The Sale of Public Office in the Spanish Indies

A Short History of the West Indies
(WITH P. M. SHERLOCK)

The Age of Reconnaissance

The Spanish Seaborne Empire

The European Reconnaissance
(SELECTED DOCUMENTS)

*Trade and Dominion: European Overseas Empires
in the Eighteenth Century*

J. H. PARRY

The Discovery of the Sea

THE DIAL PRESS
New York, 1974

Manufactured in the United States of America

First printing, 1974

*Library of Congress Cataloging in Publication Data
Parry, John Horace.
The discovery of the sea.
Bibliography: p.
1. Discoveries (in geography)—History. 2. Ocean
travel—History. I. Title.
G80.P37   910'.45   74–8966
ISBN 0–8037–2019–X*

Composition by The Haddon Craftsmen
Printed by Connecticut Printers, Inc.
Bound by Tapley-Rutter

Grateful acknowledgment is made to the following for permission to reproduce illustrations appearing herein (numbers correspond to the list of illustrations, page ix):

BARNES & NOBLE BOOKS (the photo "The stone cross . . . southwest Africa" in *Congo to Cape* by Eric Axelson, New York, 1973): 45

BAYERISCHE STAATSBIBLIOTHEK, MUNICH, GERMANY: 49

BIBLIOTECA ESTENSE, MODENA, ITALY: 67

BIBLIOTECA NAZIONALE MARCIANA, VENICE, ITALY (per concessione della Direzione, da esecuzione del suo fotografo incaricato *Ditta M. Toso*): 43

BIBLIOTECA NAZIONALE CENTRALE, FLORENCE, ITALY, ms. Port. I (particolare): 42

BIBLIOTHEQUE NATIONALE, PARIS, FRANCE: 77, 79

THE TRUSTEES OF THE BRITISH MUSEUM, LONDON, ENGLAND: 25, 26, 27, 28, 40, 44, 46, 71

COLLECTION MARCEL DESTOMBES, PARIS, FRANCE: 80

DOUBLEDAY & COMPANY, INC. (illustrations copyright © 1961 by Björn Landström from the book *The Ship*): 58, 59

HEYWARD ASSOCIATES (NEW YORK): 35, 37, 39

THE JAMES FORD BELL COLLECTION, UNIVERSITY OF MINNESOTA, MINNEAPOLIS, MINNESOTA: 29

THE JOHN CARTER BROWN LIBRARY, BROWN UNIVERSITY, PROVIDENCE, RHODE ISLAND: 30, 69, 70

NATIONAL MARITIME MUSEUM, LONDON, ENGLAND: 48

THE NEW YORK PUBLIC LIBRARY, Astor, Lenox and Tilden Foundations: 1, 6, 7, 13, 20, 31, 32, 33, 34, 36, 41, 50, 52, 53, 54, 55, 60, 61, 62, 63, 64, 65, 66, 73, 74, 75, 76, 82, 84

PANORAMA: 38

THE SCIENCE MUSEUM, LONDON, ENGLAND: Crown copyright: 2, 3, 4, 5, 8, 9, 11, 14, 15, 16, 17, 18, 19, 21, 22, 47, 57; Photo: 10, 23, 24, 51, 81, 83; Lent to Science Museum, London, by Sir Frederick Maye: 12

THE VATICAN, ROME, ITALY: 85

Contents

Illustrations

Introduction: One Sea

ll the seas of the world are one. With a few insignificant exceptions —salt lakes rather than seas—they arc all connected one with another. All seas, except in the areas of circumpolar ice, are navigable. A reliable ship, competently manned, adequately stored, and equipped with means of finding the way, can in time reach any country in the world which has a sea coast, and can return whence it came. These bare facts have become so familiar, so essential in the conduct of an interlocking world society, that they are usually taken for granted; yet their acceptance, in the long record of human experience, is comparatively recent.

Knowledge of continuous sea passages from ocean to ocean round the world—established knowledge, not geographical hypothesis—was the outcome of the century or so of European maritime questing which, in European history books, is generally described as the Great Age of Discovery. Until the last quarter of the fifteenth century most of these passages were unknown to Europeans, and some were absolutely unknown—unknown to anyone. The only major connecting passages known and regularly used by European shipping were the straits which join the Mediterranean and the Baltic with the North Atlantic, and the Black Sea with the Mediterranean. No ship had penetrated the Caribbean, the Mediterranean of the Americas. On the opposite side of the world, Chinese, Malay and probably Arab navigators were familiar with the long tortuous passages, threading between the islands, which connected the Bay of Bengal with the China Sea, and so, more remotely, the Indian Ocean with the Pacific; but none of them, so far as we know, had ventured far into the Pacific. That was a maritime world of its own; to Europeans, its very existence as a separate ocean was unknown, and so was the great continental barrier of the Americas which divides it from the Atlantic. Both European and Arab seafarers were well aware, of course, of the separation between the Atlantic and the Indian Oceans, and of the other great barrier of Africa, between them; but no one knew how far the barrier extended or whether it had an end. According to some respected authorities, the Indian Ocean was a landlocked sea. The South Atlantic was wholly unexplored; no seagoing ship, so far as surviving evidence reveals, had ever entered its waters, much less crossed it, or sailed from it to the Pacific or the Indian Ocean. In the late fifteenth and early sixteenth centuries all these feats were accomplished. In 1519–22 a ship actually sailed round the world. The Great Age of Discovery was essentially the age of the discovery of the sea.

The discovery of the sea, in the sense of the discovery of continuous sea passages from ocean to ocean, was a European, specifically an Iberian achievement. This is not to suggest, in Portugal, Spain or any part of fifteenth-century Europe, a deliberate, conscious program of maritime exploration for its own sake. Discovery as an end in itself, exploration in intellectual pursuit of geographical knowledge, or in romantic pursuit of unusual adventure, is characteristic of a safer,

richer, more comfortable society than that of fifteenth-century Europe. In such a society, the exploration of wild places may even be a form of social display. In Europe it enjoyed its greatest vogue in the nineteenth century, against a background of established prosperity, security and ennui. One cannot imagine fifteenth-century explorers searching for the North Pole. They were practical men, like the rulers and investors who sent them out, and their purposes were practical—principally, to establish contact with specific countries outside Europe, countries known to exist and believed to be of sophisticated culture and commercial importance, countries whose inhabitants could supply valuable merchandise, and whose rulers might be approached for political alliance and support. Exploration might reveal other prizes, of course —unexploited fisheries and fertile islands where fiefs and farms might be had for the seizing. Even islands, however, were best if they were inhabited, preferably by docile and industrious people. An empty wilderness had few attractions for fifteenth-century Europeans. For the most part, the explorers sought not new lands, but new routes to old lands. Initially, the process was slow and tentative. Throughout most of the fifteenth century it was confined to the eastern Atlantic. Only in the last quarter of the century did Iberian seamen and Iberian governments consider the practical possibility of sailing beyond the eastern Atlantic, and making other oceans their highway to India, the Spice Islands and Cathay.

The originality and the significance of the fifteenth-century voyages, then, consisted not so much in revealing the uninhabited and the unknown, as in linking, by usable maritime routes, separate areas of the inhabited and the known. Vasco da Gama's famous voyage is the classic example: his destination, Calicut on the Malabar coast of India, was known to Europeans by report; the shape of the Indian peninsula, and its geographical relation to Europe, Africa, and the Asian land mass, were also roughly known; and anyone familiar with Mediterranean trade knew that pepper, the product of India, was carried in Arab ships across the Arabian Sea. From the Cape Verde Islands to the southern tip of Africa, da Gama sailed through waters explored—insofar as they were explored at all— only recently and only by his compatriots; from Mossel Bay to Mozambique, quite unexplored. But in coasting north from Mozambique and in crossing the Indian Ocean, he was in an area of sophisticated maritime communication. He and his early successors relied on the skill and experience of Arab or Gujerati pilots, who were familiar with the navigation of those waters, and who were willing, for a consideration, to guide the strangers through them. East of India, sailing to Malacca and the Spice Islands, Portuguese captains could easily pick up Malay pilots to take them through the islands. The first European sailing directions for those waters, compiled in 1512 by Francisco Rodrigues, who sailed as navigator in the first Portuguese fleet to the Moluccas, were based on Javanese charts. As for the China coast, Portuguese traders working from Malacca in the early years seem to have found it most convenient either to take passage in Chinese ships or to entrust their goods to Chinese supercargoes; facilities for carriage both of passengers and of freight were plentiful and well established. These circumstances help to explain the amazing speed with which the

Portuguese extended the range of their activities in southern Asian waters. They followed well-worn paths.

The westward route to the Indies involved a much longer, much more dangerous voyage than the eastward route; but here too the same general pattern was repeated. When Magellan bore away from the African coast he left the regular routes of European seaborne trade. From Patagonia to the Marianas he was in unknown waters. His people may not have been the first to cross the Pacific, but they were probably the first for very many years, and certainly the first Europeans. Like many of his successors, Magellan was unlucky in that his route skirted the area frequented by those bold pelagic wanderers, the Polynesians. He had to plough for hungry, thirsty weeks through an empty sea. When he reached the Marianas, however, his ships were surrounded by seagoing canoes, skimming under their beautiful kite-shaped sails—"lateens," wrote his chronicler Pigafetta, with gratified if approximate recognition. The explorers had entered another network of regular maritime communication, in this instance an isolated and relatively limited network, but one within which the navigation from island to island was well understood. A week's sailing to the west, in the Philippines, they reached the edge of a much larger, much denser network. Del Cano, taking his dwindling fleet on through the great archipelago to Tidore, and then out into the Indian Ocean, could get reliable sailing directions, as the Portuguese had done when they entered the area from the opposite direction ten years earlier. Once again, the explorers were following tracks long familiar to the seafaring peoples of the region.

The discovery of the Americas seems, at first sight, a different story. We have been taught to think of Columbus as finding a new world, as exploring islands and mainland hitherto unknown. Yet Columbus's experience was not entirely different; the lands he discovered were certainly unknown to Europeans, but obviously not to their inhabitants. Columbus did not discover a new world; he established contact between two worlds, both inhabited, both in human terms already old. Sailing bravely out from the Canaries through waters never before navigated, he sighted land in the Bahamas—in the outlying islands of East Asia, as he thought—and anchored before the first island he came to. Promptly the "Indians," the naked Arawaks, came paddling in excited curiosity around his ships, offering such commodities as they had in barter for beads and trinkets. The Arawaks were simple children of nature, no doubt; but they possessed canoes, including some—according to Columbus—capable of carrying fifty people; they traded regularly over considerable distances, and they knew the way from island to island. Here, then, was yet another maritime network, however primitive and restricted. Sailing on south and west through the islands, the newcomers could get information, however vague and garbled, about what lay ahead. A generation later, Spanish adventurers were lured into the Gulf of Mexico and on to empire partly by the evidence of coastwise trade; by the presence along the Honduras coast and in the adjacent islands of articles too well made and too sophisticated to have been manufactured by their immediate owners. Later still Pizarro, sailing down the Pacific coast, looking for confirmation of hearsay reports of rich kingdoms in Peru,

found the evidence he wanted by the capture of an oceangoing raft, loaded with textiles and other manufactured goods of high quality, and equipped—exciting prospect—with "some tiny weights to weigh gold." Rafts are not ships; they are incommodious craft at best; but they can make long passages on occasion. This particular raft carried twenty men—the Spaniards detained three of them as guides—and was driven by well-cut cotton sails. It was the product of a society familiar at least with coastal navigation.

To say that most of the European explorers relied heavily, in parts at least of their voyages, upon local knowledge and skill, is in no way to belittle the magnitude of their achievements. In a hundred years or so of maritime reconnaissance European seamen linked together nearly all the major existing areas of seaborne communication. They did so not by chance discovery, by blundering and drifting where winds and currents took them, but by systematic navigation—crude navigation, certainly, but accurate enough to enable them to return on their tracks, and their successors to follow them in regular voyages; so that eventually the existing networks were embraced in a super-network, so to speak, of known ocean routes encircling the world. To do this they and their backers had to plan and execute continuous ocean voyages of a length never before dreamed of. They had to circumvent the great continental land masses which separate the Atlantic from the other oceans of the world. All, or nearly all, the existing areas of regular ocean travel lay in the northern hemisphere; the crucial outlets from the Atlantic lie far south of the equator. The explorers had to sail thousands of miles through an immense and frequently stormy ocean, touching only occasionally, if at all, on inhospitable, sparsely inhabited shores, which in themselves offered no attraction or reward, in search of passages whose very existence was matter of conjecture. The enterprise demanded, obviously, immense optimism, determination and courage. It called for an investment of men, money, ships and effort great in relation to the resources readily available, great indeed in view of the risk of total failure. Why were these hazardous enterprises undertaken by Europeans, upon European initiative? Western Europe in the fifteenth century was an area of busy maritime activity, but it was not, as we have seen, the only such area, not the busiest or the richest, certainly not the most extensive or the longest established. There were ancient civilizations whose people had been making long ocean voyages when western Europeans were still confined to inshore waters, and were still paddling about in hollow logs or skin-covered coracles. Some of these long-established seagoing traditions were still very much alive in the fifteenth century. Why, then, did Europe seek out Asia, not Asia Europe? Why had no Chinese, or Arab, or Indian, or even Polynesian or Peruvian, anticipated Columbus, Vasco da Gama and Magellan?

What were the motives which drove seamen out from fifteenth-century Europe upon a career of worldwide discovery? What were the sources of the geographical knowledge, or fantasy or rumor, which led them on? What means did they employ? Some of these questions, at first sight, are easily answered. The motives were the hope of commercial gain; to some extent, religious zeal, which in the conventional thought of the time both imposed a duty to proselytize and conferred a right to conquer; to some extent, the

fear of military threats and the hope of finding new allies; and, one must presume, curiosity. The means were stoutly constructed, well-designed ships; techniques of pilotage and navigation good enough to ensure a ship's safety when near an unfamiliar coast, and to give her company confidence, when out of sight of land, in their ability to find their way; a financial organization capable of assembling the capital for long-range enterprises; governmental encouragement; and firearms. The knowledge came from academic treatises on geography and cosmography, some recent, some inherited from the ancient Mediterranean world, some translated from Arabic; and from a profusion of travelers' tales, whether genuine or fanciful. Some of these factors, the technical factors especially, were new to western Europe in the fifteenth century; others were of long standing; but western Europeans had no monopoly of any of them, and the central questions remain. What occasion, what combination of circumstances brought them all together in the southwest corner of Europe in the fifteenth century, to achieve such dramatic success in so relatively short a time? What diverted the attention of a few enterprising rulers, investors and seamen from the old area of profit, the Mediterranean, to the unknown world of great oceans? Who provided the inspiration, the backing and the leadership? That the leadership, the skill and the equipment of European oceangoing enterprise were adequate for their purpose is evident; but were they really superior to those available elsewhere? and if not, what other less measurable factors can be found to account for European success in a world reconnaissance which others had failed to achieve, or never attempted?

I   *Preparation*

A Reliable Ship

he seagoing vessels of the world have all been developed from one or another of a small range of primitive, ancestral types. For our purpose—for the purpose of comparing western European shipping in the fifteenth century with the shipping of other parts of the world—only three of these basic types are significant. We can ignore local oddities such as pottery bowls, tub boats, inflated skins, and pontoons supported by them. Of the types which matter to us—the ancestors which produced important progeny—one was a tree trunk, hollowed out with fire and stone or shell adzes to give buoyancy and provide room for paddlers and their few possessions. Another was a raft, made by lashing together lengths of buoyant stems—bamboos, bundles of hollow reeds, banana stems, ambash boughs, or logs of light wood such as balsa wood. The third was a basket, or a basketlike frame of pliant boughs, lashed together, and covered with skins or other impermeable material, to keep out the water. From one or another of these primitive devices, or from a combination of them, almost all reliable ships and boats descend. Before the universal spread of steel and steam the ancestry of each of hundreds of local types of ship could be seen in the design and construction of its hull. It can still be seen today, in places where western industrial influence is small and where traditional local craft survive.

The geographical origins and subsequent spread of the basic types of craft followed an exceedingly complex pattern, many details of which can only be guessed; but presumably the main factors were the water conditions encountered and the nature of the available material. Rafts, if they are to be used on the sea or on large stretches of water, are appropriate only to warm climates; the crew of any raft, except in flat calm, must expect to be wet much of the time. Buoyant materials suitable for raft-making, moreover, come from quick-growing plants, most plentiful in the Tropics. Reeds are an obvious material. Lashed in bundles, they can be manipulated easily into a rough boatlike shape, with gunwales and upturned ends to keep out some of the water. Rafts and raft-canoes—even, on the lower Nile, seagoing raft-ships—were constructed in this way in very ancient times. The papyrus ships of the pharaohs, however, left no significant progeny. The papyrus-growing area has contracted over the centuries, and no boat-building reeds are now found near the sea. Reed craft are still in use in widely separated inland places, chiefly the upper Nile, Lake Tana, Lake Chad, and Lake Titicaca in Bolivia; but they are small, and their life is usually short. A raft of buoyant logs is necessarily a more substantial affair. The big seagoing log rafts which the *conquistadores* saw off the coast of Ecuador are extinct, though they were still common in the eighteenth century; but on the other side of South America a type of seagoing raft is still in general use. This is the *jangada* of northeast Brazil, a solid structure of (usually) six logs, not lashed, but pinned together by hardwood stakes hammered through. The logs are adzed to a curve, to give a sheer, and tapered towards the bow. There is a drop keel, a mast whose rake can be adjusted, and an elegant modified lateen sail. The word *jangada* is Kanarese, from the west coast of India; presumably Portuguese sailors who knew India were reminded of the clumsier log catamarans, also with lateen sails, which were (and are) used for fishing on the Konkan and Malabar coasts. Despite their name, *jangadas* are pure American. They are highly seaworthy, though uncomfortable, and often fish far out of sight of land.

The best raft-making material, however, is bamboo, and the best examples of raft design are to be found in regions where bamboos are plentiful, especially in China and in the islands off the Chinese coast. In the silted ports of Taiwan, where only shallow-draft vessels can operate, bamboo rafts ("tray-boats") are generally used for lighterage as well as for fishing. They run up to forty feet in length, tapered, with a noticeable upward curve towards the bow. The structure is braced by curved poles lashed at intervals athwart the main bamboos. Tray-boats have a remarkable turn of speed

A raft of ambash boughs from the Upper White Nile

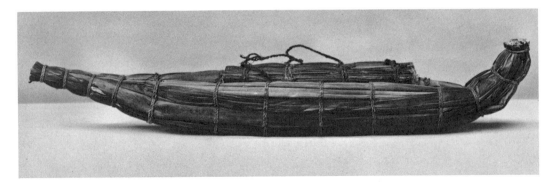

A reed raft from
Lake Tana

under sail; they are steered by a curved sculling
oar over the stern, and are fitted with three
movable drop keels to control leeway. They are
interesting, not only as ingenious and seaworthy
survivals of an ancient type, but also because they
provide clues to the character of native Chinese
shipping in general. The Chinese tradition of
ship construction is very ancient, and is almost
certainly a raft-based tradition. The humble
sampans, shallow, wedge shaped open skiffs,
which swarm in every Chinese harbor, betray
their raft ancestry to a casual glance. Larger
vessels, it is true, show more variety. The
Chinese, despite a general conservatism, have
usually been willing to adopt foreign designs and
devices, in shipping as in other fields, when it
suited their purposes. The celebrated *lorchas* of
the Canton Delta—now extinct—were efficient
and beautiful Sino-Portuguese hybrids. The
Hong Kong harbor sampan—found only in
Hong Kong, and by no means extinct—is a
modified European ship's boat. Many other
vessels, loosely described by Europeans as
"junks," came to incorporate, between the
sixteenth and nineteenth centuries, some
structural features imitated from foreign ships.
Some are built with a keel; in some the planking
rounds into a stem-post; and in some the rudder
is hung in gudgeons upon the stern-post in
European or Indian fashion. The traditional
"junk" types, however, including large seagoing
vessels, built and used in areas where European
influence did not penetrate, or was resisted, have
none of these features, and show, like sampans,
the traces of their long development from an
ancient raft ancestor. They are typically
flat-bottomed, without keel, stem-post or
stern-post. Planking, usually transverse, closes in

A *jangada* from
northeast Brazil

A bamboo raft from
Taiwan

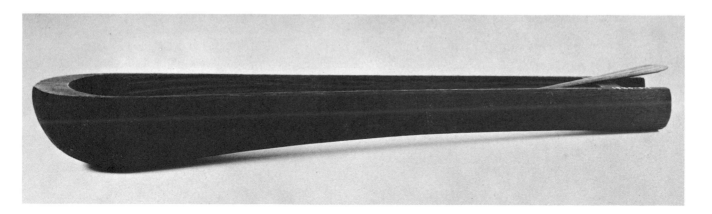

both ends, giving the vessel a transom head as well as a transom stern. These transoms represent, respectively, the first and last of a series of stout bulkheads, which give lateral strength and divide the hull into numerous watertight compartments. The rudder is suspended, and held in position by rope tackles, in a well or trunk left open in the overhanging counter. Most Chinese rudders, when in the normal sailing position, project several feet

below the bottom of the ship, and so serve not only to steer but also, like a drop keel, to check leeway. For the latter purpose, many types also use lee-boards. Generally speaking, seagoing junks are stoutly constructed, reliable and seaworthy vessels. Some are of considerable size, 150 feet or more in length. In earlier times, before the competition of clippers and steamers affected their livelihood, some undoubtedly were even larger.

A canton *lorcha*

Felling and hollowing out a tree trunk would be, for primitive people, much more difficult than lashing up a simple raft; so difficult that it probably would not have been undertaken unless some prototype model already existed. Probably the earliest rude dugouts were attempts to imitate, in solid wood, some flimsier and even more primitive craft, perhaps a semi-cylindrical roll of bark, bunched at the ends, or plugged with clay, to keep out the water. However that may be, dugouts of very ancient date have been found in many parts of the world; from such dugouts, hundreds of types of wooden craft have been developed; and still, alongside their sophisticated descendants, dugouts are fashioned and used in many areas, distinguished from their ancient predecessors only by refinements in their shape. Some, notably those made from the trunks of silk-cotton and other big trees, are large, seaworthy craft; but plain dugouts suffer from obvious defects when used at sea. They are usually heavy and rigid, without appreciable sheer, narrow and shallow in proportion to their length. For these reasons, they ship a good deal of water in anything of a sea. These drawbacks can be overcome in several ways. The hull can be flared by filling it with heated water to soften the wood and then forcing the sides outward by the insertion of wedged crossbars. The freeboard can be raised and a degree of sheer imparted, to keep out the water, by means of additional planks—wash-strakes—attached to the gunwales of the dugout by pegs or stitching. With all these improvements, however, they remain unstable craft, especially under sail.

Dugout canoes carried considerable volumes of trade in some parts of the world. The Caribbean was one such area. Another was the Niger Delta and the Bights of Benin and Biafra. The Delta peoples were—and still are—expert in making dugouts in a great variety of types and sizes, ranging from graceful skiffs used for fishing to big, heavy trading craft with thatched cabins in which whole families could make their permanent homes. These canoes were propelled by poles or paddles. Most of their navigation was by river or creek, or coastwise through the network of lagoons which runs from Dahomey to the Delta; but the biggest canoes could also make passages in the open sea. During the recent civil war in Nigeria there was a significant revival of the coastwise canoe trade; and Spanish brandy is still smuggled from Fernando Po to Victoria in the Cameroons, a distance of ninety miles in the open sea, in canoes propelled by paddles or by outboard motors.

For use under sail, dugouts need additional stability. This can be provided either by securing two canoes side by side with beams lashed between them, supporting a connecting platform, and so making a broad double-hulled craft; or, more commonly, by lashing on outriggers—floating logs, held parallel with the hull by means of booms. Double canoes reached their highest degree of sophistication among the Polynesians, before the advent of Europeans. Cook found them in general use in all the Polynesian groups, and commented on their large size. Their advantage lay in their carrying capacity; their disadvantage, in the racking strains to which they

A Samoan paddling outrigger canoe

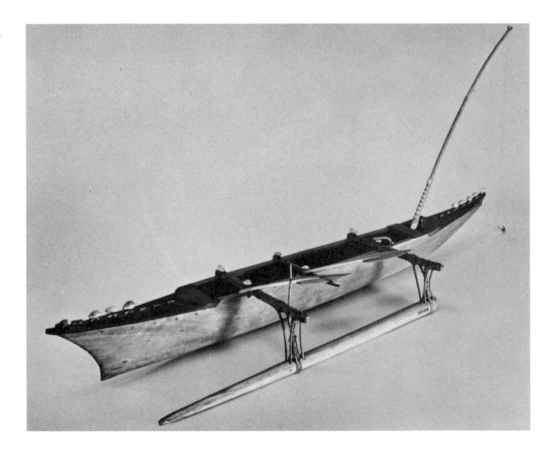

were subjected in a short sea, especially when sailing on a wind. Today, as seagoing craft, they are extinct. Outrigger canoes, on the other hand, hold their own today in many areas of the Pacific and Indian Oceans.

The idea of the outrigger is thought to have originated in southern Asia. It was adopted at a very early date throughout the Malay archipelago, and from there spread out—eastward through the Pacific islands, westward to Ceylon, Madagascar, and parts of East Africa. Outrigger craft are of two main types: double,

with a float on either side, or single, with only one float. Contrary to what a casual glance might suggest, the double-outrigger canoe—still the usual type in the Indonesian seas—is the more primitive and the less efficient. It is suitable only for relatively sheltered waters. Anything more than a slight degree of heel submerges the lee float and turns the canoe downwind. The single-outrigger canoe, presumably developed from the double, is more versatile, though it too has its limitations. In sailing with a single outrigger, the float must normally be kept on the

A Reliable Ship

A Foochow trading junk

A five-masted junk from Shantung

weather side; the canoe cannot easily go about or wear, and so in tacking must reverse its direction, end for end. It must therefore be double-ended. It cannot employ a stern rudder, and must be steered by means of a paddle. Its rig must be such that the sail and all its associated tackle can be shifted quickly and safely from one end to the other with every major alteration of course. This maneuver calls for nimble seamanship, and the necessity for it limits the size of the craft. Outrigger canoes rarely exceed thirty feet in length and three in beam. A canoe of that size needs a crew of at least four men, and its cargo capacity is very small. The most ingenious and most sophisticated outrigger canoes today are probably those built in the Caroline Islands of Micronesia, and in Ceylon. They are not particularly weatherly; the best of them can sail, close-hauled, perhaps 70 or 75 degrees off the wind, allowing for leeway. With the wind on the beam or astern they are fairly fast. When sailing fast, they are very wet, since the float and booms, striking the waves, send up sheets of spray; but in the warm waters where they are used, this is tolerable. Despite their awkward, untidy appearance, they are stout and reliable when properly maintained, seaworthy and maneuverable when skillfully handled; and they still make, for their size, remarkably long voyages.

The design of the single-outrigger canoe probably represents today a final point of development, a dead end reached many centuries ago. A far more fruitful development was the practice of building up the sides of a flared dugout hull with wash-strakes. The Indian Ocean seems to have been the area in which this process was first developed, in very ancient

times, and progressively extended, to produce a planked hull deep enough to keep the water out, even in a high sea, and broad enough to remain stable under sail without the use of outriggers (though outriggers were not entirely absent; in India some planked boats of considerable size, such as the fishing craft of the Palk Strait and the bandar boats of Karachi harbor, today employ both actual outriggers and, more commonly, vestigial outriggerlike devices known as balance-boards). When this point was reached, the hollowing of the underbody ceased to be necessary, and the dugout log was reduced to a solid axial keel. Stem- and stern-posts, butting on the keel or scarfed into it, were added to hold the planks together at the ends; and for lateral strength, U-shaped compound frames were inserted, and held in position by lashings passed through holes in the planking. Throughout the Indian Ocean, until comparatively modern times, the strakes seem to have been fastened to keel and end-posts, and edge to edge to one another, by stitches of coir twine. Many European travelers in the area—the compiler of the *Periplus of the Erythrean Sea* in the first century A.D., Marco Polo in the thirteenth, the companions of Vasco da Gama at the end of the fifteenth— commented on this peculiarity. It is curious that a relatively primitive method of fastening should persist so long, in an area where the use of iron for other purposes was widespread and well understood. Coir, of course, is much cheaper and more readily available than iron; and the flexibility of a sewn hull can be a positive advantage in some circumstances, particularly in surf. On the other hand, the working of the hull and the deterioration of the stitching must have posed troublesome problems of maintenance.

11

A Reliable Ship

OPPOSITE:
Native craft off the Malabar coast, from de Bry's *Voyages*

It is difficult to form any detailed picture of what sewn ships were like in their heyday. Over the past four centuries, Indian Ocean shipping has been greatly modified by the borrowing of European techniques of construction. Almost all seagoing wooden ships in the area today are built upon a pre-erected frame, with planking fastened to the ribs by pegs or iron spikes; and whereas before the sixteenth century all or most were probably double-ended (as some, notably the *boums* of the Persian Gulf, still are), many, including the commonest types—the *sambuq* of the Arabian coast, the Indian *kotia* and the East African *jahazi*—now have transom sterns. In the largest Persian Gulf ships, the *baghlas,* a few of which still sail out of Kuwait, the transom is carved and gilded in obvious imitation of a seventeenth- or eighteenth-century Indiaman. A few sewn craft of small size survive in out-of-the-way places in the Hadhramaut. The surfboats, known as *masula* boats, used for lightering cargo ashore in some of the smaller ports on the Coromandel coast, have sewn hulls without ribs or other internal strengthening. Until twenty or thirty years ago a fairly large type of sewn seagoing vessel, known as a *mtepe,* was still being built in the neighborhood of Lamu in Kenya, and employed in the humbler trades of the coast, mainly in carrying mangrove poles to Zanzibar. *Mitepe* could carry up to thirty tons of cargo. They were usually hauled out at the onset of the spring monsoon, and taken to pieces, to be reassembled with fresh stitching for the next sailing season. In spite of this attention, they leaked continually; and probably this characteristic, together with the high cost of their maintenance, caused their abandonment. Today they are remembered only by old men, though a few authentic models survive. The *mtepe* was the last seagoing representative—a degenerate, clumsy and relatively small representative—of an ancient and once vigorous tradition descending directly from the primitive dugout.

In all the older vessels we have been considering, in both the raft and the dugout traditions, the hull derived most of its strength from its sturdy wooden shell. In building such a vessel, the shell came first. Any internal bracing which might be needed was inserted later, after the shell was completed, or at least partially completed. In the basket tradition—a tradition which grew up in bare and treeless regions—a fundamentally different principle of construction was, and is, employed. The builder makes his frame first, and subsequently covers it with a watertight skin. The frame may be, literally, a basket, as in the basket-boats of Tongking, which are made of a stout lattice of split bamboo, caulked with coconut oil and cow dung; or in the circular *quffa* lighters, which still carry cargo on the Euphrates. These are enormous and very stout baskets, coated on the outside with tar. More commonly the basis is an open framework of gunwales, ribs and stringers, made of light lengths of wood, or wands, laths or withies, usually fastened together by lashings. This method of construction allowed great flexibility in design, and developed in a great variety of shapes, from simple round or oval coracles, still used on many inland waters for ferrying or fishing, to long sharp-ended boats which could be taken to sea. For covering, animal skins were used for many centuries and in widely separated parts of the world. In the Eskimo *umiak*—a flat-bottomed, deep-sided boat some thirty feet in length, capable of sailing, and still used for

TOP LEFT: An outrigger dugout from the west coast of Ceylon

TOP RIGHT: A *quffa* lighter

LEFT: An Aran Island *curragh*

An Arab *baghla* from Oman

Mtepe from Lamu

An Indian *pattimar*

inshore whaling in some parts of the Arctic—
sealskin is still the usual material. In the *curraghs*
of western Ireland—the most distinguished craft
in the tradition, and most celebrated in song and
epic—ox hides were used until fairly recent
times; and *curraghs* were classified by size,
according to the number of hides employed in
their construction. A one-hide *curragh* would be
about six feet in length, three or four in width.
The Irish sea sagas—the *Imramha*—make
mention of such tiny craft, but they also describe
much bigger vessels, of three, nine, twenty, even
forty hides. Allowance must be made, no doubt,
for bardic exaggeration; but Irish seafarers, both
monks and marauders, certainly made long sea
passages in hide *curraghs* in the fifth, sixth and
seventh centuries. From the eighth century,
under Norse influence, wooden planked boats
came to be more generally adopted; but *curraghs*
continued in use, and continue still, for fishing
and coastal travel. Today, tarred canvas has
replaced ox hide. Most surviving *curraghs* are
small, though the best and biggest, those of the
Kerry coast, can carry six men comfortably. They
are strong, light and very seaworthy. In the best
types, the frame is a masterpiece of complex
symmetry and balance. They are usually rowed,
but can step a mast and set a small lug sail on
occasion.

The major voyages of oceanic discovery were
all made under sail. It is possible for vessels to
make ocean passages under oars; galleys have
crossed the Atlantic, and recently an open
rowing boat has done so; but in general, oared
vessels are obviously unsuitable for such work,
not only because of the physical labor involved,
but also because of the large crew needed to row
a vessel of any size, and the quantity of stores

needed to feed them. The Norse wanderers—
great oarsmen when engaged in coastal forays—
used sailing ships for their north Atlantic
crossings. Long voyages of discovery could be
made with good hope of profitable success only
when seamen were willing to trust their sails and
(except perhaps for emergency sweeps) to leave
their oars behind. Ships for the purpose must be
not only suitably constructed but suitably rigged.
They must be able, in particular, to make some
headway against contrary winds. The story of the
development of sailing rigs, like that of hull
design, is marked by conservatism, by the long
persistence of local types in their regions of
origin, modified in the main areas of seaborne
traffic by slow but extensive borrowings and
combinations. It is equally complex and even
more difficult to trace. Underwater archaeology,
which has added greatly in recent years to
knowledge of ancient hull construction, is of
little help in the history of sail; that can be
followed only from pictures and descriptions, and
from study of surviving types.

The most obvious and probably most primitive
pattern of sail is a simple square or rectangle, its
upper edge laced to a horizontal yard, the yard
suspended at its point of balance from an upright
mast and, when at rest, at right angles to the
fore-and-aft line of the ship. The sail is controlled
by ropes attached to the lower corners, the one
serving as sheet, the other as tack, according to
the wind. Rudimentary sails of this kind can still
be seen propelling primitive craft in many parts
of the world, from Lake Titicaca to Bengal and
from Burma to the Marquesas. In its simple,
basic form the square sail is efficient only when
running and is almost useless with the wind
before the beam. Many methods have been

devised, over a thousand years or more, for improving its performance is this respect, giving the sail a flatter set, holding its weather leech stiffer against the wind, controlling the set of the yard by means of vangs or braces; but with all these refinements, the basic disadvantage of the square sail, when used alone, remains. On the other hand, there is a basic advantage: a whole tier of square sails can be carried, one above the other, on the same mast. Square rig therefore allows a maximum total area of canvas, without making any one sail unmanageably large, and without extending the number of masts, and so the length of the ship, to a point of dangerous weakness. It is this characteristic which has made square rig the favored rig for nearly all the biggest sailing ships, over the last three or four centuries; but this became possible only when square sails, the main driving force, were supplemented by other types of sail.

There are two other main types of sail in which the head is laced to a yard. In the balance lug, for many centuries the characteristic sail of China, the yard when at rest is parallel to the fore-and-aft line. The sail is hoisted from a point about one-third along the yard, so that from one-sixth to one-third of its area is before the mast. In most seagoing junks the sail is peaked. It is laced to a boom along the foot, and is stiffened by a series of bamboo battens, each of which connects with the sheet. These battens give the sails an extremely flat set, and so a very good performance on a wind; they provide maximum efficiency when running goose-winged; and they enable the sails, which are often very large, to be reefed quickly, or to be doused promptly in emergency—a valuable characteristic in a stormy area such as the China seas. The

Chinese balance lug is a difficult sail to manage; its rigging is complicated, and great skill and experience are needed to get the best results from it. Skilfully handled, it is one of the most efficient of all sails. Its disadvantage is that only one such sail can be set on each mast. Some of the biggest seagoing junks, those of Shantung in particular, step—or rather stepped until recent years, for the type is probably now extinct—as many as five masts.

In the lateen sail—so called by northern European mariners because they associated it with the Mediterranean—the head is also bent on a yard; but the yard is hoisted obliquely to the mast, and its heel is held down forward by a short tackline or tackle. The mast itself is short, usually with a pronounced forward rake. The cut of the sail varies considerably. In the Mediterranean it is triangular, with a high peak and a loose foot. In the eastern Indian Ocean and the western Pacific it is again usually triangular, but less peaked, and the foot is laced to a boom, which often has a pronounced upward curve at its forward end. In an extreme form this type of triangular lateen becomes the beautiful and versatile "kite" sail used in many outrigger canoes. In the western Indian Ocean the sail is four-sided, but its luff is so short that when the tack is strongly set up it appears triangular from a little distance. This "settee" sail is the only type ever seen in Arab ships. It probably represents the oldest form of lateen, the form from which the triangular types evolved; it may itself have developed from a square sail, through some intermediate form of dipping lug. In the area where it now survives, it is probably of great antiquity, though there is no firm evidence of this, and it may be significant that

the extinct *mtepe* of Lamu had square sails, not lateen. The whole question of lateen origins and dispersals is a matter of controversy. Lateen sails were certainly known in the eastern Mediterranean by the ninth century A.D. They may have been known considerably earlier, in imperial Roman times. They may have entered the Mediterranean from the Indian Ocean: they certainly spread westward in the wake of the Arab invasions, and by the eleventh century had almost entirely replaced the earlier square sails throughout the Mediterranean basin, and on the Atlantic coasts of Andalusia and Portugal as far north as the Tagus.

In all forms of lateen the salient characteristic is the length of the main yard, often considerably more than the overall length of the ship. This formidable spar is usually made up of several lengths fished together, and sags in a graceful curve with the weight of the sail. Its tip, though controlled by vangs, will bend and whip alarmingly in anything of a wind. With the long, taut leading edge which the yard provides, the sail has some of the qualities of a modern fore-and-aft sail. Arab ships, with lateen rig, and with their characteristic fine entry and deep keel, can do well close-hauled; as well, perhaps, as 60 or 65 degrees off the wind—nothing like the 45 degrees which a modern designer aims at (but does not always achieve), but still a respectable performance, very much better than that of vessels under square rig alone. They are at their best when reaching with a stiff breeze on the beam, and in these conditions may show a remarkable turn of speed. The rig is somewhat less satisfactory when running. The huge mainsail, carried well forward, tends to bury the bows; the vessel will yaw unpredictably with a following sea or with slight changes of wind; and with such a rig an unexpected jibe can be very dangerous.

A lateen-rigged ship cannot go about without serious loss of efficiency and—since the masts are not stayed forward—some risk. This, though a troublesome limitation when tacking in confined waters, matters less when at sea. In the Indian Ocean, indeed, where sailing seasons are determined by regular and predictable monsoons, major alterations of course are seldom necessary. When the occasion does arise, the ship will almost always wear. The sail is brailed up, the tack-tackle and shrouds are slacked off, and the heel of the yard is drawn in to the foot of the mast; the sheet is carried round forward outside everything, the yard is hauled over as the stern swings across the wind, and shrouds and tack-tackle are set up on the new weather side; the sail is then sheeted home on the new tack. The sail cannot be reefed; instead, lateen vessels often carry two or three suits of sails, which can be bent on for different weather conditions. Sails cannot easily be furled aloft; the yards are lowered on entering harbor and hoisted again on leaving. Hoisting a main yard is a laborious operation, requiring the combined efforts of a crew which is always large in relation to the size of the ship. The size of the ship is itself necessarily limited by the nature of the rig. Lateen vessels rarely step more than two masts— in the Indian Ocean never, though in the Mediterranean three-masted lateeners were formerly not uncommon. Only one sail can be carried on each mast, and there is a limit to the size of yard which can be handled. If a lateen-rigged ship exceeds a relatively modest size, therefore, it is bound to be under-canvassed

OPPOSITE:
A Chinese junk, from
de Bry's *Voyages*

and slow. About three hundred tons is probably the effective limit; though this, of course, in the fifteenth century would have been considered a big ship under any rig.

Fore-and-aft sails of the modern type, bent on the stays, or upon a mast, with or without a gaff, do not enter our story; they did not make their appearance in seagoing ships until after the first wave of European oceanic discovery was spent. There is one relatively primitive type of fore-and-aft sail of considerable antiquity, however, which should be noticed briefly. This is the sprit sail, a simple four-sided sail bent on an upright mast, loose-headed and loose-footed, extended by a sprit—a long spar, running diagonally across the sail from tack to peak, and controlled by vangs. In northern Europe this sail has been widely used in estuarine barges since the sixteenth century. There is some evidence that it was known in the Mediterranean in Roman times; and it occurs, apparently independently, in various parts of the East. It is used—and probably has been used for centuries —in light craft, *dinghis* and the like, on some of the Indian rivers. It is particularly well suited for use with a single outrigger, because of the simplicity of its rigging and the ease with which it can be shifted end for end when altering course. The very seaworthy fishing canoes of western Ceylon always set this kind of sail.

Knowledge of the development of all these diverse traditions of hull construction and rig is full of gaps, and much of its detail is conjectural; but it is good enough to provide a rough general picture of what the nautical equipment of the major maritime societies was like in the early fifteenth century. We can ask the questions: which of these societies were adequately equipped for long ocean crossings—not random driftings and wanderings, but reliable, predictable passages, out and back? which of them, given sufficient motive and appropriate occasion, could have found and used the passages between the major oceans, and so achieved the "discovery of the sea," in the sense in which the phrase is used here? We can exclude from consideration peoples who used only rafts, skin boats, simple dugouts or outrigger canoes not because such craft are incapable of long voyages in the open sea— vessels of all four types are known to have made, on occasion, voyages lasting many weeks—but because their crews could not be expected to make such voyages deliberately and regularly. Success—survival even—in relatively small open vessels would be likely only in relatively favorable conditions, which could not be relied on; conditions favorable for the outward passage might be highly unfavorable for return; and the vessels could not have carried enough stores for the immensely long voyages which the fifteenth-century discoverers undertook. Nor, of course, could they carry enough merchandise to make the repetition of such voyages commercially profitable.

We can exclude, also, peoples who used larger and more developed ships, but used them in comparatively sheltered waters. The peoples of the Malay archipelago were, and are, bold seamen, and in some places, particularly on the north coast of Java, there was an ancient shipbuilding industry producing vessels of exceptionally solid, heavy construction. Ninth-century Javanese relief sculptures show big two-masted sailing ships with massive outriggers. Ships of this type were able to make open-sea voyages across the Indian Ocean to Madagascar and east Africa, where vestigial traces of their influence can still be seen in the design of local canoes. The Portuguese conquerors of Malacca in the early sixteenth century were much impressed by the skill of Javanese boatbuilders and by the solid durability of their products; but by that time the western voyages had long ceased, and Javanese shipping was confined to the waters of the archipelago itself.

Reluctantly, we must probably rule out the Polynesians. Polynesian peoples inhabit groups of islands scattered in a vast expanse of sea, from Tonga to Easter Island and from New Zealand to Hawaii. Some of these island groups are more than a thousand miles from the nearest other inhabited land, and their settlement must necessarily have involved very long ocean voyages. The voyages were probably made in double canoes, which were relatively commodious vessels, capable of carrying considerable numbers of people, men and women, and substantial quantities of stores, including live animals. Even so, the imagination falters at the thought of undertaking deliberately a voyage through such an immensity of water, in such craft. The vulnerability and awkwardness of double canoes, when endeavoring to work to windward in a rough sea, has been noted. It is possible—probable, indeed—that the very long passages were not deliberate; that the migrants were aiming at nearer islands, and were carried much farther than they intended, to places of which they had no knowledge, by winds they could not beat against. Once they made land— any habitable land—they settled and did not, perhaps could not, return. This is not to belittle the seamanship, the endurance and the courage of the Pacific Argonauts—far from it—but there

is, in fact, no evidence that the great voyages were regularly repeated or that any return passages were made; a process of one-way migration (if that is indeed what happened) is a long way from the "discovery of the sea."

There were three great maritime regions in the early fifteenth century in which reliable ships, capable of carrying large bodies of men or quantities of goods regularly over long ocean passages, were in general use. They were: European waters, comprising the Mediterranean, and the Atlantic coastal seas, roughly from Gibraltar to Bergen; the northern Indian Ocean,

A Polynesian double sailing canoe

including the Bay of Bengal, the Arabian Sea, the Red Sea and the Persian Gulf; and the China Seas. There were channels of regular contact between the regions; men and merchandise could cross the Isthmus of Suez or travel from the Euphrates to the Levant; and ships could sail through the Malacca Strait. The commercial activities of the three regions overlapped, though their nautical traditions, as we have seen, were separate and distinct.

Probably the most reliable ships in the world, and probably also the biggest, were Chinese; and from Sung times onwards Chinese merchants made voyages far beyond their own familiar waters. Ibn Battuta, who visited both India and China in the fourteenth century, wrote that in his day the whole trade between Malabar and south China was in Chinese ships. About the time when the Portuguese were beginning their tentative exploration of the Mauretanian coast, Chinese maritime contacts were greatly—though temporarily—widened by a series of seven expeditions organized (and most of them commanded) by the Grand Eunuch Cheng Ho, between 1405 and 1433. These were made by formidable fleets; according to the accounts of officers who served in them, the first comprised sixty-three ships and "tens of thousands" of men. They were intended not primarily for exploration or trade (though they achieved both) but, in the modern phrase, to "show the flag": to extend the influence and prestige of the Yung Lo Emperor, to confer protection and gifts upon foreign rulers and to receive their homage and their tribute. They covered the whole of the northern Indian Ocean, including the entrances to the Persian Gulf and the Red Sea, and the Somali coast as far south as Malindi. For the seventh voyage we

have actual dates; on the return passage the fleet sailed from Ormuz to Calicut, about 1,600 miles, in twenty-two days. Sixty-five years later Vasco da Gama covered the 2,300 miles from Malindi to Calicut in twenty-three days; but he had the southwest monsoon behind him. After 1433 the practice of sending Chinese fleets into the Indian Ocean was abandoned, ostensibly because of their cost in men, money and ships, and because of the threat to morals and public order posed by too free an intercourse with foreigners. Another reason, no doubt, was obsessive mandarin dislike of the palace eunuchs and all their works. Ming China retreated within its own boundaries, and foreign trade was sharply discouraged, though Chinese ships continued to trade as far as Malacca, and were still doing so when the Portuguese arrived there. Whatever the vicissitudes of imperial policy, Chinese maritime resources were clearly adequate for long voyages on a very impressive scale. Chinese seamen, if they had seen any reason, or been encouraged, to do so, could certainly have circumnavigated Africa. In 1848 a Chinese ship, the *Keying*, actually sailed from Shanghai to New York and thence to London. She was owned by a party of British naval officers, who navigated her by modern methods; but she was a traditional Fukien junk, manned by a Chinese crew under a Chinese master, and despite extremely bad weather she behaved well throughout the voyage. If the fifteenth-century Chinese failed to "discover the sea," it was not for lack of adequate ships or capable sailors.

The Chinese maritime retreat in the fifteenth century left the long-haul trade across the Indian Ocean chiefly in the hands of Arabs, or of Muslims from the northwest coast of India. Arab ships regularly sailed from Ormuz or Aden to the Malabar ports, often on to Malacca, and sometimes farther east. Arab contacts with China were of long standing. Arab seamen were familiar with long ocean crossings, and they had reliable ships. It is interesting that the Arabs who came into contact with Vasco da Gama's people were unimpressed by European ships; they admired their stout construction, but thought them unhandy and slow. Their own ships were presumably superior in these latter respects, though how they would have fared, had they been moved to undertake distant voyages of discovery, can only be guessed. If—as seems likely—Arab hulls at that time were fastened by coir stitching, this would have posed maintenance problems on very long voyages, especially in regions where there were no coconuts. But there are substitutes for coir, and probably a sewn ship whose stitching has rotted or worked loose is easier to repair, when far from dockyards, than an iron-fastened ship whose fastenings have become corroded. All in all, probably the Arabs must be ranged with the Chinese among the maritime peoples who, in the fifteenth century, could have circumnavigated Africa and perhaps crossed the Pacific, if they had tried to.

In fact, neither Arabs nor Chinese "discovered the sea"; Europeans did, and we must now ask whether their success was due to superior equipment; if not, then to what was it due? What were European ships like in the early fifteenth century? This is a difficult question to answer, not so much because evidence is scanty—on the contrary, it is relatively abundant—but because of the great variety of types. In each of the major maritime areas we have been considering, a variety of craft developed to meet a variety of

circumstances, within a common tradition; but in late medieval Europe the diversity was so striking as to suggest separate and independent origins. The carvel-built hull of the Mediterranean may well have derived from a remote raft ancestor, conceivably either the papyrus raft of ancient Egypt or a log catamaran of the kind which still survives in India. Many of its features suggest a raft tradition: the thick wales running from end to end parallel with the planking; the continuous curvature of keel, stem-post and stern-post, shown in many late medieval pictures; the long persistence of quarter rudders, reminiscent of primitive steering oars, well after the date when stern-post rudders had become general in the north. In cold, windy northern Europe, on the other hand, a seagoing raft tradition was not to be expected. There was a skin-boat tradition which, as we have seen, had produced some highly successful seagoing craft; but these in the later Middle Ages were confined to the outer Celtic lands, to Ireland and the wild coasts of northwestern Spain, and were relatively small. The central tradition of northern European shipbuilding was most probably a dugout tradition, developed in a region of wide forests where trunks of great size were once abundant. It had produced, by the late fourteenth century, a basic wooden ship, with many local variations, but with essential common features: long, straight keel; straight stem-post, the angle with the keel filled in with deadwood; straight stern-post, on which the rudder hung in gudgeons; and clinker planking.

Clinker-built hulls are characteristic of northern Europe, and in seagoing vessels are found nowhere else. Today clinker construction is used chiefly in small craft intended for fishing or pleasure cruising, and in ships' boats; but in the later Middle Ages all northern European ships were built in this way. Like the ships of the western Indian Ocean, they depended for their strength on their shell of planking, built up on a massive keel and joined to posts at either end, the planks being adzed to shape or bent by the application of heat to enable them to be rounded in at stem and stern. The planks, however, instead of being fastened edge to edge, were overlapped. They may, at some remote time, have been stitched together, but this method was abandoned very early, and in the Middle Ages they were usually fastened by oak trunnels or by iron nails driven through the double thickness and clenched on the inside. Internal bracing was inserted after the completion of the shell, or at a late stage in its construction. In Norse ships, down to the tenth century at least, ribs and thwarts were lashed to raised lugs or comb cleats left standing by the adze on the inner surfaces of the planks; but this practice seems to have been confined to Scandinavia, and even there disappeared in the later Middle Ages, as efficient two-handed saws replaced adzes for cutting planks. The saw is much more economical than the adze for this purpose, for while an adze can dub out only one plank from each half of a split trunk, a saw can cut several; but a saw cannot leave raised lugs, and in vessels built of sawn planks other methods had to be devised for fastening the internal bracing. In a well-preserved late fourteenth-century *kogge* recently raised from the mud of Bremen harbor, the hull appears to have been planked up, without internal strengthening, to deck level. At that point, six heavy beams were laid athwartships, resting on the strakes, with slots cut near the ends of each

beam to fit over the edge of the planking. When the next strakes were riveted on, they were similarly fitted around the beams, which were thus locked in position, with their ends projecting through the sides of the ship. Further strength was provided by the addition of knees, bolted to beams and upper strakes, and by light ribs nailed to the planking at intervals between the beams.

A clinker-built vessel, even when strengthened in this way, could not safely exceed a relatively modest size. Henry V's "Great Ship" was a conspicuous example of over-reaching in clinker build; she came to an early and ignominious end, and lies in fragments in the mud of the Hamble. The Bremen *kogge* was about seventy-five feet overall, fifty feet on the keel, twenty-five in beam. She had a continuous main deck, a raised fo'c'sle and quarter deck, and a somewhat flimsy poop which may have been open at the sides, or only lightly planked in. She might have carried, perhaps, 120 to 130 tons of cargo. She was a good example, probably bigger than average, of the vessels with which the merchants of the German Hanse had come to dominate most of the trades of northern Europe by the end of the fourteenth century, and were beginning even to peddle North Sea fish and Baltic grain in the Mediterranean. They were not in general big ships, but capacious cargo carriers for their size, simple in design, seaworthy, cheap to build. Their clinker planking kept them reasonably watertight without constant attention to caulking, and gave them a degree of flexibility. Their broad bows and pronounced sheer—this last a characteristic feature of all northern types—made them buoyant and resilient in rough water; they were designed to ride over the seas rather than to knife through them. They stepped only one mast with a single square sail, so that their performance on a wind was poor, and even when running they were comparatively slow sailers. In ships designed for carrying bulky cargoes of only moderate value—grain, salt, salted fish, wine and woolen textiles—these defects could be accepted. Against them, the cogs had an important economic advantage: because of the simplicity of their rig, they could be handled by relatively small crews, and so their running costs were low.

Mediterranean seamen in the later Middle Ages were heirs to a maritime tradition older, more varied and in many respects more sophisticated than that of northern Europe. Their ships were more specialized, both between fighting and trade and between different kinds of trade. We need not here consider galleys, either the *galee sottile* which did most of the fighting, or the hybrid "great galleys" which carried much of the most lucrative trade—the import of oriental luxury goods from the Levant and their export to centers in Flanders and in England. These vessels, beautiful though they were, and efficient for their special purposes, were to play no significant part in oceanic discovery. Many Mediterranean ships were propelled by sails alone, including some much bigger and more stoutly constructed than any in northern Europe. They were invariably carvel built, that is with the planks set flush, edge to edge, to form a smooth outer surface. Carvel build differs from clinker not only in this respect, but in another, more fundamental one: in all modern carvel construction the builder—like the maker of skin boats—begins with his framework and adds his skin later. He sets up and bolts together a permanent skeleton of keel, end-posts, frames

and timbers; only when this is complete does he begin work on the planking, pegging or nailing each plank directly onto the frames. The planks are not, as a rule, joined one to another in any way, except by caulking in the seams. This method of construction was not always and everywhere associated with flush planking; it was not, as we have seen, in the sewn hulls of the Indian Ocean; and probably it was not, in earlier

A Mediterranean ship, early fourteenth century, with quarter rudders

times, in the Mediterranean. There is some literary evidence that there too, in remote times, the planking of boats may have been edge-joined by stitching. It is known, from a number of surviving wrecks, that in Imperial Roman times a very elaborate form of edge-joining was in general use. The planks were fastened one to another by mortice-and-tenon joints at frequent intervals along their edges, usually with a spike or dowel driven obliquely through each joint for further strength. This made a very strong and rigid plank shell; and most probably, in hulls of this type, as in northern clinker hulls, any internal strengthening which might be needed would be inserted later. Morticed planking probably did not long survive the Roman Empire, but other, less thorough methods of edge-joining may have lasted much longer, and have disappeared only when the pre-constructed frame became general. When and how this fundamental change in hull construction took place, we have no means of knowing; it is one of the major mysteries of maritime history. Some pictures of fourteenth-century Mediterranean ships show deck beams projecting through the planking, like those of the Bremen *kogge,* and this may indicate the vestigial survival, even at so late a date, of some transitional method of construction. but in the western Mediterranean at the beginning of the fifteenth century pre-constructed frames seem to have been the general rule.

Carvel building on a pre-constructed frame was a more sophisticated operation than clinker building, because the builder had to know the

Von Breydenbach's ships, 1486. A two-masted lateen-rigged ship

precise lines of his ship before he started work. The ship had to be designed, rather than built up step by step by eye. The element of calculation, and so of predictability, was increased; the element of chance reduced. Heavier planking could be used, and shorter sections of plank—an important consideration in an area where big trees were scarce. Carvel ships could safely be built bigger than clinker ships.

In the fourteenth century, also, Mediterranean shipwrights adopted the median rudder hung on the stern-post, already widespread in the north. At first the rudder, in some ships at least, was narrow and curved like a scimitar, to fit the curve of the post, but by the early fifteenth century stern-posts had been straightened and rudders enlarged. The stern-post rudder had decisive mechanical advantages over the older quarter rudder and the even older steering oar. Mounted in the center-line of the ship, it had much greater turning power; its weight, carried in gudgeons on the post, made less demand on the strength of the helmsman; its pintles provided a more efficient fulcrum; its tiller, projecting well inboard, permitted a more economical application of effort, so that the helmsman could hold the ship steady when sailing on a wind. Carvel construction, in short, enabled European shipwrights to build much bigger ships without sacrifice of strength or safety; median rudders enabled seamen to manage them in winds which would have kept their ancestors in harbor.

The Venetian merchant fleet alone included in the early fifteenth century, in addition to galleys,

Von Breydenbach's ships, 1486. A pilgrim galley

about three hundred ships capable of carrying over a hundred tons of cargo. Thirty or thirty-five of them were between 240 and 400 tons. Some Genoese ships were even bigger, and sizes tended to increase. There were no merchant fleets like this in northern waters, nor anywhere else, probably, except in Ming China. These were the great merchantmen of the Europe of their day. Big ships had their drawbacks, of course. Their heavy, rigid construction probably made them sluggish sailers, and wet in rough weather. They were expensive to build, and expensive to maintain, since their caulking needed frequent attention. As sailing ships went, they were expensive to man; they usually had three masts, and needed large crews to handle the huge lateen sails. On the other hand, they were much cheaper to run than galleys, and though slower, were almost as reliable.

Marine monsters were for predictable trade on known and regular routes, and could not be risked in uncertain ventures; but marine monsters represented only a small proportion of Mediterranean shipping. A great number and variety of smaller vessels carried the coastal trades of the area, many remarkable for their handling qualities and their speed. Most, probably all, were carvel-built like the great ships, and like them lateen rigged. Down to the late fourteenth century the two great traditions of European shipping—the clinker-built, square-rigged, and the carvel-built, lateen-rigged —remained distinct, like oil and water. Late in the fourteenth century, in the course of commercial contact, they began to interact. In the fifteenth century they were to produce efficient and fertile hybrid combinations. This was the significance, in the story of the discovery of the

sea, of the existence in Europe of two such different traditions: it provided opportunity for mutual borrowing. The seamen in both traditions had a long record of ocean voyaging. There can be no doubt that Venetian seamen could have circumnavigated Africa if they had wanted to. (Obviously they had the strongest possible vested interest in not doing so.) Hanseatic seamen could have crossed the Atlantic, if they had wanted to; their Norse predecessors, using smaller, more primitive, but otherwise not dissimilar ships had settled in Greenland and landed in North America, and they themselves sailed cheerfully to Iceland when they thought it worthwhile, which was not often. Neither group had any strong motive for oceanic discovery; and though their shipping would have been adequate for the purpose, they made no effort to develop it in that specific direction. The people who did were Andalusians and Portuguese—people whose participation in the maritime development of Europe had been, up to that time, relatively minor. The expeditions which sailed on voyages of discovery in the fifteenth century sailed not from the Adriatic or the North Sea, but from small ports on the street corner of Europe: that rocky stretch of coast between Mediterranean and Atlantic, from Gibraltar around Cape St. Vincent to the Tagus. The ships were hybrids, incorporating features of each of the great traditions.

Most of the major voyages of discovery in the fifteenth century—nearly all, until the last decade —were made in vessels described as caravels, ships of small or moderate size, used in many parts of southern Europe for coasting trade or offshore fishing. The caravel was not a precisely defined type, in the sense that the brig or the schooner later came to be, and no doubt varied considerably from place to place. The caravels of the "street corner," however, were built with a combination of qualities which came to be widely admired, and which proved to be singularly well adapted to the needs of exploration. To what extent these qualities developed as a response to the challenge of ocean voyages, and to what extent they were present already at the beginning of the century, we cannot be sure, because most of the surviving drawings and descriptions date from Vasco da Gama's time and later. We do not know, in any detail, what early fifteenth-century caravels looked like; but it is possible to put together, from scattered references in accounts of voyages, odd sketches on maps, and the like, a rough and somewhat conjectural description. The vessels were fully decked. They had little or no raised superstructure forward, but a modest poop containing the cabin accommodation and the steerage. They were carvel built, in Mediterranean fashion, but had some features of hull design usually associated with northern ships: a pronounced sheer, a tall stem and a straight keel. The merits of the first in Atlantic conditions are obvious; as for the third, the traditional curved keel of the Mediterranean had a practical use in that tideless sea, because a vessel grounded by accident could often be refloated by shifting weight forward or aft; but on the Atlantic coasts it was more convenient to have a ship which could take the ground comfortably at low water. The hull seems to have had a somewhat finer entry than was usual at the time, even in the Mediterranean. Its stern, like its bow, was rounded in to a single post; the transom stern did not appear before the end of the fifteenth century. It always had a stern-post

rudder. It is unlikely—to judge from the anchorages they are known to have used—that caravels employed in discoveries drew more than six feet, and probably they did not often exceed sixty feet in overall length, though none of their actual dimensions is known. Caravels were usually lateen rigged, invariably so in the first half of the century; in the second half, under northern influence, square sails might be added, or a kind of convertible rig adopted. There were usually two masts, sometimes three. The crew was probably never more than twenty-five (the complement of Columbus's *Niña*) nor less than a dozen or so; and even at the lower figure, living conditions would be very cramped. There was no accommodation, except for the poop cabin, and probably a few bunks in the steerage. The tiny space under the fo'c'sle deck would be crowded with cables and gear. Most of the crew would have to sleep on deck; or else, in bad weather, in the hold on top of the cargo or the ballast. There can have been no facilities for cooking other than an open sandbox, usable only in good weather. Yet Iberian caravels seem to have inspired confidence, even, in some individual instances, affection. Columbus's preference for the caravel *Niña* over his larger flagship *Santa María* is well known. The experienced and much-traveled Venetian C'a da Mosto, in the middle of the fifteenth century, declared Portuguese caravels to be the handiest and best-found vessels then afloat. In the annals of discovery, there are surprisingly few records of caravels lost at sea. They were obviously more suitable for inshore work than bigger ships; competently handled, they may have been tighter and safer even in the open sea. In widely separated parts of the world, types of vessel can still be seen which bear a striking resemblance to Iberian caravels, a resemblance which may well indicate survival or imitation. The larger *sambuqs* of the Red Sea (except for the extravagantly raked "grab" bow, which is pure Arab) look very much like sixteenth-century caravels. Probably the nearest resemblance to early fifteenth-century caravels is to be found in the *frigatas* which still ply in the Tagus today. These modest and elegant little ships do not now venture far beyond Cascaes; but their ancestors sailed halfway around the world.

The seafaring peoples of Portugal and western Andalusia, then, possessed in the early fifteenth century vessels designed for coasting trade, which were nevertheless seaworthy enough to undertake long ocean passages safely, and of a size to make such passages economically. It was not necessary for them to risk big and expensive armadas in ventures of uncertain outcome; they could use their caravels. They were not, however, the only peoples in the world to possess vessels with these good qualities; they certainly could not claim for their shipping an unique technical superiority; and in any event the mere existence of suitable ships would not, in itself, be a sufficient explanation of why the Iberians embarked on an ambitious career of oceanic exploration and pursued it with unprecedented success.

2

Finding the Way at Sea

*seaman who intends more than a local passage,* who proposes to sail to a destination which he cannot see from his point of departure, needs, in addition to a reliable vessel, a means of finding his way. If he is embarking on a coasting trip, he must know the salient features of the coast, the headlands, and the direction and approximate distance from one to the next, so that without following every indentation of the shore (which would be time-wasting, and for a seagoing vessel dangerous) he can check his progress by periodic sightings of the land. He must know, or be able to detect, any marine hazards in his way, and be able to handle his ship so as to avoid them; and he must recognize his destination when it comes in sight. All this information must be stored in such a way as to be available when needed, either in the seaman's own memory or, in a more sophisticated maritime society, in some recorded form. Pilotage—the art of taking ships from one place to another within sight of land or of navigational marks, or within soundings—is basically a matter of constant observation of visible marks, related at every stage of the passage either to the observer's own memory or to the recorded memory of others.

If our seaman's passage is to take him across open water, say from one island to another, he must make an effort of imagination. He knows his destination is there, beyond the horizon, because he or others have been there before, but he cannot see it, nor can he expect visible marks to guide him to it. He must resort to navigation, which is the art of taking ships from one place to another out of sight of land. He first needs to know, with some precision, the direction in which his destination lies; this, probably, is common knowledge in his home port, and so too are the indicators by which he sets his ship's head on its initial course. When he is at sea, without marks to guide him, his task becomes more difficult. He must be able to keep his ship moving in the right direction, and to detect, as promptly as possible, any unforeseen deviation from it, whether due to wind, current or steering error; he must estimate the extent of the deviation, and correct for it. He must know approximately how long he will have to sail in the given direction, so that if he misses his destination and sails beyond it, he will be aware of what has happened. This too will be affected by winds, currents, the state of the sea and the performance of his ship, all of which he must take into account. He must have some means of knowing when he is near his destination, even though not in sight of it; ideally he should have some indication of the final alteration of course which he must make in order to close it; and obviously he must know what the destination looks like, so that he can recognize it at a distance, as soon as it appears above the horizon. Finally, he must be able to reverse the process, with due allowance for wind and sea, so that when his business is done he can return home safely.

If the voyage on which our seaman embarks is a voyage of discovery, he must make a much bigger effort of imagination. He has obviously less to go on—no more, perhaps, than rumor, conjecture, or ancient tradition; but he has, almost certainly, some destination in mind. Even the most sanguine explorers do not usually sail out into the ocean at random to see what they can find. He is much more likely to be looking for a place whose existence is known, or at least suspected. He may be following the indications of some earlier sailor who—blown off his course, perhaps—reported the chance sighting of an unknown land; he knows in what general area of the ocean he has to search, but has no precise information on direction or distance. He may be trying to reach by sea a country whose existence is already well attested by overland travelers; he knows roughly where the country is, and something of what it is like, but does not know whether a continuous sea route to it exists, nor how long such a route may be, nor what hazards or obstacles he may have to circumvent on the way. All this he must find out for himself. If he succeeds in reaching his destination, or alternatively, if he discovers on the way some other place of interest and importance, he must be prepared to define the position of what he has found, so that his voyage can be repeated and the discovery exploited. To define a position absolutely, in terms of fixed co-ordinates, requires a highly sophisticated navigational technique. Failing this, he must define it relatively, in terms of direction and distance (or sailing time) from his point of departure, or from some other place whose position is known. He must anticipate the necessity for doing this, and prepare for his own safe return, by recording in detail, or by remembering, his movements on the outward passage. If he is following a continental coastline this task, though in practice it may be complex and arduous, is in principle straightforward; in long passages in the open sea, however, it presents serious difficulties, which can be overcome satisfactorily only by the use of instruments.

Primitive sailors have often made passages of hundreds of miles in the open sea by eye and "feel," without the help of instruments. Some do so still; and in order to define the conditions which made systematic long-range maritime discovery possible, one must understand the nature and the limitations of this kind of navigation. The primitive navigator embarking on a familiar routine passage, say from one island to another (island dwellers are more likely than continental people to be bold at sea), knows the direction in which he must sail. This direction can be expressed in two ways: in terms of the alignment of visible marks on the coast he is leaving, which he can watch over the stern until they are out of sight; and in terms of the rising or setting of the sun or of some fixed star. A star is easier and less complicated to use than the sun, because its bearing at rising or setting is constant through the year whenever it is visible, and because there are many stars, so that one can usually be selected which will give a direct and not merely a derived heading. Star headings are easier to use in the Tropics than in higher latitudes, not only because the stars are more likely to be clearly visible in the Tropics, but also because in higher latitudes the stars appear to travel obliquely from their points of rising and towards their points of setting, so that their bearings constantly change. In the Tropics the stars—except those in the extreme northern or southern sky—appear to travel vertically, and

their bearings remain steady. For the same reason, easterly or westerly star headings are easier to follow than northerly or southerly ones.

To these generalizations there is one major exception: the Pole Star, which is aligned—not exactly, but near enough for the primitive navigator's purpose—with the earth's axis, so that its bearing, from any point where it can be seen, is due north or nearly so. It neither rises nor sets, but in clear weather is visible all night throughout the year. Its value as a direction indicator is obvious, especially in low and middle northern latitudes, where it appears near enough to the horizon for its bearing to be easily observed. The Pole Star, of course, is visible only in the northern hemisphere. When European navigators first entered the southern oceans, they searched the sky for a southern counterpart, believing on grounds of symmetry that there must be such a star; but there is none. The Southern Cross rises east of south, lying over on one side, and sets west of south, lying over on the other. At its zenith it is upright, and bears almost due south; but in this position, when observed from anywhere in the southern hemisphere, it is too high in the sky for a ship's head to be aligned accurately on it. It is a beautiful and endearing constellation, and easily recognizable; but its usefulness to the primitive navigator is limited. The same is true of the lovely and brilliant Canopus. The relative importance of directional stars, however, in any regional navigation system, depends chiefly on whether travel in that system is mainly north and south, or east and west. The Caroline Islands—to cite a well-studied example—form a chain of small islands extending for hundreds of miles from east to west, but much narrower from north to south. Most long-distance travel within the group is east–west. For the bold navigators of the Carolines, therefore, it is not Polaris, but the bright star Altair in Aquila which provides the cardinal direction of the local star "compass." It rises due east; observed from near the equator, it appears to climb vertically to its zenith directly overhead, and to decline vertically to its setting due west.

Our primitive navigator, then, leaving harbor in the afternoon, gets his initial heading from marks ashore, and confirms it roughly by a derived bearing from the setting sun. He then looks for the rising or setting of his chosen star and steers towards it. When the star has set, or—if rising—has mounted too high in the sky for the ship's head to be aligned on it, other stars must be substituted, allowing for differences in their bearing. By day, and by night if the sky becomes overcast, the navigator must hold a steady course by other means. He maintains a constant point of sailing relative to the wind; he attends to the "feel" of his ship as it pitches or rolls, to ensure that it crosses the line of the swells at a constant angle. Currents, which he cannot see or feel, may set him to the right or left of his course; but if he is in familiar waters, he knows from accumulated experience how the currents set at the particular time of year, and compensates for them. The wind may deceive him. In some parts of the world—in the Indian Ocean, for example—major seasonal changes of wind occur at fairly predictable times of year; each seasonal wind, once established, will blow for several months from the same general quarter. Nevertheless, minor changes of wind may occur unpredictably, and may be big enough to falsify the navigator's reckoning, but so

gradual that he may not detect them. The swell may also change direction; but it is not likely to change at the same time, nor in the same way, as the local wind; it may, in fact, derive its force and pattern from another wind system hundreds, perhaps thousands of miles away. If the navigator, therefore, maintains a constant point of sailing in relation to a gradually shifting wind, and if he is attentive to the motion of his ship, he will soon notice that the angle between wind and swell has changed, and must make what he estimates to be the appropriate adjustment. Of course, if he runs into a serious storm, he can do nothing but lower his sail, and later, when the wind abates, try to estimate how far and in what direction he has drifted.

If the weather is kind and all goes well, the movement of sun and stars enable the primitive navigator to keep rough track of the passage of time and to estimate when he is approaching the neighborhood of his destination. He must then look for signs of land: changes in the color of the water, breaks in the pattern of the swell, towers of cumulus cloud, fish species characteristic of outlying reefs, or homing birds. These, too, can be deceptive. Cumulus sometimes builds up over open sea. As for birds, their usefulness to the navigator is often exaggerated. Some land birds migrate along predictable routes over open sea, but only at certain seasons, and with some exceptions—geese, notably—they usually fly too high to be readily observed. If a nonmigratory land bird is encountered far out at sea, it is probably lost. Pelagic birds, on the other hand— petrels, albatrosses and the like—are useless or nearly so; outside their breeding season they remain permanently at sea for months on end. Columbus, in the journal of his first transatlantic voyage, recorded his relief on sighting what, from his description of white plumage and long pointed tails, must have been tropic birds; but tropic birds, like petrels, are pelagic in habit. They are very strong flyers, ranging over great distances, and can be seen flying in almost any direction at almost any hour of the day or night. The birds which reassured Columbus could have given no sure indication, at that time of year—October—of the nearness of land, and no indication whatever of its direction. Gulls are of little use to the navigator, for the opposite reason: most of them are inshore feeders and rarely go out of sight of land. The same is true of frigate-birds, whose reputation as wanderers is undeserved. The navigator must know his birds. There are some species of regular habit—terns and noddies, gannets and boobies—which roost ashore and feed at sea, flying out at dawn to fishing grounds up to a few hours' flight away, and thence directly back. The navigator who follows the direction of homing boobies at dusk, at any time of year, is likely to find some land; but not necessarily, of course, the land he is looking for.

From this very general description, the limitations of primitive navigation are apparent. Any system of navigation without instruments must depend primarily—in many areas entirely—upon dead reckoning; upon the navigator's estimate from hour to hour of the direction and distance he has traveled from his point of departure. A primitive seaman no doubt develops a dead-reckoning sense superior to that of a navigator who habitually relies on instruments; he has, so to speak, a compass rose in his head; but if he loses track of his dead reckoning, he is lost. Unless he sights some point of land which

he recognizes, he cannot ascertain his position. A familiar star can give him a direction; but a simple direction is of only limited help if he does not know where he is. Then, the many subtle indications which the primitive navigator uses in order to keep on his course are good only in the area of sea with which he is familiar; the pattern of winds, swells, bird movements, and so forth, may be quite different in other areas only a few hundred miles away. Again, the distances over which dead reckoning without instruments can be relied on are limited. It is necessarily an art of approximation, and its errors are cumulative. The most extensive instances, which can be said to be historically established, of regular out-and-back passages without instruments in the open sea, cover hundreds of miles, not thousands. These limitations upon regular voyaging apply with more force to maritime exploration, and more still to random discovery. If a primitive navigator on a routine passage misses his destination—is blown off his course by storm, let us say—and is prevented by the wind from returning or casting about, he may eventually—in the last stages, perhaps, of thirst and exhaustion—light upon some distant and unfamiliar land. He cannot easily return; not knowing where he is, he does not know the course for home; so he is likely to stay, and to become absorbed in the local population. If the land is uninhabited, and if his companions include both men and women, and perhaps domestic animals, he may found an enduring colony, but a colony whose existence will be unknown to the people of the country he originally left. It has been suggested that Polynesian peoples became dispersed through the Pacific islands as a result of many accidents of this kind, spread over many centuries. This is a

Navigators' birds:
a frigate bird

Tinofa.

Navigators' birds:
a noddy

Navigators' birds:
a tropic-bird

Bobo.

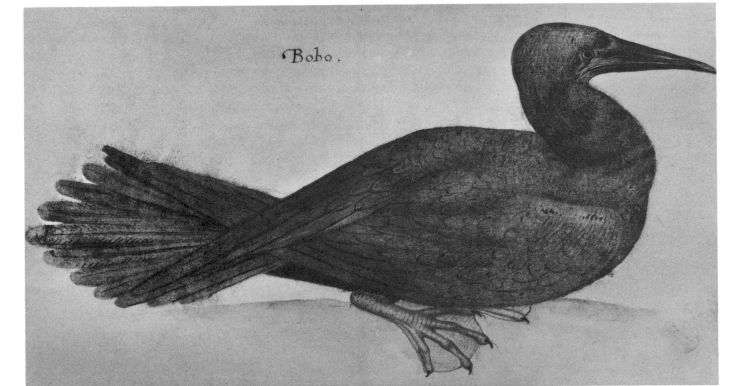

Navigators' birds:
a brown booby

controversial question. A return voyage in a sailing canoe from, say, New Zealand to eastern Polynesia would be extremely difficult. It would be impossible, except by a rare fluke of weather, to return from the Hawaiian islands to the Marquesas, whence the original settlers of Hawaii are thought to have come. On the other hand, these original settlers were followed, several centuries later, by immigrants from Tahiti. Deliberate voyages in either direction between Tahiti and Hawaii would have been within the capacity of Polynesian double canoes and their navigators; the prevailing winds are convenient, the distances, though great, are manageable, and the Line Islands lie across the route. The two groups may well have been in two-way communication at some time; but the evidence is too slight for certainty.

A comparison is often drawn between Polynesian voyages, which may or may not have succeeded in establishing two-way communication over long distances, and the Norse voyages in the north Atlantic in the ninth, tenth and eleventh centuries, which certainly did; but the analogy is not as close as it looks. The Norse adventurers were sailing between big land masses, with substantial groups of mountainous islands along the way. From Bergen to Shetland is about 180 sea miles; from Shetland to the Faeroes, 120; from the Faeroes to Horn in eastern Iceland, 240; from Snaefelsnes due west to the Greenland coast, 350. The Norse navigator would keep track not of distance (which he could not measure), but of time: so many days' sailing. If he sailed directly over the 1500 miles from Norway to Greenland—as some apparently did, to judge from sailing directions which have been preserved—he would keep, in

modern terms, between 61 and 62 degrees north. He probably took his course from the rising or setting sun, making rough allowance for the time of year, and at night would keep the Pole Star on his beam. He would pass within sight of Shetland to port and of the Faeroes to starboard. He might not actually see Iceland, but would note the great concentration of whales— long since thinned by hunting—which then fed on its southern sea shelf, with their accompanying cloud of birds. The edge of this shelf runs along the 63 degree parallel. The peaks of Greenland, finally, could be seen in clear weather from a great way off. The distances in the open sea, without sight of land, were not very great, and major alterations of course, if all went well, would be needed only to close destinations, or to avoid ice off eastern Greenland. The Norse navigator's problems were easier than those, say, of a Pacific islander navigating from one inconspicuous atoll to another, or even from one substantial island group to another; he ran less risk of becoming irretrievably lost. The north Atlantic passages were dangerous, certainly, for ships open to the weather and navigated without instruments; yet Norse seamen undertook them with confidence. References to long voyages in the sagas are impressively casual. Norse methods of navigation, though primitive, were adequate for their purposes, so long as the weather held; and sailing was confined to the months when good weather could reasonably be expected.

What advantages had European navigators in the early fifteenth century over those who used the primitive systems just described? They had some instruments, and of these the most important was the magnetic compass. The attractive property of magnetic iron ore, magnetite or lodestone, had been known from ancient times as a scientific curiosity and as an ingredient in magic practices. Its use in various forms of divination—including, it was said, the detection of unfaithful wives—may have led to the crucial discovery that pieces of lodestone, or iron wires or needles which had been in contact with the stone, if free to move, oriented themselves north and south. Long-standing tradition attributes the first use of the compass for purposes of navigation to the Italian port of Amalfi. In view of the commercial importance of Amalfi in the twelfth century, and of the demand for long-distance sea transport then created by the crusades, the tradition is at least plausible. Certainly the magnetic needle was employed at sea in the Mediterranean before the end of the twelfth century. Contemporary accounts describe it as floating on a chip of wood in a bowl of water. Its uses at first were occasional and secondary: to find the north in overcast conditions when sun or stars were invisible, or to check or maintain a course initially established by a star heading. It is interesting to find that today, in the Caroline Islands on the other side of the world, practised navigators who have only recently acquired compasses use them in just these secondary, confirmatory ways. In southern Europe, however, the needle soon became the primary instrument of navigation. The water and the wooden float were discarded, and the needle rotated instead on a brass pin, with the major directions marked round the rim of the bowl. Next, the compass points with their subdivisions, thirty-two—sometimes sixty-four—in all, were drawn geometrically on a circular card or "fly"; the fly was glued to the needle and rotated with

it, the bowl remaining simply as a protection. This device eliminated the errors of parallax and made the needle a compass in the exact sense. The compass was mounted in a chest or binnacle at a convenient height and set in the fore-and-aft line of the ship, with a lamp beside it at night. With its aid the helmsman, or the officer conning him, could watch the ship's heading from minute to minute, with only occasional recourse to the stars for confirmation. By the beginning of the fifteenth century this had become the usual manner of steering when out of sight of land, at least in the Mediterranean.

The compass liberated the seaman from his dependence on clear skies, and—storms apart—made sea travel possible at all times of year. If he knew the bearing of his destination, and if the wind was favorable, the navigator had only to follow his compass to be reasonably sure of coming within sight of his destination; but when? For safety, especially at night, he must be able to predict his approach to the land. If he knew the direct distance to his destination, he could translate distance into time. Fifteenth-century sailors, it is true, had no means of measuring speed; they had to estimate it, from knowledge of a ship's performance in this or that condition of weather; but over a relatively short passage, an experienced navigator, knowing his ship, could make a reasonably accurate estimate. In order to use it, he needed to keep track of time, in units more precise than crude days' sailing. He could do this roughly in daytime by watching the passage of the sun; and at night, a little more accurately, from the circle which the Guards of the Little Bear, Kochab and its dimmer companion, describe about the Pole Star, in every twenty-four hours of sidereal time. He memorized the midnight position of the Guards at two-week intervals through the year; comparison of their observed position at any moment with their midnight position for the same date gave the time in hours before or after midnight. This method of time-keeping had been systematically described by Ramón Lull, the Catalan philosopher, in the late thirteenth century; it was widely used at sea by the beginning of the fifteenth, though no instrument had yet been devised for making the necessary observations; the angles had to be estimated by eye and were expressed in terms of an imaginary man in the sky, head erect, feet together, arms outstretched, the Pole Star at his navel. There was an instrument, however, for measuring short intervals of time, hours or half-hours: the sand-glass. These delicate, carefully blown glasses had been an important product of Venetian industry since, at latest, the thirteenth century, and in European seagoing ships were the usual means of timekeeping, both for changes of watch and for the navigator's "reckoning." For the purposes they normally served, they were accurate enough; an error of a few minutes in the watch did not matter much. But for longer periods of time they were misleading. Their unavoidable errors were cumulative; and they could never be more accurate than the method of selecting the moment—whether noon, midnight, dawn or dark—at which the glass was started.

The wind might not be favorable; and in beating against an unfavorable wind the sand-glass, despite its limitations, was indispensable to accurate navigation. The compass gave the course sailed on each board; the sand-glass gave the time sailed along that

course, which could be translated into distance; the direct course to the ship's destination was known. Finding the distance made good along the direct course, therefore, was a matter of solving a series of right-angled triangles. Similarly, a navigator blown off his course by storm, if he could read from his compass the direction of the wind which drove him and form some estimate of the distance he had drifted, could by solving triangles, when the storm abated, find the direction and distance he must sail in order to recover his original course. Navigators did not work out these sums themselves; solutions for the principal points of the compass were tabulated. Traverse tables, collectively known as *Toleta de Marteloio*, were available to literate navigators from the late thirteenth century; the earliest surviving copy is from the early fifteenth; by then they were commonplace, at least in the Mediterranean. They gave solutions in terms of compass courses, not, as modern traverse tables do, in terms of difference of latitude and longitude; and the triangles they solved were plane, not spherical triangles, so that some error was inherent in them; but in the relatively restricted area of the Mediterranean this did not much matter. Traverse tables were sometimes drawn on marine charts, so that the navigator, having worked out his dead-reckoning position, could prick it on his chart.

The marine chart, next to the compass, was the most important of the navigational advantages possessed by the fifteenth-century Mediterranean seaman. Its development shows a close parallel with that of tables and of written sailing directions. All three sprang from the invention of the compass. The word *compasso,* indeed, was originally used to describe not only—not primarily—the instrument itself, but the charts and pilot books associated with its use. *Portolani* —directions for coastwise passages from place to place—originated in private notebooks kept by pilots for their own reference. Passed on to others, they formed a great accumulation of experience in local pilotage. By the late thirteenth century, directions contained in many different *portolani* had been collected together into a comprehensive pilot book, the *Compasso da Navigare,* covering the whole of the Mediterranean and the Black Sea. The directions in the *Compasso* go from port to port clockwise around the Mediterranean from Cape St. Vincent to Safi in Morocco. They include bearings, distances in miles (short or "geometric" miles of 4100 feet), descriptions of landmarks and dangers, instructions for entering harbors, and information about depths and anchorages. Besides coastwise passages, the *Compasso* includes directions, with courses and distances, for a number of long-distance crossings between easily recognizable points, usually capes or islands. Some of these open-sea crossings were seven or eight hundred miles in length.

The marine charts of the Mediterranean in the later Middle Ages—also confusingly, but logically, called *portolani*—were essentially sailing directions drawn in chart form. They were constructed on a base of the compass courses and distances between major harbors and principal landmarks. The coastline between the base points was drawn in freehand, with a detailed accuracy clearly derived from familiarity and experience. All the charts of this type which have survived show a remarkable family likeness. They are drawn on single skins of parchment, usually

retaining the natural outline, ranging in length from three to five feet and in depth from eighteen to thirty inches. The coastlines are in black ink, their outline emphasized by the long series of names of ports and coastal features written perpendicularly to the coast. Most names are in black; but important harbors are in red, often with colored banners to show their allegiance, a highly decorative as well as useful embellishment. Little inland detail is shown: a few major rivers, conspicuous mountain ranges, vignettes, beautifully drawn, of large cities. Navigational hazards offshore—rocks and shoals —are shown by dots or crosses. There is no indication of soundings, currents or tide races.

From the late thirteenth century—the date to which the earliest surviving portolan chart is ascribed—to the late fifteenth, the charts changed very little in outline or style and not at all in construction. None showed parallels or meridians. The designers took no account of the sphericity of the earth; the area covered was treated as a plane surface. All charts were drawn to bring the lines indicating magnetic north into the vertical, these lines being parallel in all the compass roses on each chart. The errors arising from this in the Mediterranean area were unimportant, because the range of latitude was small, and the convergence of meridians within that range was relatively slight. The direction lines which radiated across the charts from all the principal points of reference therefore approximated fairly closely to loxodromes or rhumb lines, lines of constant bearing. The whole surface of the chart was crossed by these intersecting lines. At one side, a distance scale was drawn. The navigator using the chart needed a straight-edge and a pair of dividers. He aligned his straight-edge between his points of departure and destination; if no direction line was drawn along the intended course, he found with the help of his dividers the line most nearly parallel, and set his course accordingly. He did not work out his dead reckoning, as a modern navigator does, by actual drawing on the chart; he calculated the distances made good along his chosen course, measured with his dividers the appropriate length on the distance scale, and marked his approximate position by pricking the parchment with the point of the dividers. He used the written *portolano* for coastwise pilotage, the chart for passages in the open sea.

Most surviving late medieval charts are highly decorated examples which probably were never used at sea, but graced the offices of shipping firms or the libraries of great men. That, no doubt, is why they have survived. They differ from working charts, however, only in their wealth of decorative detail. In general, portolan charts were designed as working tools for the masters of seagoing ships. The cartographers who drew them worked in the ports of north Italy or (a little later) in Barcelona or Majorca. As might be expected, the charts covered the coasts regularly visited by the trading vessels of the Italian and Catalan cities. They showed in considerable detail the Mediterranean and the Black Sea; in less detail, and often on a smaller scale, the coasts of Spain, Portugal, the Bay of Biscay and a hundred miles or so of the Moroccan coast west and south from the Straits. Some charts included, in very rough outline, the British Isles and the North Sea coasts; very occasionally, sketchily and by hearsay, the Baltic.

The seamen of the Baltic and the North Sea knew little of these refinements. They used compasses, though often primitive ones; but the marine chart was almost unknown in northern Europe before the sixteenth century. A plausible tradition attributes its introduction in England to Sebastian Cabot. It gained acceptance slowly. William Bourne, author of the first English navigation manual, could still in 1574 grumble about the conservatism of "auncient masters of shippes" who "derided and mocked them that have occupied their cardes and plattes . . . saying: that they cared not for their sheepes skins." Even written sailing directions—rutters, as they were called in the north—made slow headway, probably because few northern mariners could read; the earliest surviving English rutter is attributed to 1408, a primitive compilation, giving compass courses from place to place, but no distances. Northern navigators then—though they were not afraid to lose sight of land when they must, as in crossing the Bay of Biscay—were expert in pilotage rather than in navigation proper. They steered their ships, wherever possible, so that when one point of land disappeared below the horizon the next would be in sight; on a familiar coast, the distance from one headland to another, when both are in sight, need not be known exactly. Distances, indeed, when mentioned at all, were commonly reckoned in "kennings," a kenning being the distance at which a coast should be visible from a ship's masthead; and the whole process of navigating from place to place was often described as the "caping" of the ship.

Northern navigators, then, in the early fifteenth century lagged behind their Mediterranean contemporaries in their methods of navigation; but in some aspects of pilotage they were—and needed to be—more expert, and the rutters were more explicit than the *portolani*. This was especially true in dealing with tides, tidal streams, and the configuration of the bottom. Tides, insignificant in the Mediterranean, are a major factor in pilotage on the Atlantic coasts. A seaman entering or leaving harbor or navigating among shoals needs to know the state of the tide. On a coasting voyage, he should be able to predict the times of high and low water at each port he proposes to enter, the depths of water at those ports at those times, and the direction of flow of the tidal streams likely to be encountered between them. Three obvious and well-recognized facts helped him in his calculation: the daily retardation of the times of high water; the association between those times and the position of the moon; and the thirty-day period which elapsed from one full moon to the next. From these it was possible to calculate, for any particular place, the times of high water on each day of the moon's age, and these times could be tabulated. Time, however, as we have seen, could be reckoned only roughly at sea, and most sailors were illiterate; so they memorized not the time, but the age and compass bearing of the moon at high water. The moon's reflection on the surface of the sea was a dramatic and obvious track whose bearing was simple to observe; and since the highest high waters, or spring tides, were seen to occur on days of full and new moon—at "full and change"—the bearing of the moon at these times became the tidal establishment of the port, and was duly noted in the rutters. So, according to the early English rutter already mentioned, "a south moon maketh high water within Wight" and "all the havens be full at a west-south-west moon between the Start and the Lizard." These

statements were true only on days of full moon; but the seaman could calculate when to expect high water on any day by remembering the age of the moon and adding the daily retardation. This was taken as forty-five minutes, which is a rough approximation, but which is arithmetically convenient, and has the advantage of being equivalent to one point of the magnetic compass. The navigator marked the fly of his compass in hours as well as in points. To the establishment of the port, expressed as a compass bearing, he added one point for every day of the moon's age.

The seaman of the Atlantic coasts had to be familiar not only with the rise and fall of tides, but with the alternating run of tidal streams. There was no way, in the fifteenth century, of calculating the force of these streams, which varied not only with the state of the tide, but with the wind. Their direction, however, could be observed, and all the early rutters contain advice and warning on the subject. In the Bristol Channel, for example, which has particularly treacherous tides: "Beware of Iron Grounds, and of your streams of flood, for they sit north-east on the Iron Grounds. And on ebb spare not to go, for the streams of Bridgewater sit west-north-west."

The third characteristic which distinguished north European from Mediterranean pilotage was its reliance on sounding. In most parts of the Mediterranean basin the coast plunges down abruptly; the sea is clear, so that in shallow water the bottom can be seen; and fog is comparatively rare. Sounding, therefore, is rarely necessary. Off the Atlantic coasts, on the other hand, the seabed slopes from the shoreline—here steeply, as off Spain and western Ireland, there gently, as to the west of the English Channel—to a depth of about a hundred fathoms, and then plunges to great depths. The outer edge of the continental shelf is clearly defined by the hundred-fathom line. Here the navigator, coming from sea, could get his first and timely warning of his approach to the coast; twenty miles or so if it were the coast of Spain or Portugal, over a hundred if it were Brittany or southwest England. He would stop his ship at the appropriate point by dead reckoning and sound with a deep-sea lead and a long line, measuring in fathoms—the width of a man's outstretched arms. Farther in, within soundings off most of the Atlantic coasts, fog is frequent, the water is opaque, and the depth varies with the tides. A seaman in these waters must have some means of finding at frequent intervals exactly how much water he has under his ship. He must be able to take repeated soundings with the ship under way. For this he used a lighter sounding lead with a shorter, thicker line. The design of the lead and the marks on both types of line are today much as they were in the fifteenth century, and probably had been for centuries before that. Sounding in pilotage waters, for Atlantic coast seamen, was so habitual as to be almost second nature; a second nature to which explorers in strange waters were often to owe their lives.

The lead not only gave warning of danger; it also helped the navigator to fix his position. Off a well-known coast the sequence of soundings would fall into a familiar and identifiable pattern. Corroborative evidence was obtained by sampling the bottom. The lead was provided with a hollow at its lower end, which could be "armed" or filled with tallow. Fragments of sand, mud or shell sticking to the arming could be identified. This use of the lead was well known off the Atlantic coasts in the fifteenth century, and no doubt long before. The variety of bottom grounds described in the early rutters is remarkable: "Upon off Ushant in 50 or 60 fathoms there is red sand and black stones and white shells among. . . . Upon Lizard there is great stones as it were beans, and it is ragged stone. . . . Upon Portland there is fair white sand in 24 fathoms with red shells therein," and so on. The northern Atlantic seaman, when coasting, "caped" his way from one sighting to another. Standing in to the land, he groped his way, so to speak, with one foot on the bottom.

The maritime area of Europe, then, was the home not only of two distinct traditions of ship construction, but also of two distinct traditions of navigation. The seamen of Portugal and western Andalusia in the early fifteenth century fell heir to both traditions. Trading modestly with the Mediterranean countries, they were familiar with Mediterranean methods based on compass, traverse table and chart, though the charts they used were still Italian drawn—there was no Portuguese or Castilian school of hydrography. Trading to northern Europe, they could learn the methods of navigating off foggy, tide-bound coasts with compass, rutter and lead line. The range of techniques available to them, by comparison with the primitive methods earlier described, was impressive; but in assessing the aptness of European navigators for the discovery of the sea, the limits of those techniques must be remembered. European navigation out of soundings was still, in the early fifteenth century, based entirely on dead reckoning. With a compass and other devices, the navigator could keep a far more accurate reckoning than could his primitive counterpart who sailed without instruments; and for the ordinary purposes of seaborne trade, over relatively short passages, in known waters, this reckoning was good enough. He might stray off his course; but wherever he sighted land, he could find out where he was. It was not good enough, however, for long passages in unknown waters, for which no charts or sailing directions existed. The navigator could express the position of his ship at sea, or of any new land he might find, only in terms of an estimated compass bearing and an estimated distance from the last point of known land sighted; and his reckoning, however careful, might be subject to undetectable error. The compass itself was liable to errors as yet hardly noticed, much less understood; and at best it gave no certain clue to the lateral displacement of a ship from the course steered. Drift and leeway due to wind, certainly, would be noticed, and could be roughly estimated; but there was no way of measuring, or even detecting, the hidden pull of unfamiliar currents. The errors were cumulative as the ship sailed farther from its point of departure; there was no known way of checking its course, or its position at any moment, by actual observation.

In the first half of the fifteenth century, as European ships, especially Portuguese ships, made longer voyages into the Atlantic, ways were to be found. The only independent indicators of a ship's position in a featureless expanse of sea were the sun and the stars; and of these the most obvious, in the northern hemisphere, was the Pole Star—always there, symbol of constancy, the sailors' friend. The Pole Star, because of its approximate alignment with the earth's axis, not only maintains a roughly

constant bearing; it maintains also a roughly constant altitude. That is to say, the height at which it appears above the horizon from a particular point is always roughly the same; and it appears at roughly the same height from all points on a particular parallel of latitude. This property can be used in several ways. A navigator on a long north–south passage, by observing the Pole Star each day at dawn and dusk—the only times when both the horizon and the star could be seen—and by noting changes in its altitude, could form some idea of changes in his own position north or south. Conversely, in sailing east or west, he could maintain a steady course, and correct lateral displacements which his compass had not revealed, by maintaining a constant polar altitude. If he lost track of his dead reckoning, and so did not know his position, he could find his way home, provided that he knew the polar altitude at his home port. He had to steer roughly north or roughly south (if the wind served) until he found the right altitude, and then alter course due east or due west for home. It is hard to believe that these simple possibilities had escaped earlier attention; that the Norsemen, for example, sailing east or west across the north Atlantic, did not practice what later came to be called latitude sailing. Probably they did; but there is no evidence of it —no hint, in all the surviving medieval references to navigation, that European navigators before the fifteenth century ever used the Pole Star, much less the sun, to indicate position, as distinct from direction. In the fifteenth century they learned to do so, but slowly. There were difficulties: the Pole Star is not aligned precisely; it describes a daily circle about the geographical pole—a radius, in the early fifteenth century, of about 3½ degrees—so that both its bearing and its altitude constantly change. Astronomers knew this, but sailors did not; it is not obvious to the naked eye. Navigators could not make accurate use of polar altitude until they had learned to recognize the relative movement of the star and to allow for it, and this, in a conservative calling, took time. Then, there was the problem of measurement. Even in the middle of the fifteenth century, measurements of altitude were still rough indeed —so many fingers' breadths; so many palms, or spans, or cubits. This was better than guessing; but for anything like precise observation, instruments suitable for use at sea had to be devised, and this again took time. The earliest known use, by a European navigator, of an instrument for observing polar altitude at sea was in 1460. Methods of finding a ship's position by celestial observations, then, developed in response to a demand created by fifteenth-century exploring activity; they did not form part of the initial equipment with which that activity began.

How did the equipment of the European navigator, at the beginning of the fifteenth century, compare with that of navigators in the other major areas of sophisticated maritime communication? In China, for example? The majestic progresses of Cheng Ho's fleets demonstrated the reliability of Chinese navigation; a navigation, undoubtedly, by compass as well as star bearing, by chart as well as lead line. The property of magnetism, and its use for geomantic purposes, had been known in China from ancient times. The earliest references to magnetized needles as aids to navigation antedate similar references in Europe by nearly a century. This is not necessarily to say that the magnetic compass was "introduced" into Europe, either directly or indirectly, from China; of that there is no evidence. The mariner's compass developed differently in the two regions; in China, both the dry mounting with the needle rotating on a pivot, and the wet mounting with the needle floating in water, were known by the end of the eleventh century; but it was the wet compass which prevailed in general use. The points were incised on the bottom of the bowl, or round the rim. The rotating compass card or fly was not adopted until the late sixteenth century, as a result of European contacts. A floating needle is inconvenient for minute-to-minute steering, because of its tendency to move to the side of the bowl; presumably Chinese helmsmen used star headings as well. On the other hand, the floating needle is free from the vibration and oscillation of the dry needle. In modern ships' compasses the card is always pivoted, but it is also steadied by being floated in liquid.

In China, as in Mediterranean Europe, compass bearings provided the basis for sailing directions and marine charts. One such chart has survived, not in original, but in a later printing. This is the Mao K'un map or chart of the coasts of the Indian Ocean, which occupies forty pages in a many-volumed work entitled *Wu-pei Chih*, "Records of military preparations," printed about 1628. The original is believed to have been compiled about 1422, from a mass of information brought back by Cheng Ho's fleets, or collected for their use. The chart is in "strip" form, and necessarily diagrammatic; it does not attempt, as European portolan charts do, to show realistically the proportions and outlines of the various land masses, coasts and islands; but it gives many compass bearings from place to place, accurate to within 5 degrees, not shown as rhumb lines drawn across the chart, but written around the edges. It describes in detail harbors, anchorages, and navigational hazards such as rocks and shoals. It gives distances in "watches"; and most significant, it gives in fingers' breadths the Pole Star altitude of the more important places. In short, though inferior in graphic execution to the best portolan charts, it provides the same kind of information to approximately the same degree of accuracy, and includes some information which was not to be found on European charts in the early fifteenth century. Chinese hydrography, we must conclude, was not then inferior to European, and covered vastly bigger areas. But the Ming decision, in the fourteen-thirties, to withdraw from official oceanic enterprise, was to cause a slowing-down of Chinese development in hydrography and navigation, at a time when European skill and knowledge in these arts was entering on a period of very rapid progress.

In view of the commercial contacts between the Chinese and Arab worlds in the early fifteenth century, it is tempting to speculate on the influence which each may have exerted on the other in matters of navigational technique. It is well known that Arab ships made open-sea passages of two thousand miles or so in the Indian Ocean, relying on the seasonal alternation of the monsoons; but we have little precise information on how they navigated. No Arab marine chart has survived from the fifteenth century. The earliest Arabic references to the mariner's compass are somewhat later than the earliest European references; one Arabic word

for it, indeed—"qumbas"—is obviously of European origin. The compass was undoubtedly in widespread use at the beginning of the century: a "wet" compass, often apparently in the form of a magnetized iron leaf beaten into the shape of a concave elongated fish. Arab navigators, however, seem to have placed less reliance on the compass than their European contemporaries, and correspondingly more upon star sights, including altitudes. Several European travelers in the Indian Ocean—Marco Polo in the late thirteenth century, Nicolò de' Conti in the early fifteenth—commented on this peculiarity, and upon the extent of the astronomical knowledge which lay behind it. Marco Polo recorded the Pole Star altitude at several places, though in terms impossible to translate into modern angular measure. No doubt hand and body measurements were used as units; but fifteenth-century Arab navigators also used an instrument for measuring altitudes, the *kamāl*. This, in its simplest form, consisted of a small wooden board on a knotted string. The observer held up the board so that it just covered the space between the star and the horizon; he held the string between his teeth, and shortened it until it was taut; he then read off the angle in terms of the length of the taut string. There were several possible variations: a series of boards, each representing a vertical angle, might be fixed at measured distances along the string, which then would be held to the eye; or the string itself might be replaced by a rigid rod and the boards by sliding transoms. The *kamāl* was mentioned—though not by that name—in several Arabic treatises on Indian Ocean navigation written in Vasco da Gama's day. By that time it was clearly widespread. It probably antedated any instrument used in Europe for measuring altitudes at sea.

The best European methods of navigation at the beginning of the fifteenth century were a combination of Mediterranean and north European techniques. They were good enough for long coasting voyages. In the open sea they were adequate for keeping track of a ship's movements, by dead reckoning, over passages of medium length—of hundreds of miles, that is, rather than thousands. They were not in any respect markedly superior to methods used in the Indian Ocean and the Far East in the same period; in some respects they were inferior. No purely technical explanation, in short, will sufficiently account for European pre-eminence in the discovery of the sea.

3

The Oceans of the World in Books

The discovery of the sea was the result not of random wandering, but of systematic search. Explorers, when they set sail, usually had some destination in mind, some place they had heard of or read about, or perhaps only imagined, some new contact which promised profit and advantage to themselves and to their supporters at home. Chance played a part, of course; there is an element of chance in all discovery. Before the oceans of the world were charted, navigators often blundered upon unknown islands, sometimes whole continents which they had not expected to find; or else found open sea where land had confidently been expected. Many discoveries, including some major ones, were fortuitous, the unforeseen results of wind, current or navigational error which took ships far from their intended course. Many, again, were made by men who were searching, often on every slender evidence, for something quite different from what they actually found. A chance discovery might be investigated promptly, followed up and exploited; but often the chance discoverer would be in no condition to explore, and when he finally reached home—if he ever did—he might be unable to give more than the roughest indication of where his discovery lay, or even to convince his hearers that he had really found land and not a deceptive cloud bank. His report might then be forgotten; or the land he claimed to have found might fade into a limbo of folk recollection or legend. Many such legends or misty recollections were current in late medieval Europe, and each had its adherents. Responsible rulers and skeptical investors, however, would not send ships out deliberately on long and possibly dangerous voyages away from the known routes of commerce merely in the hope of making chance discoveries, or in order to investigate vague and implausible reports of discoveries made in the past. Such decisions were taken as the result of a process of geographical reasoning. Experts were consulted, both experienced seamen and scholarly students of cosmography. Proposals were discussed and tested with reference to an accepted body of geographical information or informed conjecture, concerning the shape and size of the world and the disposition of oceans and continents, lakes and islands, upon its surface. Some of this information was based on familiar knowledge or attested eyewitness report, some on hearsay or tradition, some on academic theory derived from the Scriptures, patristic writings and the writings of the ancient world. Much of it, by the early fifteenth century, was set out in books and maps.

As in the design and construction of ships, as in the arts of pilotage and navigation, so in the field of geographical study and surmise, there were two distinct European traditions, a northern or Atlantic tradition and a southern or Mediterranean tradition. The two were interconnected, reacted one upon the other, and had many sources in common. Both started from the late Latin assumption, inherited from Macrobius, of a tripartite world, with the three continents, Europe, Asia and Africa, forming a continuous land mass, with many peripheral islands, the whole surrounded by an encircling ocean. The difference between them was one of emphasis. The northern tradition was concerned, in the main, with Atlantic islands, real or imagined. For the peoples who inhabited the coasts of northwestern Europe, the north Atlantic —*mare tenebrosum* to the ancients, Green Sea of Darkness to the Arabs—had long been a sea of opportunity, a rich source of food and a highway for plunder, trade or migration. Mention has been made of the marauding voyages of the pagan Irish, recorded in song and epic. In Christianized Ireland, the tradition of these *Imramha* was continued by the monks, who also made adventurous voyages, in search not of plunder but of sites for monasteries or eremitic cells. St. Brendan, celebrated in legend, was a real person, who in the sixth century visited the Hebrides, Shetland, possibly the Faeroes. From the ninth century, legend associated his name with an Isle of the Blessed, in the Atlantic, west of Ireland, and the story spread all over Europe. There were others. The name Brasil, widely attached to another persistent legendary island in the Atlantic, had nothing to do with the real Brazil (so called in the sixteenth century because of the red brazilwood which grew there) but was derived from the Gaelic *breas-ail,* blessed. It was marked on many Italian and Catalan maps in the fourteenth and fifteenth centuries. The basis of these stories, if they had a basis, can only be guessed; could they derive from an early sighting of the Azores? or even conceivably part of North America? Neither Iceland nor Greenland seems likely as a foundation for such tales. Dicuil's *De Mensura Orbis Terrae*—a very competent geographical treatise for its time, written about 825 by an Irish scholar at the Carolingian court

—describes "Thyle," the real Iceland, in realistic terms, free from mystery or marvel. Dicuil implies that Iceland was known to the Irish before the end of the eighth century. Certainly the first Norse settlers in the ninth century found *papar*—monks—with, probably, some supporting lay population, established there.

The pagan Norsemen who moved out from Norway to the west and south in the ninth and tenth centuries, were no respecters of monasteries. In the Faeroes and Iceland they drove out the monks and enslaved or absorbed the lay brethren. They were not, however, mere pirates; in Iceland and the Faeroes, indeed, they can have found nothing worth stealing, except sheep. They were fugitives: some, fugitives from justice, vengeance or tightening royal discipline, all fugitives from a hard country where population pressed upon usable land. They were looking for homestead sites and pasture for their sheep and cattle. Within a few decades they occupied all the suitable places in barren Iceland, and at the end of the tenth century some late-comers pressed on to the west and settled at the heads of the sheltered fjords in southwestern Greenland. From there, they ranged far up the west coast of Greenland in summer hunting parties; and a few expeditions, early in the eleventh century, landed at various points farther west still, in what is now North America. The identity of the agreeable country which the Norse called Vinland has been the subject of much discussion; it probably included Newfoundland and may have extended to southern New England. The principal surviving evidence is in two saga narratives, reduced to writing long after the event; in a few scattered allusions in the Icelandic Annals; and in the foundations of rough buildings, believed to be Norse, lately found in northern Newfoundland. The sources agree that the attempted settlement, wherever it may have been, was soon abandoned; the settlers were too few, the winters too hard, the natives too dangerous. The Greenland settlements, by contrast, displayed a remarkable tenacity, considering the small number of the inhabitants—probably never more than a few thousand—their conservatism, and the hard environment in which they lived. They imported from Norway their iron tools and weapons and their textiles; they exported wool and wild products—white Greenland falcons were gifts for princes. So long as their European contacts were maintained, they could survive; but in the thirteenth century these contacts became intermittent and in the fourteenth almost ceased, owing to political troubles in Norway, to the Black Death, and to the increasing control of Scandinavian trade by German Hanse merchants who had no interest in Iceland or Greenland. The commercial economy of the Greenland settlements broke down, and their subsistence economy was inadequate to sustain them. Isolated and almost forgotten, they dwindled and eventually died out. There may have been Norsemen still alive in Greenland when Columbus was exploring the West Indies and Cabot was discovering the Grand Banks; but apparently no one in Europe knew or cared. No surviving evidence links the Vinland story with the fifteenth-century discovery of the Americas. Absence of evidence, of course, does not amount to contrary proof; but in general it seems that the legendary voyages of the Irish saints had more influence upon fifteenth-century geographical thought than had the real voyages of the Norsemen.

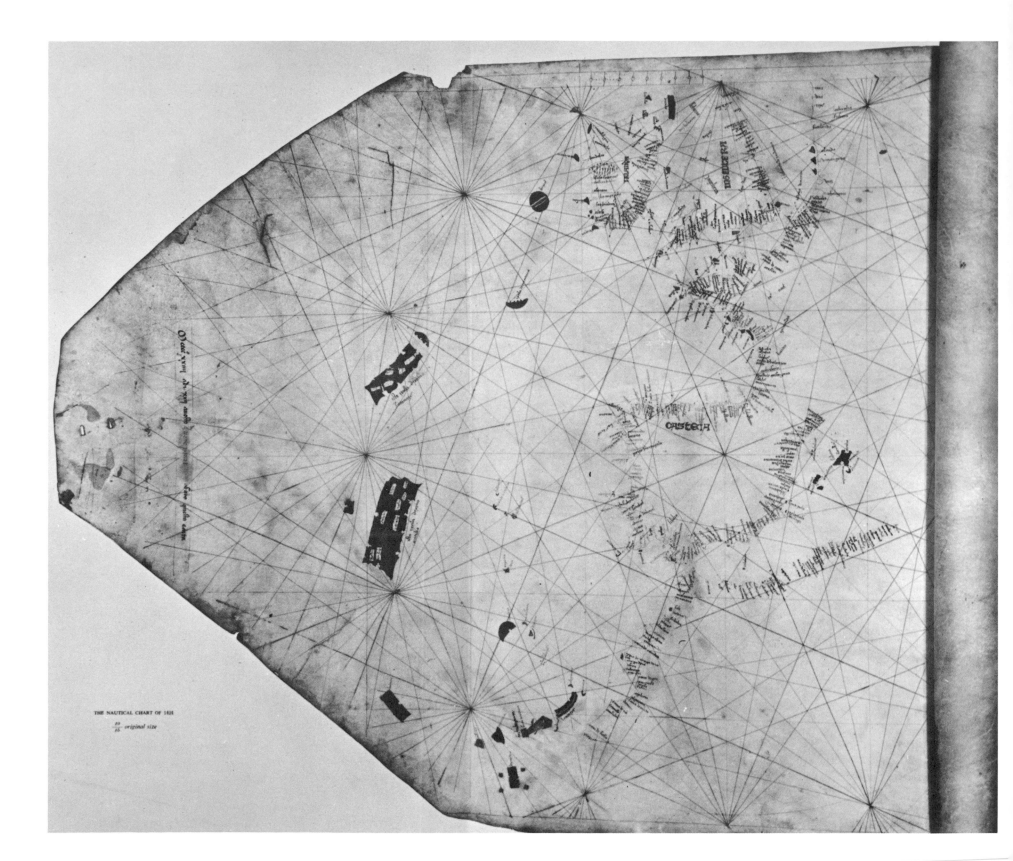

THE NAUTICAL CHART OF 1424

10/15 original size

Brasil and St. Brendan's Isle were not the only legendary islands in the Atlantic; they had counterparts farther south. The myth of the Isle of Seven Cities, current in the Iberian peninsula, was of comparable antiquity. According to this tradition, when Roderick, the last Visigothic king of Spain, lost his kingdom to the invading Moors, seven bishops had fled out to sea with their flocks and had established themselves on an Atlantic island, where, it was presumed, their descendants might still be living. This island was often described in the fifteenth century simply as Antilia, Antilha, Antilla—"the island opposite." It appears, under one or other name, or both, in many fifteenth-century maps, a rectangular island about the size of Ireland. There were others—Yma the blessed, Perdita the lost, the Fortunate Isles. These lovely, nostalgic names were not treated as allegories or literary embellishments, but as real names of real places. Western Europeans in the early fifteenth century—those of them who thought about such matters—believed that the Atlantic was full of islands. Some, at least, of these islands might well repay the trouble of discovery or of re-discovery.

There are, of course, a great many real islands in the eastern north Atlantic. Apart from the British Isles, and the Norse islands near the Arctic Circle, there are four main groups: the Azores, the Madeira group, the Canaries and the Cape Verde Islands. The existence of one of these groups—the Canaries—was certainly known to Europeans at the beginning of the fifteenth century, and had been known intermittently for many centuries. Pliny had described them. They were in fact—some of them—inhabited, by a primitive but vigorous and truculent people, the Guanches, and this, together with their

mountainous character, made them a formidable proposition for would-be settlers. A Genoese in the service of Portugal, Lanzarotto Malocello, after whom Lanzarote is named, rediscovered some of the islands about 1336, and so reminded Europe of their existence; he secured a feudal grant of Lanzarote and Gomera from the King of Portugal, but Guanche resistance and Castilian raids prevented him from establishing permanent settlements. His son, who inherited his rights, had no better luck, and attempts at settlement ceased, until 1402. In that year a similar grant was made by the King of Castile to the Norman Jean de Béttencourt, who eventually succeeded in establishing his people in Lanzarote, Ferro and Fuerteventura. The conquest of the entire archipelago was to take nearly a hundred years, and throughout most of the fifteenth century possession was to be disputed between Portugal and Castile.

We cannot be sure to what extent the other groups of islands were known at the beginning of the century. The Cape Verde Islands had certainly not been visited or sighted. The uninhabited Madeira islands were probably known from casual sightings by Portuguese, Spanish or Genoese ships returning from the Canaries, but no attempt at settlement was made until after 1418. Similarly with the remote Azores, which are a third of the way across the Atlantic: the Laurentian *portolano,* one of the most distinguished fourteenth-century maps, marks a group of Atlantic islands which might be intended to represent the Azores, but far from their true position. One of them is labeled Brasil. The islands were discovered or rediscovered by Portuguese about 1427. The first certain reference is from 1439, and concerns plans for

OPPOSITE: Chart of the north Atlantic, 1424, showing islands, real and imaginary

the settlement of some of the islands, with the implication that they had been known some years earlier. The westernmost islands of the group, Corvo and Flores, whose wind-carved cliffs mark the true extremity of Europe, were not discovered until the fourteen-fifties. Throughout the fifteenth century, then, explorers were to find new islands in the Atlantic. The supply of islands seemed endless. It was not unreasonable for people who knew the earth was round and who underestimated its size, to suppose that they could go westward from island to island until eventually they entered the archipelago which, they were told, lay off the east coast of Asia.

Southern, Mediterranean Europe possessed a tradition of geographical study older, more varied and more complex than that of the Atlantic coasts. It was concerned less with oceans and islands, more with continents, chiefly with Asia, to a lesser extent with Africa. Like the Atlantic tradition, it was compounded of factual report, hearsay, myth and academic theory; but during most of the eight hundred years from the seventh century to the fifteenth, the element of factual report was small. Europeans had little or no access to direct information about Asia. The Romans, in their days of imperial prosperity and power, had been in regular commercial contact with India and knew something, though at second hand, of *Serica*—China. They had imported spices from the one and silk from the other, in quantity sufficient to provoke many writers, from Pliny in the first century to St. John Chrysostom in the fourth, to diatribes against alien luxury. Most of these commercial contacts had been by sea, by way of the Persian Gulf or the Red Sea and across the Indian Ocean; but in the upheavals of the third century, the Romans

had lost their grip upon the trade and had become dependent on the dubious goodwill of Persian and Axumite rulers. In the seventh century, Syria, Mesopotamia and Egypt had been conquered by Islamized Arabs. A powerful and aggressive caliphate then governed the lands of the Fertile Crescent, controlled the termini of the Indian Ocean trade routes, and discouraged the already dwindling contact between Europe and Asia. Western pilgrims still visited the Holy Land, but they got no farther east. Spices still came to Europe, but in an attenuated, toll-burdened trickle through the hands of Muslim middlemen. With the drying-up of trade, the flow of information ceased. Between Cosmas Indicopleustes—merchant turned monk, who in Justinian's time visited India and Ceylon by sea, and who contrived in his *Universal Christian Topography* to fit a good deal of hard fact into a literal acceptance of scriptural cosmography—and Marco Polo—who in the late thirteenth century spent twenty years in China and composed one of the greatest travel books of all time—there was no European account of India or China worth the parchment it was written on. The encyclopaedic *Etymologiae* of St. Isidore of Seville, incorporating information derived partly from the Scriptures, partly from late Latin purveyors of geographical legend, was the most generally accepted reference book on Asia, as on many other topics. Men forgot about the mysterious and cultivated Seres. India became a memory, a vague geographical term which might include almost any area east of the Nile.

Medieval Europeans knew very little about Asia; until the thirteenth century practically nothing, except for the scraps of information which crusaders, traders and pilgrims brought back from the countries bordering the Levant. This is not to say that they lost interest in the East; only that they lost sight of it as a land of reality. Myth and legend supplied the place of concrete knowledge. According to the Book of Genesis, the Garden of Eden lay "eastward," and inaccessible to man. Early medieval describers of the world and makers of *mappae-mundi* agreed in placing "India" also in the East; but otherwise they did not define it geographically. "India" was not so much a recognizable territory as a fairyland of exotic wealth, a conventional setting for tales of fabulous kingdoms. It was the setting also for stories of marvels and monsters—giant gold-storing ants; cynocephali, monoculi, skiapods; pygmies and hermaphrodites. Some of these creatures may have had a remote basis in actual reports of pygmy peoples—who do exist—or of lemurs or baboons; but in general they were the inherited products of Greek imagination. Pliny described them; so did Solinus. St. Augustine devoted a cursory and skeptical chapter to them, in order to determine whether—if they existed—they were to be counted among the descendants of Adam. They recurred in geographies and travel books for more than a thousand years. They took fresh life and vigor from the splendid mendacity of "Sir John Mandeville." They stalked through the popular printed pages of Foresti's *Supplement to the Chronicles*.

European interest in Asia, then, was compounded of geographical curiosity, envy of eastern wealth, and an insatiable taste for the marvelous and the grotesque; but there was more in it than that. It reflected also a profound nostalgia; nostalgia for a remote and glorious past when East and West were not divided. Many

legends nourished this nostalgia in Europe, and elaborated the mental picture of the East associated with it; but three among them were outstanding in their influence and appeal. One was of Hellenistic origin, one early Christian; the third was later, dating only from the twelfth century. All three became popular and widespread at the height of the crusades and gained steadily in popularity down to the fifteenth century. The first was the story of Alexander and of the great deeds traditionally attributed to him, which escaped from the Latin chronicles and histories, and from the eleventh century became the basis of many poems and romances in vernacular languages. The tale of a western (though admittedly not Christian) hero conquering much of the East made an obvious appeal to a crusading age. In the later Middle Ages it became common form, in flattering any successful conqueror, to liken him to Alexander. The second legend was specifically Christian: the story of St. Thomas the Apostle, who, it was believed, traveled to India after the Resurrection, made many converts there, and suffered martyrdom. His followers were presumed to live there still. In fact there were, and are, Nestorian Christians in south India, who to this day revere the reputed tomb of St. Thomas at Mylapore in the suburbs of Madras; they were not very powerful nor, in proportion to the general population, very numerous; but none of these details were known in Europe. Western Catholic Christians were well aware, of course, of the existence of Christian communities other than their own; but they had little contact with Syrian and Armenian Christians living under Muslim rule, and they neither liked nor trusted the Greeks, who from 1054 onward were divided from Rome by deep and bitter schism. The belief that "India" contained an influential Christian community beyond the Muslim belt was thus doubly attractive. It lent support to the third legend, that of a great Christian priest-king in Asia, which first appeared in European writings about the middle of the twelfth century. The implications of this story, political, religious and strategic, in a crusading age, were obvious. Its basis in fact, if it had a basis, can only be guessed. Most of the European travelers to the East in the later Middle Ages, of whom record remains, searched eagerly for news of "Prester John." His realm, for the first two centuries of the legend's existence, was placed somewhere in "India"; but in the fourteenth century the setting shifted to Africa, and "Prester John" became identified with a real, though little-known Christian ruler, the Negus of Ethiopia. Wherever he was, if only he could be found and his help enlisted, the fortunes of war might be reversed, the infidel put down, and the unity of Christendom restored.

The crusades quickened European interest in Asia and contributed to the spread of myths about it; many western Europeans became familiar with parts of Syria, Palestine and Egypt; but neither the ransom-gambling adventurers who did the fighting nor the pilgrims and traders who followed them to the Levant acquired much significant information about the Asia that lay beyond. The barrier of ignorance was pierced in the thirteenth century as a result, not of the efforts of crusading armies nor of the intervention of "Prester John," but of the conquests of Genghis Khan. The grass plains of central Asia were to the Mongols what the open Atlantic had been to the Vikings; their horses

were the long-ships of the steppe. They were vastly more numerous than the Vikings, and much better organized for war and conquest. The empire they created stretched, at its greatest extent, from China to the Danube. Their incursions into Europe, though destructive and terrifying, were temporary. Poland and Hungary were raided and devastated in 1241, but not annexed or occupied. The Arab states in Syria and Mesopotamia fared much worse; Baghdad was taken and sacked in 1258, the caliphate extinguished and Mongol rule imposed. Only the Mamluk sultanate in Egypt resisted successfully. Despite the alarm of 1241, the principal European rulers—obsessed by traditional fear and hatred of Islam, and possibly with "Prester John" at the back of their minds—chose to regard the Mongols as potential allies, even as potential converts. In 1245 the Franciscan John of Plano Carpini was sent by the Pope to the Great Khan at his camp-capital at Karakorum, traveling by way of Poland and Russia. His arduous two-year journey was well recorded; he himself wrote a *Description of the Mongols,* which was soon incorporated in the great *Speculum historiale* of Vincent of Beauvais. One of his companions wrote an independent narrative, and a third contemporary account, the *Tartar Relation,* has recently come to light. William of Rubruck, who journeyed to Karakorum in 1253 on behalf of Louis IX, also recorded his experiences, and related some of them to Roger Bacon, who used them in his *Opus majus.* Both friars failed in their diplomatic purpose, but their reports were not wholly discouraging. The Tatar Khans, it appeared, were tolerant, in an offhand, contemptuous fashion, of diverse religions; they were curious, in their ominous, predatory way, about the world outside their vast dominions. They imposed a ruthless discipline, and their authority was effective enough to make travel relatively safe. In the twelve-sixties they moved their capital to Peking and so made it possible, for the first time for seven hundred years, for Europeans to travel to the Far East.

In the late thirteenth and early fourteenth centuries a long succession of friars, mostly Franciscan, made their way to the East, not as ambassadors but as missionaries: John of Monte Corvino, who bought little slave boys in Peking in order to convert them, who built the first Catholic church there and became its first archbishop; Odoric of Pordenone, who spent ten years in south India, the Malay islands and China, and wrote perceptive accounts of all these areas; Jordan of Severac, the first Catholic bishop of Quilon in Malabar, author of the best of all the medieval descriptions of India; and John Marignolli, the last of the series, so far as is known, who returned to the papal court at Avignon in 1353 to report that the Mongol empire in China was in difficulties and seemed on the point of breakup. There were many others. Nor were missionaries the only travelers, whether by sea or by the "silk road" overland. The existence of an early fourteenth-century merchants' handbook—the *Pratica della Mercatura* of Francesco Balducci Pegolotti—containing a detailed section on eastern trade routes suggests that a considerable number of itinerant merchants made similar journeys. The Venetians Maffeo and Nicolò Polo were among their number. Nicolò's son Marco was in the East from 1273 to 1292, and became a trusted official in the service of that great and magnanimous ruler, Kublai Khan.

Marco Polo's *Description of the World* is the best, the most informative and the most complete of all the accounts of Asia written by medieval European travelers. His privileged position as an imperial official, and his travels in that capacity, gave him unusual opportunities for collecting information. He was not, perhaps, a very penetrating observer; his understanding of Chinese life, religion and social customs, for example, is inferior to that of Odoric of Pordenone, possibly because Marco's personal acquaintance was more with Mongol officials than with the Chinese whom they governed. On the other hand, his descriptions of the administration of the empire, of cities, canals, rivers, harbors, industries and natural resources, are vivid and convincing. He was an assiduous observer, with a good memory and a talent for describing what he had seen in plain, sober detail. In writing of what he had heard about but not seen, he preserved, on the whole, a judicious skepticism. His accounts are factual, unsophisticated and—so far as can be judged—accurate. To people who knew nothing of the East, however, they were startling enough. The *Description of the World* was widely read and copied; over a hundred manuscripts in various languages survive. Whether it was equally widely believed may be doubted. The nickname by which Marco was known in Venice, *Il Milione,* suggests a suspicion of exaggeration; and probably many of his contemporaries read the book as an entertaining romance rather than as a documentary description. It enjoyed its greatest vogue in Italy, France and the Low Countries. It seems to have been little known in the Iberian peninsula in the fourteenth century. When Prince Pedro of Portugal visited Venice in 1428, the Doge presented him with a copy. Whether the book had any influence on Pedro's brother, Henrique, we cannot tell. Probably it did not make its full impact in Spain and Portugal until late in the fifteenth century, when the search for the sea route to India was well under way and when printed copies were available. It was first printed at Gouda in 1483, and frequently thereafter. Columbus had a copy, which survives with his marginal annotations. It may have helped to form his geographical convictions; it certainly lent them strong support.

The *Description of the World* was an important contribution to the discovery of the sea. Most European travelers to the East in Marco's day and in the generation after him went most of the way by land. There was a choice of routes, and during the Tatar peace, caravans were thought safer than ships. They were certainly quicker. Marco himself, on his outward journey, went by sea from Venice to Alexandretta, thence overland to Baghdad, where the choice between land and sea had to be made. The Polos chose land: through northern Persia, across the Turkmen Steppe by caravan-towns whose trumpet names have long since disappeared, over the Pamirs, through Kashgar, Yarkhand and Khotan, along the southern edge of the Gobi, and through the Mongol homeland to Peking. His homeward journey, however, was mostly by sea, calling at ports in Indo-China, Sumatra, Ceylon, western India and the Persian Gulf. His account revealed that "Mangi" (south China) had busy harbors, thronged with ships; that frequent sailings connected those harbors with India, and crossed the Indian Ocean to the Persian Gulf and the Red Sea; that between China and India, south of the Asian mainland, was a very extensive chain of large and populous islands. He was the first

European to describe the Malay archipelago, and the first also to report the existence of "Cipangu"—Japan. Marco never went to Japan, but heard it described as a rich and powerful island kingdom in the ocean east of "Cathay." Not all of his geographical information was accurate; some was seriously misleading. He exaggerated—or rather, by his description of immense distances, encouraged others to exaggerate—the east–west extent of Asia. He greatly exaggerated, also, the sea distance from "Cathay" to "Cipangu"; but it was Marco's fate that even his mistakes were to be fruitful in consequences.

The book was most seriously misleading as an account of a political situation not because it was inaccurate when it was written, but because it soon became out of date. Shortly after John Marignolli's return from the East, the Tatar empire broke up. In 1368 the descendants of Kublai Khan were driven from their Peking throne by a native Chinese dynasty, the Ming, who brought back the traditional official dislike and contempt for western barbarians. Nothing of this was known in Europe; the coming and going of European travelers had already been interrupted by the Black Death, which swept both Asia and Europe and brought long-distance land travel to a standstill. It was not resumed, because the Tatar Khans in western Asia embraced Islam and ceased to tolerate Christian travelers through their dominions. At the same time, Europeans were cut off from the sea routes. Access to the Red Sea by way of Alexandria and Cairo, and access to the Persian Gulf by way of northern Syria, had long been denied by the Mamluk sultans. Access to the Persian Gulf by way of the Black Sea was now threatened by anarchy in Tabriz, and by the expansion of the Ottoman Turks, with their highly organized military rule, northwest across the Hellespont into Greece, east into eastern Asia Minor. The Turks, initially at least, were more militant, more hostile to Christian visitors than the Arabs, far more so than the Mongols had been. Their expansion was interrupted at the end of the century by the incursions of Timur, the last Mongol conqueror; but the interruption, though devastating, was brief, and the anarchy which followed Timur's death still inhibited peaceful travel. The last European in the Polo succession to penetrate far into Asia was Clavijo, the ambassador sent by the King of Castile to Timur's court. Clavijo went nowhere near India or China, and arrived at Samarkand in 1405 to find the conqueror already dead. Fifteenth-century Europe was left dependent on thirteenth-century writers for eyewitness knowledge of the Far East.

The European travelers of the Tatar peace may thus be said to have added to the three ancient legends of Alexander, St. Thomas and Prester John, a fourth: the legend of the Great Khan of Cathay. Tales of the Great Khan became very popular in the fifteenth century, and spread widely not only in genuine travelers' reports but also in collections of spurious travelers' tales, which might be read chiefly for entertainment, but might be, at the same time, more than half-believed. How, indeed, was a stay-at-home reader to distinguish between the credibility of Marco Polo, who had in fact been to China, and that of the persuasive author of the *Travels of Sir John Mandeville,* who claimed to have been there, but who had certainly never been east of Palestine and possibly never east of Liège,

where, in the thirteen-sixties, he compiled his hyperbolic tale? Mandeville, however fictitious, was an important figure in the development of geographical opinion in Europe. The book of travels attributed to him is ostensibly a description of the Holy Land—a common enough literary form in that age of pilgrimage; but in fact it describes almost every part of the world on which literary evidence was available. The author, whoever he was, must have been unusually widely read in the travel literature of his time. He drew upon many books, while giving verisimilitude to his own by representing it as an eyewitness account. His book is well constructed, well written and—apart from the monsters and the marvels—plausible. The long section on Cathay was drawn mainly from Odoric of Pordenone; it contains a ringing description of the jeweled splendor of the Great Khan's court, exceeding that of all other monarchs, even of Prester John. Tales of this kind kept the Great Khan alive in western imagination long after the Tatar empire in fact had disappeared. When Columbus, long afterwards, went searching for a western route to Cathay, he carried letters of credence for the Great Khan.

While Europeans, during the century of the Tatar peace, made memorable and profitable journeys to the farthest parts of Asia, most of the continent which lay nearest at hand remained closed to them. European Christians, it is true, were not excluded from north Africa; despite religious difference, mutual piracy and frequent local wars, relations between the Barbary States and the maritime peoples of southern Europe were close. A Berber state, Granada, survived in Spain, in tolerated vassalage to Castile. Many Europeans lived in the north African ports.

Christian mercenaries served in Muslim armies—
and vice versa—to say nothing of renegades.
Under the tolerant rule of the Marinids in
Morocco, even friars were allowed to proselytize
in Marrakech, though there is no evidence that
they had much success. Foreign merchants—and
naturally most of the intercourse was commercial
—had their own establishments, their *funduks,* in
every major port. They were strictly prohibited,
however, from traveling inland. The inland
trades were valuable, the Berber middlemen
jealous of their advantages, the rulers determined
to prevent interloping. Bold smugglers, knowing
the country, might have evaded the prohibition;
but then they would have encountered the
obstacle of the desert itself. The great sand sea
was not unnavigable; caravans crossed it
regularly. The crossing, however, was arduous
and dangerous, and could be made only with
specialized equipment, experience and
navigational knowledge. Trade to the western
Sudan was absolutely dependent on the good will
of the desert people, the Tuareg, who provided
the camels, maintained the wells and guided the
caravans; blackmailing and robbing them too, of
course, but carefully keeping their depredations
within what the trade would bear. No foreign
merchant could have established the necessary
contacts with these elusive nomads without long
preparation and negotiation, which would have
excited remark. Very few Europeans before the
fifteenth century, as far as we know, even tried.
In 1283 an unknown European—one of a group
of twelve sent out by a Prince of the Church to
report on all the countries of the world—claimed
to have crossed the desert with a salt caravan to
a country, possibly ancient Ghana, where the
Negroes worshipped a dragon that lived on an
island in the middle of a lake. At the beginning
of the fifteenth century Anselm d'Ysalguier,
knight of Toulouse, was said to have visited Gao
on the Niger, married an African lady of noble
lineage, and returned home accompanied by his
wife, three African women and three eunuchs,
one of whom became a famous doctor. The
stories are probably apocryphal. For their
knowledge of inland Africa, Europeans depended
mainly upon such information as they could pick
up in the markets of the Maghrib.

This was little enough. Trans-Saharan traders
were not disposed to be communicative. If they
had been, they could have told of fair-sized cities
—Niami, Jenne, Gao, Walata, Timbuktu—strung
along the middle course of the Niger, in the
agreeable Sudan zone between the desert and the
wet dark forest; cities with mosques and houses
built of sun-dried mud brick, inhabited by black
people who had adopted Islam as a result of their
contact with Berber adventurers coming across
the desert. During the second half of the
thirteenth century and the first half of the
fourteenth—the period, in Asia, of the Tatar
peace—the cities of the middle Niger had been
incorporated in a single political unit, the
Mandingo Empire of Mali, one of whose rulers,
Mansa Musa, had astonished the entire Muslim
world by the splendor of the pilgrimage-progress
which he made to Mecca about 1330. Mansa
Musa could afford to be open-handed; through
his dominions passed the substantial trade in gold
dust which enriched the cities of the middle
Niger, which attracted the Maghribi merchants,
and—together with the slave trade—made the
desert crossing worthwhile.

The middle Niger cities were visited in
1352–53 by a distinguished Berber traveler, Abu

Abdullah Mohammed, known as Ibn Battuta. This was the last and perhaps the most adventurous of Ibn Battuta's many journeys; he had already traveled widely in the near East, in India, Ceylon, the Malay islands and China, and in Africa had visited the Arab trading posts on the east coast. The many-volumed *Travels* which Ibn Battuta dictated after his final return to Fez contain by far the best and fullest account we have of the western Sudan in the later Middle Ages. As a Moorish patrician, Ibn Battuta was inclined to condescend to the black people he described; but like other travelers from that day to this, he succumbed to their charm. He found their relatively comfortable and civilized manner of life and their friendly, courteous demeanor in sharp contrast with the surly rapacity of the desert nomads. It is unlikely that any contemporary European ever read the *Travels;* even in Arabic-speaking countries they circulated mostly in the form of summaries. Nevertheless, they aroused great interest in Morocco, and their author was much respected. Europeans residing there must have heard in conversation both of the man and of his journeys. Information about the gold-bearing Land of Negroes certainly reached Europe, and was recorded on European maps, chiefly on maps emanating from the school of Jewish cartographers and instrument-makers working in Majorca. Iberian Jews were well placed as intermediaries between Christendom and Islam, and the Majorcan Jews had particular advantages because of their connection, through Aragon, with Sicily, and because of their many contacts in the Maghrib. The famous Catalan Atlas, drawn in Majorca about 1375 by Abraham Cresques for presentation to Charles V of France, is perhaps the most beautifully executed of

surviving medieval chart collections. It represents the first major attempt to apply portolano techniques to the world outside Europe; but it also contains a considerable amount of inland information. It includes an elaborate drawing of Mansa Musa, his entourage and his treasure-laden camels. It marks a gap in the Atlas mountains, with the legend "through this place pass the merchants who travel to the land of the negroes of Guinea." It places Timbuktu in approximately its true position, and shows near it a lake from which one river, perhaps the Senegal, flows westward to the sea, and another, presumably intended to represent the Niger, eastward to join the Nile.

The only other African countries of which Europeans had any knowledge before the fifteenth century were Egypt and Ethiopia. Egypt was known commercially; the Genoese secured a commercial treaty there as early as 1290; they, the Venetians, the Catalans and the Marseillais all maintained *fondachi* at Alexandria in the fourteenth century, but as in Morocco they were not encouraged to travel outside the city. Ethiopia was of particular interest, as a Christian country. Whether any Europeans actually went there before the fifteenth century is uncertain; but Ethiopians occasionally came to Europe. The Coptic Kingdom, surrounded and threatened by Muslim enemies, from time to time took the initiative in seeking allies in western Europe. Early in the fourteenth century an Ethiopian embassy visited Rome and Avignon, and on their return journey in 1306 the envoys paused in Genoa. There they were interrogated by Giovanni da Carignano, who compiled from their answers a treatise on Ethiopia. The treatise is lost, except for a summary in Foresti's *Supplement* to the Chronicles, but traces of it appeared in maps, particularly in one drawn in Majorca in 1339, by Angelino Dulcert. The connection between Genoese and Majorcan cartography in the fourteenth century was very close. The geographical information about Ethiopia contained in Dulcert's map is sketchy and vague, as might be expected; but in one respect the map represents an important new departure: it is the first European map to place Prester John in Africa.

The process thus begun of—so to speak—bringing Prester John down to earth did not bring him effectively nearer. It was one thing to possess descriptions, even detailed and accurate descriptions, of distant and attractive countries; it was quite another to be able to reach them. In the later fourteenth century, as we have seen, many countries, all around the world from China to Greenland, became for various economic or political reasons less accessible than they had been; but at the same time, some at least of these far countries became more familiar to literate Europeans, through the composition and steady circulation of travel books, both genuine and spurious. The world which the travel books revealed was a geographical jigsaw puzzle, a collection of pieces of unrelated and often unverifiable information. Intelligent people naturally wanted a key to the puzzle, a general picture of the world which should show the geographical relation of one country to another and of both to the encircling sea; the size of the world; the proportion of land and sea upon its surface; the extent to which, in the unknown parts of the world, the land was habitable, the sea navigable. Was it true, for example, as some early Arab cosmographers—Masudi, El Bekri,

Edrisi—had maintained, that men could not cross the torrid, the equatorial zone, because of the heat? If it were not true, what lay beyond? Was the southern half of the globe all sea, or were there Antipodes? And how could men walk, presumably upside-down, on antipodean soil? In the absence of reliable eyewitness report, the task of providing answers to questions such as these fell to the academic cosmographers.

Late medieval Europe produced a good deal of writing and speculation on cosmography and geography. Geographical theory found graphic expression in great *mappae-mundi* such as the Ebstorf and Hereford maps with their central Jerusalem and their symmetrically disposed continents—all-embracing in scope, splendid in execution, and for practical purposes useless. They were not intended for use; not, certainly, for use in finding one's way; they were designed to display the balance and symmetry which orthodoxy demanded in a divinely ordered world. They stand in sharp contrast with practical marine charts in the *portolano* style; not until the fifteenth century did the two map-making traditions begin to draw together. Similarly with the scholastic treatises; they owed little to actual reports of recent travel; the information they contained was drawn, for the most part, from scriptural and patristic sources and from the handful of ancient writers long known and accepted as respectable. In the course of the thirteenth and fourteenth centuries the best of them showed an increasing sophistication, a keener critical judgement; but this was the result not so much of increasing eyewitness knowledge as of the steady recovery of long lost ancient works, mostly Greek in origin, coming to western Europe in Latin translations from Arabic.

Scholars familiar with Aristotle were not likely to rest uncritically content with Pliny or Macrobius. The most acute and objective of the treatises in the Aristotelian tradition was the geographical section of Roger Bacon's *Opus Majus* of 1264. Bacon was not indifferent to travelers' reports; he listened carefully to what William of Rubruck had to say; but he was obliged, like all the schoolmen, to rely chiefly on earlier books. He had, for his day, an unusually wide acquaintance with Arab writers. He arrived, by wide, critical reading and by a priori reasoning, at some correct and down-to-earth conclusions. He accepted the tripartite world and the encircling sea, but he rejected the notion that the torrid zone was uninhabitable, and believed that Asia and Africa extended southwards far beyond the equator. Bacon was highly original both in his specific geographical opinions and in his objective approach to scientific problems in general. His views remained current for nearly two hundred years and profoundly influenced the last great scholastic geographer, Cardinal Pierre d'Ailly, whose famous *Imago Mundi* was written about 1410. D'Ailly was a prolific writer on many topics, whose works enjoyed an immense prestige among scholars. He had a very wide acquaintance, wider even than Bacon's, with Arab authors and little-known ancient writers. He paid virtually no attention, on the other hand, to travelers' reports; he knew nothing of Marco Polo. The *Imago Mundi* is a vast mine of scriptural and Aristotelian erudition, an encyclopedic summary of the whole body of late medieval geographical theory. It exercised a widespread influence throughout the fifteenth century. It was printed at Louvain about 1483. Columbus owned a copy, which still survives.

When Columbus wanted learned confirmation of his own theories, it was to d'Ailly that he turned; and the *Imago Mundi,* with its exaggerated estimate of the east–west extent of Asia and of the proportion of land to sea in the area of the globe, gave him powerful—though by that time old-fashioned—support.

Apart from his influence on Columbus, d'Ailly represented the end of a passing era rather than the beginning of a new one. The completion of the *Imago Mundi* coincided almost exactly with the recovery, and translation into Latin, of a Greek work which was to prove still more influential and was to push geographical theory in a new direction. This was the *Geography* of Claudius Ptolemaeus. Ptolemy was a Hellenized Egyptian, the last of a long series of Greek geographers, astronomers and mathematicians who lived and worked in Alexandria. He wrote about the middle of the second century A.D.—at the time, that is, of the greatest extension of the Roman empire—though parts of the surviving text of the *Geography* may have been inserted by a sixth-century Byzantine editor. Ptolemy's fame rests chiefly on two works: the *Geography,* and an *Astronomy,* usually known by its Arabic name, *Almagest,* "the Greatest." Both books became well known and highly respected among Arab scholars, who were the most direct inheritors of Greek learning; but among them the *Almagest* attracted by far the greater attention. This was a book for the learned practitioner, serving the esoteric purposes of astrology rather than the satisfaction of general scientific curiosity, still less the task of finding one's way at sea. It enlarged upon the austerely beautiful Aristotelian picture of transparent concentric spheres revolving round the earth and carrying the sun and the stars with them, and added an immensely elaborate and ingenious system of circles and "epicycles" to account for the eccentric movements of the planets and other heavenly bodies relative to the earth. The *Almagest* was translated into Latin in the twelfth century by Gerard of Cremona, a student of Arabic learning working at Toledo. In the course of the thirteenth century it came to be known and accepted in the learned world of the schoolmen, though less understood, and much less revered, than Aristotle's own works, most of which had reached western Europe about the same time and by similar routes. The Aristotelian-Ptolemaic system with its celestial spheres and its epicycles remained—albeit with many variants—the standard academic picture of the universe until Copernicus, distrusting its over-strained complexity, began its demolition in the sixteenth century.

The indirect influence of the *Almagest* was not confined to the erudite. An abstract of Gerard of Cremona's translation was made about the middle of the thirteenth century by John Holywood or Sacrobosco, an English scholar then lecturing at Paris. Sacrobosco's little book, *De Sphaera Mundi,* became and for nearly three centuries remained a useful and very popular textbook, and in the late fifteenth and early sixteenth centuries printed copies of it were often to be bound up, as a theoretical background, with the earliest navigation manuals. It did more, probably, than any other book to discredit the flat-earth fundamentalists, such as Cosmas Indicopleustes; thanks to Sacrobosco, it was at least common knowledge among educated Europeans in the fifteenth century that the earth was round.

In view of the influence of the *Almagest,* the long obscurity of Ptolemy's *Geography* is hard to explain. Scraps of information drawn from it appeared in the work of Arabic scholars living in Europe, notably in that of Edrisi, the gifted Ceuta Moor who compiled, for Roger II of Sicily, the geographical manual known as the *Book of Roger;* but the first Latin text of Ptolemy himself came to Europe by a different route, the classic route of the Renaissance. It was translated in the first decade of the fifteenth century from a Greek manuscript brought directly from Constantinople; and the translator, Jacobus Angelus, learned his Greek from the influential Byzantine emigré Crysoloras. The text—or such of it as survives—is in form a treatise on the construction of maps. Its importance lay in the employment of a map projection based on fixed co-ordinates of latitude and longitude. Ptolemy divided his sphere into the (now) familiar 360 degrees, and from his estimate of the circumference of the earth he deduced the length of a degree of the equator or of a meridian. He described a method of adjusting the length of a degree of longitude for any given latitude, and explained how to construct a grid of parallels and meridians for maps drawn on a conical projection. The idea of co-ordinates in itself, it is true, was not wholly new to medieval Europe. Astrologers' *Ephemerides* were constructed with reference to positions in the Zodiac, and estimated differences of longitude were necessarily used in "rectifying" these tables for places other than those for which they were originally compiled. Roger Bacon had even attempted an actual map based on co-ordinates. The map, which he sent to Pope Clement IV, is lost; and Bacon, before his time in this as in other ways, exerted no influence upon cartography and inspired no imitators. Ptolemy's use of co-ordinates as a base and frame of reference in map-making reappeared in the fifteenth century as a new and revolutionary invention.

Ptolemy, then, pointed the way towards the construction of reliable and scientifically consistent maps of the world; but he also supplied, for plotting on those maps, a great deal of unreliable information. He was a compiler, not an originator, and the authorities which he selected for use did not always represent the best classical thought on his subject. The measurement of the earth, and so of a degree, which he perpetuated and popularized, was not that of Eratosthenes—who in the third century B.C., by a clever and lucky calculation, had reached a remarkably accurate figure—but that of Marinus of Tyre, which was too small by about a fifth. He assumed also that the "known" world of his day covered exactly 180 degrees of longitude. He numbered these off from the farthest reported land to the west—the Fortunate Isles—and stretched the continent of Asia eastward accordingly. Again, he reintroduced, to a Europe which had forgotten it, the Greek notion of Antipodes; in Ptolemy—or rather, in the version of Ptolemy which became known to fifteenth-century Europe—a vast continental land mass stretched across the southern Indian Ocean from Africa to the farthest extremity of Asia. Finally, he mistook the actual position of hundreds of places. The greater part of Ptolemy's text, in fact, is a long list of places, arranged by regions, with a latitude and longitude assigned to each place. The list was compiled from various *periploi*—sailing directions, from Marinus, perhaps from Strabo. Ptolemy's contemporaries and predecessors had, of course, no compass and no practicable means of observing longitude. Outside the well-known area of the Mediterranean the number of reliably observed latitudes known to him was small. The position of little-known places could be ascertained only by plotting their reported distance, along vaguely indicated lines of direction, from places better known and calculating differences of latitude and longitude by means of plane right-angled triangles. The positions which Ptolemy gave for many distant places are in fact wildly wrong; and since such a text, with its long list of names and figures, is especially vulnerable to corruption in copying, we may suppose that over the centuries many copyists' errors came to be added to Ptolemy's own.

These errors, great and small, appear clearly in fifteenth-century maps drawn to Ptolemy's specifications, and in the last quarter of the century printed. The Ptolemaic maps, like the portolan charts, have a strong family resemblance. They show, in addition to a reasonably accurate (though elongated) Mediterranean, the continents of Europe, Asia and Africa. Africa is broad and truncated, India even more truncated, Ceylon greatly exaggerated in size. To the east of India is drawn another and larger peninsula, the Golden Chersonese, that is, the Malay peninsula; to the east of that again, a great arm of the sea, the Great Gulf; and finally, near the easternmost extremity of the map, the country of the Sinae, for which no east coast is shown. The interior of Asia contains towns and river systems which cannot easily be related to any actual places. The interior of Africa is drawn with some attempt at detail, showing not only the "Mountains of the Moon" but also the lacustrine source of the Nile and the other rivers; but southern Africa is joined to the country of the Sinae, making the Indian Ocean a landlocked sea; and all around to the east and south is solid land, *Terra Incognita.*

The scholars of early fifteenth-century Europe had no reliable criteria for criticizing Ptolemy, just as they had none for criticizing Pierre d'Ailly or—insofar as they paid attention to him—Marco Polo. Ptolemy's compendiousness suited their requirements. The maps based on his information were greatly superior to the medieval *mappae-mundi* and covered areas not usually touched by the makers of *portolani.* His use of co-ordinates was a major advance which—though unintelligible to seamen—could not be ignored by scholars. Scholars, in any event, were disposed almost automatically to prefer the views of any ancient writer to those of their own contemporaries. D'Ailly completed the *Imago Mundi* before he saw the Latin Ptolemy; but he hastened to produce, after the recovery of the *Geography,* a *Compendium Cosmographiae* which summarized, though in a somewhat distorted form, the opinions of Ptolemy. In particular, d'Ailly retracted his earlier belief in a peninsular Africa and accepted Ptolemy's *Mare Prasodum,* the landlocked Indian Ocean. More august recognition followed. The *Historia rerum ubique gestarum* of Pope Pius II—that erudite and cultivated humanist—contains a digest of Ptolemy, though not an uncritical one, for the Pope maintained the circumnavigability of Africa. Columbus had a printed copy of this book, and drew from it such knowledge of Ptolemy's *Geography* as he possessed. From its first appearance, then, the Latin *Geography* was received among scholars with great, if not

entirely uncritical deference. For nearly two hundred years it remained the leading academic authority on its subject throughout Europe. To question Ptolemy, or to ignore him, a man must be either very bold and self-confident or else, as most seamen were, unlearned.

It could hardly be said that Europeans in the early fifteenth century were better informed about general geography than the peoples of the other maritime areas of the world. They naturally knew much more about the north Atlantic than did the Arabs (who were afraid of it) or the Chinese (who knew nothing of it). They knew nothing of the Pacific; but neither the Arabs nor the Chinese knew very much. The most frequented sea routes in the world at that time, outside Chinese coastal waters, were probably in the Indian Ocean and its archipelagic extensions. In view of the wide range of Arab trade in the northern and eastern Indian Ocean and down the coast of east Africa, it is curious that Arab academic knowledge of the area was not more precise. Arab geographers, following Ptolemy, represented the African coast as running south or southeast from Ras Asir (Cape Guardafui) to a point somewhere south of Mombasa and thence in an easterly direction clear across to the vicinity of Java. To judge from the Mao K'un map, Chinese geographers had a better picture of the Indian Ocean as a whole than had the Arabs. Europeans, of course, knew very little of the area, and that little only by hearsay. In Europe, as in the Arab world, there was a wide gap between academic knowledge and local practical experience. Northern Europe had busy trade routes but was very sketchily described and mapped. The only area thoroughly known to Europeans for both practical and academic

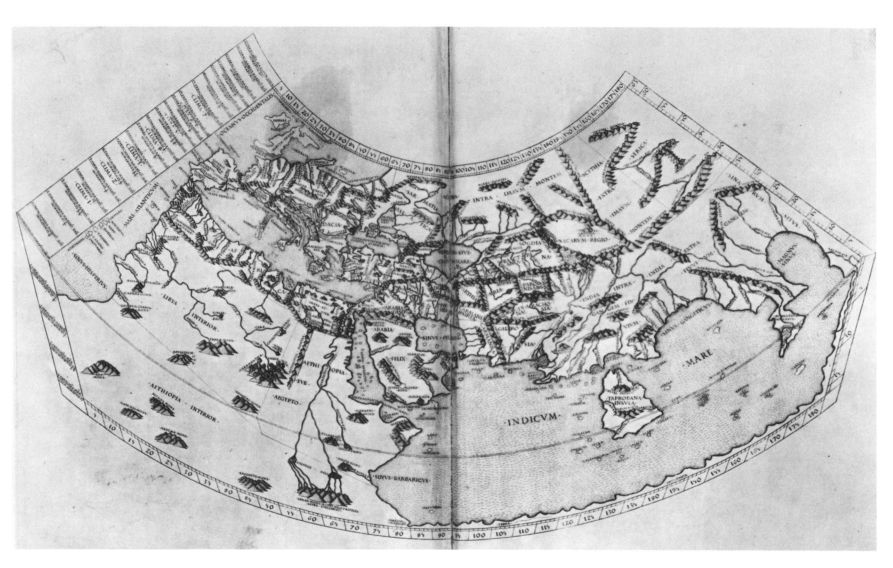

World map, engraved, from
Ptolemy, *Geographia*, Rome,
1478

purposes, and comprehensively mapped and charted, was the Mediterranean. Europeans had no monopoly of this knowledge; the Arab world was also well informed. When, at the end of the fifteenth century, Vasco da Gama's people arrived in south India—a country which they knew only by hearsay and which they fondly believed to be inhabited by Christians—they were accosted in Castilian by Arab merchants who obviously knew something of Portugal, and who treated them with a mixture of suspicion and contempt.

European cosmographical learning, in short, was not superior to that of the Arabs or of the Chinese; much of it was drawn from Arab sources. Nor were Europeans better supplied with eyewitness accounts of travel; it is certainly no disparagement of Marco Polo to compare him with Ibn Battuta, or to set the *Description of the World* beside Ma Huan's *Overall Survey of the Ocean's Shores,* of 1433 or thereabouts, which was one of the by-products of the Cheng Ho voyages. Europeans, thanks to Marco Polo and his contemporaries, could know a little more about China than the Chinese knew about Europe; but that was natural enough. China had far more attraction for Europeans than Europe could possibly have for educated Chinese.

4

The
Ties of
Trade

he *European discovery of the sea* was not the crest of a commercial wave; on the contrary, it had its beginnings in a period of relative depression and decline. The hundred years or so between the middle of the fourteenth century and the middle of the fifteenth were gloomy years in most of Europe. They were years of plague; not only the terrifying mortality of the Black Death, in itself one of the greatest disasters in European history, but a whole series of relatively smaller, but still dreadful, epidemics which swept Europe at intervals throughout the hundred-year period. They were years of war, more savage and more destructive than anything Europe had experienced since the last waves of barbarian invasion in the ninth and early tenth centuries. In France the Hundred Years War was probably an even worse calamity, or series of calamities, than the recurrent outbreaks of plague. Castile was repeatedly devastated by civil war; so was south Italy; in north Italy, *condottieri* fought innumerable local campaigns which, while economical in military casualties—since the capital of a *condottiere* was his army—were costly in sacked towns and ruined harvests. Everywhere population declined, in many places not to recover until the sixteenth century or later; and the heaviest blows both of war and plague fell on the urban population, economically the most active part. Trade shrank; not

69

consistently, it is true, and more seriously in some trades, some regions, than in others; but the general trend was downward. Outside Europe, both in the Levant and in mainland Asia, the political situation moved steadily to the disadvantage of European trade.

Depression was the more striking in that it reversed a trend more than three hundred years old. The growth of population, almost everywhere in Europe, had been steady and considerable from the late eleventh century to the mid-fourteenth. Most of this population lived on the land, a population of peasants; but in many places, particularly in areas where most of the cultivable land was already in use and little remained for settlement, a significant and growing minority had spilled over from agriculture into trade and manufacture and had taken to urban life. This process of urbanization —with all it implied in more varied and lucrative employment, more interesting social life, greater economic and social freedom, more effective concentration of political power—had been most rapid and most pronounced in Italy. By the early fourteenth century, Venice and Milan had each some 200,000 inhabitants, Genoa, Florence, Naples and Palermo each 100,000 or so. Many smaller cities in northern and central Italy numbered their people in tens of thousands. There was no comparable cluster of cities elsewhere in Europe. Outside Italy, only Paris had as many as 100,000. There were other autonomous centres of concentrated manufacture and trade—south Germany, the Low Countries, Catalonia—but they operated on a much smaller scale. Arras, for example—a major centre of northern trade and industry—had only about 20,000 people. Barcelona, in the early fourteenth century, for a time, showed signs of developing as a rival to Venice and Genoa. The Catalans had a shipbuilding tradition, relatively sophisticated business methods, and royal support; but their population and their capital were limited, and— unlike the Italians—they depended heavily on the skill and experience of the Jewish community. Their activity remained on the scale of, say Pisa, before its defeat by Genoa in 1284, rather than on the scale of Genoa itself. After 1284 the Catalans picked up such crumbs of Pisan trade as the Genoese had left, but Barcelona never really threatened the Italian lead.

The development of busy and, by the standards of the time, densely populated urban concentrations, raised difficult problems of supply. Few of the Italian cities could be fed adequately from the countryside around them and under their own control (Milan, set in its fertile plain, was exceptionally fortunate in this respect). Land transport of bulky commodities, except over short distances, was prohibitively expensive. Most of the larger cities were obliged to import part of their requirements, especially of grain, by river and sea, and in times of local failure to increase their imports at short notice. Florence, Genoa, Venice, Ragusa, Naples, the cities of the east coast of Spain—these last mostly set in country producing wine, or oil, or wool— all were importers of grain by sea, since their local supplies were inadequate or unreliable. The principal western sources were Apulia and Sicily, both controlled politically by the rulers of Aragon, who were regular importers; but the western Mediterranean as a whole often ran short, and the importing cities then had recourse to the cheap and plentiful grain of the Levant and the Black Sea countries. There existed in the

OPPOSITE: Venice, from *Civitates Orbis Terrarum,* 1576

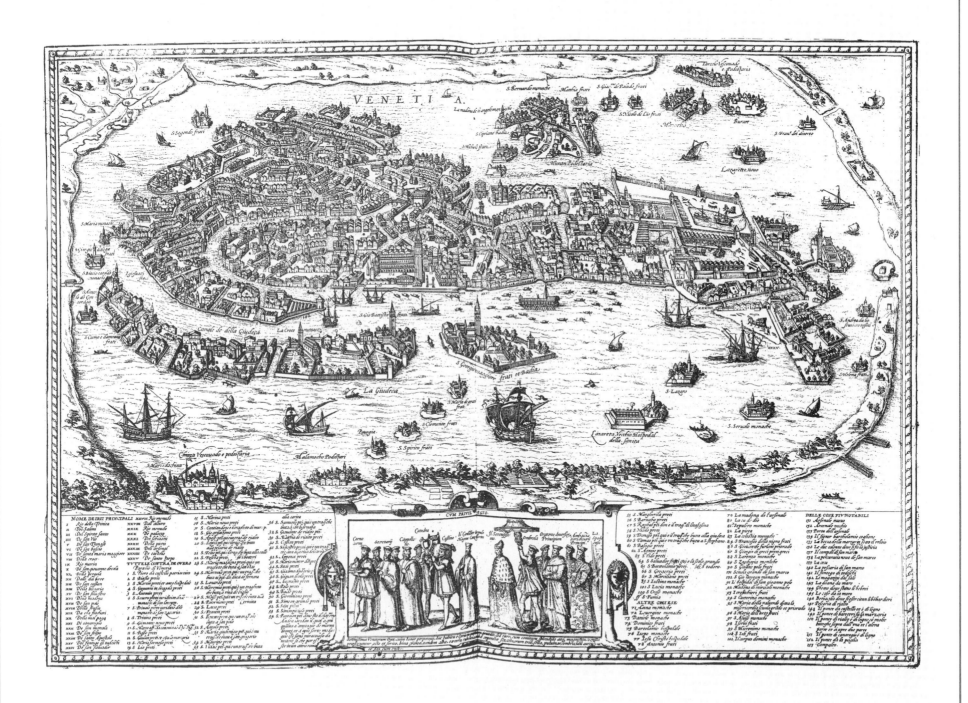

VENETIA.

western Mediterranean, therefore, a specialized, complicated and necessarily flexible seaborne trade in grain. The ships, Venetian, Genoese, Ragusan, were large, were designed to carry their bulky cargo, and usually carried nothing else. Nor was grain—though the most essential—the only bulky article of food regularly transported by sea about the western Mediterranean. Salt, and food preserved in salt, were major articles of trade. The Venetians were the principal carriers of salt, Istria and Sicily the chief exporting sources. Fishing was universal; the tunny fisheries of the Strait of Messina and the coastal waters of Provence were the richest sources of fish for salting. Mediterranean supplies of salt fish, however, by the fourteenth century were falling short of the demand, and Italian cities were beginning to import fish caught and salted in Atlantic, even in Baltic waters. Oil, wine, fruit and cheese were all carried regularly about the Mediterranean by sea in large quantities. Southern Italy and southern Spain were principal sources of oil; both, but especially Italy, exported it in exchange for grain, even as far as to Egypt. The Mediterranean wine trade—since viticulture was spread throughout the region—employed no large fleets such as those which regularly left the Gironde for England; but it was of considerable volume and importance. Cyprus and Crete—home of the famous Malvoisie grape—produced sweet heavy wines, highly prized as luxuries, which were sold all over the Mediterranean from Constantinople to Genoa and beyond Gibraltar to England. With these rarer wines went a trade in dried grapes—Spanish raisins and Greek "currants"—almonds and oranges, by the same routes, in Venetian and Genoese ships.

Northern Italy had to import not only staple foods, but also many of the raw materials of industry. Textiles formed the basis of the prosperity of many cities. Florence was the leading producer of fine woolens, Cremona of linens. Most of the flax was grown locally, but most of the wool had to be imported by sea, the coarser kinds from France, north Africa and Syria, the finer kinds from Spain and—by the early fourteenth century—from England. Alum, essential as a mordant and cleansing agent in the finishing and dyeing of cloth, was also imported in very large quantities, and probably occupied a greater tonnage of shipping than any other single commodity except grain. Most of the alum used in northern Italy came at that time from Asia Minor. The transport of the alum was virtually monopolized by Genoese shippers, who carried it not only to Italy but also to England and the Netherlands. The very large size of many Genoese merchant ships was a consequence of the need to carry this bulky and relatively cheap commodity. The products of the textile industries, both woolen and linen, were widely exported. So too were the products of the metallurgical industry of the Lombard towns, especially arms and weapons made in Milan, also largely from imported raw material.

In all these varied activities we can see a steady accumulation of capital in money and goods; a growing use of credit and a trend towards a separation of management both from ownership of capital and from manual labor; a constant endeavor to improve the methods of business and to compete with other businessmen in the same field; a planning of large-scale operations with a view to expanding the market; an elevation of trade interests to the importance of state affairs; and above all, a desire for profits as a leading motive for commercial activity. Some forms of organization, which became familiar in later mercantile development, were still lacking. There were no permanent joint stocks, no limited liability; it was not until 1408 that a Florentine statute allowed the creation of *società in accomandita,* or limited partnerships, in which dormant partners were liable only to the extent of their investment. Long before that, however, there existed in the Italian cities a great variety of devices for concentrating capital, spreading risks and sharing profits. Medieval corporations—merchant guilds, craft guilds, regulated companies—were for the most part officially chartered organizations regulating the trade of their members, forcing those members to accept uniform standards and levels of profit; they were not usually trading concerns themselves. Partnerships for conducting commercial enterprises, on the other hand, were usually not corporations but *ad hoc* devices: one organization, one "venture." They could, however, be both big and complex, and some of them, by renewal, were long-lived. They could unite either a number of capitalists, each contributing a share, and jointly employing the labor of others; or a number of partners, of whom some contributed capital only, or capital and organizing ability, others skill, labor and willingness to travel, and all shared in the profits on a prearranged scale; or a number of active participants in an enterprise who all contributed both capital and effort and lived and worked together. All these types of association, under various names—*commenda, societas, compagnia,* and so forth—were employed in Italian seaborne trade. Association for profit was thought normal, not rapacious or

reprehensible. Of course, these phenomena occurred on a far smaller scale, affected fewer persons directly, and were much less pronounced than in more modern times; but in north Italy their influence, direct or indirect, permeated the whole society. North Italy was the only area in Europe where the nobility took to trade in large numbers and where a commercial patriciate governed the big cities. The effects penetrated also to small towns and villages and into the countryside, and were felt by humble peasants. These social changes, as well as the quickening of economic activity in itself, justify historians in describing the whole process, from the late eleventh century to the mid-fourteenth, as a "commercial revolution."

The commercial revolution was accompanied by an intermittent but vigorous counterattack on the part of Catholic western Europe as a whole against Muslim infidels and Greek schismatics. Considered simply as military operations designed to push back the frontier of Islam and to recover the Holy Places for Christendom, the crusades were not particularly successful; such successes as they achieved were limited and temporary. The Latin principalities in Syria and Palestine were relatively short-lived and always precarious. The commercial effects of the crusades, on the other hand, were far-reaching and profound; the Iliad of the barons was surpassed by the Odyssey of the merchants. The Italian maritime cities profited greatly from the actual business of transporting crusading armies and competed fiercely with one another for contracts to do so. They did well out of loans to crusading powers. They accumulated capital by sharing in the loot of successful crusades. In the long run, however, they profited even more from the spread of a taste for oriental goods in Europe. They added to their regular customers returned crusaders who had learned to enjoy the luxuries of the Orient, and the crusaders' friends and neighbors who listened to the tales of easy life there. Italian merchants traveled everywhere in the wake of the armies, buying the goods with which to gratify this taste; and in order to ensure a steady supply they set up permanent trading establishments in major cities all around the eastern Mediterranean. In the crusader states these *fondachi* were often very extensive; the Italians secured grants of entire sections of cities, with fields and gardens. In the Byzantine empire also, Italian colonies occupied considerable areas, though their quarters were looted from time to time by rioting mobs. In most Muslim cities the *fondachi* were more modest: warehouses and lodgings combined, usually in enclosed compounds, in which the merchants were required to live and to which they could, if the local ruler desired, be confined. The *fondachi* in Muslim territory were to some extent extra-territorial in character, with internal self-government and corporate responsibility for good behavior. This arrangement was a convenience to the local authorities, and at first, while the settlements were small, gave some feeling of security to the merchants; but as the volume of Italian trade grew it became irksome, a symbol of frustration. The Italians were obviously in a weak bargaining position so long as their very presence in the Levantine centres depended on the goodwill of local rulers, and so long as they were compelled to buy from middlemen who could monopolize the channels of supply. The Byzantine authorities controlled the entrance to the Black Sea and access to Asia

Minor. The Mamluk rulers of Egypt controlled access to the Red Sea, and through their command of Syria, access to Mesopotamia and the Persian Gulf. The prices which Italian traders had to pay for oriental goods, and the duties levied on those goods by Levantine rulers, had already by the end of the twelfth century reached a point where they could no longer be passed on in their entirety to the ultimate customers; they were trenching seriously upon Italian profits. Nor was their privileged position in the crusader states much help to the Italians. Saladin in the twelfth century almost destroyed the Latin principalities. The "Kingdom of Jerusalem" re-established by the third crusade was only a narrow coastal strip, which could only be maintained by constant expensive naval effort on the part of the Italians. By the end of the twelfth century, maritime groups in Italy were becoming convinced of the necessity of diverting the crusading movement more directly to their own advantage; of turning the pious drive for the Holy Places and the simple pursuit of land and loot into a comprehensive strategy for the conquest of Egypt and the Byzantine empire.

The new, commercially inspired strategy was not everywhere successful. A series of crusades against Egypt, beginning in 1218, were all failures; trade in Alexandria, in the intervals of war, continued on terms settled by diplomacy, not by conquest. Against the Byzantine empire, on the other hand, the new strategy achieved a notable success. The fourth crusade yielded more booty even than the first had done, and dealt the empire an almost mortal blow. It was not quite mortal, because the Greeks retained Asia Minor; but it left the Venetians effectively in control of Constantinople. They remained in control for fifty-five years. The Greeks recovered the city in 1261, but only with Genoese help, for which they had to pay with commercial concessions. In effect, the Genoese then succeeded the Venetians as the exploiters of the empire. Much of the Black Sea trade was diverted from Constantinople itself to the Genoese suburb, Pera, while merchants from many of the smaller commercial centres of the west, including Barcelona, established colonies in the city itself. These developments, from 1204 onwards, opened the Black Sea to Latin merchants. Venetian and Genoese commercial colonies quickly established themselves: at Caffa in the Crimea, at Tana at the head of the Sea of Azov, at Trebizond, and at many smaller places. At the same time, the most valuable islands in the Levant and the Aegean became Italian possessions. Venice got the lion's share, including Cyprus and Crete, with their trade in grain and wine. The turn of Genoa came a little later; Genoese businessmen demanded fiefs as well as commercial concessions as the price of their support of the Byzantine emperor: the island of Chios, for example, the only source of mastic, one of the most sought-after aromatic herbs; and the alum-producing district of Phocaea in Asia Minor. The islands were not mere trading posts, but territorial possessions, administered outright by, or on behalf of, people who profited by shipping their products to Italy and western Europe. The commercial empires of Venice and Genoa had become also naval and colonial empires of formidable strength. They had effectively divided the Aegean into spheres of influence. They had acquired outposts on some, at least, of the routes into Asia. They had largely dissociated themselves from the central crusading

tradition. Palestine and Syria were no longer of major importance to them. The "Kingdom of Jerusalem," fast shrinking under the defeats inflicted by Sultan Baybars in the third quarter of the thirteenth century, could, so far as they were concerned, be written off. Neither the capture of Antioch by Baybars in 1268, nor the expulsion of the Franks from their last toehold at Acre in 1291 caused much stir in Italy, or indeed in Europe; it was galling to Christian pride, but had little effect on Christian pockets.

The fall of Acre coincided almost exactly with the first deliberate move, of which record remains, toward the "discovery of the sea." In 1291 the brothers Vivaldo sailed from Genoa with two trading galleys in an attempt to reach the Indies by way of the "Ocean Sea." Presumably they intended the circumnavigation of Africa. Genoese and Venetian seamen, by that time, had acquired considerable experience of Atlantic sailing conditions. Both cities were sending small galley fleets every year to the ports of Flanders and the south of England. Whether galleys, with their necessarily large crews and small stowage space, could have made the immensely long passages proposed by the Vivaldi might well be doubted; but the attempt was not regarded as madness at the time. It was taken seriously, and had serious backing. Nothing came of it; the Vivaldi sailed through the Strait of Gibraltar, turned southwest down the Moroccan coast, and disappeared. Rumors persisted for some time of the arrival of one of the ships on the east African coast, but nothing definite was ever learned of their fate and the attempt was not repeated; partly, perhaps, from conviction of its dangerous hopelessness, but also because other and surer routes to the Far East were already open. Marco Polo returned to Venice the year after the Vivaldi's departure. When the immense possibilities opened to European trade by the Tatar peace became generally known, Italian merchants were ready to take advantage of them. They had the capital and the business organization, and they already possessed the appropriate starting points for overland travel in Asia. Caffa and Tana lay on the route to Astrakhan, which gave access to the navigation of the Caspian. Trebizond was the Black Sea terminus of the road to Tabriz, whence travellers could go by caravan to Samarkand and beyond; or else to Baghdad and Basra and so by sea down the Persian Gulf to Ormuz and across the Indian Ocean. There was no need for hazardous adventures in the south Atlantic; and Syria and Egypt, if their Mamluk rulers placed unacceptable restrictions on trade and could not be conquered or persuaded, could be bypassed.

Pegolotti's celebrated commercial handbook, which has already been noticed, states that in the early fourteenth century the route from Tana to Peking was "quite safe." This was, perhaps, an unduly light-hearted description of an appallingly arduous journey, which presented special risks in addition to the ordinary risk of brigandage. In the Mongol principalities, for instance, and in the Muslim principality of Ormuz, the goods of merchants who died traveling were customarily seized as the property of the ruler. Nevertheless, the journey was made repeatedly. Genoese merchants established residences in central Asia, in India and in China; Franciscan missionaries built a *fondaco* for Catholic merchants in Hangchow. In Pegolotti's day the price of Chinese silk in Italy fell below that of silk from the Caspian region, though it had to be carried

more than twice the distance. In the spice trade, Ormuz largely replaced Alexandria as port of trans-shipment for oriental spices destined for Europe. Genoese merchants employed their own ships, built in their own colonies, for local trading both in the Caspian and in the Persian Gulf. Between 1323 and 1345 the Venetians—partly, it is true, in deference to papal injunction—sent no official convoys to Egypt. Only a trickle of spices passed through their *fondachi* at Alexandria. Most of their requirements came by other, more northerly routes. Considering the primitive nature of the available transport, the actual quantities of goods carried between Asia and Europe at this time must have been considerable; their value, more impressive still. In 1334 the tax returns of the Genoese commercial colony of Pera—taxes derived partly from dealing in Black Sea grain and fish, but also very largely from buying and selling oriental goods—reached a total of only a little less than those of the capital city of Genoa itself. They were ten times those of Lübeck.

This busy commercial euphoria, based on open traffic between Europe and Asia, came to an abrupt end in the middle years of the fourteenth century. The Black Death was the most universal and the most frightening of the disasters which closed the trade routes; frightening not only because of the appalling initial mortality, but because of the recurrence, at relatively brief intervals, of smaller, more local outbreaks. It made strangers unwelcome everywhere; any caravan might carry plague. Plague was not the only obstacle to travel, however. Already in the decade before the first terrifying outbreak, the Mongol Khanates, into which the empire of Genghis Khan had been divided, were themselves showing signs of political disintegration, and their people, in course of gradual conversion to Islam, became increasingly hostile to Christian travellers. In 1339 the European residents at Almaligh in Turkestan were massacred by mobs in the course of a rebellion against the local ruler. More serious, in the following year, the friendly Khan Abu Said of Tabriz died, to be succeeded by a bloodthirsty local tyrant, and the whole Persian Khanate collapsed in anarchy. The mountainous area between Trebizond and Tabriz had always been the worst stretch of the great silk road, constantly troubled by brigands, and passable only by armed caravans. Now it became impassable. Worse, and nearer home, was the long siege of Caffa by the Kipchak Khan, preceded by a massacre of Italians at Tana. The Khan was accused of catapulting plague-infected corpses into the city; an outbreak of plague in the city certainly weakened the defense (though not to the point of surrender), and the flight of many Europeans from Caffa to Constantinople was a factor in the spread of the Black Death. Eventually the siege was raised and peace, of a sort, was made; but it became dangerous for Europeans to go beyond the city walls. Pegolotti's safe route to Peking became exceedingly unsafe. Caravans still endeavored to get through, by devious routes, avoiding the known trouble spots, down to 1345 or thereabouts; but then movement was stopped by the plague. It was never resumed. The Khanate of China was finally overthrown by the Ming rising in 1368. After that, even if European merchants could have reached Peking, they would not have been allowed to trade. The doors which had opened so invitingly in the

middle of the thirteenth century were slammed shut in the middle of the fourteenth.

The transcontinental silk trade was naturally the principal casualty; but its disappearance was less damaging to Italian interests than might have been expected. Silk manufacture had long been established on a modest scale in Italy, chiefly at Lucca, having been carried there from the Byzantine empire many years earlier. The Lucchese silk throwers had used raw silk imported from China or from Turkestan. The interruption of supplies from these sources created an urgent demand, which was met to some extent by the development of sericulture in Italy itself, chiefly in Sicily and Calabria, whence the silk was shipped north from Messina. Necessity, in this instance, proved the mother of invention in more ways than one: Lucchese silk manufacture was notably efficient for its time, especially in its use of water power to drive the throwing mills, though the silk was never comparable with the best eastern silks, and there was never enough of it to meet the demand arising from the extravagant Renaissance taste in clothes.

In the spice trade, import substitution was more difficult. The term "spice," as used in the later Middle Ages, defies definition. It covered a wide range of miscellaneous substances, not all exotic to Europe, not all rare and costly, and not all edible. Pegolotti listed three or four hundred of them, nearly all primary products, though some had been through simple processes of manufacture. Many of the raw materials of industry were "spices," according to Pegolotti; copper, for example, was on the list, and so were some of the raw materials of textile manufacture —raw cotton, raw silk (twenty-three kinds), and a number of dyestuffs, gums and resins, some exotic, some not. The gums included, oddly, glue. The most sought-after spices, however, were either medicinal drugs, cosmetics, perfumes, or seasonings and preservatives for use with food. The importance of the last group was obvious, especially in northern Europe, where in order to conserve fodder large numbers of animals had to be slaughtered every autumn, salted, and eaten half-rotten through the winter. Some of these seasonings could be grown in Europe. Sugar, for example, formerly imported from the Levant, was grown and manufactured increasingly in the later Middle Ages in Crete, Cyprus, Sicily and southeastern Spain; Pegolotti listed eleven kinds. Saffron was another example of a widely used seasoning which, when Levantine supplies were difficult, came to be cultivated widely in Italy, Spain and other parts of Europe, including, for a time, eastern England. Saffron was an exception, however. The most valuable seasonings and preservatives grew in the humid Tropics, and could not be made to grow elsewhere. For them, Europe was absolutely dependent on trade with Asia. Pepper was by far the most important, in terms of quantity. Species of *capsicum,* red pepper, grew in many parts of the Tropics, including (as Portuguese and Spaniards were later to discover) Africa and the New World; but the white and black peppers of commerce came from the fruits of *piper nigrum,* which was confined to the East and had been used as a condiment there from very early times. It grew in south India and throughout the Malay archipelago. Cinnamon was, and is, almost confined to Ceylon. Nutmegs and their by-product, mace, were grown chiefly in the Banda Islands. Cloves, the scarcest of all,

were prized not only for their flavor and aroma, but as a powerful preservative for arresting the decay of meat, and were used also in the manufacture of pomanders as a prophylactic against plague; they grew only in a few small islands in the Moluccas group. All these valuable commodities were the objects of heavy demand in China, Persia, the Arab countries, and all over Europe. The port of Malacca, on the eastern shore of the strait which bears its name, in the course of the fourteenth century grew from a fishing village into a major international spice mart, chiefly supplying the needs of China, but also providing spices of island origin for shipment to India.

Spices intended for sale in western Asia and in Europe were purchased by Indian, Persian and Arab traders in the Malabar harbors of Calicut, Quilon, Cochin and Cananore, and taken to two main ports of trans-shipment: Ormuz at the mouth of the Persian Gulf, Aden at the mouth of the Red Sea. In these branches of the Indian Ocean, trade was carried in coastal shipping, in the Persian Gulf mainly Arab and Persian, though for a time, as we have seen, Genoese traders had been able to penetrate the area and buy spices at Ormuz. In the Red Sea, that heated funnel of reef-bound water, the shipping was mostly Egyptian, plying from one port to another from the Bab-el-Mandeb up to Suez, the harbor for Cairo and the Nile valley. Spices carried from Suez via Cairo to Alexandria were offered there to European merchants, among whom the Venetians were the most prominent group. During the century of the Tatar peace, Europeans in the spice trade had enjoyed a choice of sources, a choice of routes. The existence of this choice had been particularly to the advantage of the Genoese, though the Venetians also sent fleets to Trebizond. In the middle of the fourteenth century events conspired to narrow the choice. The supply of spices coming to European buyers from Ormuz through Tana, Caffa, Trebizond and Constantinople was greatly reduced and at times cut off. Syria was still under Egyptian control, and its own supplies were precarious. So the buyers turned once more to Alexandria, the one place where supplies—at a price—could be relied on. The Venetians were the first to effect this change of trading policy. In 1345, they implored the Pope to lift his embargo on Egyptian trade, and sought new commercial treaties with the Sultan. The Pope responded by selling individual dispensations; the Sultan gladly resumed his exploitation of European traders, and the Venetians returned in force to their old, tolerated, dependent—but highly profitable— business in his dominions.

From the point of view of European consumers in general, the state of eastern trade in the late fourteenth and early fifteenth centuries was thus highly unsatisfactory. They were back to where they had been before Genghis Khan. From an Italian, and particularly from a Venetian point of view, it was less unsatisfactory than at first sight it may have appeared. The total volume of European economic activity declined in the late fourteenth century, and began only very slowly to recover in the fifteenth; but within the total, the Italians maintained their predominance. If Venice, having outstripped Genoa, was the leading naval and commercial centre of the western world in the fifteenth century, Florence was the greatest banking centre and the Medici bank the biggest financial organization. Its

activities reached every region of Europe and the Levant; they included not only banking operations and a big trade in luxury goods, but also staple trades, especially in grain, control of many units of textile production, and the exploitation of alum mines. Many other banks in Florence and in other northern and central Italian cities had widespread business interests maintained by agents in all major centres. Both Venice and Genoa let out the administration of some of their public revenues and of their colonial possessions to financial corporations originating in groups of public creditors. The

Spice trees, from de Bry's *Voyages*

Genoese Casa di San Giorgio, incorporated in 1408, was a bank of this kind, as was the *maone* of the Giustiniani family and their associates, which administered the island of Chios. The Italian cities, in times of adversity, did not lose—they rather developed and extended—the business skills which they had acquired in more expansive times. Their established networks of trade and intelligence, their accumulations of capital, could resist heavy blows and still survive and flourish. The size and efficiency of Italian commercial and financial organization, the superiority of Italian manufactured products, the Italian monopoly of the trade in eastern goods—all combined to tie the whole of Europe, in greater or less degree, commercially to northern Italy. Venice remained, throughout the fifteenth century, the main channel of commercial contact between northern Italy and the East.

The standing of the Venetians at Alexandria in the early fifteenth century was less dependent on the goodwill of the Sultan than it appeared to be. Mamluk Egypt had its troubles. It had succeeded in resisting the Mongols, it had survived Timur, the Turks were not yet threatening it; but it was weakened by maladministration, by succession disputes and Syrian rebellions, and impoverished by the strain of recurrent double war against Mongols and Christians. The Sultan had every temptation to squeeze the merchants who came to Alexandria. The rate of the duties which he collected from them approached 100 percent of the value of the goods, and throughout most of the century they were required to buy annually a fixed quantity of pepper from the Sultan at his price. On several occasions, when the Venetians resisted increases in this price, they were intimidated by confinement to their *fondachi* and by threats of expulsion. These high-handed measures were rare, however, and never taken to extremes. The Mamluks and the Venetians needed one another's business; and Venice, if pushed too far, could take severe naval reprisals, as the Mamluks knew from experience. The Sultan's pepper, moreover, was usually only about one tenth of the total amount bought and sold; the price of the rest fluctuated with the ordinary operation of demand and supply; gluts sometimes occurred, and in fact over the century as a whole, spice prices remained suprisingly steady. Tense though the situation in Alexandria sometimes became, therefore, it was by no means intolerable; the Venetian merchants trading there had no good reason to suppose that, in the political circumstances of the time, they could do better anywhere else. They could usually get all the pepper they wanted. The conditions of the retail trade in spices, also, had changed. The economic crises of the fourteenth century had tended to make the poor poorer, the rich—who were the chief purchasers of spices—richer. New markets for luxury goods, particularly in south Germany, had developed. The Venetians virtually monopolized the wholesale supply. When prices or duties rose, therefore, the increase could usually be passed on to the consumers.

Balance of payments, for all European merchants in the spice trade, was a more serious problem than either restriction of supply or governmental squeeze. Some European goods could be sold profitably in the Levant, and the proceeds used to buy spices, but the range was limited. It included fine woolens and fine linens, arms and armor from Milan, copper from south Germany, lead and tin from northern Europe.

ALEXANDRIA

MEDITERRANEUM MARE

Oddly, it also included coral, which at that time was fairly plentiful in the Mediterranean but was prized almost as a precious stone in east Africa. Genoese coral fishers collected it off the north Africa coasts by dragging great wooden dredges along the bottom, and sold it in Alexandria. The Black Sea trades also, for a time, provided goods which could be exchanged for spices. Caffa, though no longer the terminus of a route to China, was still an important commercial centre, frequented by Kipchak Tatars, Russians, Poles, Rumanians, Bulgarians, Armenians and Greeks. Genoese traders sold salt, coarse woolen cloth and even ready-made garments to these comparatively primitive people, and returned with honey, caviar and slaves. Caucasian slaves, women especially, were in high demand in Alexandria. Honey was produced all around the Mediterranean, and had been since early times, but was relatively scarce and expensive in the Red Sea countries. Despite all this, however, the overall balance of trade was usually unfavorable to the Italians, and considerable quantities of gold and silver coin had also to be exported in payment for spices. The payments situation deteriorated in the fifteenth century, as a result of political developments, especially the extension of Turkish power on both shores of the Sea of Marmora. In 1367 Murad I had made Adrianople his capital and threatened Constantinople from the landward side. The incursions of Timur had interrupted the Turkish advance, but after Timur's death the Ottoman power had recovered quickly from its defeats, and the noose around Constantinople had tightened once again. The Turks were not necessarily hostile to trade and to merchants, but they were arrogant and capricious, and certainly unwilling to maintain the privileged standing which Italian merchants, Genoese in particular, had long enjoyed in the cities of the Byzantine empire. Even while Constantinople held out, its trade was slowly strangled. The tax returns of the Genoese colony at Pera provide eloquent evidence. In 1334, at the height of prosperity, they had amounted to £Gen 1,648,630; in 1391 they stood at £1,119,046; in 1423 they were down to £234,000. When finally, in 1453, the great city fell and its ancient empire was extinguished, the Turks, controlling the Bosphorus, could monopolize what little trade remained, and could exclude European shipping from the Black Sea. The Italian colonies in the Black Sea were isolated, those in the Aegean increasingly threatened. The fall of Constantinople did not stop trade. The Venetians, always resourceful, found ways of doing business with or through the Turks; but they were obliged to pay much heavier imposts on a diminished volume of Black Sea trade. Turkish power, moreover, expanded to the east as well as to the west. The Turks threatened Syria and made intermittent war against Persia, so discouraging the revival of the spice trade from Ormuz to the Syrian harbors in the Levant. Italian spice merchants had to rely more and more heavily on supplies from Alexandria; and as the products of Caffa and its hinterland ceased to be available, or became less readily, less cheaply available, they were obliged more and more to make their payments in coin.

At the same time, the supply of specie dwindled. Most of the major European countries, by the middle of the fourteenth century, possessed gold coinages, and Italian gold coins were much used in international trade. A

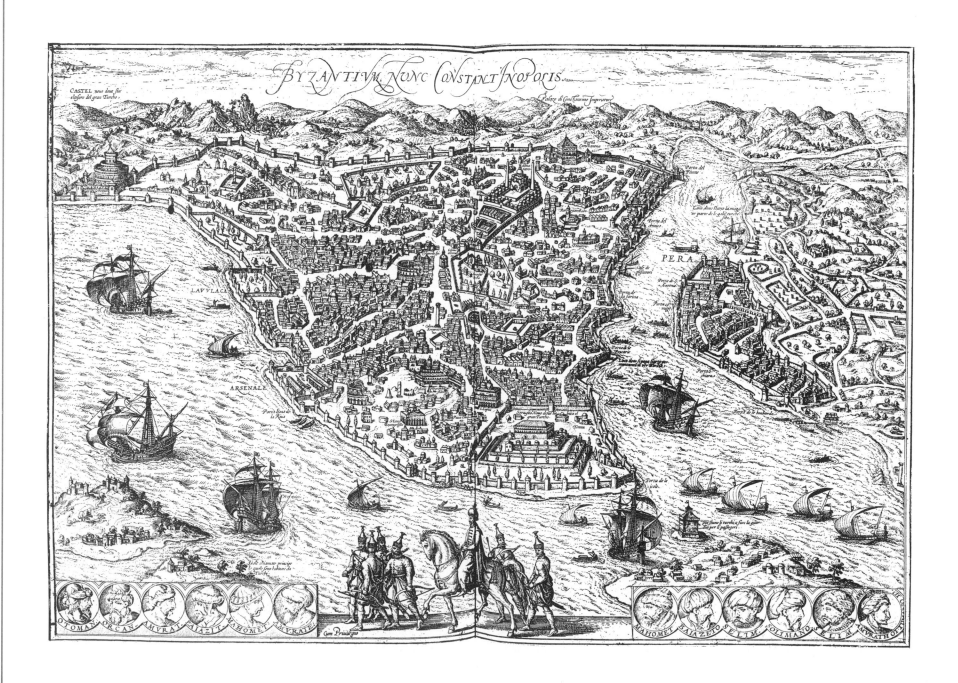

BYZANTIVM NVNC CONSTANTINOPOLIS

CASTEL novo doue sta elettore del gran Turcho

Palazo di Constantino Imperatore

PERA

LAVVLACH

ARSENALE

standard of weight and purity was provided by the Byzantine gold hyperperon, the only gold coin which was recognized and accepted everywhere. With the decline and fall of the Byzantine empire, the supply of these fine pieces dried up. Europe itself was deficient in gold for coining; the few German mines never produced enough for the purposes of trade. Nor could silver coinages adequately fill the gap. There were many small silver mines—at Freiberg, at Meissen, in the Tyrol, Carinthia, Transylvania and Bohemia—but production in all these regions declined between the middle of the fourteenth century and the middle of the fifteenth. Continued mining had deepened the shafts to the point where the workings went below the water table, and mines were put out of use by flooding, which the primitive pumping devices of the time could not control. The same difficulties affected the production of copper, which was itself an important article of export to the Levant.

The shortage of monetary metals throughout Europe emphasized for enterprising Italians the importance and the value of African trade. North Africa, in the late fourteenth and early fifteenth centuries, suffered from the same maladies as Europe: plague, disorder, war—and its trades, like those of Europe, contracted; but it was still a major market, a market moreover in which European manufactured goods were paid for, partly at least, in gold.

Some of the goods exported from Europe to north Africa, it is true, were regarded there as somewhat disreputable luxuries. They included considerable quantities of wine, which was not then produced in north Africa but was widely and publicly sold, not only to Christian residents.

The trade was tolerated, in order to secure the supply of other more vital imports. The north African coast was deficient in timber and other shipbuilding materials. Venetian and Genoese merchants regularly exported timber to the Barbary ports, and even sold there ships built in Venetian and Genoese shipyards. Such exports were the subject of repeated, and repeatedly ignored, prohibitions by European governments; in the Barbary ports they were actively encouraged by exemptions from import duty. Not only the coastal trade of north Africa, but the trans-Saharan caravan trade also, depended heavily on goods imported from Europe. European cloth always commanded a ready sale south of the Sahara. Venetian glassmakers supplied the beads which, until quite recent times, have been used in large quantities in the Sudan trade. Of metals, copper was especially in demand for re-export to the Sudan. The goods received in return in Europe from north Africa also included many which originated in the western Sudan. All the northbound trans-Saharan caravans brought back slaves; not only because Negro slaves were a saleable commodity in north Africa, but also because they supplemented expensive camels as carriers of other goods. Some of these slaves were re-exported to Europe, as were some of the goods with which they stumbled across the desert: ivory, ebony and colored "Morocco" leather. There are even records, in the fourteenth century, of *malagueta* pepper—the product of the Guinea forest belt, a coarse and pungent substitute for *piper nigrum*—reaching north Italy and the south of France from the Sudan through Barbary. None of these imports, however, compared in importance with gold. Whatever other commodities might be carried, the gold of the western Sudan was the basic reason for the existence of the caravans.

In Gao, Timbuktu, and other cities on the middle bend of the Niger, Maghribi merchants were paid in gold, at extravagant prices, for the textiles, glass beads, copper, dried fruit and Indian Ocean cowries which their caravans brought in. The gold, they were given to understand, came from a region much farther south, vaguely known as Wangara. It was produced by primitive people whose chief need from the outside world was salt. Dealers in the Niger cities imported rock salt by camel train from Taghaza in the desert and sent it by headload to meeting places on the edge of the forest zone, where it was said to be exchanged for gold dust in a process of anonymous silent barter. Possibly other middlemen interposed themselves between the bartering places and the actual sources of the gold; nobody concerned with the trans-Saharan trade appeared to know; and the shy bush-dwellers who produced the gold went to great lengths—very understandably —to preserve the secrets of their business. The name Wangara—source of gold—may well have been applied at different times to different places: to Bambuk, perhaps, between the upper Senegal and the Faleme rivers, or Bure at the junction of the upper Niger with its tributary the Timkisso, or Lobi on the upper Volta. All three to this day produce small quantities of gold by primitive washing methods. Neither the Mandingo rulers, however, nor the middlemen of the Niger cities, nor the Maghribi merchants, nor, later, the Europeans on the coast, ever found or controlled the gold-bearing areas, and their identity has never been certainly established.

Wherever Wangara might be, its attractions for gold-hungry Europeans were obvious, and the obvious way to get nearer to it—however daunting—was to push inland from the Maghrib ports and participate directly in the caravan trade. In the fifteenth century some Europeans actually succeeded in penetrating to the interior and trading there. A Genoese, Antonio Malfante, about the middle of the century, took a load of cloth from Honein on the Algerian coast to an oasis in Tuat in the central Sahara. According to his own account sent back from Tuat, he had little luck with his cloth. The inhabitants of the oasis were few, and wore few clothes; probably, as in many of the Saharan oases, most of them were captives, or descendants of captives, brought up from the Sudan to tend the date palms. Malfante's persistent inquiries about the source of gold elicited only evasive, or perhaps merely ignorant replies. Tuat was many hundreds of miles from the nearest of the Sudan gold markets, and farther still from the mysterious sources of the gold. Nothing further was heard of Malfante; probably he died in the desert. The earliest known European description, at first hand, of one of the gold-dealing cities of the Sudan—Timbuktu—was written by a Florentine. Until the early fifteenth century, Florence had been precluded by its geographical position from competing with Venice and Genoa for seaborne trade. The wide commercial influence of the Florentines had been exercised in other ways. After the capture of the port of Pisa in 1407, however, Florentine merchants embarked vigorously on direct oversea trade, and were particularly successful in north Africa. They acquired by treaties a favored position in Oran, Bona, Bugie, Algiers and Tunis; and in Tunis their agreement included the exceptional privilege of trade in the hinterland. Florentines did business in Marrakech, Sijilmasa and Kairwan, and there is evidence that some actually crossed the desert. Benedetto Dei, agent of the great merchant house of Portinari, claimed to have visited Timbuktu in 1470. Dei was an experienced traveler in Europe and the near East, a curious and careful observer, with a talent for describing remote places and a keen interest in oddities of all kinds; yet his account of Timbuktu is curiously brief and pedestrian. "I have been," he wrote, "to Timbuktu, a place situated beyond Barbary in very arid country. Much business is done there in selling coarse cloth, serge and other fabrics such as those of Lombardy." The casual nature of this account suggests that Dei's journey was not unique; that others of his countrymen had already reached the Sudan and were trading there. If so, however—if there was in Dei's time a significant direct participation by Italians in the caravan trade—it can have lasted only a short time. Leo Africanus, who wrote detailed descriptions of the Sudan cities and their trade half a century after Dei's visit, made many allusions to European goods but none to European traders. Caravan travel was necessarily arduous, costly and dangerous; doubly so for Christian Europeans. Treaties with coastal rulers could not protect them, once in the desert, against the jealousy of the established traders or against the rapacity of the Tuareg. The costs, in fact, were prohibitive; far easier and cheaper to procure gold in Morocco. Moreover—and in the long run more significant—other, competing channels of supply were becoming available, on the coast of upper Guinea; and finally, within a year or two of Dei's journey, Europeans began to tap a new and hitherto (to them) unknown source, more productive than those of the Sudan. This was Ashanti, the upland forest area behind what came, in later centuries, to be called the Gold Coast. The gold of Ashanti had no adequate trade outlet until the late fifteenth century. The people who produced it did not import desert salt. They had no regular commercial contact, so far as we know, with the gold-dealing cities of the Sudan; but they traded with the coastal peoples, who therefore, when the opportunity arose, could pay in gold for European cloth and hardware. The first Europeans to reach this coast and exploit its commercial possibilities were not Italians, but Portuguese, traveling not by camel caravan, but by sea.

5

The
Street
Corner of
Europe

he coasting of west Africa was a major stage in the discovery of the sea. Portuguese seamen took the lead in it, and for many years their lead was not effectively challenged. At first sight, this pre-eminence is surprising. Late medieval Portugal displayed few of the obvious attributes of a nation about to embark on an ambitious career of oceanic expansion. It had, of course, sea coasts, harbors and ships, trades and traders; but no powerful tradition of long-distance, deep-water voyaging, no widespread system of commercial contacts or financial organization comparable with that of, say, Genoa or Florence, certainly no great surplus of capital for outside investment. Compared with the north Italian city states, or even with Catalonia or Biscay, its economy was restricted and primitive. Even its future as an independent state must have seemed precarious to anxious contemporaries. That might be said, no doubt, of any of the Iberian kingdoms; the stability of their frontiers was constantly called in question by the chances of dynastic marriage or succession war; almost every monarch in the peninsula could put forward some sort of claim to his neighbor's throne and territory. To survive in this free-for-all, any king of Portugal had constantly to be on his guard. In the late fourteenth century, it is true, began a period of

87

comparative respite for Portugal, insofar as its most threatening neighbor, Castile, was concerned. The battle of Aljubarrota in 1385 put an end to a major Castilian invasion, the fifth in sixteen years. It stablized the boundaries of Portugal more or less as they exist today, and effectively confirmed John of Avis on the Portuguese throne. The victory was worthily commemorated by the great abbey of Batalha which John built on the site, and to this day is remembered as a major event in Portuguese history. Yet the battle did not, in itself, ensure safety. It was followed by a series of uneasy truces, punctuated by raids. The conclusion of even a provisional treaty of peace had to wait until 1411, and then Castile was brought to it chiefly by the weakness and disorder consequent upon two successive royal minorities. In the event, civil disturbances continued intermittently in Castile for the first three quarters of the fifteenth century; the peace of 1411 was renewed in 1423 and made definitive and "perpetual" in 1431, so that after 1411, for many years, Castile was to pose no serious threat to the house of Avis. John I and his successors, however, could not foresee that; they had to assume that sooner or later, in one form or another, Castilian claims would be reasserted. Portugal was smaller, politically and militarily weaker, than Castile; much weaker than France or England, on one or the other of which—usually England—the Avis kings relied for an alliance strong enough to deter Castilian aggression. English archers had done good work at Aljubarrota; and John of Avis married an English queen, Philippa of Lancaster, daughter of John of Gaunt, who himself had claims on the throne of Castile. Even with this insurance and backing, however, Portugal was

not, at first sight, a country that might be expected to spend its resources on perilous adventures overseas. It had not, indeed, many resources to spend.

Portugal was a small country with, at the beginning of the fifteenth century, probably less than a million inhabitants. Like most European countries it had suffered severe losses from the Black Death, losses which were only slowly recovered. The great majority of its people were peasants, mostly small-holders paying rent in kind, labor or money, for land which they did not own. The only important exception to this pattern were the southernmost provinces or "kingdoms," the Alentejo and the Algarve, captured from the Moors in the thirteenth century. Here, many large estates were worked by landless laborers. Irregular rainfall and violent fluctuations in the levels of the major rivers made agriculture precarious in many parts of the country. Relatively few areas were fertile; despite the smallness of its population, Portugal was short of profitable and productive land. More than half its area was stony, scrub-covered mountain, good only, at best, for rough pasture. Only the river valleys with their terraced vineyards, and the plains of the south with their cork and olive groves, were readily productive. The country as a whole was barely self-sufficient in cereals, and grain had to be imported in most years to supply the towns.

In Portugal, as in most of western Europe, the attrition of the Black Death had caused a shortage of labor, increased money wages, and encouraged a drift from the countryside into the towns. Even with this increase, however, most towns remained small. Lisbon, the capital, was by far the biggest, with perhaps forty thousand inhabitants; Oporto, second in size, had about eight thousand. Probably none of the other incorporated towns had more than three thousand, and some of them were little more than villages. Artisans and urban laborers formed a very small proportion of the total population, merchants and shopkeepers a smaller proportion still. The guilds in which craftsmen and shopkeepers were organized developed late in Portugal. In the late fourteenth and early fifteenth centuries, it is true, the guilds of Lisbon and Oporto grew rapidly in influence and esteem; but this development reflected the support they had given to the Avis party in the revolution of 1383–85 as much as recognition of their economic and social importance, and of the tax-paying capacity of their members. The total quantity of manufactures was small, and their sale was confined to local markets. All in all, the economic activity of towns and countryside alike provided a very narrow base for any attempt at oversea expansion.

There remained the sea itself. Portugal possesses a long Atlantic coastline and a valuable inshore fishery. These assets were not enough in themselves to make the Portuguese a nation of sailors or even a nation of fishermen. The coast is either low, sandy and windswept, or rocky and abrupt; for part at least of every year it is exposed to the full force of westerly winds. Few of the rivers are navigable for much of their length and there are few good natural harbors; Oporto has a confined anchorage with a dangerous sandbar; only Lisbon and Setúbal are naturally both safe and extensive. Though fishing was widespread, much of it was—and is—on a very small scale, conducted from villages on open roadsteads, in craft small enough to be hauled up

the beach when not in use. Long fishing voyages in larger craft—after tunny, for example, off the coast of Morocco—could be undertaken only from harbors such as Lisbon and Setúbal, or from some of the small ports of the Algarve, such as Lagos in the lee of Cape St. Vincent. Today, the catching, preserving and export of sardines and other fish is a major industry in Portugal; yet only 1.2 per cent of the active population is wholly or mainly engaged in fishing. In the fifteenth century the proportion was almost certainly smaller. Nevertheless, the fishery was vital. It provided essential protein in a country where other food often ran short, and a substantial surplus for export. It trained skilled seamen, though never enough to meet the heavy demands which oversea adventure was later to make. It encouraged the building of small, sturdy, maneuverable ships.

The maritime trade of Portugal was necessarily modest. In Lisbon, Portuguese merchants had to compete with privileged groups of foreign businessmen, including the resident representatives of powerful Italian and German houses. In the early fifteenth century, however, they achieved a considerable measure of success, in some trades at least. Lisbon was a convenient and regular port of call for the north Italian galley fleets plying to Southampton and Bruges; but the expensive goods which the fleets carried did not compete directly with the exportable products of Portugal, of which salt, salted fish, wine, oil, fruit and hides were the most important. Setúbal—a modest little place then as now—depended almost entirely on its specialized trade in salt. Its sheltered bay had many shallow tidal inlets where sea salt could be produced by a simple, if laborious, process of ponding and evaporation. To this day, dingy white pyramids of salt are the most striking feature of the shores near Setúbal. The salt was widely exported, not only in coastal vessels to Lisbon and to many small fishing centres on the Portuguese coast, but also to northern Europe. Lisbon had a larger and more diversified trade, exporting to Flanders, England and the Maghrib, importing wheat, cloth, iron and timber from northern Europe and gold coin from Morocco. Merchants, though not very numerous, were an influential group in Lisbon, Oporto and Setúbal, free of feudal interference and, after 1485, assured of royal sympathy.

A considerable proportion of the foreign trade of Portugal was carried in Portuguese ships. The ships were reliable, necessarily maneuverable, built for coasting along exposed and often dangerous shores; they were of eclectic design, design capable—and this was the important point —of sustained and highly efficient development, when the need for it arose. The shipwright's craft was a relatively respected one. In the social hierarchy of the organized "misteries" he occupied, with the carpenter and the weaver, a standing inferior to that of the goldsmith, but decidedly superior to that of the tailor or even the armorer. As yet, Portuguese-built ships were small and modest, like the trade they carried. Early fifteenth-century Portugal had not the timber resources, nor the capital, nor as yet the need, for a large-scale shipbuilding industry producing big ocean-going ships; nor had it the men to maintain and man such ships. The total number of caulkers, for example, working in Lisbon did not exceed fifty or sixty even by the middle of the century. The Portuguese were only marginally a maritime people; fishing and

seaborne trade together employed only a small proportion of a small population, undoubtedly a smaller proportion than in, say, Biscay, the Netherlands or the Scandinavian countries. When, in the early fourteenth century, attempts had been made to create, or expand, a royal navy, the officers appointed to organize and command it had been Genoese mercenaries. In later years, of course, Portugal was to become a major maritime nation, in the sense that a high proportion of its interests and resources were to be devoted to overseas enterprise, and dramatic successes were to be achieved; but even in the height of maritime success, Portuguese endeavors were constantly to be hindered and frustrated by a persistent shortage of competent officers and trained seamen.

It would be an anachronism to speak of a national economy in late medieval Portugal. There was a national system of taxation—though occasional, and uneven in its incidence—and a national coinage; but there were many local economies. In many parts of the countryside a barter economy still sufficed for most transactions. A money economy was general in the towns, and was a necessary condition for trade; but the monetary basis of it was shaky. Most of the major kingdoms and city-states of Europe at that time used gold coinages; but no gold coins were struck in Portugal between 1383 and 1435, and regular coining of gold was not resumed until 1457. Such few gold coins as circulated were obtained by trade with Morocco. Silver coins were uncommon. The coinage in general use was either copper, or a copper and silver alloy which the Portuguese called *bilhão*, the Spaniards *vellón*. To meet the needs of the long wars with Castile, this coinage was progressively increased and debased; a process against which the *Cortes*—which met twenty-five times in John I's reign—protested repeatedly and in vain. Throughout the first half of the fifteenth century, indeed, the Portuguese economy was in a state of chaotic inflation which no internal administrative device could control.

Inflation had social as well as economic consequences. Those who lived by rents suffered more from it, relatively, than those who paid them. Inflation was an important factor in reducing the power of the heads of the great noble houses. It was not of course, the only factor. In Portugal as elsewhere in Europe, these territorial magnates had always been troublesome subjects. Their allegiance sat lightly upon them; with their private armies, they were often as ready to take the field against the King or one another as against a foreign enemy. They would not willingly tolerate command by one of their own number; most of them were initially hostile to John of Avis, some were implicated with Castile. Aljubarrota, therefore, was a victory for knights and *povo* as well as for the house of Avis, a defeat for the higher nobility as well as for Castile. This did not mean that the power of the magnates was destroyed; only that it was weakened and, temporarily at least, eclipsed. Nor did it mean that the *povo* were to rule, through a sympathetic king. John I certainly made more use than his predecessors had done of legally trained counselors, some of relatively humble birth; certainly, also, he owed a great debt to the guilds of Lisbon, and he rewarded them well in corporate privilege; but neither artisans nor merchants, who together made up the order of the *povo*, were powerful enough to do much more, politically, than grumble about taxes

through their representatives in the *Cortes.* Peasants, of course, were not consulted. The chief political beneficiaries of the decline of the great houses were a middling nobility and knighthood, among whom John I, as a reward for loyalty, distributed a large part of the crown lands. They were thus landed men, but not on a scale large enough to support private armies—men who saw their way to advancement rather through loyal service to the Crown. Their conventions of behavior were based on an archaic and romanticised chivalry. The legends of the Round Table had a remarkable vogue in late medieval Portugal, chiefly among people of this class. Tristram and Lancelot were not merely heroes of romance, but exemplars to be imitated and surpassed. Challenges were issued and accepted; armored knights charged and battered one another with a fine punctilio over points of "face" and personal reputation. War itself assumed, at least for the armored and the mounted, many of the characteristics of the tournament. John I, stern and autocratic certainly, but also calculating and hesitant, did not perhaps make an entirely convincing King Arthur; but he did nothing to discourage the tourneying belligerence of his subjects. He entered into the ritual; in a sense it was a game between them. The chronicler Fernão Lopes relates that on one occasion, at the siege of Coria, the King, displeased by the slowness of the operation, complained of the lack of "good knights of the Round Table"; to which one present retorted, with a characteristic Iberian bluntness in addressing kings, that the flower of Portuguese chivalry need not fear comparison with Lancelot or Galahad; "What we lack is good King Arthur, fleur-de-lys lord of them all, who knew good servitors and gave them good gifts for their desire to serve him well."

Here, then, was a society vastly different from that which had sent out the Vivaldi in 1291 to seek the Indies by sea; a society poorer, less sophisticated, less well informed, much less experienced in long-range maritime endeavor. Yet, as soon as the Castilian menace was lifted temporarily from their backs, the Portuguese were to follow in the wake of the Vivaldi, and eventually were to succeed where the Vivaldi had failed. Once embarked on a career of maritime expansion, the Portuguese very quickly discovered a taste and an aptitude for it, and pursued it with a reckless persistence unparalleled in Europe since the days of the Vikings. Like the Vikings, the Portuguese had a strong inducement to seek outlets from a difficult and cramping environment. The health of their economy urgently demanded additional fertile land and a reliable source of gold. An occasional haul of gold might be got by lucky piracy or plunder, but a regular supply could be secured only through regular trade. The most lucrative trades of the Mediterranean and of northern Europe were firmly grasped by other, stronger, more skilled hands, Italian, Catalan, German. Even in Morocco, the gold which Portuguese traders could earn by selling Portuguese products was a mere trickle. A significant increase in the flow of gold to Portugal could be achieved only in one of two ways: either by seizing and controlling a gold-dealing centre, perhaps in Morocco; or by opening an entirely new channel of trade with some hitherto inaccessible country, where gold was actually produced, or at least plentiful; perhaps a country from which Morocco itself obtained its gold. Either would be a costly

and hazardous enterprise. As for fertile land, there was little prospect of securing additional territory in the Iberian peninsula, except by an improbable fluke of dynastic inheritance; land in Morocco would be well defended, and not particularly productive. There remained the possibility of settling islands in the Atlantic, some of which—as we have seen—were known at the beginning of the fifteenth century, others suspected. Whatever centuries-old legend might say, these islands were uninhabited, or inhabited only by savages; but for impecunious knights hoping to carve out territorial fiefs, and for

Cape St. Vincent

peasants seeking fertile holdings relatively free from feudal restriction, they had the same powerful attraction that Iceland and the Faeroes had had for the Norsemen centuries before.

Portugal was uniquely well placed, in a geographical sense, for maritime adventure in the central Atlantic, whether of conquest, commerce or colonization, and whether aimed at Morocco, west Africa or the islands. It stood, so to speak, on the street corner of Europe. The towering promontory of Cape St. Vincent, much more than the Gibraltar Rock, marks the boundary between north Atlantic Europe and the smiling Mediterranean world. The little ports of the southern Algarve—Lagos, Portimão, Faro—and the harbors of southwestern Andalusia, are Mediterranean in appearance and habits, reflecting in obvious ways the long centuries of Roman and Moorish occupation. In the fifteenth century they still looked, commercially as well as geographically, towards Morocco. In contrast, Sines, Vasco da Gama's birthplace, north of the cape on the Alentejo coast, is uncompromisingly Atlantic in appearance and committed to the Atlantic fishery and coastal trade. Portugal stood on the fringes of two different worlds and felt the attractive pull of each. The shipping that connected the major Mediterranean centres with the major centres of the north all passed within sight of Cape St. Vincent, rounding it with considerable difficulty at some times of year, particularly when northbound, and always giving a wide berth to the breakers at its foot. A man could stand at the seaward end, high among the cystus and the rosemary, and watch the shipping of a dozen nations struggling around the cape. Some of the ships, of course, were Portuguese, coasting from Lisbon, Setúbal or Sines to the

ports of the Algarve, crossing to Morocco, or sailing to Italian ports. It would have taken a rare effort of imagination, at the beginning of the fifteenth century, to foretell that the distinctive future of Portuguese shipping lay not in that direction, but south and southwest, *por mares nunca dantes navegados.* Later in the century, the effort was to be made; the great cape was to become a pointer and a symbol, for many outward-bound navigators the last sight of Europe. The shape of the headland, its sharp angle, its flat top, its vertical cliffs, suggest the bow of a great ship standing out southwest into the Atlantic. It was not by rounding the cape, but by following the direction in which it pointed, that the Portuguese, in a few decades, were to place themselves in the forefront of maritime endeavor.

More practically, the winds off the Portuguese coast favored exploration to the south and southwest. The wind systems of the Atlantic basin, though always subject, like wind systems everywhere, to local variations and exceptions, preserve a vast, rough general order. In the sub-Arctic north, especially in spring and summer, easterly winds are frequent; these were the winds of the westbound Norsemen. In the southern oceans, south of Cape Horn and the Cape of Good Hope, strong west winds pour around the world in uninterrupted circuit. Between these two extremes, the prevailing Atlantic winds move in two great ellipses, clockwise in the northern hemisphere, counter-clockwise in the southern. The ellipses are separated by an area of equatorial calms, the hated Doldrums. The long axis of each ellipse, marked by a belt of variables, runs east and west; and the whole system moves north or south with

TZAFFIN.

Eremitę Cella

Fontes

the changes of the seasons. The eastern end of one of the axes rests on the Atlantic coast of Portugal, moving from south of Cape St. Vincent in the winter to roughly the latitude of Finisterre in the summer. In the winter the coast, along most of its length, is subject to frequent westerly gales. Throughout spring, summer and early autumn it receives lighter winds, variable but predominantly northwest to north. In approximately the latitude of Madeira the prevailing winds veer north-northeast, though still variable; assisted by the Canary current, they will carry a ship comfortably down the coast of Morocco. The ancient port of Safi, the principal harbor on this stretch of coast (before the founding of modern Casablanca) was well known to Mediterranean merchants; it was described in the *Compasso di Navigare* and marked on medieval portolan charts. There, the regular trade route ended. Only seagoing fishing vessels went farther, as far, perhaps, as Cape Noun or Cape Juby. The wind pours on, still north-northeast and variable along the coast; but out to sea, west of the Canaries, it settles into a steady, fresh and exhilarating flow from the northeast. The northeast trade wind is one of the most reliable winds in the world. It will drive a westbound ship, with hardly a hand to sheets or braces, clear across to the West Indies in a few weeks; or take a southbound ship down at least to Cape Verde before deserting it in the sticky calms of the Doldrums. For most of the year, therefore—at least from March to October—a ship out of Lisbon or Lagos, leaving Cape St. Vincent on a southwesterly course parallel with the African coast, could expect favorable sailing conditions for some fifteen hundred miles; and it could reach this area of favorable conditions much

more easily and quickly than a ship coming, say, from the Mediterranean, the Bay of Biscay or the North Sea.

To exploit these advantages and possibilities Portugal possessed, as we have seen, only modest maritime equipment, a relatively small seafaring population, limited capital and relatively little experience in long-haul oversea trade. In the event, however, these deficiencies were to prove less limiting than might have been expected. In a sense they were advantages, in that they permitted flexibility. The Portuguese had no traditional commitment to any major existing trade, no hard-won privileges in Levantine ports, no expensive *fondachi* to be maintained, no heavy capital investment in fleets of big, specialized ships. In fact the ships they did possess, mostly small and designed for coastal work and modest tramping, were to prove very suitable for exploring the African coasts and the Atlantic islands, and a few decades of experience in that employment were to improve Portuguese design almost beyond recognition. Because they were small and lightly built, these ships could make a profit on small and uncertain cargoes. They were, moreover, relatively expendable; they could be employed in dangerous ventures where the use of larger, more costly vessels would have entailed an unacceptable risk. As for capital and financial organization, although the Portuguese were comparatively poorly provided in these respects, they had regular contact with others much better off. There was a small but influential Genoese colony, for example, in Lisbon. When Portuguese expeditions began to make discoveries of commercial value and especially, later, when a sea route to India was opened, foreign financiers were more than willing to invest capital and to

OPPOSITE: Safi in Morocco, from *Civitates Orbis Terrarum,* 1576

participate in the development of trades which the Portuguese had initiated.

These developments, of course, lay in the future. At the beginning of the fifteenth century they could not easily have been predicted. The commercial and maritime communities in Portugal were far less experienced, much less well informed about the world outside Europe, than were corresponding groups in Italy. The kind of learning which devoted itself to studying and co-ordinating geographical theory and evidence was rare in Portugal; insofar as it existed, it was confined to Jewish circles. The art of chart-making and the use of charts were poorly developed; here, too, Portugal depended on borrowing and imitation from foreign sources. Even the physical advantages, from a navigational point of view, which Portugal enjoyed, were not obvious; they had to be discovered. Geography, meteorology, navigation, are empirical sciences. Portuguese seamen, obviously, would know from experience the usual behavior of the winds off their own coasts. Equally obviously, they could not know the winds off west Africa or in mid-Atlantic until they had used them over a considerable period in actual voyages. Professional sea captains would not willingly undertake such voyages without reasonable assurance of a safe return; nor could moneyed men, native or foreign, be expected to invest in them without good indications of a profitable outcome. In the discovery of the sea—specifically in the coasting of west Africa—it was the first steps which counted; and paradoxically, it was the very limitation, the relative backwardness of Portuguese economy and society, which made the first steps possible. A romantic knight-errantry, bookish and somewhat brutal,

was a positive asset in recruiting leaders for dangerous ventures of unknown or unpromising outcome. The first west African expeditions out of Portugal, those at least of which record remains, were not set out by merchants or commanded by seamen. Seamen, of course, worked and navigated the ships; but seamen were technicians or mechanics, socially little regarded, needing to be told by their betters where the ships were to go. The early African expeditions were set out by princes and commanded by men variously described as knights, squires or gentlemen of the household. These leaders were not primarily interested in commercial profit; on the whole they tended to despise commerce, and they certainly knew nothing of cost accounting. Nor were they moved by intellectual curiosity for its own sake. They were passionately interested in personal reputation and in standing well in the service of their royal masters. This is not to suggest, of course, a selfless devotion; they were as eager for plunder as for fame. They were more than ready to fight, especially if the people to be robbed were Muslims. A belligerent piety was traditional among them, a piety which sought expression not so much in converting an ignorant heathenry as in killing, humiliating or subduing the known enemies of Christ. With these somewhat primitive emotions, they were willing to be employed on ventures which a more skeptical, more sophisticated community might not have thought worthwhile.

The Portuguese move overseas in the fifteenth century, however, was not simply a random process of pious piracy, of crusade, conquest and plunder. If it had been, it would probably never have got farther than Morocco. On the contrary, it was deliberately planned, remarkably persistent, and directed—despite some false starts—to long-term practical ends, of which profitable trade was one. The additional factor, which gave it unity and direction, which harnessed seamen and knights-errant to a common purpose, was royal encouragement and discipline. Portugal was the first European country in which oversea exploration, whether with trade or conquest in mind, was actively supported over a long period by government; if not always by the King himself, then by princes close to the throne. The support was somewhat intermittent, and its immediate objects varied with the interests of the moment. It was frequently interrupted by preoccupations nearer home, particularly by Afonso V's minority and the fighting, in the late fourteen-forties, over the regency; but over the century as a whole its share of the royal attention increased steadily from reign to reign. John I played no active part in promoting Atlantic voyages; nor did the eldest of his half-English sons, Duarte, his successor. Two of Duarte's brothers, however, Pedro and Henrique, were prominent in the work, were indeed in the early stages its principal directors. Afonso V, after his assumption of full royal authority, concentrated his attention on north Africa, though he also encouraged and supported the enterprises of his uncle Henrique. His successor John II himself took over and directed the movement Henrique and Pedro had begun; in his reign Portuguese explorers began seriously to think of sailing beyond west Africa, if possible to India. Manoel I, "The Fortunate," after Vasco da Gama's return assumed the hyperbolic title "Lord of Guinea and of the navigation and commerce of Ethiopia, Arabia, Persia and India"; a title which jealous

brother monarchs condensed to "the Grocer King."

The interest of John and Manoel in oversea voyages needs little explanation; by the fourteen-seventies the profit to be derived from them was apparent. The enthusiasm of the two princes, Pedro and Henrique, suggests a more far-sighted imagination. The question, which of them provided the main initiative, is difficult to answer on the available evidence, and the attempt is perhaps not very profitable. The regent Pedro—the indefatigable traveler, with his exuberant energy and his lively, inquiring mind—played a much bigger part than the court chroniclers give him credit for; but Pedro's defeat and death at Alfarrobeira in 1449, and the suspicion of treason which clung to his name, no doubt deterred the chroniclers from singing his achievements. The career of Henrique—"Henry the Navigator"—on the other hand, provided perfect material for the conventional romanticism of court chroniclers: the knightly valor of his early exploits, the loyal peace-making sagacity of his excursions into national politics in middle life, and the dedicated ascetic seclusion of his later years. Tradition has long associated the prince with Cape St. Vincent and with its narrow sub-promontory, Sagres Point. He certainly held land in the neighborhood, and built there a fortified village, *Vila do Infante,* for the protection and convenience of ships waiting off the point, as they often had to do, for a favorable wind. Nothing of the *vila* now remains; the cape has recovered its windswept loneliness, and the site cannot be identified. There is no evidence that Prince Henry ever actually lived at Sagres; his permanent residence was probably in or near Lagos, some fifteen miles east of the

Sagres Point, traditionally associated with Prince Henry of Portugal

cape; but the tradition was more significant than the fact. The picture of the enigmatic prince, gazing out to sea from his lonely headland, has power to fire the imagination today, and it did not escape the chroniclers of the time. Zurara, whose *Chronicle of the Discovery and Conquest of Guinea* is our chief contemporary source of information about the early Atlantic voyages, places Henry firmly at the centre of the story. If

Henry was not alone in initiating the Atlantic ambitions of the Portuguese, he became their inspiration and embodiment, and is so regarded in Portugal to this day.

What impelled Henry to turn his attention to the sea? Zurara's *Chronicle* lists six separate motives; but in the delicate matter of motives, chroniclers are never wholly to be trusted; narrative, not analysis, is their business. Zurara, in particular, was a court chronicler, more interested in knightly tales than in—say—economic history or geographical research. The *Chronicle,* as it exists today, is a compound of two separate works, one of which was written as a panegyric in Henry's lifetime, employing the forms of praise then customary. This does not, of course, make Zurara's testimony worthless; if the *Chronicle* reflects the conventional values of Henry's generation, it also—we may presume—emphasizes the personal traits in which Henry himself took pride. It gives valuable clues to the prince's character, and scraps of supplementary information from other sources enable us to fill some of the gaps. Three of the six motives attributed to Henry by Zurara were conventional crusading aims: to investigate the geographical extent of Moorish power, to convert pagans to Christianity, and to seek alliance with any Christian rulers who might be found. The shadowy figure of Prester John was by this time, it will be remembered, localized in Africa. The chronicler does not mention him by name; but the hope of contact with some such ruler connected African exploration with the older Mediterranean crusade, and is a plausible partial explanation of Henry's interest.

Another motive—the last in Zurara's list, but according to him the strongest—was the prince's determination to fulfill the predictions of his horoscope, which bound him "to engage in great and noble conquests, and above all . . . to attempt the discovery of things which were hidden from other men." There is nothing surprising in this. Astronomical knowledge in Zurara's time was much more commonly applied to fortune-telling than to navigation, and horoscopes, especially those of princes, were

taken seriously. The wording of this particular horoscope may well have provided a conventional explanation of a trait which, in a prince, seemed eccentric: a disinterested scientific curiosity. Such curiosity probably did form part of Henry's intellectual make-up; but Zurara does not emphasize it and probably did not understand or admire it. The only specific example he gives of an interest in "hidden things" is the prince's desire to discover what lay along the African coast beyond the limits of known navigation; beyond the channel which separates the Canary Islands from the coast. Even here he implies that the purpose was practical. The prince, he goes on to say, wished to open new trades. On this matter of trade Zurara is vague and (one feels) apologetic. Social purists in his day considered trade to be incompatible with knighthood. It was thought legitimate, however, even for knights, to deprive the infidel of resources for making war by indirect means—by economic war, as we should say—if direct means failed. According to Zurara, this was Henry's intention: he would trade only with Christian peoples, whom the explorers hoped to encounter beyond the country of the Moors. Less courtly witnesses took a less refined view of the matter. Diogo Gomes, one of Henry's captains, in describing his own voyages of 1444 and 1463, simply states that the prince wished to find the countries whence came the gold which reached Morocco by the desert routes, "in order to trade with them and so maintain the gentlemen of his household."

Prince Henry's personality remains an enigma. We know very little about him, except what the chroniclers related. The characteristics attributed to him by contemporaries were, in the main, the virtues conventionally admired in his day: his courage and prowess in battle (not, it may be observed, his tactical or strategic skill—he was not much of a general); his princely hospitality; his piety, his personal asceticism and his obsession with the idea of the crusade. To these may be added a strong sense of duty, a stern will and a hard persistence in the pursuit of territory, trade and revenue. He must have possessed a lively curiosity; but he conceived the objects of that curiosity in terms both practical and traditional. He emerges from the chronicles of his day as a conservative, staunchly medieval figure. Certainly he was no Renaissance humanist. He was said to be fond of contemplation and study, and he supported formal learning through his gifts to the university at Lisbon; but he was not particularly learned himself. Unlike his royal brothers, he left no writings. He was a generous host and patron to seamen and chart-makers, but there is no evidence that he showed much personal interest in the technical development essential to the discovery of the sea. Jafudo Cresques, son of Abraham of the Catalan Atlas, is said to have been one of his entourage; but the story of a school of navigation and astronomy at Sagres is a myth. He employed charts and ships as means to ends, but did not think of them—so far as we know—as objects of technical interest in their own right.

Prince Henry did not, of course, go to sea himself, except to take passage with armies to Morocco. Late medieval conventions of propriety would have prevented a royal prince from participating—even had he wished—in long voyages in small vessels ill-provided for his state. We cannot even be sure that, until the last

decade of his life, he gave Atlantic voyages the priority in his purposes which later historians, with the advantage of hindsight, have attributed to them. The Portuguese, as we have seen, had open to them a choice of three oversea fields of action, which were geographically more accessible to them than to other Europeans, and in which they would not be likely to encounter entrenched European opposition: the islands, the west African coast, and Morocco. Initially they chose Morocco; Prince Henry as a young man acquired a considerable reputation as a military commander against the Moors; a reputation celebrated in Zurara's chronicle of the taking of Ceuta. The Portuguese attack on Ceuta in 1415 was Henry's first experience of war. It was said, indeed, to have been undertaken at the request of the prince and his two elder brothers, who wished to achieve knighthood in battle against the infidel, rather than in the tournament which the King their father had offered them. The story is plausible, so far as it goes. It is consistent with what we know of the characters and upbringing of the princes; but not with the calculating caution of John I, who would hardly have agreed to so hazardous and expensive an operation unless practical advantages were to be expected from it. Ceuta was a port of some strength and importance; but merely as a territorial acquisition it had not much to commend it. The surrounding country was not very productive and Ceuta, like Lisbon, often had to import grain by sea. Nor are strategic considerations a sufficient explanation. The place certainly had a strategic importance: a maritime power possessing it could harass and prey upon shipping passing through the Strait of Gibraltar; and it was a bridgehead, connecting Morocco with Granada, the only

Muslim kingdom in western Europe. From the point of view of European Christendom as a whole, there would be great advantages in having Ceuta in Christian hands; but the immediate beneficiaries would be Mediterranean traders, mostly Italian, and the kingdom of Castile, with which the Portuguese were formally at peace, but which they regarded with long-standing suspicion. For Portugal—apart from opportunities for pious piracy—there would be little direct strategic advantage.

The most plausible explanation is an economic one. Portugal was desperately short of gold; Ceuta was one of the termini of the trans-Saharan gold trade. It is unlikely—though there is no direct evidence—that the Portuguese government could have been ignorant of this. Since the conquest of the Algarve in the thirteenth century, commercial and even social contact between Portugal and Morocco had been regularly maintained, largely through Portuguese and Moorish Jews, who were natural intermediaries between Christendom and Islam. Genoese merchants also, an influential group in Lisbon, were well informed about the trade of north Africa. To the Portuguese government, with this information almost certainly at their disposal, the commercial advantages of possessing a major harbor in Morocco must have seemed obvious. The operation was a military success; Ceuta was taken, and Prince Henry played a leading part in its capture. It did not answer expectations; Ceuta became the object of fierce and repeated counterattack, and as a result of the fighting was largely cut off from commercial contact with its own hinterland. Prince Henry fought fiercely for its retention, and for many years afterward urged the extension of the conquest to other ports in Morocco. It became an obsession, in which obstinacy and pious belligerence outweighed all prudent and practical considerations. The memorial which he wrote in 1436 urging an attack on Tangier, and his own gallant but inflexible conduct in command of the enterprise, both recall the pages of Froissart rather than the calculations of a realistic ruler. This operation was a failure; the Portuguese army withdrew with difficulty, leaving Henry's youngest brother behind as a hostage. Henry failed, or refused, to secure his release by the cession of Ceuta, by way of ransom, and Fernão died in captivity at Fez. Pedro, probably the most intelligent and realistic of the five brothers, as regent left Morocco alone; but after Alfarrobeira the King, Afonso V, urged on by an irresponsible nobility, which by then had recovered much of its power, resumed the offensive. He achieved considerable local successes, including the capture of Tangier in 1458. Henry, meanwhile, had lost much of his influence at court; he stayed in his lonely retreat and fought no more battles in Morocco; but he remained the first powerful proponent of a policy of aggression there which ultimately, more than a hundred years after his death, was to lead to utter disaster at Alcazar-Kebir.

The trade which eventually enabled Portugal to resume the coinage of gold came not across the desert and through Ceuta, but from west Africa. The taking of Ceuta has often been represented as the event which initiated the Atlantic voyages. It is perfectly possible that Prince Henry obtained information in Ceuta, or heard rumors there, about trade on the Mandingo coast; it is equally possible that these rumors were already current, from other sources, among those in Europe who cared about such matters. The Catalan Atlas marks a River of Gold; probably it was not unique in this. There is no direct evidence; but it seems unlikely that the Atlantic voyages were conceived in Ceuta. None of them sailed from there. Initially, they were probably considered complementary to the Moroccan enterprise. Later, they became a competing alternative. They were never directly connected with it. Prince Henry's direct encouragement of the voyages fluctuated in inverse relation to his success in persuading the government to spend money on war in Morocco.

Ill-success in Morocco, or Henry's exclusion from the fighting there, were necessary conditions for the vigorous prosecution of Atlantic discovery. In the last decade of his life, after Alfarrobeira, the Prince seems to have accepted this; perforce, perhaps. It was in that decade that the west African gold trade became significant in the Portuguese economy, and that papal blessing was sought for a Portuguese monopoly of navigation in west Africa. In the long run, it was his second choice of vocation, not his first, which made a national hero of him and achieved lasting success.

6

West Africa and the Islands

n *the story of the discovery of the sea* the capture of Ceuta was a false start. The way to the sources of Saharan gold, the way, eventually, to kingdoms whose shores were washed by other oceans than the Atlantic, lay not through Morocco, but down the west African coast; not southeast from Cape St. Vincent, but southwest. According to Zurara and later chroniclers, Prince Henry began, soon after his return from an arduous relief expedition to Ceuta in 1418, to promote coastal voyages; but Zurara gives neither names nor details. Henry was certainly not the only promoter. It was Pedro, not Henry, who on several occasions in the fourteen-twenties drew attention to the cost and uselessness of Ceuta. Of all the west African expeditions which left Portugal between the taking of Ceuta and the tragedy at Alfarrobeira, it is probable that about a third were undertaken on Henry's initiative, another third on Pedro's, and the remainder at the instance of private investors. There is no firm evidence. In any event, nothing much was achieved until the fourteen-thirties. Meanwhile, prospects of another sort were opening in some of the Atlantic islands, prospects which attracted men who had no princely backing and who were not obsessed by the crusade. Africa, no doubt, was the place for gold and glory; no one seriously expected gold in the Canaries or Madeira, and settlement there promised more hard

work than glory. The islands offered rewards, however, relatively humble but still worth seeking. To sober entrepreneurs they might well seem more attractive and less risky than the arid, inhospitable shore of Mauretania. In the early fourteen-twenties a number of private adventurers turned their attention to these lovely and remote archipelagos toward which both wind and current urged their ships.

Free land was the main attraction. Inflation at home bore hard upon the knightly class. It raised prices and reduced the value of money. It enriched tenants who paid fixed money rents and brought many landowners to penury. Not only *fidalgos* who, by the chances of inheritance, held no land, but also those whose inheritance was relatively modest, had a strong incentive to move out, either to restore their fortunes by piracy off the Barbary coast—which was all that Ceuta, in Portuguese hands, was good for—or else to acquire estates in new places on new terms; estates which might be made to produce saleable goods instead of derisory money rents. There was no great difficulty in obtaining labor for such settlements. Emigrants could be recruited from among landless laborers or among peasants whose holdings were arid and infertile, or whose tenures were on unfavorable or irksome feudal terms. Capital was a more difficult problem; but a new and vigorous industry was to help in solving it. Throughout the thirteenth and fourteenth centuries, the cultivation of sugar cane and the manufacture of sugar had been spreading from Syria and Egypt westward through the Mediterranean countries, along the coast to Morocco, along the chain of islands, through Cyprus, Crete and Sicily, to southeastern Spain and southern Portugal. Sugar was a scarce and

costly "spice," a valuable article of commerce. The first Portuguese plantation and mill was started in 1404, in the Algarve; the entrepreneur being—not surprisingly—a Genoese. By the fourteen-twenties there existed in southern Portugal a vigorous group of sugar producers, interested in extending their operations. For this purpose, the islands were to prove very suitable; and sugar interests were to provide much of the capital needed for island development.

The earliest attempts at Iberian settlement were made in the Canaries, as might be expected, since these were the most accessible of the islands. Merely by drifting southwest with wind and current, vessels might reach either Fuerteventura or Lanzarote. The first, and ultimately unsuccessful, settlement in Lanzarote had been made in the middle of the fourteenth century by a Genoese under Portuguese auspices; the second, from 1402, by a Norman under Castilian. Since Béttencourt's day the Castilian title to these easternmost islands had changed hands several times, but Castilian settlers had remained continuously in possession and had increased in number, living chiefly by growing grain—barley and a little wheat—by raising cattle and goats, and by fishing. Portuguese ships, as well as Spanish, probably visited these settlements from time to time, to trade with them, perhaps to raid them or fish in their waters. Such ships, in the prevailing winds of summer and autumn, could not return to Portugal directly. Their most convenient course would be by a long board of about three hundred miles northwest with the wind abeam, then a longer board of nearly six hundred miles northeast. Such a course would take them close to the Madeira islands; Madeira lies about three hundred miles northwest of the northern tip of Lanzarote. The Portuguese discovery, or re-discovery, of these islands probably occurred in the course of such a return voyage, either from Lanzarote or from the Moroccan coast opposite. The reputed discoverers, Zarco and Teixeira, started a settlement in Porto Santo about 1420—the exact date is uncertain—and were joined shortly afterward by Bartolomeo Perestrelo (another Italian, naturalized in Portugal), an efficient and energetic pioneer who was to become a leading figure in the life of the islands, and whose daughter, years later, was to marry Christopher Columbus. This was a purely private initiative; but private adventurers, even in uninhabited islands, needed the backing of authority. Without a formal title, a leader could not govern; his orders could be disputed by any sea lawyer in his company. Zarco and Teixeira secured their title not from Prince Henry, who at that time had nothing to do with Madeira, but from the Crown.

The Madeira settlements prospered, after initial setbacks. According to one story, the first setback in Porto Santo came from the multiplication of rabbits, which the settlers had unwisely introduced; the destruction of crops by these pests was among the causes of the first move into the larger island of Madeira. Here, too, there was an early setback. Madeira, as its name implies, was then heavily wooded. The settlers, in their initial attempts to clear land by cutting and burning, succeeded in setting a large area of standing forest ablaze in the neighborhood of Funchal. According to the chronicles, the fire could be seen from many miles out to sea, and smouldered on for years thereafter. This, apart from the danger to the settlement, was a gross

waste of a valuable natural resource, as the settlers discovered. Many of the trees were tall hardwoods. Hardwood timber was scarce and valuable in Portugal, and the settlers could export it—as long as it lasted—for shipbuilding, housebuilding and furniture making. They also gathered and exported a red resin known as dragon's blood, used as a dye in the textile industry. The islands soon graduated, however, from the sale of wild products to agriculture and cattle raising, the export of wheat and hides, and eventually sugar. Sugar manufacture began seriously in the early fourteen-fifties; within twenty years Madeira became a major producer, exporting sugar directly to Antwerp and Bristol as well as to Lisbon. Finally, sugar in the coastal lowlands and valley bottoms was supplemented by vines on the steep terraced hillsides. Cadamosto, who visited the island in 1455, wrote an admiring description of the vineyards. The Malvoisie grape, introduced from Crete, was the source of Malmsey, the most famous and sought-after product of Madeira to this day.

A success story, then. Development in the other islands followed much the same pattern, but more slowly. The Canary Islands form an extensive group, covering three hundred miles or so from east to west. The islands are separated by considerable distances, and several of them are individually much bigger than Madeira. In the larger islands the native inhabitants resisted European settlement successfully for many years. Cadamosto reported in 1455 that Castilian settlers were living in Lanzarote, Fuerteventura and Ferro, and were establishing themselves in Gomera. Attempts to land in Grand Canary had been driven off. Tenerife was known from a distance—its towering cone could hardly be missed—and Palma similarly, though only slave raiders landed there. When Columbus sailed in 1492 from Gomera for the West Indies, these last three islands were still in process of conquest and settlement. A long process; and economic development was correspondingly gradual. The settlers exported hides, skins, tallow and *orchella*, a wild lichen from which a purple dye was made; and sold provisions to passing ships. There was no sugar in Cadamosto's time; that came later in the century, Genoese merchants in Seville providing the capital and the experience; vines came later still.

The remote Azores—the Hawks' Islands—form an archipelago even more extensive than the Canaries—the length of the whole chain, southeast to northwest, is about four hundred miles—but the islands are individually smaller and the sea distances between them correspondingly greater. The westernmost islands, Flores and Corvo, are a hundred miles from Fayal, their nearest neighbor. A ship can pass between the islands without sighting any of them; though in the daytime cloud formations, birds and marine life would indicate their presence to an observant navigator. Their nearest point is about eight hundred miles west of Portugal, a third of the way across the Atlantic. Westerly winds prevail in their neighborhood for much of the year, becoming stronger and more consistent in late summer and autumn. The islands were thus more easily reached from Madeira or the Canaries than directly from Portugal; but conversely the return passage from the islands to Portugal usually presented little difficulty, other than the danger of bad weather. Some of the islands of the eastern group were discovered, or re-discovered, about 1427. The

exact circumstances cannot be established with certainty; there are several conflicting allusions in chronicles and in legends on contemporary maps. Discovery, in so scattered an archipelago, was necessarily piecemeal, but seven of the islands— all except Flores and Corvo—had been sighted, and plotted roughly on maps, by 1439. The first attempts to make use of them, by the introduction of livestock in the fourteen-thirties, were made apparently on the initiative, or with the encouragement, of Prince Henry. The islands, except in sheltered valleys, were not wooded; they contained, as they still do, extensive areas of open grassland. They were less inviting than Madeira, and their economic development was slow. The progression was from sheep to grain, eventually to sugar.

The discovery of these three island groups, and the first attempts to exploit them, owed little or nothing to the initiative of Prince Henry, so far as can be determined; but the Prince began to take an interest in them from an early date. In 1424 he procured the despatch of a powerful expedition—2500 men—to seize Grand Canary, and a second fleet to the same island in 1427. It was not clear—or at least was not accepted in Portugal—that the undoubted Spanish presence in the eastern islands implied a Spanish title to the whole group; and it might well be argued that in so large an area there was room for everyone. Both expeditions, however, were beaten off by the Guanches. They drew a vigorous protest from Castile and inaugurated a long series, lasting more than fifty years, of diplomatic wrangles and intermittent naval fighting over the control of the archipelago.

In 1433 the Prince obtained, from his brother King Duarte, title to the lordship of the

OPPOSITE: Terraced vineyards in Madeira

Fogo Lake, São Miguel,
Azores

Madeiras. It was Henry who issued, in 1452, the first contract for the construction of a sugar mill in Madeira. In 1439 Prince Pedro, as regent, granted to Henry the lordship of the Azores; that is, of the seven islands so far discovered. This grant is the earliest firm documentary evidence of Portuguese activity in the Azores. As in Madeira, Henry granted licenses to colonize, at the colonizers' expense, and titles to the land to be settled, sometimes, but not always, described as "captaincies." He retained appellate jurisdiction and drew a share of the proceeds. The Order of Christ, of which he was governor and administrator, exercised ecclesiastical jurisdiction. The arrangement was feudal and personal rather than national. Many foreigners—not only Italians —played a part in island development. In Terceira the principal entrepreneur and some of the actual settlers were Flemings. In all this we can see Prince Henry establishing his personal position as, so to speak, the royal specialist in oversea activity, extending his control over the Atlantic islands wherever circumstances allowed it. Prince Pedro as regent seems to have been content, as a rule, to leave such matters to his brother, but he retained a personal interest; the settlement of the Azores after 1439, in particular, owed more to him than to Henry, though Henry was formally responsible. After Alfarrobeira, however, Henry was left alone in the field. The island settlements proved to be sound investments and sources of much-needed revenue —unlike the African adventures, which were sources of heavy expense—almost from the start; but this was not their only, or, in the long run, their chief value. As more European ships sailed farther into the Atlantic, the islands became more and more important as maritime outposts, as

ports of call: the Canaries, or the Madeiras, and later the Cape Verde Islands, on outward passage, the Madeiras or the Azores upon return. The island settlements were essential factors in the discovery of the sea.

In 1434 Gil Eannes, a gentleman of Prince Henry's household, rounded Cape Bojador on the Saharan coast. This achievement was recorded by the chroniclers, and has been described by historians ever since, as an event of great significance. Cape Bojador is nearer than the Azores to Cape St. Vincent, not more than eight hundred miles, down-wind and down-current. If it is true that exploring expeditions had been going out in that direction since 1420 or thereabouts, the rate of progress over fourteen years seems unimpressive, and the delay calls for explanation. The chronicles mention two capes beyond which the explorers were reluctant or afraid to venture: Cape Noun, about two hundred miles beyond Safi, and Cape Bojador. There is no difficulty in passing Cape Noun, despite the unpromising negative—Cabo Não—by which it was known in Portuguese. It presents no danger to shipping; it is clearly visible, a sandstone cliff rising to 170 feet; it does not project far into the sea; there is deep water close inshore. It stands, however, at the end of a relatively frequented and not infertile stretch of coast. From Cape Noun to Cape Juby only fishing vessels were to be encountered. Beyond Cape Juby the coast was dry, sandy, unproductive; its few inhabitants possessed no boats and few goods; they were suspicious, predatory nomads, apt to strip and murder anyone unlucky enough to be cast ashore. Down to the nineteenth century the *Africa Pilot* enjoined "the utmost circumspection" in dealing with them. These were negative reasons for staying north of Cape Noun. There was also a positive reason: the counter-attraction of piracy. To the "gentlemen of the household," adventurous young men with their fortunes to make, raiding Moorish commerce along the known stretch of coast was vastly more exciting and rewarding than exploring the fruitless unknown. It took a great deal of princely insistence, and the promise of princely rewards, to induce these gentleman-adventurers to change their predatory ways, to look a little beyond immediate plunder and profit.

Princely discipline and (if Zurara is to be believed) princely ridicule prevailed eventually; but even then there were difficulties. The discovery of the sea depended on co-operation between gentleman-adventurers and professional seamen, and seamen naturally raised professional difficulties based on the dangers of navigation. We can probably discount, as serious obstacles, the ancient superstitious dreads; fifteenth-century Portuguese seamen did not fear—except to the extent of proper professional respect—the Green Sea of Darkness. Ships' companies may have worried about the boiling sea of the tropics and the sun which turned men black; sailors were always vulnerable to alarming rumors, as they still are, though today the alarm attaches usually to the physiological effects of scientific gadgets rather than to climate; but capable and determined officers can usually talk their people out of fears of this sort. Some of the dangers, however, were real. The hundred-mile stretch of coast between Cape Noun and Cape Juby embays about twelve miles. There are no harbors, and the bight is open to the prevailing wind. The Canary current, compressed between the islands and the coast, accelerates to 1¼ knots and sets obliquely against the westward curve of Cape Juby. A heavy continuous swell from the northwest sets across wind and current into the bight, raising a confused and mountainous surf. For all these reasons, a sailing ship embayed within the bight cannot easily work off. Cape Juby itself is a long low sand spit, usually half-hidden in a haze caused by spray from the surf and by windblown desert sand. For ships standing close inshore, this is the most dangerous stretch on the whole coast between Spartel and Bojador; many ships have been wrecked there. It is curious that none of the chronicles mention Cape Juby; probably the nomenclature of the various capes became muddled over the years, and the characteristics of Juby were described under the name of Bojador; but this is conjecture. Every book of sailing directions, from the *Esmeraldo de Situ Orbis* in the early sixteenth century to the modern *Africa Pilot,* recommends that ships coasting along this stretch should keep at least five miles offshore, where the current is strongest and will carry ships safely past Cape Juby. If this advice is followed there is no danger; but what was the use, our fifteenth-century seamen might inquire, of exploring a coast on which they could not land?

Beyond Cape Juby the current slows again, and resumes its coastwise direction. There are no dangers, except for a reef extending about one and a half miles north from the False Cape of Bojador, and some scattered rocks on which the sea breaks at the foot of the cape itself. Cape Bojador is clearly visible, a red sandstone cliff about seventy feet high. Throughout the 140 miles from Juby to Bojador there is still heavy surf, but in the lee of the cape is a small area of sheltered water in about nine fathoms. The discovery of this welcome, if limited, anchorage, the only safe landing point for hundreds of miles, may well have been an event of major importance for thirsty explorers; a "breakthrough," as we should say.

The dangers of an inhospitable shore were not the only, not the main navigational obstacles in the way of African exploration. Throughout their voyages down the coast the explorers must have been haunted by the problem of return. The outward passage, with favoring wind and current, provided Cape Juby was passed at a safe distance, may well have seemed all too easy; how were they to get back? Gil Eannes and others like him made their voyages in *barchas,* small craft, perhaps not even fully decked, fitted with oars as well as sails. If necessary they could pull around the difficult points. But if the looked-for land of gold were to appear beyond Cape Bojador, what then? As a regular commercial undertaking, to beat back or pull back more than eight hundred miles against wind and current was out of the question. The answer was to stand boldly out to sea. By long boards, first northwest and then northeast, a ship could make enough northing to find a westerly wind for home. This was the *volta do mar,* which in time became standard practice. It involved long passages in the open sea; but there were islands on the way. It did not require sophisticated navigation, for which no instruments then existed; with reasonably predictable winds, dead reckoning and rough estimates of polar altitude were good enough. If a navigator passed west of Grand Canary, too far west to sight Madeira, there was still the four-hundred-mile net of the Azores spread across his way, with opportunities for

refreshment and refit for the final passage home. The existence of the island settlements, and knowledge of the winds in their neighborhood, gave navigators the necessary confidence for further discovery in west Africa. To make use of them, however, seamen needed more substantial ships than the *barchas* used by Gil Eannes. It was here that the caravels came into their own: big enough to be safe, small enough to be easily handled, weatherly enough to make the long boards on a wind, which the *volta do mar* demanded. The first explicit mention in the chronicles of a caravel off west Africa was made in connection with Nuno Tristão's voyage of 1441.

The coast does not change significantly beyond Cape Bojador; it is sandy, featureless, valueless, but with rich fishing grounds offshore. Gil Eannes, in a second voyage in 1435, coasted a hundred miles or so beyond the cape, and found nothing of interest except some seal rookeries. This was a useful minor discovery; sealskins were a marketable commodity, the only one which the voyages had so far revealed. In the following year Gonçalves Baldaia sailed a few miles farther and found the mouth of a considerable river. It was—and is—an awkward place, with a narrow channel, swift tides and a dangerous sand bar; but it afforded an anchorage, and its banks were inhabited. It was the first river with water in it which the explorers had seen since the neighborhood of Cape Noun. It was also an eddy —a minor eddy—of the river of gold which flowed across the desert. Small parcels of gold dust could occasionally be got in trade there; the Portuguese optimistically called the place Rio do Ouro, which name it retains to this day.

These modestly promising discoveries marked

the end of the first stage of west African exploration. In 1437 all Prince Henry's energies were concentrated on Tangier, and thereafter on the anxieties caused by King Duarte's death and the royal minority. For five years no expeditions left for west Africa; but with Pedro's emergence as regent in 1441, exploration was resumed with a new vigor which reflected the regent's personal encouragement. Two ships were sent in that year to Rio do Ouro, Nuno Tristão in his caravel, and Antão Gonçalves, the latter to collect a cargo of sealskins, the former to explore. They joined forces in exceeding their instructions, attacked a party of natives ashore and captured a dozen or so for shipment to Portugal. According to Zurara, the two captains regarded their prisoners not primarily as marketable merchandise—though they were that—but as curiosities to amuse Prince Henry. Some of them were enslaved on arrival. Some who appeared, on what grounds we cannot tell, to be of superior social standing, were by the Prince's order put through what must have been a very rapid course of instruction in Christian doctrine, and then sent home in a Portuguese ship to be ransomed. Part of the ransom was paid in slaves. The Tristão-Gonçalves exploit thus inaugurated both slave raiding and slave trading by Europeans on the west coast. Chasing people on foot across open country is obviously an inefficient and self-defeating method of obtaining slaves, especially when the raiders have to be landed from ships whose approach can be seen a great way off. Portuguese captains in their further voyages down the coast, wherever they found slaves offered for sale, bought them; but where no arrangements existed for marketing slaves, they caught them for themselves when they could. The affray at Rio do Ouro was the first of a long series of minor skirmishes and squalid kidnappings which Zurara, true to his calling, dignified as battles for the Faith.

In 1442–43 Tristão and several other captains independently reached Cape Branco, which is the most striking landmark on the coast. It is a long ridge-backed peninsula running more than twenty miles southward into the sea and terminating in an abrupt white cliff, which can be seen from a great distance. On its eastern side the cape encloses a large, almost circular bay, now known as Levrier Bay. The bay is more than twenty miles across, but the entrance from the south is partly blocked by sandbanks, leaving a channel about one and a half miles wide. Ships entering had usually to make several short tacks in this channel, but once inside they found an extensive and sheltered anchorage. There are several islands in the bay, and visiting Portuguese formed the habit of landing on one of them, Arguim Island—the only one with a reliable water supply—to barter with natives who came off in canoes: wheat, colored woolen or linen cloth and glass beads for slaves and, in limited quantities, gold dust. The place became a regular trading post, and about 1445 Prince Henry ordered the construction of a fortified barracoon on the island. The "castle" which Cadamosto saw, when he called there in 1455, was probably a dry-stone wall or wooden stockade; its successor in masonry was not completed until John II's time. Arguim was the end of qualms about the compatibility of trade with knighthood. The merchants followed hard on the heels of the fighting men, as they had done in the earlier crusades in the Levant. Prince Henry was in constant need of money, a need which the revenues of the Order of Christ only partially relieved. He not only accepted, he actively encouraged the trade which his captains initiated with infidel peoples; he jealously guarded his own monopoly of it, granted by Pedro in the young King's name in 1443, confirmed in 1446; and he drew his share of the profits.

Arguim was not yet the land of gold, and the caravels coasted on. In about 17 degrees north, some three hundred miles south of Cape Branco, the character of the coast changes. It is broken by the estuaries of several big rivers, the Senegal, the Gambia, the Geba, descending from an extensive and, even today, little-known mountain range, the Futa Jallon. The character of the people changes also; instead of tawny-skinned desert dwellers, the fertile, tree-shaded river banks are—and were then—cultivated by settled Negro peoples. Nuno Tristão found the mouth of the Senegal in 1444; he and others reported the great volume of fresh water spreading far out to sea, and encouraged geographers to think the river was a western branch of the Nile. Little use was made of the estuary at that time; it is a dangerous place, with a shifting sandbar and precipitous surf. A hundred miles farther south is Cape Verde, the westernmost point of Africa, which Dinis Dias sighted, also in 1444; its rounded green hills a welcome contrast with the bony austerity of Cape Branco. Like Cape Branco, Cape Verde shelters an extensive bay, and within it Gorée island, in later years the site of a big slave barracoon. Between the island and Dakar Point, where the city of Dakar now stands, is good anchorage; but the early explorers seem to have taken no interest in Gorée. Possibly its scanty water supply, still described in the *Africa Pilot* as "repulsive," put them off.

They were more impressed by the mouth of the Gambia, which Tristão reached in 1446. This fine river is twenty miles wide at its opening. It narrows to two miles at Bathurst, but is navigable for quite large vessels for 230 miles farther. This was an important discovery; but the local people fiercely resisted attempts to enter the river. Tristão and most of his company were killed there by poisoned arrows, then an unfamiliar hazard to Europeans. His death had an interesting sequel: seven survivors, of whom two were badly wounded and none had formal knowledge of navigation, took the caravel back to Portugal. An apprentice seaman, a *grumete,* navigated her. In trade-wind conditions it was more important to have good seamen and shipwrights than good navigators. The seven were at sea for two months without sight of land. No wonder caravels were admired.

News of the discoveries soon got about. They were faithfully recorded in Andrea Bianco's world map, drawn in Venice in 1448. Zurara ended his chronicle with that year, explaining that thereafter "the affairs of this area were always conducted more with commerce and mutual agreements than with force and feats of arms"; poor material for a chronicler. By 1448, fifty-odd ships had passed Cape Bojador; they had brought back to Portugal about a thousand slaves, and with them small parcels of gold dust, a little ivory, natural gums (used in silk throwing), *malagueta* pepper and a few oddities such as ostrich eggs, which caused a mild sensation in the princely kitchen: all welcome imports, but still a small return on the capital invested in fitting out expeditions. Individual trading voyages certainly made profits; but the west African enterprise as a whole stretched

Prince Henry's resources, and those of the Order of Christ, to their limit and beyond. Comprehensive balance sheets were foreign to the temper of the time, and certainly to the Prince's temperament; but financial strain may partly account for the second long pause in African exploration, between 1448 and 1455. It was not the only cause, however; there were also political interruptions.

In 1449 the whole royal family became involved in the quarrel between the regent and the Duke of Braganza, arising from the Duke's influence over the young King, which led to Alfarrobeira. Henry's ability to mount expeditions was reduced by the loss of Pedro's support, and his attention was further distracted, between 1450 and 1454, by a sharpening of controversy with Castile over the complicated question of rights in the Canaries. This particular stage in what had become a perennial dispute began with Prince Henry's purchase, from one of Béttencourt's successors, of the lordship of Lanzarote. The Castilian Crown, not wanting so formidable a vassal in the islands, objected through diplomatic channels. The dispute was accompanied by a good deal of informal fighting in Canarian waters. It ended inconclusively, with the death of Juan II of Castile in 1454 and the accession of Enrique IV. In the more friendly atmosphere of the new reign, the Portuguese government agreed, tacitly, to let the matter rest. Peace in the islands lasted—piracy apart—for twenty years, and during that time Portuguese and Italians often called there for trade.

African exploration was resumed in the last five years of Prince Henry's life. Trade to west Africa had not been interrupted, and continued to increase. The best informant on the affairs of the coast at that time is the Venetian Alvise da C'a da Mosto, no court chronicler, but an experienced and intelligent merchant. Cadamosto made two trading voyages to west Africa: the first in 1455, on a profit-sharing basis, in a Lagos caravel owned or chartered by Prince Henry, with a Portuguese master and crew; the second in 1456, in a caravel fitted out by himself, in company with another vessel chartered by a Genoese associate named (or nicknamed) Antoniotto Usodimare. He compiled, probably several years after the event, a lively and detailed account of his adventures, which seems to have circulated in manuscript and attracted considerable attention; several Italian maps drawn in the fourteen-sixties show signs of its influence; it was included in the first printed collection of voyages, the *Paesi novamente retrovati* of 1507, and reappeared in 1550 in the first volume of Ramusio's great collection, *Delle Navigiationi e Viaggi.* From Cadamosto we can form an impression of the bold self-confidence which Portuguese seamen had already attained in African waters. His ships called at Madeira and at Gomera and Ferro in the Canaries. From there they sailed directly to Cape Branco and put in to Arguim for trade, and then on down the coast. The long passage in the open sea was apparently regarded as routine; navigation was by dead reckoning, checked by eye estimates of polar altitude. Off the coast mariners proceeded more cautiously, navigating only by day "with lead in hand," and anchoring at night.

The trading post at Arguim was firmly established and ships were calling regularly. Cadamosto says that a thousand slaves passed through the place every year, though this number is difficult to credit. The local Sanhaja people obtained their supply of slaves from the Negro areas farther south, in exchange for horses, which in Guinea were scarce and valuable, worth anything up to fifteen slaves apiece. Portuguese traders were already shipping horses to Arguim for use in this trade; Cadamosto himself went one better: he carried a number of Spanish horses (shipped perhaps in the Canaries) down the coast to the Senegal region, where he disposed of them to great advantage.

The chief interest of Cadamosto's account lies in his description of the life of the coast south of Cape Branco—the first clear description by any European of a country inhabited by Negroes. He describes the country itself: the dramatic change at the Senegal from tawny desert to green scrub and cultivation; and the people: the Muslim Moors in their white or blue gowns, and the semi-naked pagans. He describes the commodities, not only those familiar in European trade, but those of the local markets, of no commercial interest to Europeans: palm wine and palm oil, bark cloth and palm-leaf matting, skins of marmot, civet and baboon. He describes the birds, beasts and reptiles—an interest very rare among Iberian explorers—and gives one of the first sober and detailed accounts, by a European, of hippopotamus and African elephant. Cadamosto enjoyed the hospitality of the leading people with whom he traded; he watched their dances, admired their women, shared their food, and described them all. He thought poorly of elephant meat; but nevertheless salted a piece for Prince Henry, who accepted it with princely condescension.

Although the purpose of Cadamosto's voyaging was trade, not exploration, curiosity and force of circumstance also led him to explore. He forced his way some miles up the Gambia, the ships' companies defending themselves with "bombards" and crossbows against the canoe fleets which opposed their passage. Finally, on the second voyage, diverted from his course by gales, he made—almost certainly—the first European sighting of the western islands of the Cape Verde group. His account of this event is geographically confusing, and his claim was contested by the Portuguese Diogo Gomes (recounting much later) and by the Genoese Antonio da Noli; but there seems to be no good ground for doubting it. As with the other extensive island groups, the exploration of the Cape Verde Islands was a gradual, piecemeal process; probably a series of independent discoveries revealed the extent of the whole archipelago. In any event Cadamosto attributed no great significance to his discovery. He was a trader, and the islands were uninhabited. It was da Noli who undertook the task of colonizing them, under license from Prince Henry about 1460, with Portuguese settlers and west African slaves. His captaincy lasted—with interruptions due to the Spanish Succession War—for forty years; and the Cape Verde Islands, like the Canaries, became valuable ports of call for ships outward bound from Europe.

Prince Henry died in 1460. Shortly before his death Pedro da Sintra had sailed down the coast as far as Sierra Leone—so called, it was said, because of the thunderstorms that growled and roared, as they still do, about Mount Auriol—and this is commonly accepted as the limit of Portuguese navigation in the Prince's lifetime. Henry had fulfilled the predictions of his horoscope, and for some years there was no one

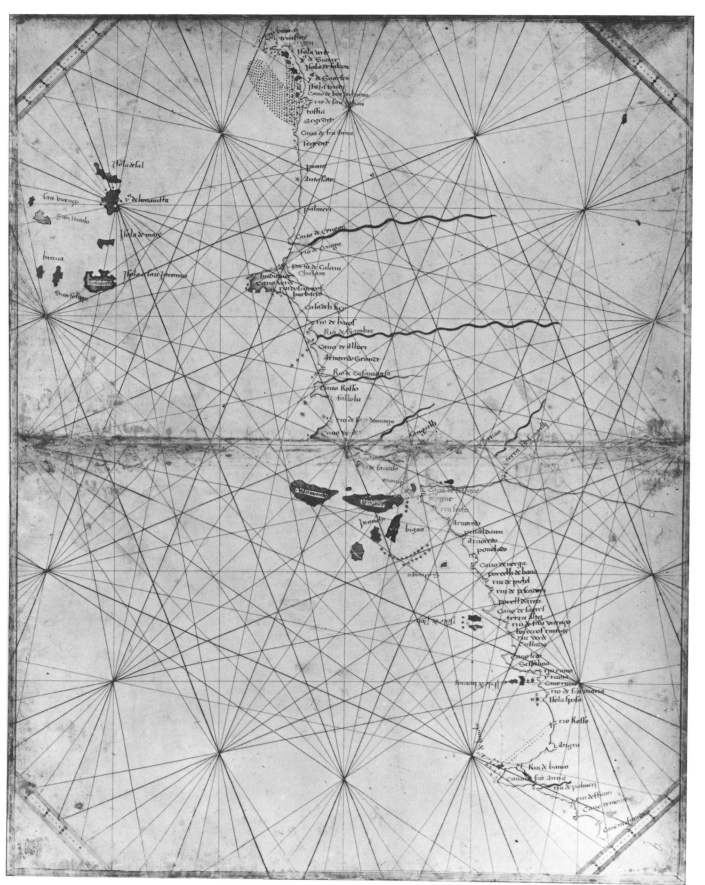

Marine chart of
West Africa showing the
Cape Verde Islands, by
Grazioso Benincasa, 1468

to take his place as patron. The Crown, to which Prince Henry's African rights reverted, was willing enough to encourage discovery, but unwilling to incur expense, especially since Henry had left a load of debt. Afonso V, the Prince's royal nephew, was more interested in the crusade—preached against the advancing Turk, diverted against Morocco—and in plans for seizing Arzila and Tangier, than in the exploration of Guinea; though he must have known that the gold, which he coined into *cruzados* in 1457 to pay for the crusade, came from Arguim. The explorers had reached a difficult stretch of coast, with no evident prospect of improvement. From just south of the Gambia to just south of modern Freetown—the coasts of Portuguese and French Guinea and Sierra Leone —the shallows are full of islands, rocks and shoals, and the whole stretch from Iles de Los to Cape St. Ann is marked on modern Admiralty charts "all approach dangerous." There was the alarming prospect, moreover, that the mariners' friend, the North Star, barely visible above the horizon off Sierra Leone, would disappear if they went farther. The merchants, for their part, were content to develop their modest but prospering trade at Arguim and at the mouths of the Senegal and the Gambia. For all these reasons no further discoveries were made, and no official action was taken on Guinea, until 1469. In that year, Afonso decided to lease the whole enterprise, excepting only Arguim and the Cape Verde Islands (where Portuguese residents had already settled and private leases already existed) to a private entrepreneur. The lessee, Fernão Gomes, covenanted to pay an annual rent and to explore one hundred leagues of coast annually during the five-year period of his lease. Little is

known of Gomes as a person; but he was clearly a man of energy, a good organizer and a good judge of men, and his story is one of success. He carried out his obligations, and more; he made a fortune from his highly speculative investment; spent much of it serving his King in arms in Morocco; was ennobled for his pains, and became a member of the royal Council.

South of modern Freetown the shore trends southeast to Cape Palmas, then east: the coasts of modern Liberia and Côte d'Ivoire, lined with lagoons and mangrove creeks, featureless and flat. The coast of Liberia has many small inlets, and produced considerable quantities of *malagueta,* which gave it for a time the trade name of the Grain Coast. Farther east, beyond Cape Palmas, there were no usable breaks in the mangroves; the channel which now takes ships into the lagoon at Abidjan is recent and man-made, and the aspect of the coast is depressing in the extreme. About Cape Three Points, however, there is a change: from there to the mouth of the Volta river is an open sandy coast with occasional rocky headlands. Except for the surf, the beaches are readily approachable. This was the *Mina do Ouro,* the Gold Coast, which in recent times has appropriated the name of Ghana (an unconnected empire on the upper Senegal, which had disappeared long before Europeans reached the coast). The *Mina* was not, of course, a gold mine (though some envious Spaniards seem to have thought so) but a stretch of coast where gold was traded in considerable quantity, mostly in the form of dust washed from streams inland. It is unlikely that this region ever made any significant contribution to the trans-Saharan gold trade. It was separated from the gold fields of the western Sudan by hundreds of miles of thick bush, a far more formidable obstacle to travel than the desert ever was. Ashanti gold was used locally, traded as dust or worked into a profusion of chiefly ornament. To Europeans, it was a virtually untapped source.

East of the Volta is another long stretch of low-lying coast, with a few good harbors, particularly Lagos, with lagoons enclosed by mangrove-covered banks stretching as far as the Benin River. This navigable river gave access to the most extensive and powerful of all the coastal kingdoms. Benin, besides numerous slaves captured in its constant wars, produced—and still produces—peppers of savage pungency. It was a populous city with highly developed arts and craft industries: wood and ivory carving, stone and terracotta sculpture, metal work. Its brass and bronze casting was among the best in the world. East of it is the great area of the Niger Delta, the biggest mangrove swamp in the world, a vast sodden sponge into which the waters of the Niger pour, to seep out to the Gulf through innumerable tortuous creeks. There was little cultivable land on the banks of these dark watery tunnels, and no towns, only stilt-built villages, whose inhabitants lived, and still live, by trade and fishing. The territory of these aquatic people, many of whom are born in canoes, includes the whole of the Delta and its eastern outlier, the Calabar river. East of the Calabar comes a dramatic change of scene: the mountainous coast of the Cameroons and the deep curve of the Bight of Biafra, a treacherous, unhealthy trap for sailing ships, but enclosing big, inviting islands.

All this was the coast which Gomes's captains were to explore. They reached Sama, near Cape Three Points, the first village of the Mina do Ouro, in 1471, and in the next four years

coasted as far as the Benin river (though the city was not visited until about 1485). Whether Gomes's people investigated the Cameroons coast is uncertain. The coastal current in the Bight of Biafra sets strongly from east to west and winds are notoriously unreliable; but certainly during this period, in 1472, Fernando Po discovered the fertile island which now bears his name. Mount Cameroon is only ninety miles to the north, and visible in good weather. Probably the discoverer followed the coast from there on his return passage with the current, past the many mouths of the Niger Delta. The other major islands, Principe and São Tomé, were found soon afterward—the exact year is uncertain; and finally, in 1474 or 1475, Lopo Gonçalves and Rui de Sequeira discovered the southerly trend of the coast beyond Malimba, and followed it south to Cape López and then to Cape St. Catherine, which is in 2 degrees south. About that time, Gomes's lease expired. He did not seek to renew it, probably because of the increase in the cost and danger of the trade after the outbreak of war with Castile in 1475. During the years of his concession nearly two thousand miles of coastline had been roughly explored: more in six years than Prince Henry's captains had covered in forty. Discovery had developed its own momentum, with gold the accelerator. The Guinea trade had assumed roughly the form it was to retain for more than a century, and its value had been clearly demonstrated; so clearly that the King, after the expiry of the lease, made no more general concessions to private subjects. He entrusted responsibility for the affairs of Guinea to his own son, the future John II.

Royal supervision of the Guinea enterprise had become necessary not only because of the value of the trade, but because of its vulnerability. Throughout the whole process of coastal exploration the Portuguese had remained uneasy about the group of islands on their seaward flank, in which the only European settlements were Spanish. As the Guinea trade became more valuable, the Portuguese authorities became more determined to prevent Spaniards from sharing in it. They based their claim to monopoly on grounds both of prior discovery and of papal bulls of 1455 and 1456 granting to Prince Henry and the Order of Christ the sole right and duty of converting the natives of the region. Despite the claim and despite the bulls (the binding force of which was disputable), Andalusian skippers were already trading in Upper Guinea by the fourteen-fifties. They even hit on the ingenious idea of collecting sea shells in the Canaries and shipping them to the coast, where they were used as coin. Prevention was always difficult: the national distinction between Portuguese and Andalusians, along the coast between Cape St. Vincent and Tarifa, was then much less clear than it is now. Andalusian skippers operated caravels which could not easily be distinguished at sea from Portuguese. They fished regularly in Mauretanian waters; and for the purpose of clandestine trade on the Guinea coast, they had the convenience of the Spanish harbors in the Canaries. Worse, those harbors could be used in wartime as bases for direct assaults on Portuguese ships and trading posts. Hence the persistent attempts of the Portuguese to establish bases of their own in the islands; attempts which had all been frustrated, either by native resistance or by Castilian obstruction. In 1475 the Succession War between Spain and Portugal presented them with a fresh opportunity.

The immediate cause of the war was the determination of the Castilian nobility to exclude Juana, daughter and heiress of Enrique IV, from the throne, and to install Isabella "the Catholic" in her place. They had their reasons for preferring a capable and strong-minded woman to a timid child believed by many to be illegitimate; but Juana was Afonso V's niece. He espoused her cause, married her (though uncanonically) and laid claim through her to the throne of Castile. The result was four years of bitter and destructive fighting; and naturally the Guinea trade and the Canary Islands were among the prizes contended for. In 1475 Isabella issued a formal authorization to her subjects to enter the African trade, and in 1476 and 1477 privateering fleets were fitted out in the Río Tinto to intercept Portuguese ships homeward bound from Mina. On the Portuguese side, an armed fleet under Fernão Gomes—as commanding officer, not as lessee—was sent out in 1477 to bring Guinea produce home, and made a successful passage out and back. The fighting throughout the war was extremely savage, prisoners usually being hanged or thrown over the side. The last big Spanish expedition of the war, thirty-five sail, went out in 1478; it was out-maneuvered and out-fought, and many of the ships were taken by the Portuguese. In general, in sea and island fighting the Portuguese more than held their own everywhere except in the Canaries, where the Spanish settlements were too strong to be dislodged. Consequently, although at home the Portuguese were heavily defeated and withdrew all their claims in Castile, the Treaty of Alcáçovas, which ended the war in 1479, contained clauses dealing with oversea trade and settlement highly favorable to

Portugal. Castile retained rights only in the Canaries. The Castilians were extremely reluctant to abandon their claim to trade with Mina; but many of their ships were still in African waters at the time of the treaty, and in danger of interception. Eventually, after very tenacious bargaining, Castile recognized the Portuguese monopoly of fishing, trade and navigation along the whole west African coast, and the Portuguese gave safe-conduct to Spanish ships returning from the coast at the end of the war. The Treaty of Alcáçovas was the first of a long series of European treaties regulating maritime spheres of influence, and in this respect was a signal diplomatic triumph for Portugal.

Castilian adherence to treaty obligations was not entirely to be trusted. Clandestine fishing continued off the Mauretanian coast. A proposed English expedition to Mina in 1481 was believed to have been instigated by the Duke of Medina Sidonia; and the treasonable correspondence of the Duke of Braganza, discovered in 1481, had included proposals for Spanish trade to Guinea. John II, who acceded to the throne in that year, was not a man for half measures, and he made the Guinea trade a matter of major concern. Decrees were issued prohibiting the shipment of shells from the Canaries and prescribing savage penalties for interlopers caught in African waters; and serious attempts were made, for the first time, to prevent the export of information about new discoveries. Probably these were not very effective. Genoese sailors went everywhere and peddled everyone's secrets; there were many Portuguese, from the Duke of Braganza downwards, whose national allegiance sat lightly upon them; and there was a regular trade in smuggled charts. Legislation was useless in itself;

it could be made effective, and the royal trade monopoly preserved, only by force, and for this secure bases were necessary. In 1481, accordingly, at the very outset of his reign, John ordered the building of the factory-fort of São Jorge de Mina. This famous fortress was, in a manner, prefabricated; the beams cut, the stone dressed, the roofing tiles baked in Portugal, and shipped out, with a force of a hundred or so workmen, in a fleet of eleven sail commanded by Diogo d'Azambuja, soldier, diplomat and military engineer. According to a persistent and plausible tradition, Christopher Columbus sailed as a seaman in one of the ships. D'Azambuja, whether by negotiation or by threat, beat down the objections of the local chiefs, and himself supervised the construction, which was completed within a matter of months. Nothing of his work remains today; the Dutch in the seventeenth century replaced it by a bigger castle, which still stands; but it was evidently, in its day, an impressive landmark, and its construction was a notably efficient undertaking. The site, Elmina Point, is a small rocky peninsula, flanked on the east by a shallow bay and on the west by the small Beyah river. From the west bank of the Beyah a reef, on which the surf breaks violently, curves south and east two or three cables from the point. This line of rocks shelters a small anchorage at the mouth of the river, now silted up and approachable only by small boats; but as late as the early nineteenth century, ships up to a hundred tons could enter, and in Portuguese times caravels could berth alongside the castle gates. The fort was manned by sixty Portuguese soldiers; a native village soon grew up on the neck of the peninsula, inhabited by laborers and fighting auxiliaries. This is today a fair-sized

town. The Portuguese garrison was rarely at full strength, and the soldiers had a poor time of it. Provisioning was difficult and expensive: the water supply was poor, and food, other than local fish and vegetables, had initially to be brought out from Portugal; but interlopers kept away from the place, and it served its purpose for a hundred and fifty years.

Elmina was not, of course, the only Portuguese post on the Gulf of Guinea in the late fifteenth century. Axim, on the bay of that name just west of Cape Three Points, and Cabo das Redes (Fetta Point) at the mouth of the little Kahkoo river, were secondary gold-collecting stations. Like Elmina, these places have protected landings; a rare and valuable advantage on that surf-bound coast. A small fort was built at Axim before the end of the fifteenth century. Gwató at the mouth of the Benin river was mainly a slave barracoon, sending slaves not only to Portugal but also to Elmina, where the local up-country traders needed carriers and would pay for them in gold. Gwató had no local food supply, and was provisioned from São Tomé. This luxuriant island settlement was already, in the early sixteenth century, producing a surplus of yams, rice, fruit and sugar, to which, later in the century, it added maize. It became the principal source of food for all the Portuguese stations in the Gulf, as Santiago in the Cape Verde Islands was for Upper Guinea. The out-and-back trade between Lisbon and Elmina was thus supported by a network of seaborne exchange within the Gulf; a network in which—in the absence of a local maritime tradition—Europeans were the carriers.

The ships—mostly caravels—which plied between Lisbon and Elmina in the late fifteenth and early sixteenth centuries were owned or chartered by the Crown and fitted out on Crown account. (Later in the sixteenth century, whole sections of the Guinea trade were leased out to contractors, as had been done before John II's accession; but by then Guinea had become overshadowed, in royal estimation, by India.) Efforts were made to maintain monthly sailings; and though this regularity was not always achieved, it was sometimes exceeded. Vasco da Gama, on arrival at Calicut, told the ruler there that twelve to fifteen ships made the Elmina voyage every year. The goods which the ships carried belonged either to the Crown or to private firms and individuals trading with Crown license. Outward bound, they included textiles—woolen and linen materials and ready-made garments—iron and brass manilas, coral, glass and hardware. The returns were in gold, slaves and pepper, with minor dealings in ivory, gum, wax, palm oil and sundry curiosities, parrots and the like. Apart from gold, slaves probably represented the biggest total value, though not very numerous by the later standards of the trade; perhaps five hundred a year at the end of the fifteenth century. Pepper was a highly prized commodity, and dealing in it was a royal monopoly. High-quality Benin pepper, in particular, was an important source of revenue in the late fifteenth century; but in the sixteenth its import was forbidden, in order to protect the price of Indian pepper. *Malagueta* continued in use as a cheap substitute. Ivory was also reserved to the Crown under the Gomes lease, but not subsequently.

The main attraction, the main reason for the existence of the trade, was gold. Mina gold, once purchased from the local traders and stored

OPPOSITE: Elmina Castle,
from de Bry's *Voyages*

behind the thick walls of the castle, belonged to the Crown. Soldiers of the garrison and other functionaries serving on the coast were allowed, as a privilege, to buy gold up to the amount of their pay and ship it to Portugal; but this was a trifling exception. Private traders could procure gold in Upper Guinea, at Arguim (where the Crown also traded) or on the Gambia or the Senegal, where most of the trade was private. The gold which private traders brought to Portugal was, naturally, taxed. All gold, wherever it came from and whoever owned it, had to be turned in to the mint on arrival at Lisbon, for coining. No doubt, as always in such situations, the rules were widely evaded; but the machinery for enforcing them was fairly elaborate, and so was the record-keeping. Like many others in Portugal, these records have suffered from the destroying hand of time, and no details survive from the fifteenth century; but from the early years of the sixteenth, it is possible to estimate roughly the scale of the trade and its fluctuations from year to year, or at least from decade to decade. The best period, the period of consistently high levels of gold import, was from the end of the fifteenth century through the first twenty years of the sixteenth. In that period, not less than seven hundred kilos of gold, worth 200,000 *cruzados,* perhaps much more—one cannot even guess the extent of fraud —came annually to Portugal. About two thirds of this gold, belonging mostly to the Crown, came from Mina; the rest, belonging largely to individuals but paying tax to the Crown, came from Arguim or the "Guinea rivers." In the fifteen-twenties the average annual total dropped to about half these high figures, apparently because some old workings became exhausted; it

rose steeply again in the early fifteen-thirties— new sources were found in neighborhood of Fetta at that time—but the rise proved temporary. Through the fifteen-forties the trend was steadily downwards. According to Barros, the chronicler, the royal trade actually began to lose money after the middle of the century; in some years at least, the cost of forts and garrisons, of fleets and the goods they carried, exceeded the value of the gold brought in. These years became more and more frequent. The high prosperity of the seaborne trade in Guinea gold was impressive while it lasted, but it did not last very long.

The Guinea enterprise is often described as a victory of the caravel over the camel: the Portuguese, that is to say, diverted the ancient gold trade of the trans-Saharan caravans to the new sea route, which they had discovered, and which was more economical and efficient. Barros says this almost in so many words: Elmina and Arguim "bled" Guinea of its gold. The Portuguese took what there was—a dwindling amount—and left none for the Moors, whose camels so often perished in the desert sand. Barros was a high official of the *Casa da India e Mina,* and knew what he was talking about, at least where Portuguese trade was concerned; but in the matter of the Moors and their camels, he exaggerated. The caravans were not in fact put out of business. Leo Africanus, the communicative Christianized Moor—well named, for he was lionized at Rome—before his capture and conversion had traveled to the western Sudan on a diplomatic mission, and later wrote a description of the country. Leo remarks on the abundance of gold at Gao and Timbuktu when he was there, and says that the caravan trade was flourishing. That was in 1510 or a little later. The old empire of Mali had shrunk by then to the Mandingo homeland on the Senegal. Most of the urban centres of the western Sudan were dominated by the powerful Songhai empire under its Askia rulers, a dynasty of Negro Muslims native to the middle Niger, with their principal capital at Gao. Leo's contemporary, Askia Muhammad I, "the Great," made his pilgrimage to Mecca in a lavish golden splendor recalling that of Mansa Musa, the Mandingo ruler a century and a half before. For more than fifty years he and his successors maintained and tried to extend their control of the commercial centres of the western Sudan, and profited from the coming and going of the caravans which linked the Sudan with Egypt and the Maghrib.

In Askia the Great's time, the caravan trade across the desert and the caravel trade on the coast flourished simultaneously, and both dealt in gold; but they drew their gold, to a large extent, from different sources. It is true that Mandingo merchants (among many others listed in *Esmeraldo de Situ Orbis*) traded at Elmina; presumably they bought European goods with Sudan gold, probably from Bure or Bambuk; but in view of the nature of the country and the total absence of beasts of burden, it seems likely that most of the gold shipped from Elmina was Ashanti gold, dug or washed within a week or two's march from the castle. Ashanti gold was never important to the caravan trade. At Arguim and on the Guinea rivers, all the gold traded was Sudan gold; Portuguese factors had to compete with traders from the Maghrib, and the gold they obtained was diverted from the caravans. They would have liked to divert much more, and made strenuous efforts to do so, especially under

John II. For a time, a few of them traded inland at Wadan, on one of the main caravan routes, five hundred desert miles east of Arguim; but they never established a permanent post there. Attempts were made to open diplomatic contacts with major rulers in the Sudan (insofar as it could be ascertained who the major rulers were) with a view to increasing trade. John II sent letters to the paramount chief of the Mossi (a warlike group on the upper Volta, a thorn in the side of Songhai) under the impression that he was a vassal of Prester John. Portuguese emissaries made almost incredible journeys: from the Gambia to Timbuktu, and from Elmina to Gao, to wait upon the Askia, who was mightily surprised to see them. None of these diplomatic approaches could alter the economic facts. Success in the gold trade depended not so much on the efficiency of the carriers—camels or caravels—as on the commodities carried.

The standard exports from the Mediterranean area to the Sudan—textiles, copper, glass, horses—were common to the sea and land routes; but the one commodity most urgently desired by the actual producers of gold in the western Sudan was salt, rock salt. The Ashanti gold miners used sea salt, to which they had relatively easy access; but for the Sudan peoples only rock salt would do. It was quarried from deposits at Taghaza and Taodeni, far in the desert, to which the Portuguese had no access. Traders in Timbuktu and Gao received it from the desert caravans and took it on to the gold-producing areas. Whoever controlled the salt mines in large measure controlled the trade and named the price. In the late fifteenth century and the first half of the sixteenth they were controlled by the rulers of Songhai. In the middle of the sixteenth century, this control was challenged with increasing success by the rulers of Morocco, who had always been among the chief purchasers of Sudan gold. Finally, in 1591, the armies of the Moroccan Shereef El-Mansur crossed the desert, invaded the Sudan and conquered the Songhai empire. The Moors, if their historians are to be believed, found the Sudan cities a disappointment: extensive but unimpressive collections of mud-built mosques and houses. But the gold was real, and for the first time the western desert route by which much of it traveled was brought under a single political control. Couto, the Portuguese historian who continued the story of Barros's *Decades*, remarked on the prodigious quantities of gold which then reached Marrakech and Fez, as tribute or by way of trade. English merchants trading in the Barbary ports told a similar tale. To his first title, El-Mansur, "the Victorious," the Shereef added a second, El-Dzehebi, "the Golden."

The Portuguese in Guinea in the sixteenth century were in a losing position, at least so far as the gold trade was concerned. By the middle of century their flow of Ashanti gold was declining; their attempts to increase their purchases of Sudan gold failed; their seaborne trade with Guinea was increasingly preyed upon and damaged by maritime robbers from other European countries, from France, and a little later from England. They were obliged to provide heavier and heavier naval protection which, even when successful, added greatly to their costs. This was a major factor in the unprofitability of the trade in the later sixteenth century; the sea became as hazardous and costly as the desert. They did their best to tap the

desert trade at the Mediterranean end—as Prince Henry had always advocated—by seizing Moroccan harbors; but their adventures in Morocco came to a disastrous end at Alcazar-Kebir in 1578. The victory of the caravel over the camel was brief. By the end of the century it had been reversed; the camel had reasserted its indispensability.

Successful trade is not simply a matter of moving goods efficiently from place to place. In the story of the discovery of the sea, we shall meet other examples of traditional overland trade routes persisting, remaining in busy use, long after more economical, or seemingly more economical sea routes had been opened. The sea routes usually won in the end, but the process of competition might extend over centuries. This is not to say, however, that the achievements of the fifteenth-century Portuguese explorers were thrown away. Guinea was not the only source of gold; the Portuguese, as the discovery of the sea proceeded, were to find other sources. Nor was gold the only valuable product of Guinea. The slave trade, after the Atlantic had been crossed, was to take a new lease on life, and to make profits for several centuries. Senegal gum and *malagueta* pepper brought the Portuguese into the spice business, and gave them experience which they were to use in dealing in real pepper from India. The most significant legacy of John II's captains, however, was not a commodity but an attitude of mind: a bold, skillful self-confidence in making long ocean passages. In the reign of John's successor this boldness, this confidence and skill were to be applied on a far wider scale, in oceans other than the Atlantic.

7

The
Way to
India

n the early fifteenth century "India" was a vague and compendious term which could include any territory east of the Nile and west of "Cathay." The actual peninsula of India, which we now know by that name, was then almost unknown to Europeans. The excellent fourteenth-century description by Jordan of Severac had been forgotten. Marco Polo's account of his visit to south India, if not forgotten, was ignored and discounted by the erudite, read chiefly for amusement. In the course of the fifteenth century Europe slowly and painfully regained contact with the East, and at the end of the century a Portuguese fleet visited the Indian peninsula. As a result of this process, some Europeans learned to employ the term "India" more precisely. It was still used by many in the old general sense, but for well-informed Portuguese it had been narrowed to include the peninsula, together with those areas, chiefly the Indonesian islands, which supplied the peninsula with spices; the areas connected with Portugal by what, in the sixteenth century, came to be called the *Carreira da India*.

What were the stages in this narrowing process? India in the early fifteenth century was not only unknown to Europeans, except by hearsay and tradition; it was, for practical purposes, inaccessible. The only known way to get there was by hazardous subterfuge, by traveling in

Arab disguise and adopting at least the outward forms of Islam. The first firm information about India to reach Europe in the fifteenth century was brought by a man who traveled in this way: Nicolò de' Conti, a Venetian trader who spent twenty-five years in the East; who visited Mesopotamia, India, Burma, the Indonesian archipelago, the approaches to the Red Sea, and Egypt; and who returned to tell the tale. About 1441, Conti recounted his experiences to Poggio Bracciolini, secretary to Pope Eugenius IV. Poggio was a humanist scholar of formidable learning, who had himself traveled widely in Europe in the course of his ecclesiastical duties, and who was an enthusiastic amateur of travel farther afield. He was interested in facts, insofar as they could be ascertained, rather than in tall stories, and he used the information given him by Conti as the basis of one section of his own book of historical reflection, *De varietate fortunae.* The section soon became detached from the rest of the work, circulated widely in manuscript, and was printed in 1492 under the title *India recognita,* the Indies re-discovered. The earliest known map to include information drawn from this work is an elliptical world map made in Genoa in 1457. The map is Ptolemaic in general outline, except for a sea passage round the southern tip of Africa, but much of the Asian detail clearly comes from Conti: the great city of Vijayanagar in peninsular India, the island of Ceylon, and the scatter of islands off southeast Asia. These include Sumatra (firmly distinguished from Ceylon), Java Major (Borneo) and Java Minor (Java). Farther east is a group of smaller islands with a legend alluding to cloves: the first known appearance on a European map of the much-sought Spice Islands, the Moluccas.

How soon, and to what extent, did the Conti story affect geographical thought in Portugal? There is no evidence of actual manuscripts circulating there, though they may have done; Poggio was a celebrated personage, and incidentally an admirer of Prince Henry, to whom he addressed adulatory letters; his name must have been known in Portugal. There were, in addition, verbal channels of communication. Paolo dal Pozzo Toscanelli, for example—member of a prominent family of Florentine merchant bankers, physician, and learned amateur of cosmography—was familiar with Conti's story and probably interrogated Conti himself. In 1459, Toscanelli talked with Portuguese emissaries in Florence. His purpose was to collect information about Portuguese discoveries in Africa, in order to revise his own world map, completed two years earlier. It seems likely that he offered in return information about the East, derived from Conti. We shall meet Toscanelli again later, advocating a westward sea route to Cathay; but in 1459 he was principally a channel of information about India.

To know something of India by report, obviously, was one thing; to contemplate actually going there, quite another. The tale of Conti's adventures was of absorbing interest to geographers, but it was hardly likely to excite investors. The way he had gone was too dangerous for regular profitable trade, and he had no suggestions to offer about alternative routes. With the advantage of hindsight, we can see that the only way in which Portuguese could travel regularly to India was by an all-sea route; but in the middle of the fifteenth century Portuguese oversea activity was heavily concentrated upon Africa. Just as Ceuta had been

OPPOSITE: Detail from the Genoese world map of 1457, showing the influence of Conti's travels in southern Asia and the Malay archipelago

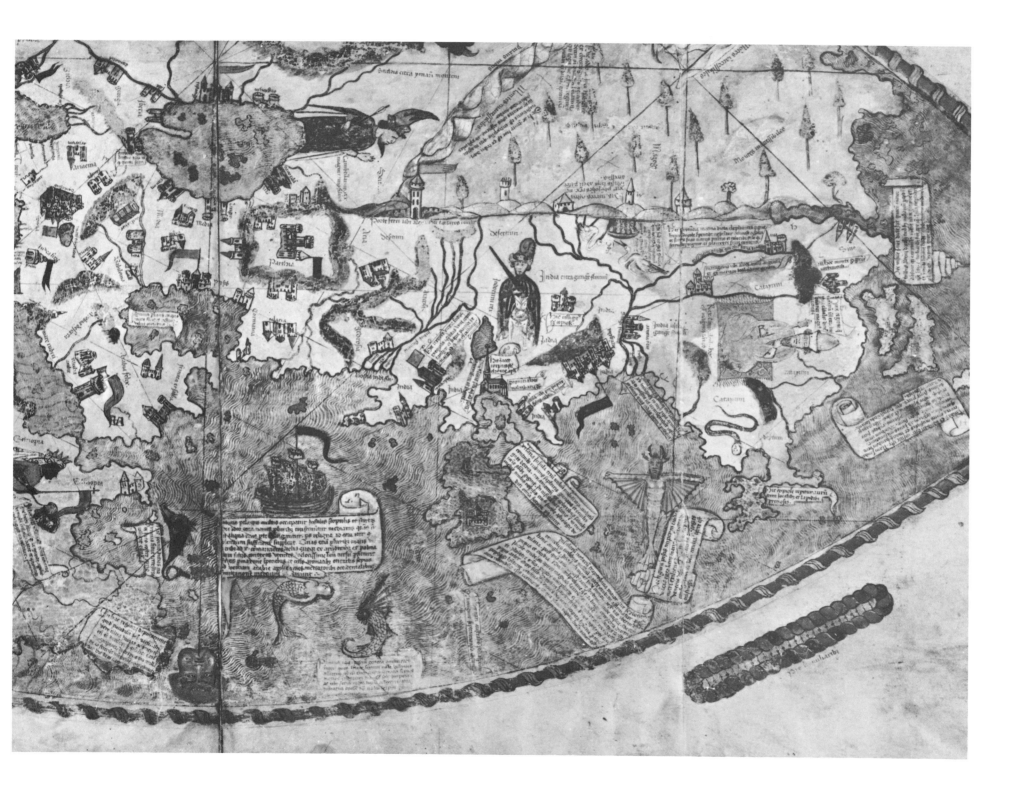

a false step in the direction of Guinea, so Guinea itself—at least in a navigational sense—was to prove a false step in the direction of India. Guinea is not on the way to India; not, certainly, for a sailing ship. The Gulf of Guinea, with its uncertain winds, is if possible to be avoided. In later, better-informed times, ships leaving Portugal for India made straight for the Cape Verde Islands. Following from there the quickest and easiest route to the Cape of Good Hope, making the best use of prevailing winds, they missed Elmina by two thousand miles. This was to be the route of Vasco da Gama, and approximately the route of hundreds of Indiamen, Portuguese, Dutch, English and French, in succeeding centuries. The navigational peculiarities of the south Atlantic were unknown, however, at the time when the Portuguese Crown first began to send out expeditions in search of a sea route to the Indian Ocean. At that time, Portuguese traders were already active on the coast of the Gulf of Guinea, and the waters of the gulf were reasonably well known to a considerable number of pilots. It was natural that explorers, before entering the unknown, should wish to sail as far as possible through familiar waters. The obvious way to search for a passage round (or through) the African continent was to cross the Gulf of Guinea from Elmina to the Gabon coast, and then to follow the coast southward. The earliest expeditions sent from Portugal in search of the Indian Ocean all pursued this course. Though well equipped and ably commanded, they all ran into trouble, first drifting through the Doldrum calms, then struggling for weeks and months against head winds and contrary currents, along an inhospitable coast which yielded no provisions,

scarcely even wood and water. Explorers might accept these difficulties, as among the hazards of their calling; but merchant ships, in pursuit of commercial profit, could not be expected to undertake such uncertain voyages. For them, a reasonable assurance of favorable conditions was a requirement for investment. Regular sailing between Atlantic and Indian Oceans became possible, in fact, only when the India navigation had been firmly separated from the Guinea navigation, as a distinct enterprise in its own right.

Such a separation could not easily have been made by a simple decision, by a flash of intuition or an act of faith. One searches directly for something only in the reasonable confidence that it is there to be found. In the mid-fifteenth century there were too many uncertainties, geographical, economic, political, for such confidence. Ptolemy, obviously, with his *Terra Incognita* and his landlocked Indian Ocean, had added to the geographical uncertainties; though in practice the discouraging influence of Ptolemy was less than might have been expected. Serious geographers never accepted Ptolemy whole and uncritically; they admired his erudition and his ingenuity, but they often pointed out that geographical facts, well known to them, had been unknown in Ptolemy's time.

The standard mid-fifteenth-century view of the matter, among the well-informed, was set out in the Genoese world map of 1457, to which reference has been made, and more magisterially in Fra Mauro's famous planisphere, drawn at Murano near Venice in 1459. Fra Mauro enjoyed a great reputation as a cartographer in his day, and his map was commissioned by the Portuguese Crown. He drew his information from many sources. The outlines of Europe are of the normal portolan shape. The outline of Africa resembles that in the later Catalan maps. There is some information about the interior of Africa, which may have come to Venice through Cairo or Jerusalem from Ethiopian sources. The east African coastline bears a number of Arabic place names. The detail of west Africa is disappointing; in that region the Portuguese could teach Fra Mauro more than he them. Legends on China, the Malay archipelago and the interior of Asia derive, apparently, from Marco Polo and from Conti. For the general size and shape of Asia and the world as a whole, Fra Mauro relied on Ptolemy, but not uncritically and not in all respects: the map shows a continuous ocean to the south of Africa and Asia. Fra Mauro was aware that in departing from Ptolemy in a major feature of his map he invited the criticism of the learned, and in a respectful but firm note he explained his reasons. He was convinced not only that Africa was circumnavigable, but that—in part at least—it had been circumnavigated. Near the edge of the map, off the *Prassum Promontorium,* the southernmost point of Africa, is a drawing of a ship passing the cape from west to east. In the accompanying legend the ship is described as an Indian "Junk," and the date of its voyage is given as 1420.

Ship and legend constitute a minor mystery. No other evidence exists of such a voyage; yet it is unlikely that Fra Mauro merely drew what he thought his Portuguese patrons wanted to see. Possibly some unidentified cape had been wrongly reported as the "end" of Africa. Whatever the explanation may be, the significance of the ship to Fra Mauro's contemporaries should not be exaggerated. There is no evidence that Portuguese promoters of voyages at that time contemplated the circumnavigation of Africa, except perhaps as a remote possibility. They were interested immediately in Guinea, as a source of gold. More distantly, they were interested in the (reputedly) rich and friendly kingdom of "Prester John." They hoped to reach this kingdom, preferably not by an ocean passage, but by a short cut, a navigable waterway across the continent. Their persistent attempts to explore the west African rivers were inspired, partly at least, by reports of inland rulers who might be identified with Prester John, and by the belief that one of those rivers connected with the upper Nile. They had no notion of the longitudinal breadth of Africa. In the event, the Guinea coast was to answer expectations, the Guinea rivers were to defeat them. There was no interior waterway to the Indian Ocean. Those who hoped to find one were to be driven farther and farther south in their search, until finally they were left with no recourse but the ocean passage. They faced the prospect with understandable misgivings. Geographical uncertainty was not the only difficulty in their way. Who would provide the men, the money and the ships for so ambitious a project? What assurance could be given of a commercial return on so costly an investment? Could the available ships last out so long a voyage? Could they carry enough stores to feed their people for many months, perhaps years, of search? How would they find their way, in an ocean totally unknown? All these uncertainties made it inevitable that the way to India should be for many years a continuation of the way to Guinea; not the best way, but the

AVSTER
Diab. Questo e el nome de la isola.
DIAB
ETHYOPIA AVSTRAL
Ethyopia
ABASSIA
DAVARO
FATAGAR
REGNO
ABASSIA
ADEL

most cautious; a groping progress along the coast of Africa.

It is hard to say precisely when voyages to India were first considered, by responsible people in Portugal, as a practical proposition. Did Prince Henry, for instance, seriously entertain the possibility? Papal Bulls on the subject of exploration and missions, issued at the request of the Portuguese Crown in 1455 and 1456, contain references to "India." *Romanus pontifex* of 1455 granted to Portugal exclusive rights of conquest and possession in Saracen or pagan lands along the African coast from Cape Bojador to the south; it imputed to Prince Henry the belief that "he would best perform his duty to God in this matter [of exploration] if by his effort and industry that sea [to the south and east] might become navigable as far as to the Indians who are said to honor the name of Christ, and to incite them to aid the Christians against the Saracens and other such enemies of the Faith." The confirmatory Bull *Inter caetera* of 1456 granted to the Order of Christ "ecclesiastical and all ordinary jurisdiction, lordship and power, in ecclesiastical matters only . . . from Capes Bojador and Noun as far as through all Guinea, and past that southern shore all the way to the Indians." Papal Bulls issued, as these were, to monarchs high in papal favor, usually reflected the wishes, often the actual words of those who solicited them. Presumably the references to "Indians" were included at Portuguese request; but in view of the vague sense in which the name "India" was then used, we cannot assume that the framers of the Bulls had any particular "Indians" in mind. How much, then, can be inferred from the Bulls, concerning Portuguese intentions and plans?

At the time of the issue of the Bulls, Portuguese ships were exploring and trading farther and farther down the Senegambia coast and nosing into the great rivers of Upper Guinea. The region yielded commodities of value. Prince Henry, and the Portuguese government negotiating on his behalf, naturally wished to establish a recognized monopoly of trade. The Papacy could give valuable moral, legal and diplomatic support, and could discourage—though not, of course, prevent— meddling by other Europeans. The immediate economic objects of Portuguese activity, however —the expansion of the gold and slave trades and the search for the sources of Guinea gold—were no concern of the Papacy. The desired support could be given only for purposes within the papal competence; and the purpose most likely to command papal sympathy was the crusade. The fall of Constantinople, and the feeble reaction of most western European governments, had made the search for other Christian allies more urgent (if no more realistic) than ever. There were no Christians on the Guinea coast, nor prospects of any; but Christian communities—the kingdom of Prester John was only one of them—were known or believed to exist on the shores of the Indian Ocean. Portuguese diplomatic approaches to the Papacy, therefore, would naturally represent, as pre-eminent among Portuguese objects, the establishment of contact with such communities. This is not to suggest that the search for eastern Christians was merely an exercise in public relations; for some Portuguese—certainly for Prince Henry—the crusade in all its many forms was a deeply cherished purpose. It was certainly not the only object of Portuguese activity overseas, not the most immediate, not perhaps

OPPOSITE: Detail from the world map of Fra Mauro, 1459, showing a ship off the southern cape of Africa. South is at the top.

the most compelling; but it was stressed above others, in the negotiations leading to the issue of the Bulls, because it was the object which most directly concerned the Papacy and was most likely to command papal support.

The term "Indians," as used in the Bulls, certainly included the Christian people of Ethiopia, who were the Christians most likely, it was believed, to assist the crusade. In Fra Mauro's map, and in other maps, the land of the Ethiopians, the realm of "Prester John," occupied a great stretch of the east African coast, south to the *Prassum Promontorium*. In theory— failing an interior waterway—it could be reached by a coastal passage. This, clearly, was one of the possibilities suggested in the Bulls; but it was not the only possibility. The Portuguese government naturally wanted Bulls supporting its oversea activities to be drawn in the broadest possible terms, to include any territory which Portuguese expeditions might traverse, on their way to any land of eastern Christians. The term "Indians" was sufficiently comprehensive and vague to suit requirements not yet precisely formulated. The Bulls, in short, were a general insurance for the future; they were not drafted to cover any particular or immediate plan for expansion in the East, nor, probably, did they refer to any particular eastern territory. There is, in fact, no evidence that Prince Henry or any of his contemporaries ever contemplated, as a practical proposition, the circumnavigation of Africa; or that a sea route to India (that is, to the subcontinent) ever entered his plans.

The first Portuguese expedition to reach India by sea, that commanded by Vasco da Gama, followed a definite and pre-concerted plan. The instructions issued to da Gama, it is true, have disappeared, and so has his report; but from the confident, unhesitating conduct of the voyage, the general outline of the plan can be deduced. Da Gama was to sail as directly as possible to the southern tip of Africa, without entering the Gulf of Guinea; he was to follow the east coast of Africa northward until he found a harbor, preferably in Christian territory, where he could obtain information and provisions and if possible engage a pilot for the Indian Ocean crossing; he was then to sail for India—not a vague, general "India," but a specific India, the peninsula of India; more, he was to make for a specific harbor, Calicut, on the Malabar coast, which was known to be an important spice market; in Calicut, once more, he was to make contact with the Christian community reported as living there; presumably he was to seek the good offices of these Christians in establishing an oceanic trade in spices. Here, then, was the clear decision, the separation of the India navigation from the Guinea navigation.

In order to formulate such a plan, the Portuguese government must have collected a considerable store of information about the south Atlantic navigation; about the configuration of Africa, and about the trading cities on both shores of the Arabian Sea. It must have sorted out, so to speak, some at least of the territories loosely comprised in the old term, "India." It must have made, at some point, a conscious decision to break into the oriental spice trade, and with this end in view, to include the subcontinent of India and the navigation of the Indian Ocean in the areas of its exploring and trading expansion. The objects of Portuguese oceanic policy had become, in short, much more ambitious and widespread, but also much more specific. All this had happened between the death of Prince Henry in 1460 and the accession of Manoel I in 1495. What were the stages in this process of investigation and decision?

Some of them can only be guessed. Surviving records are scanty, and the accounts of later chroniclers are not always consistent or sufficiently detailed. The chroniclers all wrote, moreover, at a time when trade with India was an accomplished fact; they tended to assume that it had always, inevitably, existed in the minds of the policy makers. Prince Henry, already in the sixteenth century a semi-legendary figure, was widely credited with dreams and aspirations which, almost certainly, he never entertained. India, in fact, did not enter seriously into Portuguese calculation until a generation after Prince Henry's death. In the fourteen-sixties there was no significant exploration in any direction, nor, as far as we know, any serious consideration of India. Exploring was resumed from 1469, organized by Fernão Gomes. That astute and enigmatic businessman used his abilities to great effect, but concentrated them upon the development of trade in the Gulf of Guinea. From what we know of him—very little, to be sure—he never seriously thought of India. Indeed, it was in Gomes's time that Lopo Gonçalves and Rui de Sequeira discovered the southerly trend of the Gabon coast; a discovery which, to anyone who might have supposed Ethiopia and "India" to lie just round the corner from Guinea, must have been a severe discouragement. The reaction of the Portuguese government was to seek the advice of Toscanelli, then the most distinguished advocate of a westward route to "the Indies." His arguments, we may suppose, were received skeptically, and

nothing was done at the time to pursue them.

After the expiry of the Gomes lease, exploration was held up and the Guinea trade endangered by war with Spain; no serious plan of expansion was possible until after the treaty of Alcáçovas, and no royal encouragement given until the accession of John II. John had already, as prince, been entrusted, since 1474, by his father, Afonso V, with responsibility for regulating and promoting African trade and discovery. His personal enthusiasm for the enterprise was well known; he regarded himself as Prince Henry's successor in this respect, as his own proclamations declared. Circumstances had long frustrated the pursuit of these interests, and even after his accession he felt obliged initially to concentrate on the defense of existing oversea trade, rather than on its extension. Once Elmina Castle had been built and manned, however, and the safety of the Guinea trade assured, he began to send expeditions down the African coast south of the Equator. The expeditions were fitted out at royal expense; the ships were caravels equipped for exploration rather than for trade; the commanders—Diogo Cão and Bartolomeu Dias—were professional seamen and capable, experienced navigators. This whole series of voyages demonstrated a new determination, a new efficiency and seriousness, in pursuing the discovery of the sea.

Diogo Cão sailed from the Tagus in 1482. No original documents concerning his voyage have survived—no instructions, no journal or report— but there can be little doubt of its purpose: to find a passage to the Indian Ocean, and to establish, by unanswerable record, the Portuguese claim to exclusive use of it. Cão took with him *padrões,* carved and dated stone columns, which he was to erect on prominent points in newly explored land. He was the first Portuguese commander, so far as we know, to use these solid records of discovery and warnings to competitors; but several subsequent expeditions carried *padrões,* and at least a dozen of them were set up round the shores of southern Africa before the end of the fifteenth century. A few survive intact, fragments of others have been found in modern times at or near their original sites, and some have been brought back to Europe for study and reassembly. They provide the most concrete evidence possible of the course of discovery.

Cão sailed first to Elmina, then directly across the gulf to Cape López, and south, down the coast, past Cape St. Catherine, the last known point up to that time. His first major discovery was the mouth of the *rio poderoso*, the Congo; and here, near the modern village of São Antonio do Zaire, he set up his first *padrão* (the shaft of which is now in Lisbon). The sight of so great a volume of fresh muddy water pouring down from the interior and far out to sea must have raised excited speculation; Cão sent some of his company up the river to make contact, if they could, with the ruler of the country. He waited in vain for their return and eventually sailed on south down the Angola coast, past the future sites of Loanda and Benguela, to Cape St. Mary, in 13 degrees south, which he named Cabo do Lobo—Wolf (or Seal) Point. On this modest headland he erected his second *padrão.* The *Africa Pilot* states, wrongly, that Cão's column still stands; it stood until 1892, when it was removed to Lisbon, where it remains. It marked Cão's farthest point south on this voyage; he returned to the Congo, searched again

unsuccessfully for the men he had sent upcountry, seized four prominent natives as hostages, and sailed home to Portugal in 1484.

It had been a distinguished voyage; yet the enthusiasm which greeted Cão's return seems disproportionate to his achievement, by the standards of the time. He was ennobled, though a man of humble origin, and granted a liberal pension. No other Portuguese discoverer in the fifteenth century, except Vasco da Gama, received comparable rewards. John II was not given to excessive generosity; he treated Dias, for example, much less handsomely. Cão, however, seems to have believed, or to have given others to understand, that he had actually reached the farthest cape of Africa, or at least come within easy reach of it. His claim was announced to Europe in the following year in the most solemn and public manner possible, in a formal Oration of Obedience from John II to a new pope, Innocent VIII: ". . . last year our men, having completed the greater part of the circuit of Africa, reached almost to the *Prassum Promontorium*, where the Barbarian Gulf begins." This bold claim is reflected in a Venetian chart drawn about 1489, one of the collection known as *Ginea Portugalexe.* The chart shows the line of the coast beyond "Capo do Lobo" trending southeast, then east, then northeast, and ending in the unknown ocean. Cão's delusion—if it was indeed a delusion, and if he was responsible—has never been explained. Possibly he misunderstood a native description—presumably conveyed by signs—of a large bay, which he took for the Indian Ocean. In fact, from Cape St. Mary the coast runs due south for fifty miles to the head of the gulf known locally as Lucira Grande, thence west for ten miles to Cape St. Martha, and then

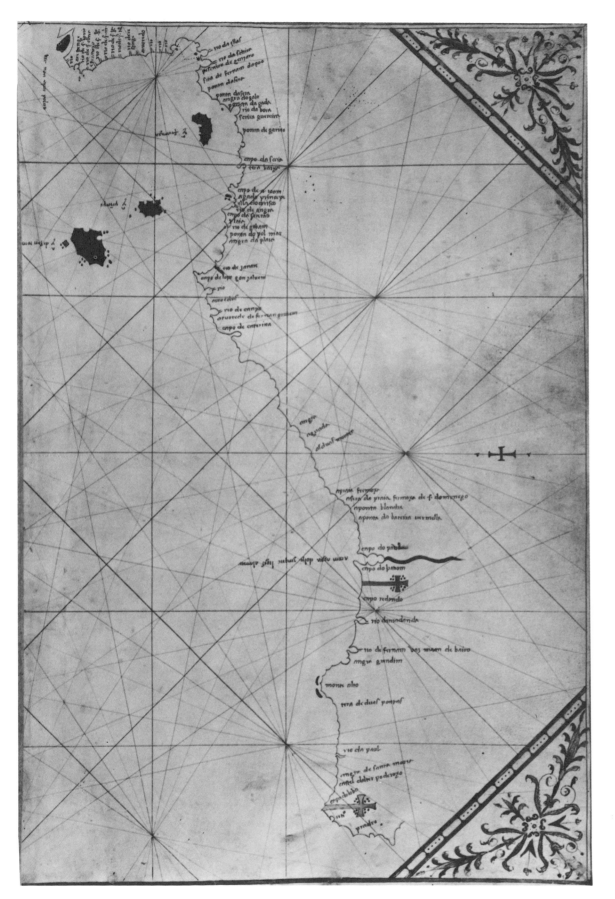

Marine chart of
the west coast of central
Africa, signed Cristoforo
Soligo, c. 1489, a
Venetian copy of a
Portuguese original,
showing the error fostered
by Cão's first voyage

south by west for eighty-five miles to Cape Negro. There are many indentations, but mostly mere coves. The only point in hundreds of miles of coast which could conceivably suggest the *Prassum Promontorium* is Cape Euspa, the northern extremity of Baia de Moçamedes, Little Fish Bay. Here the coast embays to the east about ten miles; but Annunciation Point, the other extremity of the bay, is only eight miles south of Cape Euspa, and in the clear weather which prevails on that coast is almost always clearly visible. Little Fish Bay would never have deceived Cão if he had actually been there; yet the royal claims, so publicly announced, must have been based on his reports; there was no other possible source. Everything we know of Cão shows him to have been a careful and thorough explorer, and he would not have ventured to lie to the King on such a matter. The whole affair remains mysterious; but it shows beyond any doubt the eagerness with which John II, by 1484, was looking for a route to the Indian Ocean.

Disillusion came quickly. Cão was sent off again in 1485. He put into the Congo to return his hostages from the previous voyage and to collect his own men, who had—perhaps surprisingly—survived. It was probably at this time—*pace* Barros—that Cão visited the *mbanza* of the King of Congo; a journey which involved navigation of the lower river. At Yelala, near the modern port of Matadi, there are still some Portuguese inscriptions cut into a rock face, apparently on this occasion. Matadi is eighty miles from the sea. To reach it, vessels must pass through the narrow gorge known as the Devil's Cauldron, where the force of the current reaches ten knots in December and is rarely less than

five. Cão's ships, or boats, must have been bravely and skillfully handled to have penetrated so far. They could not have gone much farther; ten miles upstream from Matadi the river is broken by a series of impassable falls.

From the Congo, the caravels coasted on south to Cape St. Mary and beyond, to find the coast running on, dry and uninviting, for hundreds of miles. Cão explored a long stretch of coast from Cape St. Mary to Cape Cross, leaving *padrões* on the commanding height of Cape Negro (16 degrees south) and on Cape Cross (22 degrees south). The first of these, its inscription now undecipherable, is in Lisbon; the second, in a good state of preservation, was taken off by a German cruiser in 1893, and is in Berlin. The Cape Cross *padrão* is probably the last surviving trace of Cão himself; a cryptic legend on the Martellus map, which was drawn about 1489, suggests that he died at "Serra Parda, which is a thousand miles from Mount Negro." "Serra Parda" may have been the coastal mountain range of which Mount Dourissa is the most conspicuous peak, about twenty miles north-northeast of Cape Cross, though it is much less than a thousand miles from Cape Negro, whatever miles be used.

With or without Cão—we cannot be sure—the expedition returned from Cape Cross to the Congo, and on this visit took several more Congo natives back to Portugal, this time as willing passengers; a testimony to the civil and honorable relations which Cão had maintained on both voyages. One of these passengers, named Caçuta, having been duly baptized and instructed in Portuguese, returned eventually to become a great man in his own country and a zealous supporter of Portuguese influence there.

This, from the King's point of view, was all that Cão's people had to show for four years of hardship and effort. If Cão himself, contrary to accepted belief, returned to Portugal, it could only have been to obscure neglect. He had found no *Prassum Promontorium,* no navigable interior waterway. His distinguished voyages yielded only disappointment, which John II was not the man to forgive.

In all the euphoria of 1484–85, Portuguese interest in the Indian Ocean seems still to have concentrated upon its western coast. The *Sinus Barbaricus,* the Barbarian Gulf, mentioned in the Oration of Obedience of 1485, meant in Ptolemaic nomenclature the great indentation in the east African coast which has Mombasa at its centre. There is no word in the Oration of a specific India or of designs on the spice trade. This does not prove, of course, that John II was not, by then, thinking of India and of spices; probably he was, though it would have been extremely maladroit to say so publicly, especially in Italy. India, however, was still a vague and distant place, the way there—if way there was— still unknown. Ethiopia of Prester John, though also vague and distant, was nearer than India and probably more attainable. Even if India were to be the ultimate goal, it would be sensible first to find the country of Prester John, and make it the base for attempts to cross the Indian Ocean. Every scrap of information or misinformation about Ethiopia was eagerly discussed. In 1486, while Cão was still at sea, reports arrived of a Portuguese visit—probably the first visit—to Benin. Benin was an important place and its ruler a considerable potentate; but he was in some sense, it seemed, the vassal of an inland suzerain, whose name was Ogané. This may have

The padrão erected by Diogo Cão on Cape Cross, now in Berlin

been a variation of Ogun, the name of a Yoruba divinity, spirit of iron. More probably, Ogané was in reality the Oni of Ife, the Yoruba dignitary to whom the Obas of Benin accorded, and accord to this day, a degree of spiritual allegiance. Certain characteristics were common to the Oni of reality (down to this day), to Ogané of fifteenth-century report, and to Prester John of legend: the practice, for instance, of veiling the face or of speaking from behind a curtain, when receiving courtiers and ambassadors on ceremonial occasions. What more natural than that the Portuguese visitors should equate Ogané with Prester John? His court was several weeks' march away, through difficult forest country; but Diogo Cão was already on his way there by sea.

Benin not only yielded encouraging reports about a possible Prester John; it produced pepper. Fernão Gomes in the previous decade had made his considerable fortune partly by dealing in *malagueta* pepper from the Grain and Ivory Coasts; Benin pepper was greatly superior to *malagueta*, and the ready sale which it immediately commanded in Europe must have suggested to the King's advisers the much greater profit which might be made from real Indian pepper, to say nothing of the rarer spices; if, indeed, they had not thought of it already. Whatever the actual process of discussion and decision, it was at this time, the time of Diogo Cão's second voyage, that John II began the systematic collection, by overland channels, of information about the Indian Ocean as a whole, and of all the countries—not only Ethiopia— which lay upon its shores. Cão was daily expected back, with firm reports of the passage to the Indian Ocean; it was important that

subsequent seaborne expeditions in that area should know what to look for.

In 1485 or 1486 the King sent Frei Antonio de Lisboa and Pero de Montarroio to the Levant, to try to reach Prester John by land. They went first to Jerusalem, where they had the luck to meet two Ethiopian clerics, and obtained some information; but their courage failed them—not surprisingly, since they knew no Arabic—and they returned to Lisbon. Another failure, then, no more excusable than that of Cão. The King needed, so to speak, his own Conti; and he found one in Pero da Covilhã. Covilhã was a picaresque individual who had formerly been employed as a spy in Spain and Morocco. He spoke fluent Arabic and was able to pass himself off as a Muslim; unlike Conti, he apparently had no qualms of conscience in the matter. Covilhã left Santarem in 1487 with a single companion, Afonso de Paiva, carrying letters of credit from the Florentine bank of Marchionni, which had extensive interests in Portugal. The two made for Cairo by way of Barcelona, Naples, Rhodes and Alexandria. They cashed their letters of credit in Naples and bought a quantity of honey, with which they intended to pose as traveling merchants—quite plausibly; honey, unlike sugar, was a scarce luxury in the Red Sea countries. In the teeming crowds of Cairo they disappeared from Christian view, assumed their new disguises, and joined a caravan to Tor; thence by sea to Suakin, and on to Aden, where they parted. Paiva set out for Ethiopia, but fell ill and returned to Cairo, where he died. Covilhã took ship for India, and arrived at Calicut, the spice port. He made an extensive reconnaissance of the Malabar coast and its many commercial ports, as far north as Goa, the terminus of the Arab horse trade to India. From Malabar he returned to Aden, and thence embarked on a long coastal reconnaissance of the east African ports, as far south as Sofala. Sofala was the port of shipment of gold, mined in its hinterland, north to Kilwa and Mombasa, which in the sixteenth century was to become a matter of great importance in the Portuguese India trade.

Eventually, in 1490, Covilhã returned to Cairo, where he learned of Paiva's death, and found Portuguese royal emissaries, both Jewish business men: the Rabbi Abraham of Beja, and Joseph of Lamego. To Joseph, Covilhã entrusted a report on his travels to that date; and from Joseph he received messages in which John II, characteristically, ordered him to take on Paiva's unaccomplished mission. Covilhã, also characteristically, complied; but he took his time about it. After 1490 his story, bold already, became fantastic. First, in company with Abraham of Beja and in accordance with his instructions, he visited Ormuz, the great spice entrepôt of the Persian Gulf. Then, having seen Abraham off in a caravan to Aleppo en route for Portugal, he made a pilgrimage to Mecca—a most dangerous proceeding, and quite outside his instructions; then to the monastery of St. Catherine on Mount Sinai, a tolerated Christian enclave and a famous place of pilgrimage. It was not until 1493, after many more adventures, that he landed at an Ethiopian harbor—probably Massawa—and made his way inland to the Ethiopian court. He was well received; all too well, for he spent the remaining thirty years of his life as an influential and trusted, but probably captive, servant of the Negus. The first formal Portuguese embassy to Ethiopia, that of Rodrigo de Lima in 1520, found him there, an old man, comfortably

ensconced and much respected, but still glad to see his countrymen and eager to be of service to them.

We do not know whether Joseph of Lamego got back to Portugal with Covilhã's letters or whether Rabbi Abraham made his way home from Aleppo with an account of Ormuz. From the course of subsequent events it seems very likely that one or the other, perhaps both, arrived safely with their immensely valuable news. If so, John II had in his possession by 1491 a first hand, up-to-date report on the coasts and harbors, the political and commercial situation, on both shores of the northern Indian Ocean. He knew nothing, of course, of Covilhã's subsequent arrival in Ethiopia; word of that did not get back until the return of Rodrigo de Lima's embassy in 1527. Meanwhile, however, news of Ethiopia reached Portugal by another channel. Ethiopian clerics, as we have seen, occasionally visited Rome, usually to solicit support against the common enemy. One of these, Luke Mark, was persuaded by Portuguese emissaries there in 1488 to travel on to Portugal. From Luke Mark the King could have obtained information at leisure. Perhaps John was not particularly impressed; there are indications that in the fourteen-nineties the attractions of "Prester John" began slightly to fade, that India was replacing Ethiopia as the prime object of Portuguese exploration. India, indeed, to judge from what was known of Covilhã's experiences, might prove to be more accessible than Ethiopia, and more commercially rewarding.

The question remained of the accessibility of India from Portugal by an all-sea route. The famous expedition of Bartolomeu Dias had brought back a partial and—so far as it went—a clearly encouraging answer. Dias commanded the last of the series of African expeditions sent out by John II. He left Portugal in the summer of 1487, the same year as Covilhã. He was well equipped: two caravels and a store-ship. This, no doubt, was a lesson learned from Cão's voyages; fresh provisions were difficult to find on the west coast of southern Africa, and the stowage capacity of caravels was limited. Once again, no instructions and no report have survived; but the voyage was well recorded by the chroniclers, and Dias, like Cão, set up padrões, so that the principal events of the voyage, and some of its details, are reasonably clear. Dias's route across the Gulf of Guinea was an improvement on that of Cão: he seems to have sailed directly from Cape Palmas to the mouth of the Congo, bypassing Elmina, avoiding the worst of the Gulf calms, and so initiating a distinction—a small and tentative distinction—between the Guinea and India navigations. He lost no time in the Congo, probably because a formal embassy there (which actually left in 1490, with Caçuta in its train) was already in contemplation; but he did, apparently, take with him some Congo natives returning from Portugal; these unfortunate people were put ashore somewhere in the neighborhood of Cape Negro, supplied with money and trade goods, and instructed to travel overland to "Prester John."

Coasting on south, Dias, like Cão, experienced increasing difficulty from the prevailing southerly winds and from the Benguela current, which sets fairly consistently to the north at about one knot all along the Angola coast. He found a sheltered bay, probably the desolate Baía dos Tigres in southern Angola, where he victualed his caravels from the store-ship and left the store-ship at anchor with a small party on board. Then on south, past the padrão which Cão had left on Cape Cross, into unknown waters. In Lüderitz Bay he rested for five days from his incessant battle with the wind. This was a safe and extensive anchorage. Its southerly extremity, Dias Point, projects two or three miles farther to seaward than Northeast Point, which is the northerly extremity. The bay is open to the northwest, but is perfectly protected against the southerly or southeasterly winds which prevail through most of the year. Dias, on his return passage, erected a padrão on Dias Point, which stood for three hundred years. A British naval officer made a watercolor sketch of it in 1786, which still survives; but by 1825 the column itself had been shattered. Adolf Lüderitz, the German colonial organizer, in 1883 set up a spar on the most likely site, and subsequent archaeological search confirmed his guess; some fragments of the original column have returned to Lisbon.

After leaving his anchorage in Lüderitz Bay, Dias at some point, probably off Cape Voltas, stood out to sea. According to some accounts, he was driven off the coast by a storm, but it is far more likely that the decision was deliberate. The northerly set of the current and the prevailing wind inshore are both partly caused by the presence of the coast itself; farther out to sea, in that latitude, the current disappears and the summer wind is southeast rather than south. Dias did the most intelligent thing he could have done; sailing close-hauled, he could make southing without much difficulty. A second tentative step had been taken in separating India from Africa. Eventually the caravels reached the zone of westerly winds, and ran to the east, until

Dias judged, correctly, that they were east of the longitude of Cape Voltas; he then braced up on the port tack, sailed north, and made land about two hundred and fifty miles east of the Cape, near São Bras, Mossel Bay. This, again, is a tolerably good anchorage and must have seemed a good augury. Surprisingly, no *padrão* was left at São Bras; perhaps Dias was anxious to press on before his stores ran low; perhaps the surf rolling in from the southeast prevented the landing of so heavy and awkward an object. He did set up a *padrão* on False Islet, a small headland east of Algoa Bay, near the cape subsequently known as Cape Padrone. The site is relatively inconspicuous, a dark low rock; but several early sixteenth-century sailing directions described it, and recent digging has confirmed it, though only fragments of the column survive.

In this neighborhood, probably at anchor in Algoa Bay, the signs of unrest appeared. Dias's people were far from home and probably worried about their supplies. They were hampered by wind, current and coastal surf, and the coast appeared to run on endlessly to the east. Evidently thinking they had done enough for one voyage, they demanded that the fleet should turn back. There was no mutiny. The habit of submitting major decisions to a general council was deeply ingrained in all seamen during the Age of Reconnaissance. Sea captains did not, as a rule, belong to a social class accustomed to command; they rarely ventured to over-ride, when far from home, if they could not over-persuade. Dias did his best, and got his people to persevere for a few more days. The ships turned either at the Keiskama or at the mouth of the Great Fish River. This (though ships cannot enter it) is a river of some size, and shows from seaward as an obvious gap in the coastline. After rain it brings down a large volume of red mud, which streams away to the southwest, visible evidence of the force of the coastwise current. East of the river mouth, the water is always clear and the current noticeably warm. Dias, seeing the coast running on to the northeast, can have been in no doubt that he was at the entrance to the Indian Ocean. Others were to reap the fruit of his endeavor. He wept like a child, so it was said, when re-passing the lonely pillar on Cape Padrone.

In one respect, Dias was a lucky as well as a brave and skillful navigator. The Cape of Good Hope is one of the most famous capes in the world, a bold, commanding promontory, visible for many miles; but it is not the southernmost point of Africa. That is Cape Agulhas, which is about one hundred miles east-southeast, and less impressive to the eye. Between the two capes, the inshore branch of the Agulhas current usually sets west-northwest at about one and a half knots, following the line of the coast, with occasional unpredictable indrafts towards the land. Prevailing winds alternate between west in the (southern) winter and southeast in the summer. Gales are most frequent in the winter, but may occur at any time. It is a dangerous stretch of coast, with many banks, bays and headlands. A sailing ship coming from the west, if it rounds the Cape of Good Hope too closely, runs the risk of being embayed in False Bay; if it succeeds in weathering Cape Hangklip, which is the eastern extremity of the bay, it may still run foul of Danger Point, twenty-six miles farther on. Sailing west to east close inshore is always risky; in the summer months, indeed—the months when Dias was off the coast—progress is often

To find a westerly wind at that season, a ship must stand far to the southward, often as far as 40 degrees south. Dias did this, and so avoided the contrary current and the coastal dangers between the Cape of Good Hope and Cape Agulhas. Unwittingly, he thus took the third tentative step toward separating India from Africa. He did not merely "discover" the Cape of Good Hope; he established one of the cardinal rules of sailing from the Atlantic to the Indian Ocean: that of giving the Cape of Good Hope a wide berth.

No long southerly detour is needed in sailing east to west. In winter ships must expect a tedious and difficult beat to windward, but in summer wind and current will take them over the Agulhas Bank and swiftly up the coast. It was on this relatively easy return passage that Dias first sighted Cape Point, the towering cliff at the end of the Cape peninsula. The Cantino map of 1502, one of the finest products of early sixteenth-century cartography, marks a *padrão* on this point; but no early sailing directions mention it. Barros, indeed, says that Dias encountered rough weather off the Cape, was unable to land, and in consequence named it Cabo Tormentoso, the Cape of Storms. It was the King, after Dias's return, who—according to Barros—gave it the name Good Hope, surely the most exciting and evocative name in the whole story of the discovery of the sea.

From the Cape, Dias ran north-northwest up the coast. At Baía dos Tigres he found only three of his ship-keepers left alive. Possibly scurvy had killed the others; they cannot have found much in the way of fresh provisions on that desolate coast, and the fishing, though good, is seasonal. Otherwise the return passage seems to have been prosperous, with favoring wind and current up the Angola coast. Dias called at Principe Island and at Elmina, and passed Cascaes at the end of 1488. His reception, considering his achievement, was unenthusiastic. Perhaps John II, the unforgiving taskmaster, blamed him for turning back on the threshold of success. His rewards were a niggardly pension and the command of a trading caravel to Elmina; no coat of arms, no national rejoicing, though his abilities were not in doubt, and he was constantly consulted over the next steps in the direction of India.

It is curious, at first sight, that Dias's discoveries were not more promptly exploited. Throughout the fourteen-eighties voyages down the African coast had followed one another in eager succession, each quickly extending the knowledge brought home by its predecessor. After Dias's return there was a pause; the cape he had discovered remained for nearly a decade the cape of hope deferred. Initially, no doubt, the authorities in Portugal deferred action while awaiting the return of Covilhã and Paiva. Dias had demonstrated that the two great oceans of the known world were connected, but he had brought no knowledge of the conditions which might be encountered within the Indian Ocean, of the courses and distances from place to place, the navigational problems, the political circumstances and the commercial opportunities. Covilhã, however, in three years of travel had acquired much detailed information on these subjects—or on some of them, for he was not a seaman. This information was probably in the King's hands early in 1491, so that by then, of the whole circuit of the African coast only about fourteen degrees of latitude remained wholly

OPPOSITE: World map, from *Insularium* by Henricus Martellus, c. 1490, showing the results of Dias's voyage

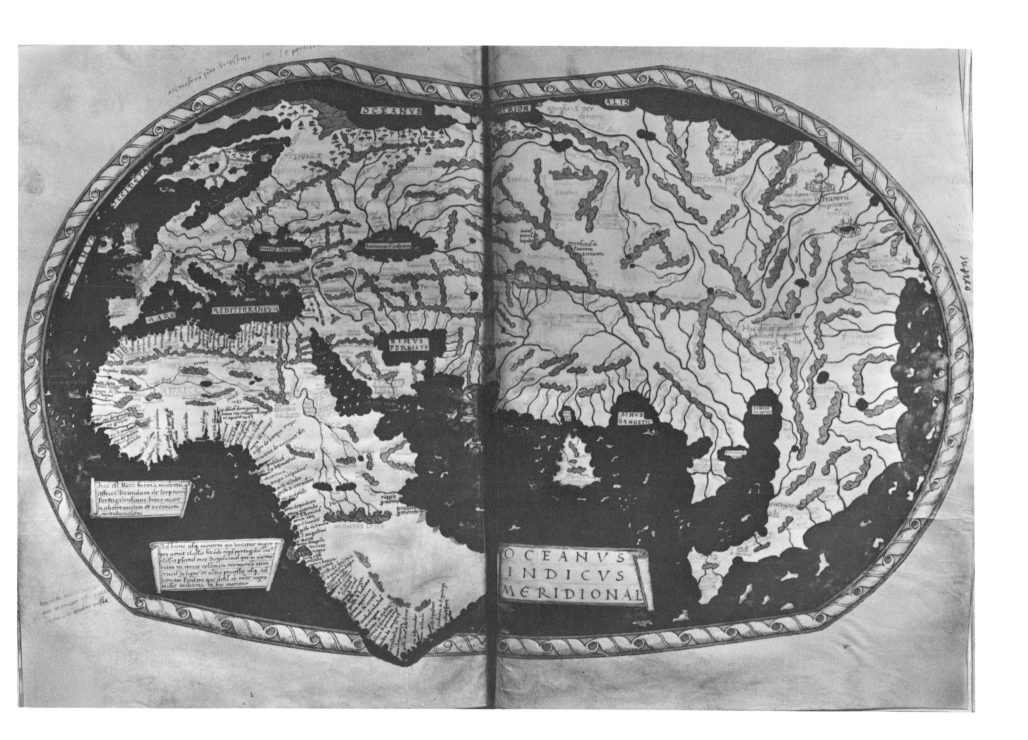

unknown to the Portuguese authorities: the stretch from the Great Fish River to Sofala. There was still no firm news of Prester John, except what the King might have gleaned from Luke Mark, or what Luke Mark might have seen fit to tell him; but Covilhã had visited a number of east African ports from which ships regularly sailed to India and had traced the main geographical lines of the spice trade. Prester John was a cherished figure of pious legend for many Portuguese; but the spice trade was what interested the King and his immediate advisers, and in that trade Prester John apparently played no significant part. If Prester John could not be found, therefore, he could be ignored. Portuguese ships, once in the Indian Ocean, could sail to India without his help.

The enterprise of India had long been the personal concern of John II. It would have been consistent with John's earlier enthusiasm if a fleet had left for India in, say, 1492; yet still the King delayed. No doubt there were many in his entourage who urged caution; Portugal was a small and relatively poor country; there were jealous enemies at home and abroad. John himself was aging, and suffering already from prolonged attacks of the dropsy which eventually killed him; probably he was less capable than he had been of firm decision and leadership.

Apart from all this, there were sound geographical reasons for caution. Covilhã's report —assuming that it reached Portugal—probably contained reassurances on conditions of navigation in the Indian Ocean; what Indians and Arabs could do as a regular routine, Portuguese sailors presumably could imitate. Dias's report on Atlantic navigation, however—apart from the crucial fact of the connected oceans—must have

been much less encouraging. The Cape of Good Hope was much farther away than anyone earlier had expected. Dias himself, in sailing so far south, had had a hard time of it, at least on the outward passage. An expedition to India might have to make a voyage nearly twice the length of Dias's. It would have to be, moreover, a commercial embassy, adequately armed and victualed, provided with goods for trade and with the paraphernalia of ceremony. For this service, exploring caravels would not do; it would require a bigger fleet, of bigger ships. Such a fleet could not be expected to follow Dias's track, struggling against wind and current along several thousand miles of comfortless coast. There might be—as it eventually turned out, there was—a quicker, easier route. Dias had done best, from a navigator's standpoint, on those occasions when he left the African coast and stood out to sea. His experience would suggest to any bold and intelligent commander that the whole southward passage might best be made in mid-ocean, well away from Africa; but before committing himself, the commander would want to know what winds and currents he was likely to encounter and what islands might lie on his route. It is probable that John II, in the last years of his reign, secretly sent out ships to collect this information; possible, even, that the ships entered the Indian Ocean. A book of sailing directions attributed to the Arab pilot Ahmãd ibn-Mãdjid mentions Portuguese vessels wrecked off Sofala in 1495. The story is not confirmed by any known Portuguese source; but it would have been consistent with the King's habitual systematic way of proceeding.

A similar systematic caution dictated the Portuguese reactions to the claims of Christopher

Columbus. Columbus, driven by stress of weather, put into the Tagus in the spring of 1493, boasting that he had been near the confines of Cathay. Probably no informed Portuguese took Columbus at his own valuation; and in any event India, not China, spices, not silk, were the objects of Portuguese exploration at that time. Nevertheless, in the circumstances, any Castilian activity in the central Atlantic was unwelcome; it might endanger alike the existing Portuguese monopoly of the Guinea trade and the hoped-for monopoly of the best route to India. It was a matter to be settled, before the India voyage was attempted. John tried first to lay claim to Columbus's new-found islands, on the ground that they were merely outliers of the Azores. Then, abandoning this patently absurd contention, he worked through diplomatic channels to push the sphere of Spanish exploration as far west as possible, well clear of any possible southward route through the central Atlantic. In this, he was brilliantly successful; there was to be no Spanish interference on the route to India.

The treaty of Tordesillas in 1494 was John II's last contribution to the Portuguese discovery of the sea. He died in the following year. The uncertainties which, in the late Middle Ages, always followed upon a demise of the Crown, invited still further delay; but John's successor, Manoel I, less methodical, less sagacious than his cousin, was young, impetuous and confident. Shortly after his accession he ordered the preparation, under Dias's experienced direction, of a fleet for India. There seems to have been no lack of money for the purpose. Some of it may have been borrowed from foreign sources: from the Florentine Marchionni, perhaps, who had

made the credit arrangements for Covilhã's travels; or from the Bardi, who had a branch in Lisbon; from the Affaitadi of Cremona, who ran much of the sugar trade of Madeira; or from the Fuggers, whose adventurous Spanish agent Cristóbal de Haro was active in Lisbon at the time. There is no firm evidence of these transactions; but the King's credit was good. The gold of Guinea was pouring in, and probably he also received, at about the same time, windfalls in cash as a result of measures taken against the Jews of the kingdom, many of whom were recent refugees from Spain. One of Manoel's first major acts was a decree ordering the expulsion of unbaptized Jews. The expulsion was a fraud; the King had no wish to lose skilled and industrious subjects. His purpose was to please Castile—a royal marriage being in prospect—by an anti-Jewish gesture; to induce the Jews, by force or threat of force, to accept an outward form of conversion; but to retain their persons and their services. In most instances the threat succeeded, but some highly placed Jews—Abraham Zacuto among them—left Portugal unbaptized; of these, some left their businesses and property behind. These assets were confiscated, and turned over for administration to the Order of Christ, which in turn leased some of them to Italian bankers and businessmen. Portuguese Jews, already responsible for Zacuto's and Vizinho's tables and many illustrious charts, thus probably made a further, involuntary contribution to the discovery of the sea. However the money was raised, the fleet was got ready, with no expense spared; and in 1497, with Vasco da Gama in command, it left the Tagus for the Cape of Good Hope, east Africa and Calicut.

II

Achievement

8

*he distance from Lisbon to Cape Town* by the most direct sea route, the route which a modern steamship would take, is about five thousand nautical miles. For a sailing ship, using the quickest (not the shortest) route, the outward passage is never less than six thousand, and may in some circumstances be considerably longer, though on return the sailing ship's route will approximate more nearly that of the steamer. Dias, unwittingly following a difficult and circuitous route, probably covered more than seven thousand miles between the Tagus and Mossel Bay. All the Portuguese voyages to southern Africa in the fourteen-eighties, those of Diogo Cão and that of Dias, impressed contemporaries by their duration. They were far longer than any voyages previously made by European ships; each in turn set up a new and alarming record of distance traveled. Quite apart from the geographical information which these explorers brought home, their experiences offered new lessons on the planning and conduct of very long voyages, lessons promptly noted by the Portuguese government of the time, and by shipping contractors, sea commanders, navigators and cartographers working in its service.

The most obvious and immediate lessons concerned the type of ship employed. For nearly fifty years the vessel most favored—one might almost say the standard vessel—for all exploring work had been a lateen caravel, usually two masted, carrying twenty or twenty-five men, but capable of being handled by a much smaller crew at need. These small coasting craft, sturdy yet maneuverable, were characteristic of the Atlantic seaboard of Portugal and Andalusia. Their virtues were widely celebrated; Cadamosto was only one of their many admirers. It was said, indeed, that caravels were the only vessels capable of making the Guinea voyage; other types of ships might reach Guinea, but none was weatherly enough to return thence. There was probably some truth in this—good performance on a wind was the most valuable feature of light lateen-rigged craft in general—but probably also the story was deliberately spread about by the Portuguese to discourage interlopers. There is a tale in the chronicles, of the pilot Pero d'Alemquer, who had sailed with Dias and was later to sail with Vasco da Gama, and who—significantly—had become something of a figure about the court. D'Alemquer said in the King's presence that he could take any ship to Guinea and bring her back. He was publicly put down and silenced by the King who, however, apologized in private and explained the necessity for maintaining the accepted fiction.

Diogo d'Azambuja made his famous voyage to Mina in 1481 with a mixed fleet. The artisans and the soldiers for the garrison traveled with the captain-general in a flotilla of caravels, but the building materials for Elmina Castle were shipped out in *urcas,* big tubs of ships, said to have been of three or four hundred tons. The urcas were sent on ahead for a rendezvous with the caravels in Gorée Bay. From there the fleet sailed in company to Elmina; but the urcas did not return. Having discharged their cargo, they were broken up, and their timbers presumably used in the fort. D'Azambuja, of course, was not an explorer. Diogo Cão, who was, used nothing but caravels. Dias, besides caravels, took a store-ship; we do not know what type of vessel she was, nor whether she returned to Portugal; probably she was abandoned in Baía dos Tigres.

From Nuno Tristão's departure in 1441 to Dias's return in 1488, then, the pre-eminence of lateen-rigged caravels in African exploration was unchallenged. For following unknown coasts and nosing into bays and estuaries, their weatherly qualities made them unbeatable. The lessons of Dias's voyage, however, while not belittling the importance of good performance on a wind, suggested the desirability of other qualities in addition. Dias, while coasting, had had to beat for hundreds of miles against contrary winds. His caravels enabled him to do this; in any other type of European ship then available, he would probably have had to abandon the attempt. Dias, however, was an explorer; difficulties were his business. For regular commercial expeditions to do, even in caravels, what Dias had done, was out of the question. Dias's own experience off southern Africa had suggested the alternative. The future of central and south Atlantic navigation for Europeans depended on the discovery of open-ocean routes, on which ships could expect favorable winds for the greater part of their voyage. Such routes existed: in trade-wind latitudes and in the zones of the regular westerlies, there were great areas of stable wind conditions where ships could run for hundreds of miles; but to make the best use of these conditions, the ships must be appropriately rigged. Lateen sails are relatively inefficient when running. The best rig before the wind, for ships of any size, is square rig.

Square rig had always been the standard rig of seagoing ships in northern European waters. In the Mediterranean, from the eleventh century to the fourteenth it was rarely seen; but from the late fourteenth century, as a result of increased commercial contact between northern and southern Europe, it had returned to the western Mediterranean and spread there once more at the expense of the lateen. Its attraction for commercial shipowners lay initially in its simplicity and in the relatively small crew needed to handle it. A price had to be paid for these desirable qualities in loss of maneuverability. Purely square-rigged vessels were much less maneuverable than lateens and were helpless with the wind before the beam. This disadvantage, however, could be reduced by ingenious modification. Unlike lateen rig, which remained essentially unchanged throughout the fifteenth century, square rig was greatly modified in the process of its return to the Mediterranean.

Not all the modifications were improvements; some merely reflected local habit. Some devices which in the north had proved their usefulness failed for many years to find favor in the south. An example of this is the use of ratlines. In northern square-rigged ships, ratlines were fitted in the shrouds, to allow men to go aloft for handing sail and to give access to the tops, the railed platforms near the masthead which accommodated lookouts and, in battle, bowmen. In lateen-rigged vessels, the yards were normally lowered to the deck for furling sail; there were no tops, because they would have got in the way of the yards; and shrouds were set up only on the weather side. If it was necessary for any

reason to go aloft when under way, a man would shin barefoot up the yard; this is still the practice today. When Mediterranean seamen took to square rig, they immediately fitted tops, the value of which was obvious, and permanent standing shrouds; but they were much slower to adopt the northern practice of furling square sails aloft; they continued to lower the yards, as they had always done. Not needing quick access to the yards, they dispensed with ratlines in the shrouds and relied on jacob's ladders up the masts to give a restricted and inconvenient access to the tops. Defense may also have been a consideration here, since without ratlines hostile boarders could not easily swarm up into the tops. Whatever the reasons, the absence of ratlines continued until after the end of the fifteenth century to distinguish southern square-rigged ships from northern ones of otherwise similar rig and build.

Reef points provided another instance of local conservatism. Southerners did not reef their square sails, but used bonnets, additional strips of canvas which could be laced on to the foot of the main course in fair weather and removed in foul. The use of bonnets, far from being superseded by reef points, spread to northern Europe; and although reef points remained common in northern sails until about 1450, after that date the southern device became general.

In many other adaptations of square rig, Mediterranean sailors showed a more lively inventiveness. To the ties which supported the northern square yard they added lifts at the yardarms, so making possible the use of longer, more slender yards, which (like lateen yards and unlike northern ones) consisted usually of two spars lashed together and overlapping at the bunt. Accustomed as they were to tackles at the foot and peak of the lateen yard, they soon replaced the single northern yard ropes by more powerful braces and brace pendants, and fitted tackles also to the bowlines. The sails were gored to produce separate wind bags on either side of the middle line. To give a flatter set when sailing with the wind abeam, bowges were used in addition to bowlines. These were lines made fast to a thimble in the centre of the foot of the sail; they passed round the mast, through the thimble, and down to the deck, so flattening in the middle of the sail while the bowline stiffened the weather leech.

All these modifications were obvious improvements, but all were in matters of detail. The spread of square rig in the Mediterranean in the fifteenth century produced another, far more fundamental adaptation. Northern square-rigged ships, at least down to the end of the fourteenth century, usually had only one mast. Mediterranean sailors were accustomed to two- and three-masted ships, and early in the fifteenth century they began to experiment with ways of combining the two types of sail, with their respective virtues, in a single ship. The commonest arrangement for big ships—though by no means the only arrangement—consisted of a short foremast with a single square sail; a much taller mainmast, with a much bigger main course; and a mizzen mast with a lateen sail. Vessels so rigged might be described by many different names—ship, barque, carrack and so on—since ships were normally classified by their size and hull lines rather than by rig; but the basic rig had become fairly widespread by the middle of the fifteenth century.

About the same time, Mediterranean sailors discovered another vital advantage of square rig:

the ease with which it enables a large area of canvas to be divided into units convenient for handling. The first step in this direction was the addition of a main topsail, at first of pocket-handkerchief size, and sheeted not to the yardarms—that came later—but to the top-rim. Other additions followed in the later fifteenth century: a spritsail, bent on a yard carried below the bowsprit, chiefly useful for swinging the ship's head when getting under way; in some big ships, a foretopsail; in some an additional or bonaventure mizzen. The possibilities were almost endless. The ancestors of all the square-riggers of the great age of sail came from this vital marriage between square rig and lateen, between Atlantic and Mediterranean, in the fifteenth century. New and fertile crossbreeds, they quickly spread not only throughout the Mediterranean but, with minor local differences, round all the coasts of Europe.

These developments were in progress while Cão and Dias were exploring into the south Atlantic. In the late fifteenth century they came to be applied not only to big merchant ships, but also to Iberian caravels, in the process of adapting some of these nimble little vessels to new oceanic needs. The change was generally made by increasing the number of masts from two to three, sometimes to four. This allowed several possible combinations of sails: four masts with one square-rigged, three lateen, or two square and two lateen; or three masts, with one or two square-rigged. Sometimes a two-masted caravel might cross the yard on the foremast, though this combination was comparatively rare. Caravels with any of these hybrid rigs were described as *caravelas redondas,* square-rigged caravels, to distinguish them from the older, more familiar *caravelas latinas*. They differed from ships or carracks only in their smaller size, in their finer lines, and in their lack of elaborate superstructure. They always retained at least one lateen aft, for reasons of balance and maneuverability; but on a trade-wind run the lateens would be furled and the vessels would run under square sails alone. They would make far better time, with less trouble and less strain on their men and their gear, than they could have done with lateen rig alone.

Because caravels were small and carried light spars, their rig was flexible. It could be altered without great difficulty to meet the conditions expected on a particular voyage. One well-known example: Columbus's fleet in 1492 included the flagship *Santa María,* square-rigged, described variously by nautical historians as a ship or a caravel, but always by Columbus himself as a *nao;* the square-rigged caravel *Pinta;* and the lateen-rigged caravel *Niña.* On the run down to the Canaries the *Niña* had difficulty in keeping up with the others, and Columbus decided, or was advised, to have her re-rigged as a *caravela redonda.* This work was done in harbor at Las Palmas, and presumably—since so small a place could have offered only rudimentary dockyard facilities—was carried out by the ships' own people. It involved re-sparring, re-rigging shrouds and lifts, changing running rigging, and re-cutting one or two large sails. According to its muster roll, the fleet carried shipwright-carpenters but no specialist sailmaker; probably any competent bosun knew how to cut and rope sails. The work on the *Niña* was completed in a week or so, and must have been well done, for she behaved excellently throughout the first transatlantic voyage, was

employed again in the second, took Columbus back to Spain in 1496, and was engaged in some shady semi-piratical escapades in the intervals.

The story of the *Niña* illustrates well the marvelous versatility of Iberian caravels; yet, curiously, she was one of the last caravels to be employed in major discovery. Already by the end of the fifteenth century these small vessels, so reliable and so admired, were beginning to lose favor as explorers' ships. The search for India and Cathay demanded longer and longer voyages; the experiences of Cão and Dias had demonstrated the need to use bigger ships. This was not primarily a matter of safety; size in itself made relatively little difference to safety, in a time when all ships were comparatively slow and built to ride over the seas rather than to knife through them. Fifteenth-century mariners probably seldom experienced "swept decks." Caravels were better found and more reliable than many larger ships; but they were miserably uncomfortable. Stowage capacity was limited, and armament necessarily light: at best a few small built-up pieces, swiveling on spikes set in sockets along the gunwales. Caravels in general were too small to carry the men, the provisions, the water, the goods and the guns for long voyages to destinations where trade as well as exploration was intended.

In the late fifteenth century some square-rigged caravels were built larger than formerly; but this meant sacrificing some of their characteristic agility, without commensurate gain. The essence of the caravel was its small size. To build a caravel nearly as large as a small *nao,* but without the ship's accommodation and hold space, was to combine some of the defects of both types. Square and lateen caravels continued

to make commercial voyages to Guinea, and both commercial and exploratory voyages to the West Indies, well into the sixteenth century; but a passage to the West Indies, with reasonable luck, involved a trade-wind run of only a few weeks. Columbus on his second transatlantic voyage commanded a large mixed fleet including three fair-sized ships, several square-rigged caravels and two lateen caravels for inshore work. On his third voyage he took one ship and five caravels; on his fourth, four caravels; this may have reflected a personal preference derived from experience with the *Niña,* but we cannot be sure of this, because by 1502 he was out of favor and had to accept whatever he was offered.

In the fleets for India, caravels were employed only for despatch-carrying, inshore reconnaissance, and other odd jobs which later admirals would entrust to frigates; they were auxiliary to the main fleets. Vasco da Gama sailed for India in 1497 with three ships, *naus,* and one caravel. Cabral in 1500 commanded a much larger fleet, but similarly balanced; to judge from contemporary sketches, his caravels were lateen rigged. Magellan, sailing in 1519 on what was to prove the longest voyage of all, took no caravels. His fleet consisted of five small or medium-sized ships. The *Victoria,* the smallest of them, and the only one to complete the voyage, was of only eighty-five Spanish tons, not much bigger than a large caravel. By that time it was generally accepted that small or medium-sized ships, rather than caravels, offered the best combination of qualities for long voyages into the unknown; and that their handling qualities, under combined rig, had improved sufficiently to enable them to perform nearly all the varied tasks involved in exploration. Still further

improvements, and further differentiation of types for different tasks, were to be developed in the course of the sixteenth century.

Reliable ships, capable of making very long voyages and of bringing their companies safely home, were the first essential for the discovery of the sea. With such ships, with a general idea of what to look for and with the courage and determination to persevere until they found it, explorers could not fail in time to reveal the shape of the Atlantic basin and to find the vital passages leading out of the Atlantic into the other oceans. The general pattern of Atlantic exploration, though vast in scale and daunting in execution, was essentially simple. The Atlantic is a huge ocean channel running continuously north and south from the Arctic to the sub-Antarctic, between two continuous (though intricate) coastlines. Cão and Dias followed the eastern coastline southward, month after month, until Dias came to the end and found a way out. Columbus sailed westward directly across the Atlantic, week after week, until he found land on the other side. Vespucci, Solís, Magellan, followed the western coastline southward until eventually Magellan came to the end and also found a way out.

Merely to discover, however, was only part of the explorer's task. He had to describe what he had discovered, so that it could be recognized, and determine its position in such a way that his successors could find the place again with a minimum of trouble, in order to exploit the discovery. He had, of course, no chart, unless he had the skill to draw his own. He would have kept, as a matter of routine, a dead-reckoning "account"; but dead reckoning, with only magnetic compass and sand-glass for measuring

OPPOSITE: A large Portuguese caravel, 1536

direction and distance sailed, was liable to cumulative error, which over a long voyage might amount to many hundreds of miles. At best, dead reckoning could only give a position relative to the last known point of departure; and this would be of limited use to a successor approaching by a different route, or at a different time of year in different wind conditions. If Dias, for example, had merely given a position for the Cape of Good Hope in terms of an approximate magnetic bearing and distance from Cape Cross or Cape Voltas, this would not have been much help to Vasco da Gama. The explorer needed to be able to fix the absolute positions of newly discovered places, in part at least by observation. This required a technique of celestial navigation much more sophisticated and precise than anything Europeans had known before the late fifteenth century.

Of the two co-ordinates of an observed position, latitude could be measured—once the principle of it was grasped—with relatively simple instruments and by relatively easy calculation; longitude was much more troublesome. The major voyages of the crucial decade, the fourteen-eighties, were all made in a roughly north–south direction. The passage from Lisbon to the Cape traverses seventy-five degrees of latitude, and latitude was the chief interest and concern of the navigators. The first steps in developing a technique of navigation good enough for very long voyages were refinements in the measurement of latitude. The most easily observable celestial body for this purpose was the Pole Star, familiar to European seamen because of its constant northerly bearing and its use in telling the time. The altitude of the Pole Star— its angle above the horizon—grew less as a ship

sailed farther south, and so gave an indication of how far south she had sailed. Conversely, a ship sailing due east or due west could keep a steady course, and correct compass errors, by maintaining a constant polar altitude. Altitude could be measured roughly by eye and hand; this was an old, familiar skill. We do not know exactly when European navigators began to use instruments at sea for measuring it more precisely; probably in the last few years of Prince Henry's life. Cadamosto, off the Gambia in 1455, noted that the Pole Star appeared "about a third of a lance" above the horizon. Cadamosto was not a navigator, but he was observant of nautical detail, and if instruments had been used in his ships for measuring altitude he would probably have mentioned it. They were in use, however, within a few years of Cadamosto's voyage. Diogo Gomes, who was a professional navigator in Prince Henry's employ, recalled—though in a conversation recorded many years later—that he had taken a quadrant with him to Guinea about 1460.

The seaman's quadrant was a very simple device; a quarter of a circle, with a scale from 0 degrees to 90 degrees marked on the curved edge, and with two pinhole sights along one of the straight edges. A plumb line hung from the apex. The sights were aligned on the star and the reading taken from the point where the plumb line cut the scale. Polar altitude in degrees gave the observer's latitude—as every astronomer who had read his Ptolemy knew—provided that the right correction was applied to allow for the small circle which Polaris describes about the true pole. This correction could be ascertained from the position of the Guards. Some years elapsed, however, before seamen learned to apply the correction, or to think in terms of latitude measured in degrees. At first, the navigator used his quadrant simply as a means of measuring his linear distance south (or north) of his port of departure, usually Lisbon. He observed the altitude of the Pole Star at the port of departure when the Guards were in a given position. Subsequently during the voyage, he observed the polar altitude of each place he came to, with the Guards in the same position, landing for the purpose if possible. According to Diogo Gomes, he marked the names of important places against the appropriate points on his quadrant scale. He was taught that each degree division represented a fixed distance ($16\frac{2}{3}$ leagues was the usual reckoning in the third quarter of the fifteenth century, an underestimate traceable to Ptolemy); and so he built up his knowledge of the polar altitudes and the distances south (or north) of his base, of all the places he had visited. Conversely, if he wished to find a place whose polar altitude he already knew—say in west Africa or in one of the islands—he would sail south (or north), as nearly as the wind would allow, until he found the right altitude. He would then sail due east (or west) until he fell in with the land.

This was all very well in the northern hemisphere; but Portuguese seamen, sailing south along the west African coast, saw the Pole Star sink lower in the sky night by night, until in about 5 degrees north they lost sight of it altogether. Other conspicuous stars, whose distance from either pole had been tabulated, could be used; a rule for determining latitude by the Southern Cross, analogous to the Rule of the Pole Star, was worked out in the sixteenth century. With the limited mathematical knowledge of the time, however, such observations were accurate only if made at the moment of meridian transit. That moment was difficult to determine, and might occur at a time when neither star nor horizon was conveniently observable.

The most obvious substitute for Pole Star altitude was the meridian altitude of the sun. Like the Pole Star, the sun's altitude had long been used for giving the seaman a rough idea of his distance north or south of a point of departure; but squinting at the sun through the pinholes of a quadrant was almost impossible. For measuring solar altitudes, therefore, the late fifteenth-century navigator used a more sophisticated instrument, the astrolabe, modified for use at sea. The medieval astronomer's astrolabe was a complex and often very beautiful device. It consisted of a brass disc engraved with a stereographic projection of the heavens, and a rotatable grill, by means of which the movements of the more conspicuous heavenly bodies could be followed. It was chiefly intended to assist astronomical calculation; but on its reverse side it was graduated in degrees round the perimeter and fitted with a rotating sight bar or alidade for observing altitudes. Only the reverse side of the instrument was useful—or indeed comprehensible —to seamen; so the simplified type of wooden astrolabe used at sea retained only the peripheral degree scale and the alidade. Most astrolabes were small, from six to ten inches in diameter; but some navigators, including Vasco da Gama, used a specially large type for making more accurate observations ashore. The mariner's astrolabe, unlike the quadrant, did not have to be held in the hand. It was fitted with a suspension ring at its top edge; in taking sun sights, the navigator hung it independently at a convenient height, and rotated the alidade until the point of light shining through the upper sight-hole fell exactly on the lower sight.

Both quadrant and astrolabe used an artificial horizon; they depended, that is, on perpendicularity. Their accuracy at sea, therefore, was impaired by the movement of the ship. Balancing himself on a heaving deck, a navigator can take more accurate sights with an instrument designed, as most modern sextants are, to measure altitudes from the visual horizon. Fifteenth-century Arab navigators possessed such an instrument, the *kamāl.* Vasco da Gama's people found this device widespread in the Indian Ocean and brought examples home with them. Possibly imitations of the *kamāl* led to the development of the European cross-staff for star sights, and its later refinement, the backstaff, for sun sights. These, however, were sixteenth-century inventions. In the fifteenth century and the early years of the sixteenth, European navigators had to make do with quadrant and astrolabe, or quadrant alone. As might be expected, in such records as have survived—in the log, for example, kept by Francisco Albo, who navigated one of Magellan's ships—latitudes observed ashore are noticeably more accurate than those taken at sea.

Besides the practical difficulties of observation, a navigator trying to ascertain his latitude by means of sun sights had to master a calculation considerably more complicated than the Rule of the North Star. He wanted to know his angular distance in degrees north or south of the equator, which is equivalent to the zenith distance of the celestial equator; but unlike the Pole Star, the celestial equator cannot be

observed directly. The sun does not follow the celestial equator, and the angular distance between the celestial equator and the ecliptic, the track which the sun does follow in relation to the earth, changes from day to day and from year to year. The navigator needed, therefore, to know this angular distance north or south of the celestial equator—the sun's declination—for any day of the year at midday. This was an astronomical and mathematical problem which no amount of rule-of-thumb experience could solve; it required the help of the men of science.

The exact processes whereby late medieval science was made available to seamen are, in general, little known. Chroniclers often stated that princes—Prince Henry of Portugal was not unique in this—invited astronomers to their courts in order to pick their brains; but they very rarely explained precisely what the learned men taught, to whom, and with what result. The Rule of the Sun is an exception: a clear and rare instance of a group of scientists, deliberately employed by the State, applying theoretical knowledge to the solution of a particular and urgent practical problem. John II of Portugal in 1484 convened a commission of mathematical experts to devise the best method of finding latitude by solar observation. Declination had long been studied by astronomers, and tables of declination existed in a variety of forms. Among the most accurate and detailed were those in the *Almanach Perpetuum* worked out for the years 1473–78 by the Jewish astronomer Abraham Zacuto of Salamanca. King John's commission drew up a simplified version of Zacuto's tables, brought them up to date, translated them from Hebrew into Latin, and devised a fixed procedure to enable an intelligent and literate

seaman to use them. They did more; a leading member of the group, José Vizinho, who had been Zacuto's pupil, was sent off on a Guinea voyage to test the new method of latitude-finding and to check the values given in Zacuto's tables by actual observation on the Guinea coast. That was in 1485; Diogo Cão was already at sea and Dias was soon to follow.

The Rule of the Sun first explained how to measure solar altitude with an astrolabe, and stressed the importance of catching the exact moment of meridian transit. Without adequate timekeepers, this in itself was a lengthy business. It was done by starting well before the expected moment and taking a series of observations, which increased in value as the sun approached the meridian and decreased after it had passed. The maximum reading was taken as the meridian altitude. The navigator wrote this on his slate. He next turned to his tables, looked up the sun's declination for the day, and wrote that down too. He then had to select the appropriate rule for applying the declination to the altitude, according to whether he was north or south of the equator, whether the declination was north or south, and whether the declination was greater or less than the latitude if both had the same name. Application of the correct rule gave him the altitude of the celestial equator above his own horizon, and this he subtracted from 90 degrees to obtain his latitude.

The procedure was summarized for the benefit of practical navigators in a manual compiled in Portugal under the title *Regimento do astrolabio e do quadrante*. This was the first European manual of navigation and nautical almanac. It is now an exceedingly rare book. The earliest surviving copy was printed in 1509, but there were probably earlier editions, and the work seems to have circulated in manuscript from the fourteen-eighties. It contained, as a theoretical basis, a Portuguese translation of Sacrobosco's well-known treatise *De Sphaera Mundi;* a list of latitudes from Lisbon to the Equator, most of them correct to within half a degree, some to within ten minutes; a calendar; and a table of the sun's declination for a leap year. In addition, the *Regimento* gave the Rule of the North Star and the Rule of the Sun; these were the essential content of the book, and their laborious detail well illustrates the difficulty of making practical seamen understand the elements of mathematics and astronomy; learning had perforce to be by rote and not by reason.

Finally, the *Regimento* contained a Rule for Raising the Pole. This was in essence a traverse table; but unlike the old *Marteloio,* which had been in terms of relative direction only, the new tables were in terms of northing and easting. They told the navigator how far he would have to sail on any course in order to raise or lay a degree of latitude, and how much easting or westing he would make in the process. They were obviously helpful in latitude sailing; though being based on plane right-angled, not spherical triangles, they were reasonably accurate only for comparatively short distances, and their use still depended on the navigator's ability to estimate his speed in order to calculate his distance sailed. The Rule gave a value of 17½ Portuguese leagues, of four Italian miles to the league, to a degree of latitude, in place of the older approximation of 16⅔. This was still an underestimate; but at least in north–south sailing distance could be checked by observation, and an underestimate made for safety. Most navigators preferred, in the sixteenth-century English phrase, to have "their reckoning before their ship" and so "to sight land after they sought it."

Celestial navigation presented an immense task, not only of research and invention, but also of education. Although many fuller, more accurate manuals were to appear in the course of the sixteenth century, the rules set out in the *Regimento* supplied for many years the basis of the navigator's training. They were expounded in formal schools of navigation, established at Lisbon and at Seville in the early sixteenth century, to train and license navigators for the East and West Indies trades, respectively. These men, however, formed a small aristocracy among seamen. It cannot be supposed that any save the ablest and most up-to-date navigators, in the late fifteenth or early sixteenth century, used or understood the *Regimento.* Columbus, who learned most of his navigation in Portugal, understood the principle of latitude sailing and made Pole Star observations (though he often got them wrong); but so far as we know, he never took a sun sight, and probably could not have worked one out. In the Portuguese fleets for India, practice was more sophisticated. Vasco da Gama on his outward voyage, after three months in the open sea, made land at St. Helena Bay on the west coast of South Africa. His pilots did not recognize the place; but they calculated, correctly, that they were thirty leagues north of the Cape of Good Hope. They could have done this only by observing the latitude of the bay and comparing it with the latitude supplied by Dias for the Cape. In the hands of experts, the new methods worked.

The best navigational practice, then, consisted of a careful dead reckoning checked, whenever the weather allowed, by observations of latitude. There was no practicable way of observing longitude. The Portuguese seamen who explored the west African coast were little troubled by the problem. It took on a practical urgency only when Columbus had crossed the Atlantic and Vasco da Gama the Indian Ocean; and when, from 1494, the Spanish and Portuguese rulers tried to agree on a longitudinal division of their respective spheres of oceanic exploration and trade. Sixteenth-century attempts to relate longitude to magnetic variation were doomed to failure; attempts to determine it by simultaneous observations from different places of an eclipse or other astronomical event were theoretically promising, but impracticable for navigators. Longitude is bound up with time; it cannot be measured precisely without an accurate timekeeper, and no such instrument for seagoing use was devised until the eighteenth century. In practice, longitude had to be calculated roughly from *departure:* east–west distance from an agreed meridian, most commonly that passing through Cape St. Vincent. Because of the convergence of the meridians, the value of a degree of longitude in terms of distance varies with the latitude. At the poles it is zero, on the equator it is approximately equal to a degree of latitude. If the latter were known, the intermediate values could be worked out mathematically. Rough tables for this purpose became available in the sixteenth century; but not till the end of the century did spherical trigonometry reach a point where a reliable formula could be devised for converting departure into difference of longitude on an oblique course. Even then, the accuracy of the result still depended on an estimate of distance sailed. No estimate of longitude at sea

could be more accurate than the means employed to measure a ship's speed.

No navigation, in general, could be more accurate than the available instruments allowed it to be. Sixteenth-century instruments were coarse and unreliable. This was true not only of the devices used in celestial observation, but of humbler and more familiar appliances also. The most basic, most familiar instrument of the deep-sea navigator—the compass—on long voyages could prove the most treacherous of all. Of the many errors to which the magnetic compass is liable, those due to shoddy workmanship—of which sixteenth-century navigators endlessly complained—could be avoided by careful inspection; those due to deviation could be prevented—in ships containing a negligible quantity of iron—by discipline and vigilance, to ensure that men working near the binnacle had no iron about them; but there was no avoiding variation, the difference between the direction of the magnetic and geographical poles. This was inherent in the nature of the instrument. It had mattered little in practice, so long as all navigation was by distance and magnetic course or bearing; but the use of celestial observations and the practice of latitude sailing required the navigator to relate his course to the true, not the magnetic north, and so to know the exact allowance to make for variation.

Fifteenth-century navigators knew of the existence of variation; or, rather, some navigators did; many were ignorant of it; some preferred to ignore it; some denied its existence. Those who recognized it usually assumed it to be constant. The earliest surviving allusion to a change of variation is in the *Journal* of Columbus's 1492 voyage. Having crossed the isogonic line of no variation in about 30 degrees west, Columbus noted that the Pole Star "appeared to move." The "movement," most probably, was the result of the change from easterly to westerly variation, combined with the diurnal rotation of Polaris, the observation being taken at a time when the star was at the eastern extremity of its orbit. Columbus made several subsequent comments on this subject: evidence of his powers of observation, since the variation along his course never exceeded 8 degrees west, and in the West Indies was negligible. He seems to have regarded change of variation as an interesting—initially as an alarming—phenomenon; but there is no evidence that he made any allowance for variation in practical navigation.

In the early sixteenth century the notion gained ground that variation was symmetrically disposed. The line of no variation near the Azores was thought to be a "true meridian," from which the angle increased east and west in a direct and consistent relation with longitude. Some instrument-makers manufactured "corrected" compasses, in which the needle was offset against the north point of the fly to allow for the variation of some particular area. Such compasses were worse than useless outside the area for which they were made, and seriously dangerous on long voyages. In the course of the sixteenth century, however, experience both in Atlantic and Indian Ocean crossings revealed the complexity of the variation pattern. The best navigators grasped that the problem could be solved only by empirical observation. Eschewing mechanical "corrections" and using a meridian compass, they made systematic observations of variation in all parts of the oceans through which they passed.

Francisco Albo made observations while crossing the Pacific, and recorded an unusually large variation near the southern tip of South America. Pedro Nunes, mathematician and cosmographer, and the scholarly practical navigator João de Castro, chief pilot of the *Carreira da India* in the fifteen-thirties, between them pursued the question systematically over a period of years. Nunes devised a compass fitting, which Castro used, for observing variation by comparison of the sun's meridian azimuth, as shown by a shadow, with the azimuth indicated by the magnetic needle. By such means, in the course of the sixteenth century navigators built up knowledge of variation in different parts of the world, and learned to apply the appropriate correction to their compass courses and bearings wherever they happened to be.

By the late fifteenth century, a competent navigator could grope his way about the world with reasonable confidence. He had at his disposal a well-developed technique of dead reckoning, and several rough but adequate methods whereby, in good weather, he could check his estimated positions by observations of latitude. However long his voyage, if he escaped storms, scurvy, starvation and shoreside hostilities, he could hope to find his way home. During the voyage, he could calculate the position of his ship, or of a newly discovered coast or island, with some approach to accuracy. He could not, however, with anything like the same accuracy, plot these positions and the courses to them, upon a chart. This was not the result of ignorance or lack of skill among marine cartographers, but rather of technical conservatism in a distinguished and well-established craft. The entrenched excellence of the portolan chart, in the area where it had been developed, hindered the technical changes needed for charting other and vastly larger areas.

Charts in the portolan tradition derived their peculiar excellence partly from the quality of their workmanship, partly from the empirical method of their construction. Nearly all the surviving examples were drawn with meticulous care, and some are of outstanding beauty. The men who drew them were artist-craftsmen, trained through rigorous apprenticeship, proud of their skill and determined to maintain the standards of their craft; they passed on their knowledge and their technique from generation to generation, often from father to son. They were conservative in their style and methods of work, sceptical and precise about the information they conveyed. Portolan charts were based on firsthand experience or reliable report. They owed little to academic knowledge or a priori reasoning. The chart-makers rarely indulged in conjecture about what was unknown to them, nor did they set down merely traditional outlines. Even when they extended their range in the later fifteenth century to include the African discoveries, they still marked only capes and islands which had actually been discovered. They drew coastlines from the viewpoint of the practical navigator, as series of places connected —with due regard for hazards on the way—by a network of compass courses and distances.

This commonsense empiricism produced charts well suited to the needs of seamen navigating by relatively primitive dead reckoning in relatively small areas of sea, but increasingly inaccurate over larger areas, and wholly unsuited to the purposes of celestial navigation. In the fifteenth century, enlargement of the operating range of European ships, and improvement in methods of navigation, both increasingly outstripped the development of cartographical technique. Fifteenth-century marine cartographers were not indifferent to discovery or unreceptive of new information—on the contrary, new discoveries appeared on charts very quickly, in response to a lively demand—but in adding new information they were content merely to enlarge the range of the charts without revising or questioning the basis of their construction. It was a construction which had served well for two hundred years and more; it contained, nevertheless, basic mathematical errors, negligible when navigating by dead reckoning over small areas, but increasingly dangerous when navigating on long ocean voyages by a combination of dead reckoning and celestial observation.

Portolan charts, as we have seen, were based on the known direction and distance from one harbor or coastal landmark to the next, along the length of coast to be depicted. Coastlines were drawn in freehand, and were copied unchanged from chart to chart. Hazards were shown by dots or crosses. In addition, compass roses were provided: usually a "mother" rose in the middle, and interconnecting subsidiary roses arranged as the points of an octagon near the periphery. The "quarter-winds"—the directions radiating from the centre of each rose—were produced as straight lines across the chart to its edges, covering the whole surface with a criss-cross of loxodromes—lines of constant bearing, or rhumb lines. This loxodromic net was not the basis of the chart's construction, but was superimposed, as an aid to navigation. The navigator, with the help of straight-edge and dividers, used it to find his course to steer.

The area covered by the chart was treated as a plane surface; the cartographer had no means of representing the curvature of the earth, and though he might be theoretically aware of it, in practice he ignored it. In reality, the earth's surface is curved and the meridians—the north–south lines—converge toward the poles. A true rhumb line, therefore—unless along a parallel or meridian—is not a straight line but a heliacal curve. The lines drawn on portolan charts were not true rhumb lines, but approximations to them, and to that extent they falsified everywhere on the chart the proportional relation of northing (latitude) to easting (longitude). The charts, however, showed neither parallels of latitude nor meridians of longitude, so that the discrepancy was not apparent.

The bearings upon which portolan charts were constructed were all magnetic bearings. The orientation of the charts differed from geographical orientation, therefore, by the value of the angle between geographical and magnetic north: the variation. The charts were, so to speak, tilted. Magnetic north, moreover, was treated as constant; in all the compass roses on each chart, the arrows indicating north were drawn parallel and were all brought into the vertical. Variation, in fact, differs from place to place. In the Mediterranean, the original home of portolan charts, a line of no variation at present runs through Crete; the variation off Cyprus is 2 degrees east, that off Gibraltar 10 degrees west. Thus, from one end of the Mediterranean to the other, the direction of magnetic north differs by 12 degrees. Variation changes from year to year, and the rate of change differs from place to place. In the western Mediterranean at present, variation is decreasing by 7 minutes annually, in the eastern increasing by 4 minutes. In the fifteenth century there was no line of no variation in the Mediterranean; all variation was easterly, and its extent was considerably greater than it is today. The orientation of the charts was not only tilted away from geographical orientation; it was also internally inconsistent, bent or twisted.

Mediterranean navigators were not seriously troubled by these peculiarities of portolan chart construction. The range of latitudes in the Mediterranean is small; the convergence of the meridians is slight, and could be ignored without serious consequence. The discrepancy between a "loxodrome" drawn on the chart and a rhumb line or compass course was small—much smaller than many other possible errors, such as might arise from currents, leeway or human carelessness. The discrepancy between magnetic and geographical orientation gave no trouble; it was, indeed, hardly noticed; so long as all navigation was by dead reckoning based on magnetic compass courses, "true" direction could be ignored as a purely academic concept, appropriate to scholars' world maps but omitted from practical marine charts. The annual change in variation, it is true, was a potential source of error, since the bearing of one place from another changed over the years; but the change was imperceptible over short periods, with the compasses then in use, and over longer periods the charts could be adjusted gradually in the light of experience, as they wore out and were replaced.

In the second half of the fifteenth century charts of portolan type were drawn depicting more and more of the African coast, as it was explored. Most of the surviving examples were made by Italians, drawing on Portuguese sources of information. Only two or three are of Portuguese origin; a curious circumstance, since a flourishing chart industry existed in Lisbon in the later years of the century. This industry, however, was under official patronage and control; its products were regarded as confidential documents, for necessary seagoing use but not for general circulation, and this may account for the disappearance of most of them. On the other hand, as might be expected, the earliest surviving charts showing both sides of the Atlantic, including islands and stretches of coast in the New World, are Iberian. The de la Cosa map, usually dated 1500, is Spanish: a world map rather than a marine chart, though drawn, somewhat crudely, on portolan principles. The Cantino chart of 1502 is Portuguese, and a much more sophisticated piece of work.

These charts, whether Italian or Iberian, all displayed in varying degrees the qualities of their Mediterranean predecessors: empiricism and meticulous craftsmanship. They displayed, also, the corresponding defects. Like their predecessors, they were built up by plotting the compass courses from point to point along each coast, and drawing the intervening coast in freehand. With the greater distances involved, the basic defect, which arose from ignoring the curvature of the earth, was greatly magnified. It might not seem serious in navigating down the west coast of Africa, since the coast ran roughly north and south; the only place where it did not, in the Gulf of Guinea, was so near the equator that a degree of longitude was almost equal in length to a degree of latitude, and chart and traverse table agreed. A ship making a long passage on an oblique course, however, across

the Atlantic or the Indian Ocean, and steered by compass alone, might diverge from the corresponding "loxodrome" on the chart by hundreds of miles. A competent navigator, of course, would check his dead reckoning by observations of latitude, and in making an east–west passage would endeavor to follow a parallel of latitude. In so doing, however, he would encounter the second defect of the chart: its magnetic orientation. In order to maintain a constant polar bearing and altitude, he would have to make repeated alterations in his compass course, and his course made good would bear no fixed relation to an east–west "loxodrome" drawn on the chart.

It was beyond the skill of late fifteenth- and early sixteenth-century chart-makers to reconcile, in a single chart, the requirements of dead-reckoning navigation using a magnetic orientation with those of celestial navigation using a geographical or "true" orientation. Various attempts were made. Early in the sixteenth century, graduated scales of latitude began to appear, usually at the edge of the chart, but sometimes on a north–south line, such as the "line of demarcation," down the central Atlantic. Graduated scales of longitude appeared about 1520, usually along the equator. No attempt was made, until a much later date, to carry meridians or parallels (other than the equator and the two tropics) across the face of the chart. The scales were probably used mainly for measuring distances with dividers, rather than for plotting actual positions. In some early sixteenth-century charts—the earliest example is a chart of the north Atlantic by Pedro Reinel, about 1504—a second latitude scale is drawn, usually in the northwest corner, inclined at an angle from the main scale. In the Reinel chart it is parallel to the Labrador coast. This seems to have been an attempt to show the direction of geographical north, and its divergence from magnetic north. It was the cartographical counterpart of a "corrected" compass, a device so crude as to be useless or positively misleading. Some chart-makers—the celebrated Diogo Ribeiro was one, in the fifteen-twenties—corrected whole charts for variation as best they could on the basis of limited observations. All these devices were mere palliatives. For accurate long-distance navigation, an entirely new substitute had to be found for the portolan-type plane chart.

A possible substitute, in theory, would be a globe. On the curved surface of a globe, it was theoretically possible to plot the parallels and meridians geometrically; to draw land masses in their true shape and position (insofar as these were known); and to indicate true courses and distances between them. The earliest known terrestrial globe was that of Martin Behaim of 1492; this had scales both of latitude and longitude, but no graticule. Much better globes were to follow; they were used, along with their celestial counterparts, in training navigators, and some sixteenth-century navigators took them to sea. Their use must have sharpened the geographical perceptions of their owners, though to turn from a globe to a plane chart must have required considerable mental agility. It was extremely difficult to plot or measure on the surface of a globe; and in any event the scale of a globe small enough to be carried conveniently at sea was too small for practical navigation. As substitutes for plane charts, globes would not do.

The only satisfactory substitute would be a chart oriented by geographical north, with indications of the magnetic variation in each area; a chart which should show parallels and meridians as a rectilinear grid, and should allow a compass course, corrected for variation, to be plotted as a straight line by a ruler laid across the parchment; a chart on which a ship's position, ascertained by observations, could be shown in terms of latitude and longitude, without thereby falsifying its position in terms of the nearest lee shore. For such a chart, a projection would have to be used for the systematic reduction of curved surfaces to plane sheets. The simple port-to-port empiricism of the portolan tradition would have to be abandoned.

Projections were familiar devices in drawing academic world maps. Ptolemaic maps used a conical projection, others were round, oval or cordiform. They were designed to present a schematic picture of the world as a whole: intellectual exercises rather than practical instruments, useless for navigation. Each was based on a symmetrical pattern of parallels and meridians, the meridians curved and converging in an attempt to simulate reality, the continents and oceans stretched or squeezed to conform with the pattern. All projections—rectilinear projections no less than others—must inevitably distort. The world-map projections distorted in accordance with overall verisimilitude and artistic convenience; the navigator needed a rectilinear projection in which the distortion was mathematically consistent, so that he could make accurate allowance for it, wherever he happened to be.

The sailors had to wait a long time for their projection. Pedro Nunes prepared the way in the fifteen-thirties, with his study of the nature of rhumb lines. The Fleming Gerhard Kremer—

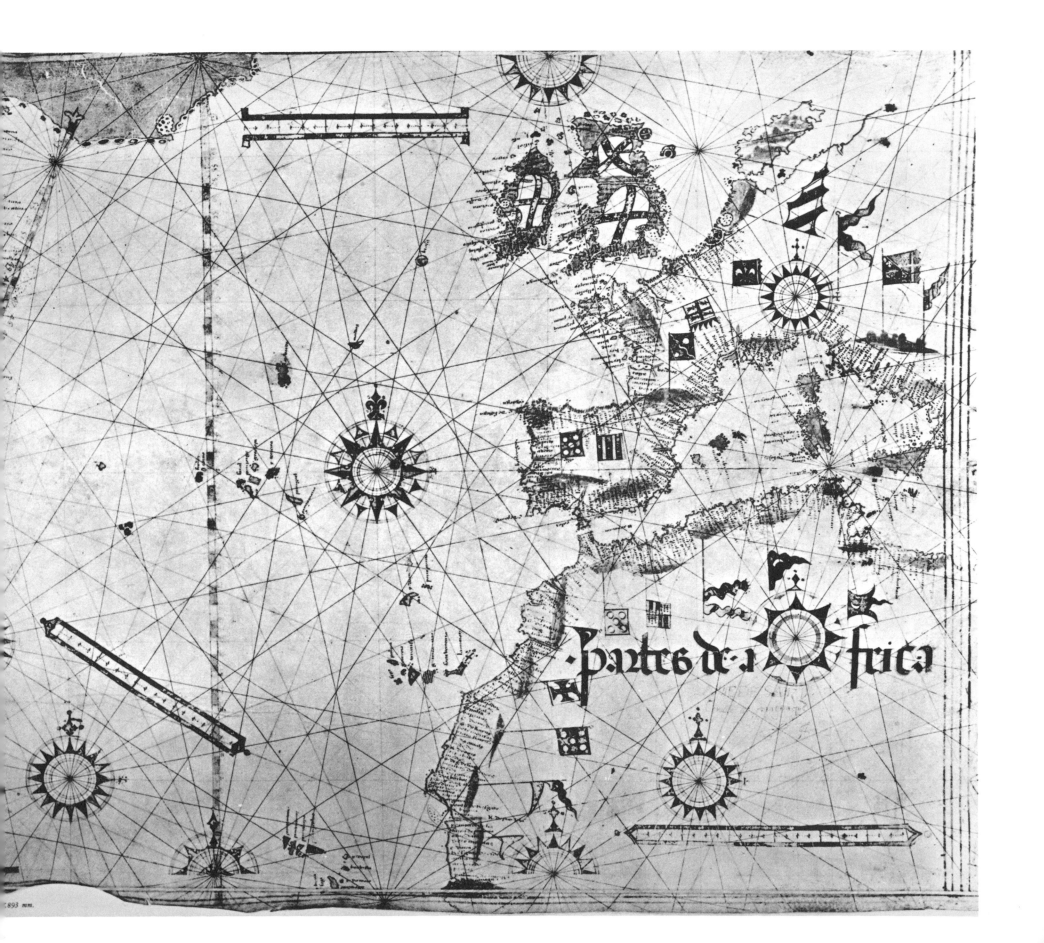

partes de africa

Mercator—who probably knew of Nunes's work, devised his famous projection and engraved a huge world map or atlas based upon it, in twenty-four sheets, in 1569. The basic principle of the projection—on which most marine charts are still designed—was first fully explained by Edward Wright in 1599. It is comparatively simple, constructed on a graticule of latitude and longitude, in which the meridians, like the parallels, are drawn as parallel straight lines. The length of the degree of longitude is thus shown increasing toward the poles in exact proportion to the secant of the latitude. In order to preserve the correct relationship of angles, and so correct direction, the length of the degree of latitude also is increased progressively from the equator to the poles, in the same proportion. Overall verisimilitude is lost; areas in high latitudes are greatly exaggerated, and since the exaggeration is progressive, the shape of large areas is distorted. The angles, however, are correct throughout, and rhumb lines of any length can be plotted accurately as straight lines. On the Wright-Mercator projection, the navigator, for the first time, could draw a nautical triangle which showed course and distance, latitude and longitude (insofar as longitude could be estimated) in their correct relation; and could measure distance accurately at the mid-latitude point.

This was the most important advance in both navigational and cartographic technique since the Portuguese astronomers had first taught the use of solar declination. At last, cartography had caught up with the development of navigation; yet many sailors remained conservative and suspicious of new devices. The first comprehensive collection of charts on the new projection, Dudley's splendid *Dell' Arcano del Mare,* was published in 1646, but at the end of the seventeenth century up-to-date navigators were still complaining that the majority of their calling refused to use Mercator charts. It was not until the eighteenth century that the hand-drawn plane chart, that beautiful and treacherous medieval survival, finally disappeared from seagoing use.

All this, of course, occurred long after the main tasks of the discovery of the sea had been accomplished. Late fifteenth- and early sixteenth-century discoverers, and those who followed up their discoveries, did not possess, and could not construct, charts upon which the position of a ship or a new discovery could be accurately plotted. They navigated, nevertheless —at least the experts among them—with an amazing accuracy. They knew where they were going and could relate with precision where they had been. No doubt their success depended partly on the directional sixth sense of the navigator, the "compass rose in the head," which grows from long sea experience, but which also seems to come to some favored individuals as a gift. Dias possessed it, as from his long experience might be expected; but Columbus, with only a sketchy formal training and with relatively little sea experience, had it too. Even more, the success of the discoverers and their immediate successors depended upon the habit of meticulous, detailed dead reckoning and record keeping.

Newly discovered lands appeared on charts within a few years, sometimes within a few months, of the discoverers' return, and year by year the charts included more information; but prudent navigators, following in the track of the

PRECEDING PAGE: Chart of the north Atlantic by Pedro Reinel, c. 1504 discoverers, treated these charts, as they treated all charts, with proper skeptical reserve. They could get from the charts a general idea of the relation between different land masses, the initial courses they had to steer, the distances they would have to cover, the hazards they were likely to encounter on the way. Portuguese charts, for example, as early as the fourteen-nineties showed in some detail the navigational dangers off the Cape Verde Islands. For detailed coasting, however, a navigator would rely much more heavily upon written sailing directions, derived initially from the account of the first discoverer, refined and enlarged in the light of subsequent experience, and eventually—in some instances—printed. No sixteenth-century chart showed the African coast, for example, with anything approaching the detail and precision of the *Esmeraldo de Situ Orbis* of 1505 or thereabouts.

For a long passage in the open sea, the navigator might plan his courses with the help of a chart. Once at sea, however, he made no attempt to record his track, as a modern navigator does, by actual drawing on the chart; he relied instead on a separate calculation. He kept careful record of his progress watch by watch, with the aid of a traverse board; he totted up the sums on a slate, checked them when he could by observations of latitude, and daily entered the results in detail in a log or journal. He might mark the resulting positions on his chart by pricking the parchment with the point of his dividers; but he would know that the mark on the chart could only be approximate, as was the chart itself. When he found, by observation, that he had reached the "height" of his destination, he would alter course and run down

the latitude, if the wind permitted. The chart could give him only a rough idea of the distance he would have to travel along his chosen parallel, though chart and sailing directions together would help him to recognize his destination when it came in sight. His safety in approaching land would depend, as always, on a good lookout and the leadsman in the chains. William Bourne, it will be recalled, complained in 1574 about "auncient masters" who despised charts and thought they "could keep a better account upon a boord"; it is true that sixteenth-century Englishmen were backward in chart navigation; but there was something to be said for their point of view. Charts were useful; but even among more advanced maritime peoples, their reliability was limited. They had to be used with caution, and they provided no substitute for a good "account."

Ships, charts, navigating techniques, whatever their defects, were adequate for their purpose; of that, the success of the discovery of the sea is sufficient proof. There was another technical problem, however, which proved more intractable: the problem of keeping men healthy, even of keeping them alive, at sea. Seamen inevitably ran unusual risks from constant exposure to cold and wet, to say nothing of the chance of drowning. Crowded together, having little opportunity to wash their clothes or themselves, they were vulnerable to contagious or dirt-borne disease; but on long voyages, the most serious hazard to their health arose from the food they had to eat. The staples of diet in all ships were hard biscuit and beef or pork pickled in brine. Many ships also carried barreled salt fish, sardines and anchovies in southern Europe, herrings in the north; dried peas, beans and chickpeas also regularly occur in stores lists. The only items of fresh food frequently carried—apart from a short-lived supply of fruit for the officers' mess—were cheese, onions and garlic. Fresh fish was expected to supplement the salted supplies; fishing lines and hooks are sometimes mentioned—once by Columbus—as an item of ship's stores; but fishing was only possible in harbor or when becalmed, and a regular supply was not to be expected. Cooking was done on an open fire box, a shallow iron box filled with sand on which a fire could be built. In bad weather, cooking might be impossible. Drinking water was a constant problem. Water in cask quickly becomes foul, and large quantities of wine were also carried. The normal daily allowance of wine in Spanish and Portuguese ships was one and a half liters per man, so long as the supply lasted; no doubt it became extremely sour long before it was exhausted.

The food was no worse, probably, than that of peasants ashore in the winter months; but in the later fifteenth century ships began to make voyages in the open sea which lasted much longer than a European winter. It was then that a new hazard appeared: scurvy, the deficiency disease which, after a few months on salted food and inadequate water, could reduce a ship to a floating cemetery. Nearly all the discoverers encountered it. Columbus was exceptionally fortunate, at least on his 1492 voyage; the health of his ships' companies remained good throughout; but Columbus on this voyage did not spend very long periods at sea. Vasco da Gama's experience, on a far longer voyage, was far worse and much more typical. Of Magellan's fleet only fifteen of the original company got back to Spain, and many more died of scurvy than of wounds or drowning.

This was a problem for which the sixteenth century had no solution. It was soon recognized that men fed on fresh food did not suffer from scurvy. By the end of the century, the special therapeutic value of oranges had been noticed by some intelligent commanders. It was out of the question, however, for small, heavily manned ships to carry enough fresh food, or preserve it long enough in good condition, to keep men healthy through voyages lasting many months. The problem of health was bound up with that of preserving fresh food, and with that of concentrating the known anti-scorbutics, such as orange or lemon juice, to enable enough of them to be carried, without destroying their efficacy. Not until the eighteenth century was any real progress made toward a solution of these problems. The only improvements in the sixteenth century came from the commonsense determination of enlightened commanders to carry fewer men and to keep them fitter by feeding them as well as possible. That was more easily said than done. The handling of coarse and clumsy gear, and the necessity for self-defense, demanded heavy manning; fresh food could only be got ashore, and not always there. Dried fruit, conserves and similar luxuries no doubt helped to keep the officers healthy. Magellan's flagship, for example, carried a quantity of quince conserve for the after cabin; whether or not for that reason, his officers seem to have escaped the worst effects of scurvy. Seamen in general, however, had to accept the horrors of scurvy, with all the other perils, as normal hazards of their trade. In terms of sailors' lives, the success of the discovery of the sea was dearly bought.

9

The Indian Ocean Crossing

asco da Gama's departure from the Tagus in 1497 was attended with considerable ceremony. There had been a solemn audience in the old Moorish castle at Montemor o Novo, eighteen miles west of Lisbon. Da Gama had received a consecrated banner from the King's hand. He had ridden back to join the fleet, which meanwhile had dropped down the tide from its Lisbon berths and anchored off Restelo. At Restelo, intercession, general confession, plenary absolution. Prince Henry, years before, had built a small chapel there, on the right bank of the river, near where the great church of the Jeronymites now stands. The chapel was much used by departing sailors, and had been the scene of many leave-takings, but probably none more moving, nor more widely advertised, than this. A large crowd, many more than the little chapel could accommodate, came out from Lisbon for the farewell mass. This was no surreptitious departure for a secret destination; the first sailing for India was made—deliberately, we must assume—a great public occasion, of which Europe would take note.

Such a departure suggested high confidence in the prospect of success. The sanguine temperament of the new King had something to do with this; but there were solid grounds for confidence. Much thought, trouble and expense had gone into the preparation of the fleet. Two of

LISBONA.

OLISIPO, SIVE VT PERVE;
TVSTÆ LAPIDVM INSCRIP;
TIONES, HABENT, VLYSIPPO,
VVLGO LISBONA FLORENTIS;
SIMVM PORTVGALLIÆ EMPORIV,

Cum Priuilegio.

CASCALE *Lusitaniæ opp:*

Betheleem

the ships, the *São Gabriel* and *São Rafael*, had been built expressly for the service, under Dias's supervision; their keels had been laid, indeed, in the previous reign. They were *naus*, of medium size by the standards of the time. They seem to have differed from others of their class only in being exceptionally strongly built. They carried guns, about twenty in all, no doubt small built-up pieces, which fired stone balls weighing ounces rather than pounds; this was before the day of big cast guns on shipboard. The armament was not heavy by the standards of fighting ships in the late fifteenth century; it served for self-defense and for ceremonial salutes rather than for serious naval fighting. It was more formidable, nevertheless, than any previously carried on voyages of discovery, and it was to make an impression in the Indian Ocean, where ship-borne artillery was then almost unknown. The other two ships were probably unarmed, or nearly so. They were the *Berrio*, a Lagos caravel, and a store-ship, whose name no one troubled to record; she was presumably chosen for her carrying capacity, and regarded as expendable. No stores lists have survived. We have no details of provisions, gear, instruments or charts; but on the evidence of Duarte Pacheco of the *Esmeraldo de situ orbis*—and on that of their performance—the ships were provided with the best, the most up-to-date available.

The men were selected as carefully as the ships and the stores. Only one appointment, that of the captain-general himself, may have seemed at first sight capricious. Dias was passed over. Da Gama was the King's personal choice. Little is known of his career before 1497. There is no record of his having had previous experience of seagoing command. He was described officially as a gentleman of the household. He came, it is true, from Sines, a fishing port built in a cleft of the Atlantic cliffs of Alentejo, which lives from the sea and turns its back on the barren sandhills which form its hinterland. No man brought up in such a place could be wholly ignorant of the sea; and da Gama seems in addition to have acquired some knowledge of mathematics and navigation. In general, however, he had the training in arms and manners conventional for a gentleman of his time. Probably these accomplishments were thought more essential, for the service in which he was to be employed, than technical skill.

Whatever the arguments, the King's choice was justified by events, perhaps in ways different from those intended. Da Gama was to prove an outstanding sea commander, bold, decisive, intelligent, persistent. Almost alone among the great captains of discovery, he was never threatened with serious mutiny. No doubt he would have dealt with it pitilessly, for he had the defects of his qualities: a fierce, impatient temper, savage ruthlessness on occasion, and a lack of tact and imagination in unfamiliar situations. He was far better as commander than as diplomat. He made few mistakes at sea, but many ashore.

Unlike many of the captains of discovery, da Gama was allowed to select his companions. He chose well, with due regard both to competence and to personal attachment. We know considerably more about the men than about their equipment. Of a total complement somewhere between 140 and 170, the names of about forty are known. The captains were Gonçalo Alvares in the *São Gabriel*; da Gama's brother Paulo in the *São Rafael*; Nicolau Coelho in the *Berrio*; and a personal retainer of da Gama, one Nunes, in the store-ship. Paulo da

O GOVERNADOR · IORGE · CABRALL · MAMDOV · FAZER · MEMO
RIA · DAS · ARMADAS · QVE · PORTVGALL · PASARAM · A ESTAS
PARTES · ESTA · PRIMEIRA · COM · QVE · VASCO · DA
GAMA · COM · QVE · DARTIO · REINO · ANO · DE · 497

Paullo   Dagama

Vasquo   Da gama

Ho navio de necu!aocoelho q̃ 25 fizerao

Gama was a competent and kindly officer, who inspired as much affection as Vasco did fear. He died on the return voyage, to Vasco's intense grief. Alvares and Coelho both did well, and like several other officers were employed in subsequent expeditions to India. The navigators were all men of proved ability and experience. Pero de Alemquer shipped in the *São Gabriel.* Pero Escolar, pilot of the *Berrio,* had sailed with Diogo Cão, though not with Dias, and was later to sail with Cabral. Each ship carried an *escrivão,* clerk or purser. These too were competent and responsible officers; one of them was Diogo Dias, a brother of Bartolomeu; another later became factor at Calicut; yet another, eventually government treasurer at Goa. Besides officers, petty-officer tradesmen, and seamen, the fleet carried men-at-arms, gunners and musicians. There were three Arabic interpreters; and finally, a little group of *degradados,* convicts. The practice of carrying convicts was common in Portuguese expeditions. Its purpose was not simply to take undesirables into exile, or merely to fill gaps in the complement by drafting from the prisons (though this became an important consideration later); on the contrary, it was considered useful to have a few expendable desperadoes on board. Being under suspended sentence of death, they could be employed in undertakings where the chance of survival was small. Some did survive, however; one successfully deserted at Mozambique, and entered the service of the local ruler. Another, put ashore by da Gama, made his own way to India later, and eventually became commandant of the fort at Goa.

Reliable ships, then, manned by picked crews, with the best of equipment: ground for confidence indeed. The most serious mistakes made in preparing for the voyage were the results not of negligence or parsimony, but of defective knowledge and lack of imagination. The Portuguese in their drive to the East not infrequently combined methodical care and skill in technical matters with obtuseness in their human dealings. The freighting of da Gama's fleet was an example of this. Besides their own stores, the ships carried a quantity of coarse cloth, ready-made garments in bright colors, miscellaneous small hardware, hawks' bells and glass and coral beads. These were all articles habitually used in trading on the Guinea coast. The list suggests that the Portuguese, despite the accounts of Covilhã and others (if Covilhã's report had indeed been received) had no real understanding of the power and sophistication of the societies whose territories they proposed to visit. The goods were of small account in east Africa, and in India unsaleable. Worse, da Gama had no objects suitable for presentation as gifts to rulers and their officials. The omission is hard to explain. Covilhã, it is true, before his arrival in Ethiopia, had not moved among princes; but the desirability of diplomatic presents might have seemed obvious. Da Gama bore letters to "Prester John" and to the King of Calicut; neither monarch was likely to be interested in red caps or brass basins. One is struck by the contrast with the proceedings of Cheng Ho, nearly a century earlier. Royal meanness is not a convincing explanation, for Manoel I, unlike his predecessor, habitually inclined to extravagance; nor, probably, is the fear that gifts might be interpreted as tribute. Presumably no one gave thought to the matter; this lack of imagination was to cause da Gama much humiliation and trouble.

OPPOSITE: Vasco da Gama's fleet in 1497, from an early sixteenth-century print

The other serious failure in preparation was in a technical matter, the date of departure. It must have seemed obviously sensible to leave Portugal in the northern summer, in order to arrive off the Cape of Good Hope at the beginning of the southern summer. Dias had done this; but for a quick passage to India, it was a mistake, which indicates the sketchy nature of the available information. The voyages of Cão and Dias, and possibly others of which no record survives, had revealed something of the behavior of winds in the central and southern Atlantic, and da Gama at least knew what areas he must avoid. There had not been enough voyages, however, nor enough sailings at different times of year, to establish reliable knowledge of the shifts of the major wind systems north and south with the changing seasons. Of winds in the Indian Ocean, da Gama probably knew nothing. Without such knowledge it was impossible—except by lucky chance—to plan a six- or eight-month voyage so as to make the best use of the winds at each stage. The best departure month, in fact, for a sailing-ship passage from Portugal to India, is February. In the course of the sixteenth century this became well known, and ships in the *Carreira da India* normally sailed in late February or early March; or at least were instructed to do so. Da Gama, with insufficient accumulated experience to guide him, left the Tagus in July.

Of the day-to-day conduct of the voyage, we know very little. All logs, reports, and trading accounts brought back by the fleet have disappeared. While they survived, they must have been treated as highly secret. There is one private firsthand account, the so-called *Roteiro,* commonly attributed to Alvaro Velho, of whom nothing is known but his name and his

birthplace. It is not a true rutter, but a simple diary. Its author was not in the flagship and did not participate in the inner councils of the fleet. He was probably a soldier, rather than a seaman; he had relatively little to say about navigation and other nautical matters. On the other hand, he seems to have been a trusted man; he accompanied da Gama ashore on several crucial occasions, and wrote detailed and interesting, if somewhat naive descriptions of the course of events at Mombasa, Malindi and Calicut.

Apart from the *Roteiro,* our knowledge of the voyage comes from secondary sources, chiefly sixteenth-century chronicles. These differ considerably, especially over dates, but also over simple details such as the names of ships. The most nearly contemporary, and the most vivid, the *Lendas da India* of Gaspar Correa, is probably among the least reliable; though Correa spent many years in India, as did Castanheda, whose *Historia do descobrimento* appeared in the fifteen-fifties. The two best accounts of the da Gama voyage are in the *Decades* of João de Barros and in Damião de Gois's *Chronicle of King Manoel.* Barros was a *Casa da India* official and Gois an official archivist; both had access to original documents; but both wrote long after the event, and neither was a sailor. Our knowledge of the voyage as a maritime rather than a political or commercial operation has to be inferred from the comments of people who were not primarily interested in that particular aspect of da Gama's achievement.

The voyage began with a routine run down the Moroccan coast and through the Canary channel, in company with Bartolomeu Dias, who was taking a caravel to Elmina, having—at last— been appointed captain of that fortress in recognition of his services. Off Rio do Ouro the fleet ran into fog and the ships became separated but proceeded independently to a prearranged rendezvous at Santiago in the Cape Verde Islands. In later years, ships for India were forbidden to stop at these islands, for fear of delays and desertions; but on this occasion da Gama made use of his stay at Santiago to repair storm damage to his spars and rigging. Repairs completed, he left the islands on a southeast or east-southeast course, probably to a point a hundred miles or so off Sierra Leone, where Dias parted company. It was at that point, apparently, that da Gama made the bold alteration which was to make his route the model for India voyages over the next three hundred years. The fleet sailed west-southwest into the open Atlantic.

This famous alteration of course—which the *Roteiro,* curiously, does not even mention—has often been cited to support the belief that da Gama had prior information on the central Atlantic winds, derived from voyages in that area between 1488 and 1497. This is possible; but such an assumption is unsupported by any evidence, and as an explanation of da Gama's route is unnecessary. We may be sure that the general plan of his voyage had been worked out, in consultation with Dias, before the fleet left Lisbon. It would have included the resolve to make southing, as far as possible, in the open Atlantic, rather than fighting wind and current down the Gabon–Congo–Angola coast. This would have entailed a further decision, on the point at which the open-sea route should diverge from the normal route to Guinea: the Cape Verde Islands? Sierra Leone? Cape Palmas? We can easily guess why da Gama chose Sierra Leone. To the south of the Cape Verde Islands is

an area of variable winds; the northeast trade wind dies away and southerly or southwesterly breezes are frequent. A minor eddy, however, often blows along the coast, following the shoreline, first from the north and then the northwest; and the Guinea current sets in the same direction. The best way to make southing in this area in summer is to sail southeast, parallel to the coast. This was well known to navigators on the Guinea run. Off Sierra Leone in August, however, the northwest wind would have died away. The prevailing summer winds on the Guinea coast are southerly. Da Gama, unable to sail south, would have had only two alternatives: either to enter the navigational trap of the Gulf of Guinea contrary to advice and instructions, or to stand out to sea on the port tack. Naturally, and boldly, he stood out to sea; but his long board to the southeast had not been wasted. The easting he had gained enabled him to make the best use of the southeast trade wind and to avoid the risk of fetching up to leeward of Cape São Roque in Brazil. It is extremely unlikely that da Gama understood this danger at the time; but the danger is real, and for this reason the modern *Pilots* recommend sailing vessels to follow a course very similar to da Gama's.

On a west-southwest course from Sierra Leone, da Gama would have approached the Equator somewhere in the region of 24 or 25 degrees west, and would there have begun to feel the strong, steady pressure of the southeast trade wind. Once within its influence, he could alter course to southwest or even southwest by south. No doubt he would keep his ships as close to the wind as he comfortably could; but even so, the trade wind would probably put him within a few hundred miles of the east coast of Brazil. That coast was still unknown to Europeans, and there is no evidence that da Gama suspected its presence. Well before reaching it, he would have found the wind losing some of its force and beginning to back east-southeast, so that he could steer more nearly south. The farther south he went, the more the wind would back: probably to east between 15 and 20 degrees south, possibly to northeast between 20 and 25 degrees south. Each shift of wind would permit a further alteration to port. Eventually, somewhere between 30 and 35 degrees south, he would be beyond the southern limit of the southeast trade wind and in an area where the winds at that time of year—early October—though variable, are frequently north or northwest. With these winds he could shape his course directly for the Cape of Good Hope. He could have had only a rough estimate of how much easting he had to recover, and must have tried, as far as possible, to steer due east along the latitude of the Cape.

This interpretation of da Gama's course, if it is correct—and at least it is highly probable—does not necessarily suggest foreknowledge. It does suggest a bold and intelligent use of the winds as da Gama probably encountered them. It suggests also a remarkable tenacity of purpose. From the Cape Verde Islands to south Africa, the fleet was out of sight of land for more than three months; by far the longest ocean passage that European seamen had made to that time. During at least half the passage, the ships were continuously close-hauled on the port tack, making little apparent progress in the direction of their destination. They were following, in fact, the best possible route; but their people could not be sure of that. They must have passed many

anxious days awaiting the west wind which Dias would have told them to expect.

Da Gama, unlike Dias, never got down into the zone of the true, round-the-world westerlies. He made a natural mistake in trying to approach the Cape directly from the west. Ideally, he should have made his easting in a higher latitude. The prevailing winds off the southern tip of Africa in the southern summer are from the south or southeast. Within four or five hundred miles of the coast, da Gama must have lost his favoring wind and been obliged to sail close-hauled on the starboard tack, struggling to maintain his course and being driven to the north of it. Instead of making his landfall at the Cape, or passing south of it as Dias had done, he first sighted land more than a hundred miles farther north. He had a troublesome beat down the coast, and rounded the Cape itself with difficulty, by long boards out to sea, after several unsuccessful attempts. Not until the end of November did the fleet reach Dias's old anchorage in Mossel Bay. Here the stores were redistributed and the store-ship broken up, wood and water taken in, and attempts made to procure fresh provisions by local barter.

The author of the *Roteiro,* like most Portuguese, thought poorly of south Africa. It was a troublesome obstacle, and landings there were marred by quarrels with the natives. These quarrels did not arise, apparently, from aggressive behavior on da Gama's part. Most probably water was the difficulty. European sailors, coming from a region of relatively good rainfall and many rivers, habitually took water wherever convenient. It probably never occurred to them that in an area where surface water was scarce, their taking it without payment or permission might be resented. There was an ugly skirmish with Bushmen at St. Helena Bay. At Mossel Bay, though the visitors succeeded in buying an ox from the cattle-herding Hottentots and paying for it with bracelets, the dispute over water was repeated. Da Gama made good Dias's omission by setting up a *padrão* at Mossel Bay, but the natives began to demolish it as soon as the ships weighed anchor.

Christmas found da Gama's people off the Pondoland coast, the agreeable country which they named Natal. On this coast in summer, easterly winds prevail and approach to the coast is dangerous. A strong current, moreover, sets southwest close inshore. Da Gama would have done better to have made his easting and his northing much farther from the land. Modern sailing vessels bound from the Cape to Indian ports or to Aden at that time of year often pass east of Madagascar; if bound for Mombasa–Kilindini, they sail through the Mozambique channel, but close to the west coast of Madagascar, just outside the reefs. Da Gama, however, was not bound directly for India; he did not know what east African harbor to make for, nor even, except in a very general sense, where he was. He had left the area of Dias's knowledge and not yet entered that of Covilhã's. He did make one attempt to stand out to sea—presumably recognizing the dangers of a lee shore—but after a week was driven back to the land by shortage of water and by sickness among his people. He spent a few genial days at the mouth of the Zavora River—the "Copper River" in the "Land of Good People"—and a whole month in the estuary of the Quelimane, to take in water, careen the ships, and give the scurvy cases an opportunity to recover. The Portuguese

got on much better with the Bantu peoples in this part of the coast than they had with the Hottentots. There was no shortage of water in the rivers, and the natives, being farmers as well as herdsmen, had provisions to sell. Da Gama named the Quelimane *Rio dos Bons Signães,* River of Good Omens, and set up a *padrão* at its mouth. This column is marked and named on at least two almost contemporary charts, the Cantino of 1502 and the Canerio of *c.* 1504. It has disappeared, like most of the others; not, however, by deliberate destruction, but as a result of coastal erosion.

When da Gama's ships stood out from the Quelimane they entered a new and different stage of their voyage: a stage less of exploration in the geographical sense than of political and commercial reconnaissance. For the first time, European ships had penetrated a major area of non-European ship-borne commerce. They had, indeed, without knowing it been within that area for some weeks, for between the "Good People" and the "Good Omens" they had bypassed Sofala, the port of shipment for the gold of the Zambezi drainage. Sofala—now an insignificant little town, overshadowed by Beira—stands at the head of a deep indentation of the coast, and in pressing north with—for once—a favoring wind, da Gama's people had missed it. Six days beyond the Quelimane, however, they came to the considerable town of Mozambique; and here the change in their surroundings became obvious. They were no longer traversing an empty ocean, wooding and watering in lonely anchorages, dealing in sign language with half-naked people who would barter produce for glass beads. Instead, they found themselves sailing up a frequented coast with the help (when they could get it) of local pilots, and putting into busy harbors, whose inhabitants wore fine clothes, understood Arabic, used coined money and were accustomed to distant trade. The people of the Barbarian Gulf—in the coastal towns at least—were clearly far from barbarous; they thought little of the goods which the Portuguese ships carried and were unimpressed, or at least unattracted, by the Portuguese themselves.

The harbor towns of the east African coast had relatively little industry other than shipbuilding, and crafts such as blacksmithing and carving; they were mainly commercial centres. They imported silk and cotton textiles, brassware, Chinese porcelain, spices and dates. They exported cotton; grains, especially sesame and millets; ivory; charcoal; timber, including mangrove poles for building; and in some instances gold. The slave trade was not then of much importance, and seems to have been confined to the Somali ports on the northern part of the coast. Kilwa controlled most of the gold trade, but Mombasa, and to some extent a few smaller towns, also shared in it. The merchants who handled these varied trades came from all over the Indian Ocean; there were Persians, Gujeratis, Malabaris among them; but the majority were Arabs. Many Arabs resided on the coast, and some of the ruling families were of Arab origin. The Portuguese, not usually very perceptive in such matters, quickly noted the distinction between "white Moors" and "black Moors." This is not to say, however, that the coastal towns formed part of an Arab "empire." On the contrary, they were independent city-states. They possessed in common a mixed Afro-Muslim culture, with strong Arab influences, but in many ways distinctive. Many features of this culture—architectural details, for example, such as the design of minarets and pillar tombs—did not and do not occur elsewhere in the Muslim world. The towns derived some sense of unity from common religion and common languages: Arabic as a polite and learned language, Swahili as an everyday *lingua franca;* but they had no political unity, except insofar as Kilwa dominated the trade and politics of the southern part of the coast, Mombasa the northern part. They were all jealous of one another, and were also largely cut off from the hinterland, the inhabitants of which were primitive and often hostile.

Vasco da Gama's people made their way slowly up the coast, looking for the Christians they had been told to find. Here and there, obliging people told them what they wanted to hear, either from politeness or from desire to be rid of them; but they found no Christians, except perhaps a few Nestorian merchants from south India. They did not go far enough north to make any contact with Christian Ethiopia. At Mozambique, the first town they came to, they had initially a civil reception, apparently because the local people thought they were Turks. Guarded politeness turned to hostility when the truth was discovered, and da Gama delivered a farewell cannonade before departing up the coast. He succeeded, however, partly by negotiation, partly by kidnapping, in picking up several pilots. Angered by defiance at Mozambique and suspicious of treachery, he subjected these people to various forms of ill treatment, and not unnaturally they deserted as soon as they could; but they took the fleet as far as Mombasa. They missed rich Kilwa, embayed north of Cape Delgado; they passed to seaward of Zanzibar—not then a place of much

OPPOSITE: Aden, Mombasa, Kilwa, Sofala, from *Civitates Orbis Terrarum*, 1576. These are all fanciful views; or at best based on hearsay.

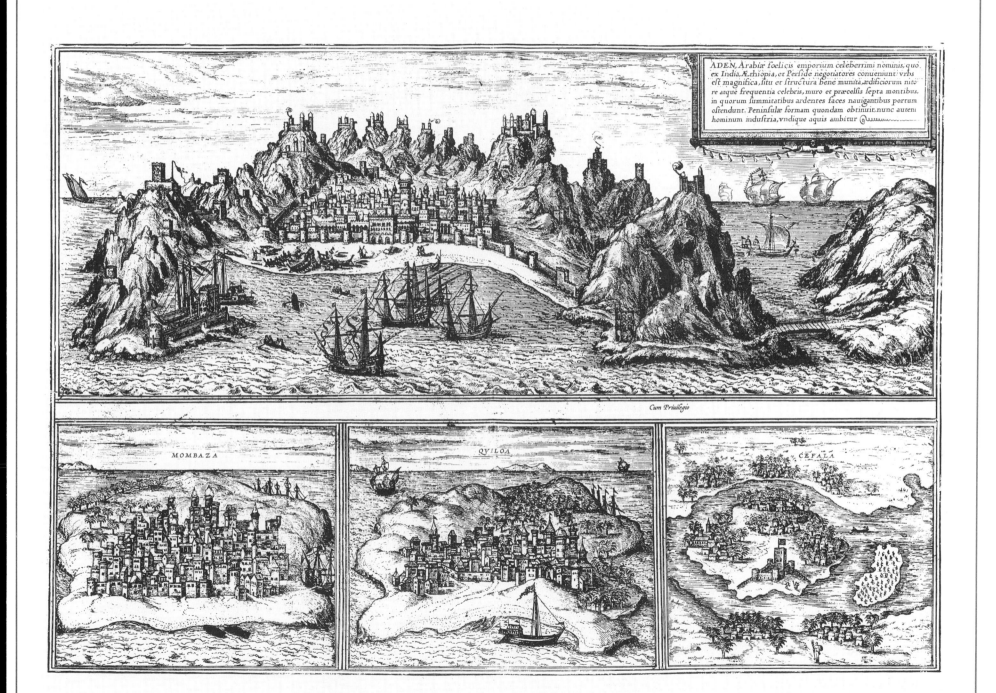

ADEN, Arabiæ foelicis emporium celeberrimi nominis, quo ex India, Æthiòpia, et Perside negotiatores conueniunt: vrbs est magnifica, situ et structura bene munita, ædificiorum nitore atque frequentia celebris, muro et præcelsis septa montibus, in quorum summitatibus ardentes faces nauigantibus portum oftendunt. Peninsulæ formam quondam obtinuit, nunc autem hominum industria, vndique aquis ambitur

Cum Priuilegio

MOMBAZA

QVILOA

CEFALA

importance—and to landward of Pemba, known then as now for fine mast timber; passed Mtang'ata, modern Tongoni, where the *São Rafael* grounded on a reef and had to be kedged off, and where canoes came off from the town to sell them oranges; and arrived off Mombasa in early April.

Mombasa, then as now, was the biggest town on the coast. It had then—according to later Portuguese estimates—about ten thousand inhabitants. It was built on an island, which gave it immunity from mainland raiders; between the north end of the island and the Nyali shore was the anchorage—now the Old Harbor—guarded by a small fort. On this same site today, the ochre, lichen-streaked walls of Portuguese Fort Jesus scowl down from the headland. Here da Gama came to anchor. The Portuguese were impressed by the European appearance of the place—which the old town still retains—and even more by the fact that the ships in the harbor were dressed overall, in celebration of the feast which closes Ramadan. The Portuguese interpreted this as a sign of welcome and responded in kind. Boats put off from the shore, bringing fresh provisions from the Sultan, including large quantities of oranges—a most valuable gift for companies prostrate with scurvy; though the author of the *Roteiro* ungratefully attributed the recovery of the sick to the "good air" of the place. Da Gama replied by sending ashore two of his *degradados* with a string of coral beads. Civilities were short-lived; the reputation of the Portuguese had evidently preceded them. Negotiations broke down, as they had at Mozambique, and after a few days punctuated by skirmishes and attempts at cutting-out, the fleet sailed on, pausing only to pick up the occupants of a small boat outside the harbor, bound for the next town up the coast, Malindi.

Malindi was a much less important place than Mombasa. It had no sheltered harbor, but an open road in a shallow curving bay, protected only by reefs, untenable in the northeast monsoon, though safe enough in the imminent southwest. It was a pleasant little town, as its successor still is; Alvaro Velho wrote that it reminded him of Alcochete, the small town on the Tagus near his birthplace. It had a good water supply and a productive agricultural hinterland. Most important of all, its ruler was on bad terms with his powerful neighbor of Mombasa. This was da Gama's first stroke of political good luck; he found himself welcomed as a potential ally.

Presents were exchanged: from da Gama a surtout, two strings of coral, a hat, two pieces of trade cloth, and three hand-wash basins; from the Sultan, six sheep and parcels of various spices. It is interesting to note that in every harbor on the coast the Portuguese were offered provisions on arrival. These gifts of food appear to have been customary; they did not inhibit subsequent hostilities, and for some days at Malindi, da Gama did not abandon his suspicious caution; but the Sultan meant business, and soon an interview was arranged in the middle of the harbor between Sultan and captain-general, each in his own boat. Da Gama took his trumpeters and men at arms; the Sultan came in full state with umbrella-bearer, sword-bearer and the royal *siwas*—trumpets made from single ivory tusks, elaborately carved. Most of the coastal rulers possessed these enormous instruments. Two of them are still to be seen in the ancient port of Lamu. They greatly impressed the Portuguese;

the author of the *Roteiro* even refers implausibly to their "sweet harmony."

On this occasion, at least, there was harmony of a sort. As the boats rocked side by side, da Gama stated his intention of going to India; the Sultan indicated his desire to be of service, and promised to provide a pilot. There followed a round of festivities, in which a prominent part was played by the people from four Indian ships lying in the harbor: Christians, according to Alvaro Velho; more probably Hindus, to judge from their behavior. The most interesting detail which Velho gives about these ships is that they carried guns, with which they returned the Portuguese salutes; none of the Arab vessels mentioned in the *Roteiro* seem to have been so armed. The Indians were friendly, even if not Christian; and by this time da Gama had apparently decided to give up the search for Christians in east Africa and to make directly for India. The season was right for it—late April or early May, near the beginning of the southwest monsoon, and perhaps the amiable "tawny men" in the Indian ships encouraged his decision.

Eventually, after a week of procrastination and a display of irritated impatience by da Gama, the promised pilot came on board. Alvaro Velho refers to him casually as "the pilot whom the King gave us" and calls him, absurdly, a Christian. The Portuguese chronicles describe him, more plausibly, as a Gujerati. A sixteenth-century Arabic account, which most modern scholars have accepted, makes him an Arab and a *hadji*: Ahmād ibn-Mādjid, one of the best-known navigators of his day in the Indian Ocean, and the author of many sailing directions and works on navigation. Ibn-Mādjid was already elderly in 1498, and much respected. It is hard to imagine why such a man should have been unemployed in Malindi, or how he could have been induced to take service with the Franks. Whoever the opportune pilot might have been, it was obvious, even to the suspicious Portuguese, that he knew his business. Da Gama's rapid and uneventful crossing of the Indian Ocean was due mainly to this man's experience and skill.

The passage took twenty-seven days, of which twenty-three were out of sight of land. The details of the route can only be surmised. The main danger to ships sailing from Mombasa to the Malabar ports (apart from cyclones) comes from the many islands of the Maldive and Laccadive groups. These atolls are low-lying, and so difficult to sight from a distance by day, but also steep-to, with deep water between them, so that the lead gives no warning of their nearness by night. The two groups are scattered over more than twelve degrees of latitude. Nowadays, sailing ships making the passage at the same time of year as da Gama are advised to stand northeast along the African coast, just within sight, until in 2 degrees, 30 minutes north, and then to steer a direct rhumb-line course for Cochin, which is now the principal harbor. This course takes them through the Nine-Degree Channel, between the northern outliers of the Maldives and the southern outliers of the Laccadives. Since da Gama's destination was Calicut, not Cochin, he probably followed the coast for a much shorter distance, perhaps for about two days' sailing, and stood out to sea in about 2 degrees south. The rhumb-line distance, coast to coast, is about 2,300 miles. Da Gama made a quick passage, by the standards of the time. From Velho's allusions to thunder and rainstorms it seems that the southwest monsoon set in while the ships were at sea, and during the latter part of the passage at least, must have pushed them along at a great rate, clear of dangers. It was to cause difficulties, however, on arrival.

The Malabar coast is a long strip of sandy, low-lying country, running north and south between the escarpment of the western Ghats and the sea. It is broken at intervals by abrupt, rocky headlands; and one of these, Mount Dilli, which rises to 850 feet or so and can be seen for a good twenty-five miles in clear weather, was probably the first point sighted by da Gama's lookouts. Mount Dilli is about fifty miles north of Calicut, and the fleet had to beat down the coast. In squally weather, with poor visibility, even experienced pilots had difficulty in recognizing the leading marks for Calicut. When they eventually arrived there, boats put off from the shore to warn them not to anchor near the town. This was good advice; during the southwest monsoon the whole coast is a lee shore, to be approached with caution; in the southerly part of Calicut road there are clusters of reefs, and a rocky bottom gives poor holding ground. Da Gama, though chronically suspicious, allowed himself to be persuaded, and moved his ships some miles back up the coast to "Pandarane." No settlement of that name exists today; the place which corresponds best with the contemporary descriptions is Kollam, a village on the shallow bay between Cotta Point and Quilandi. It has a reasonably safe anchorage, protected by an extensive mud bank. This is probably where da Gama's ships anchored; and there the ruler of Calicut's emissaries found him and commanded his presence at the court.

Da Gama's voyage from Lisbon to Calicut had been a maritime triumph; his diplomatic endeavors in Calicut itself, by contrast, were markedly less successful. The technical reach of the Portuguese, as they soon discovered, exceeded their commercial and political grasp; and this was to be their experience throughout the East. Everywhere they went, they were to find themselves forestalled by competitors, mostly Muslim in religion. The trades of the Indian Ocean, as we have seen, were largely run by Arabs, Persians and Gujeratis, who had access to more attractive goods than the Portuguese could offer, and were probably sharper and more experienced traders. Muslim merchant princes were establishing themselves round the shores of the Malayan islands. In major mainland territories, particularly in India, Muslim military adventurers from central Asia were extending their dominion. The Portuguese were entering a world in which Islam was expanding rapidly at the expense of native religions, whether Hindu, Buddhist or local pagan.

Da Gama had the luck to make his landfall in a part of India which had not yet fallen under Muslim domination. If he had landed in—say—Gujerat, his reception might have been less courteous and less equivocal. The most powerful state in south India was the Hindu kingdom or confederacy known by the name of its principal city, Vijayanagar, east of Goa. The Italian traveler Varthema, who visited Vijayanagar in about 1505, described its ruler Krishna Raya in terms which recalled tales of Prester John. Today the Sanskrit City of Victory is a vast deserted ruin; it was sacked by a league of Muslim princes in 1565, and its territories dismembered; but in Krishna Raya's time, and da Gama's, it was the capital of a rich, well-organized state stretching

OPPOSITE: Calicut, Ormuz, Cananore, Elmina Castle, from *Civitates Orbis Terrarum*, 1576

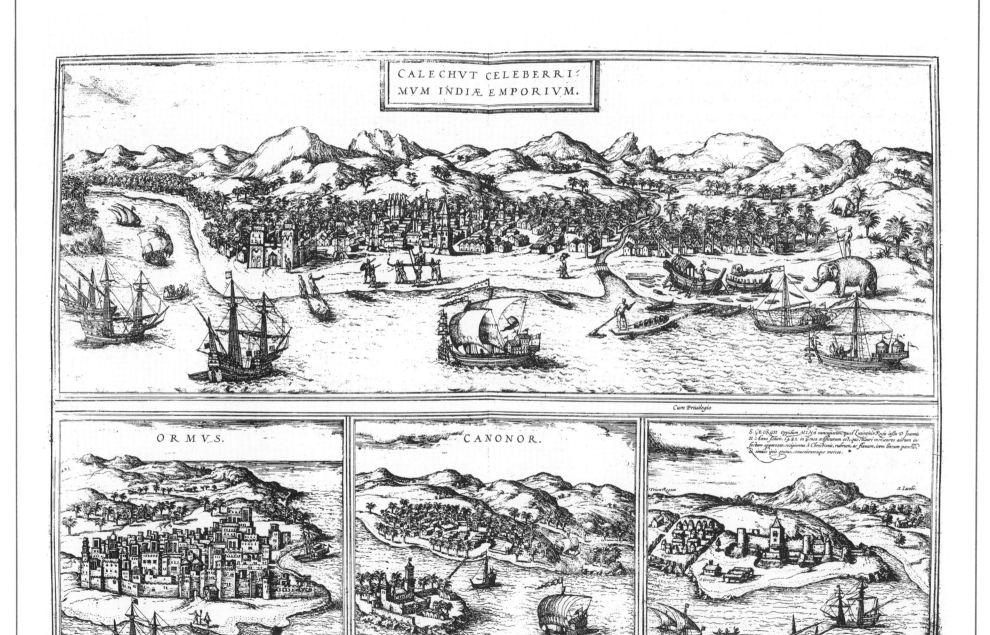

CALECHVT CELEBERRI-
MVM INDIAE EMPORIVM.

Cum Priuilegio

ORMVS.

CANONOR.

S. GEORGII Oppidum MINA nuncupatum, quod Lusitaniae Regis iussu D. Ioannis II : Anno salutis 1482. in Guinea ædificatum est, quo Mauri mercatores aurum in-
fectum apportant, recipientes à Christianis, rubrum, ac flauum, item lintea panos &c.
& simeas, quas gratas, conuenientes, que merces.

Trium Regum.   S. Iacobi.

Georgii.

from the Coromandel coast to the western Ghats and from the Kistna to Cape Comorin. West of the Ghats, sheltered from Muslim attack on the landward side by the power of Vijayanagar, but independent, lay a string of small Hindu states, of which Calicut was then the most powerful, stretching along the Malabar coast, from the southern boundary of Goa to Cape Comorin. The ruler of Calicut, the Zamorin, was a Hindu, and so were most of his subjects. There were other elements among them, however: Nestorian Christians, mostly quiet folk who minded their business and gave no trouble; native Muslims, the Moplahs; and Muslim merchants from abroad, Arabs or Gujeratis, some resident and some transient. These merchants handled the very considerable trade of Calicut, in particular its export trade in pepper and re-export of other spices. The Zamorin depended for much of his revenue on the duties which they paid, and they exerted a considerable influence upon his commercial and foreign policy. They were quick to see, in da Gama's unwelcome presence, a potential threat to their privileges and their livelihood.

The initial reception was civil; the local officials proved helpful, though grasping, in their attention to da Gama's immediate material needs. Calicut was a pleasant enough town, then as now, with spacious sandy streets and buildings widely scattered among the coconut palms. Da Gama and his companions, making their way to the ruler's durbar—da Gama in a palanquin provided for him—were agreeably impressed. In their obsessive search for Christians, they were willing to call Christian anyone who was not obviously a Muslim; even to see, in the Hindu deities in the temples they visited, the effigies of saints. They

entered the ruler's presence confidently, expecting the favorable reception to which they thought themselves entitled; and da Gama stated his business, proposing friendly intercourse as between Christians, an exchange of embassies, and trade.

Da Gama's arrival had placed the Zamorin in something of a quandary. He was not, by Asiatic standards, a major potentate; but he was a civilized and sophisticated ruler, familiar with the proprieties of international intercourse and conscious of the value of orderly trade. The advantage of widening competition between the buyers of his country's products must have been obvious; but was da Gama a serious buyer? Would he bring business valuable enough to outweigh the loss of Arab goodwill? More serious still, was he really—as he claimed—the emissary of a remote but not inconsiderable king, or merely—as the local Muslims alleged—a well-armed pirate? His fleet, though small, was clearly formidable; if it took to commerce raiding off the coast, it could do a good deal of damage. No useful purpose would be served by provoking him. The Zamorin, though noncommittal, was courteous. Arrangements were made for lodging the Portuguese in the town, instead of their trudging back to the anchorage in a monsoon downpour, and orders given for their merchandise to be landed and offered for sale.

The goods were duly landed; they were shoddy and unsuitable, and no one would buy them. Nor did da Gama, by his own behavior, do anything to reassure the Zamorin. His abrupt and hectoring manner must have been profoundly displeasing. So must his evident suspicion of bad faith; no doubt he was wise to be on his guard against surprise; but there is no evidence that he was ever in danger of physical attack, and his men wandered unmolested all over the town. His suspicion was unfounded. He was quick to resent unintended slights. When lent a horse, he took offense because it wore a cloth but no saddle, not knowing that in Malabar horses were rare and valuable and saddles not ordinarily used. Having anchored his ships, contrary to advice, at a considerable distance from the shore, he took offense because the port authorities, late at night in monsoon weather, refused to provide boats. When reminded that usage demanded a diplomatic gift for the Zamorin, he produced the usual collection of hats, basins and pieces of trade cloth; and when the officials refused to deliver a gift they thought derisory, and the Zamorin himself complained of the show of disrespect, da Gama virtually forced his way into the presence in order to make lame and lying excuses. His relations with the Zamorin deteriorated steadily during the three months he was at Calicut. No serious trading was done, no agreement reached, no alliance prepared. When da Gama, despairing of progress, finally weighed anchor to depart, probably everyone in Calicut heaved a sigh of relief. Insufficient attention, perhaps, was paid to his threat of an early return.

If the outward passage had been a nautical triumph, the return passage came near disaster. Da Gama left Calicut in impatient haste, with a few kidnapped hostages, but with no local pilot and with inadequate provisions. His ships were foul with long sea-keeping and with three months at anchor; it was imperative to find a safe and remote harbor where they could be careened. In fitful land and sea breezes between the monsoons, they worked their way up the coast, and found the haven they needed in the Anjedivas, a group of small islands near the coast just south of Goa. They are not very attractive islands; the largest is only a mile long, and nothing much grows there except coconuts; but it has a beach, and there the ships were hauled out, one by one, scraped and caulked. Wood and water came from Bingi Bay, on the mainland opposite. Boats came off from the mainland with fish and vegetables for sale, and once the work was interrupted by an attack from local pirates, driven off by gunfire from the *São Rafael,* which was still in the water.

A little later, a plausible and affable gentleman appeared, proffering, in good Italian, his services as purveyor. He described himself as a Christian born, captured in youth and forcibly converted to Islam. Da Gama's people took him for another pirate reconnoitering the fleet, or else—as he confessed under torture—a spy from Muslim-governed Goa. He seems, in fact, to have been a Jewish adventurer. They kidnapped him and took him to Portugal where, baptized under the name of Gaspar da Gama, he made himself useful to later expeditions as guide and interpreter.

Eventually the ships were ready, or as ready as they could be made in that inhospitable place, and da Gama sailed for Africa. Without local knowledge, he sailed too early; he should have waited for the northeast monsoon, which there sets in about the middle of November. Instead, he encountered the usual October alternation of calms and cyclonic disturbances; the ships drifted helplessly for weeks before they caught the monsoon. Their first sight of Africa was the Somali coast at Mogadishu, where their presence was unwelcome and their only communication with the shore an exchange of shot. They had been three months at sea, thirty men had died of scurvy, and many more were sick, by the time they anchored once more in Malindi road, wondering no doubt, in their enfeebled state, what their reception would be. Off came the bumboats, with sheep, fowl, eggs, and oranges for the sick; the Sultan had remembered his alliance. Da Gama asked two further favors, both of which were granted: the gift of a tusk of ivory for the King of Portugal, and permission to erect a *padrão.*

The Malindi *padrão* was almost the last of the series. One *padrão* had been left with the Zamorin, who presumably ignored it, for nothing more was heard of it; another was erected on one of the Santa María islands, between Calicut and Anjediva, and this too has disappeared. The Sultan of Malindi set up his *padrão* near his palace, but later, in deference to local religious feeling, moved it to a site outside the town. Its subsequent story is uncertain. Visitors today are shown a stone column faced with stucco, on a small headland near Leopard Point, a mile or two south of the town, described as Vasco da Gama's pillar. The column is relatively modern, but the cross which surmounts it is old, with the arms of Portugal just discernible on its weathered surface. It is possible, though by no means certain, that this is the cross from the original *padrão.* The Portuguese owed a heavy debt to Malindi. They repaid it in the sixteenth century, initially by military alliance, by laying waste Malindi's nearer rivals; subsequently, by neglect. When the Sofala gold trade was diverted to the direct route from Mozambique to Goa, Malindi decayed, along with Kilwa and, for a time,

Mombasa. The place was sacked and razed by Galla raiders in the seventeenth century and rebuilt on a different site in the nineteenth. It is now a pleasant but insignificant resort.

The fresh provisions of Malindi came too late to save many of the sick; or else the stay there—only five days—was too short for full recovery. The deaths continued, and a few days after departure it became clear that the survivors were too few to man three ships. On a sandbank off Mtang'ata, near where she had grounded on the outward passage, the *São Rafael* was beached and burned. They preserved her figurehead, which da Gama kept as a treasured heirloom, and twice more took out to India and back; it survives still, in the church of the Jeronymites at Belém. Da Gama had now no thought but to get home, and, with his attenuated company, to avoid frequented places. He had passed Mombasa; he sailed within sight of Zanzibar, without pausing; anchored for two days off an island near Mozambique, where he hastily set up his last *padrão,* but did not approach the town; and on to Mossel Bay. Here the people spent ten days fishing, sealing and killing penguins, to provide salted provisions for the Atlantic passage. They had still to face the Cape; at that season, towards the end of the southern summer, the wind should have been favorable, but they were unlucky, and had to wait a further week for a southeasterly wind to take them round. Then they ran steadily for a whole month before southerly winds, which did not fail them until they were off the Cape Verde Islands once more, and in familiar waters.

The voyage, like many of the great exploring voyages, ended untidily and obscurely. The *Roteiro* ends abruptly off the Guinea coast, and nothing more is known of its author. The two ships, having kept company successfully for two years, became separated. Coelho in the *Berrio* was first home with the news. Da Gama returned via Terceira in the Azores, where his brother died and was buried. None of the chronicles gives the date of his arrival at Lisbon; but all agree on the tumultuous welcome he received.

Da Gama had found the way to India; what was to be done with it? Was it practicable as a route for regular trade? What reception awaited the next Portuguese fleet in the Indian Ocean? We do not know exactly what da Gama told the King, nor how much his story grew in the King's own excited imagination. Presumably it lost nothing in the telling. A successful discoverer could not be expected to belittle his own achievement; nor, in the face of royal enthusiasm, to dwell on the difficulties which his countrymen would encounter in trying to exploit his discovery. Yet the difference between what we know of da Gama's experience and the interpretation which King and public placed upon it was too wide to be explained simply by deliberate exaggeration, or by a wish to slur over unwelcome facts. It was the product of a genuine delusion. Many of the great discoverers possessed, in addition to the essential qualities of skill, courage, persistence and power of command, a capacity for self-deception. They often saw what they wanted to see, rather than what was really there. This habit was notorious in Columbus; but da Gama had it too, and so had the sovereign he served.

The doubts and hesitations of John II's reign were all left behind. We can catch something of the excitement of the time from the eager promptitude with which another and much larger fleet was got ready; from the frenetic program of public works on which the King embarked, including the vast Jeronymite church at Belém, intended as a thanksgiving for da Gama's success; from the splendid ten-cruzado gold coin struck to commemorate the event; and from the jubilant letters, narratives and descriptions which poured out from Portugal, carrying the news of success to the principal centres of Europe.

Some of these compositions appeared, in the early years of the sixteenth century, as printed pamphlets, and naturally created a considerable stir in political, commercial and religious circles. The Portuguese government, as we have seen, usually tried to restrict the circulation of papers bearing on its oversea activities, and many of them disappeared into the limbo of its archives, never to emerge. The "India" pamphlets, however, were not inconsistent with this policy; the information they contained was of a general nature; none of it would have been much help to navigators or to commercial competitors. To some extent, they were spontaneous expressions of an understandable national euphoria. They also served practical ends: to warn off possible competitors and to represent Portuguese penetration of the Indian Ocean in a favorable light, as in the interests of Europe and of Christendom as a whole. Some of them were sent out by the Portuguese government itself, or at least with its approval, using King Manoel's new and preposterous title: Lord of Guinea and of the Conquests, Navigation and Commerce of Ethiopia, Arabia, Persia and India.

The pamphlet which purports to be a letter from King Manoel to the King and Queen of Castile, announcing da Gama's success, was printed in 1505 but bears the date July 1499. It may have been written after Coelho's return but before da Gama's. It dwells chiefly upon the material aspects of the discovery: "big cities, large buildings and rivers, great populations. . . . trade in . . . cinnamon, cloves, ginger, nutmeg and pepper . . . fine stones of all sorts . . . mines of gold" and so on. It alludes to the Christians of India and to the hope that, with their help, a blow may be struck against Islam. "Moreover," it goes on, "we hope, with the help of God, that the great trade which now enriches the Moors of those parts . . . shall, in consequence of our ordinances, be diverted to the natives and ships of our own kingdom, so that henceforth all Christendom, in this part of Europe, shall be able . . . to provide itself with these spices and precious stones." The religious aspect of discovery is more heavily stressed, as might be expected, in the Oration of Obedience which Diogo Pacheco delivered to Julius II in 1505 on behalf of King Manoel (whose name he used to great oratorical advantage). This, too, was widely distributed as a printed pamphlet. The orator spoke of "the enthusiasm with which the Christians of India welcomed us. The coming of our men confirmed them in their faith, oppressed as they had been by the arrogance of the Saracens that almost cut them off, through long despair, from the faith of Christ. They even sent as a gift to King Manoel, in testimony of common adoration and faith, a cross. . . ."

All this was a long way from the matter-of-fact detail of the *Roteiro,* which is the only eyewitness account we have of da Gama's experiences. Some of it was nonsense, and much was wildly exaggerated. We need not assume, however, that pamphlets and exuberant royal pronouncements represented, with any precision of detail, a worked-out national policy. There must have

been in the King's entourage hardheaded men whose business was to separate fact from fantasy; men who had listened skeptically to earlier discoverers' claims—those of Columbus in 1493 or of Diogo Cão in 1484; men who remembered the Oration of Obedience of 1485, which had made the King of Portugal look foolish. Behind closed doors, these men must have put searching questions to da Gama and his officers. Apart from national self-congratulation, what were the practical lessons to be drawn from the voyage? What were the established facts?

A continuous sea route, from western Europe to India, existed and was navigable. Portuguese ships were capable of making the voyage. Well-armed, they need not fear molestation at sea; they were more formidable than any hostile vessels they might encounter. In India spices, both those produced in India and those imported from farther east, could be bought at a fraction of the price prevailing in Europe. On these grounds, no one doubted, apparently, that da Gama's discovery could and should be exploited; but the difficulties, ignored in the pamphlets, had in practice to be faced. Spices, though relatively cheap in India, had to be paid for. Portugal produced nothing that could be used for the purpose. The letter to the rulers of Castile admitted that da Gama had obtained only a very small quantity of spices, and explained the failure by saying that his ships had carried no merchandise; but this was not strictly true—they *had* carried merchandise, but it had proved unacceptable. Da Gama had been told pointedly, by the Zamorin and others, that he should have offered gold or silver; but a suggestion that precious metals should be exported regularly from Portugal, even to pay for spices, was unlikely to find favor with the Portuguese government. A source of gold existed—so da Gama had been told—in the neighborhood of Mozambique; some of this gold might be procured and used to buy spices; but the diversion of so profitable a trade from east Africa to India would involve piracy or naval aggression on a very ambitious scale.

Paying for spices was not the only problem; there was the cost of the voyages to be considered. Da Gama's expedition had been appallingly costly; he had lost two ships out of four, and more than half his men. At that rate of loss, spices, however cheap in India, would be very expensive indeed by the time they reached Europe. With better information about winds and seasons, routes and harbors, fleets could no doubt make the passage more quickly, more economically and with less risk of loss; but the operation would always be expensive. For a regular dispatch of ships, an enormous capital outlay would be necessary, by investors willing to lock up their money for several years without return. Investment capital on the scale required could not be found in Portugal; much of it would have to come from abroad. To that extent, the fruits of Portuguese discovery would have to be shared with foreigners.

Finally there was the problem of opposition. The maritime world in which da Gama's ships had moved was, on the whole, a hostile world. They had been received in some harbors with wary, noncommittal politeness, in others with open enmity. The only ruler who had shown any enthusiasm for their visit was the Sultan of Malindi, who had his own local reasons; he was, in any event, a minor ruler and, inconveniently, a Muslim. Muslim rulers, in fact, governed most of the territories bordering the Arabian Sea, and their power was expanding. Nothing had been seen of Prester John and his Christian empire, and nothing heard but unsubstantial rumor. In south India Muslims, though influential, were few in number; but only the eye of faith could discern, in the religion which the rulers and most of the inhabitants professed, a resemblance to Christianity. The myth of great Christian populations, longing for alliance and reunion, still persisted in western Europe, as the Oration of Obedience showed; but Vasco da Gama had already begun, unwittingly, to expose it. As for seaborne commerce, throughout the Arabian Sea it was dominated by the "Moors," from whom the Portuguese must expect an unrelenting hostility.

The Portuguese might start a regular trade in one of two ways. They might find in south India a ruler who, for his own reasons, might prove more accommodating than the Zamorin of Calicut; who might allow them to establish a commercial factory in friendly territory. For this they would probably have to pay in the only coin they could offer: a promise of alliance and naval support. This, sooner or later, would involve them in fighting against the ruler's local enemies. Alternatively, they might seize and hold a territorial base of their own in India; perhaps also a base in east Africa. This, a fortiori, would have to be fought for. But even if they succeeded, by one or another of these means, in establishing regular trade, they would still be operating on the fringe of the Arab commercial network. There was no good reason to assume that supplies of spices delivered by Portuguese ships at Lisbon would be more reliable, more plentiful, cheaper, than supplies delivered by

Arab merchants at Alexandria. In handling goods of small bulk and high value, in sixteenth-century conditions, with small ships and large crews, trans-shipment was not a major obstacle; cost would be determined chiefly by the overall length of the voyage, and by the dangers, whether of the sea, of war or of piracy, against which the cargoes had to be protected. In straightforward commercial competition the Arabs and the Venetians would have all the advantages of inner communications, experience and goodwill. From the Portuguese point of view the physical destruction of Arab commercial shipping, besides being a pious duty, might become a competitive necessity. This would involve piracy and naval aggression on an enormous scale. All the arguments, therefore, pointed the same way. If the Portuguese seriously proposed to break into the trade of the Indian Ocean, by the route which da Gama had discovered, they would have to use their guns.

10

The Atlantic Crossing

ive years before Vasco da Gama opened the sea route to the East, Christopher Columbus had found a false Asia in the West. The existence of the immense barrier of the Americas, stretching through 122 degrees of latitude, north to south, was then, so far as we know, wholly unsuspected in Europe. Norse adventurers from Greenland had landed, centuries before, in parts of North America: in Labrador, in Newfoundland, possibly farther south; but if any tradition of the Norsemen's Vinland lingered in late fifteenth-century Europe, that equivocal country was probably assumed to be an island. Greenland was usually thought, by the few who knew of its existence, to be a peninsula of northwestern Europe. There are vague indications that English fishermen may have sighted unknown land in the northwestern Atlantic in the fourteen-eighties, but neither their discoveries nor their conclusions have been recorded. As for other parts of the Americas, there are many tales of discoverers before Columbus; none is impossible, but no shred of evidence supports any of them. Columbus, then, found in 1492 an extensive group of islands unknown to Europeans, and in 1498 he found an undoubtable, but equally unknown mainland. He concluded that both islands and mainland were parts of Asia, and persisted in that belief until his death.

Columbus's enterprise and da Gama's were both voyages of discovery; both were concerned, directly or indirectly, with Asia; both, in very different senses, were successful; both were well rewarded; but there the resemblance between them ends. Da Gama's achievement was the culmination of a long series of voyages, each extending the experience of its predecessor. Columbus's voyage was without precedent, other than the piecemeal exploration and settlement of the Atlantic islands; his geographical reasoning was based not on intelligence reports, but on a combination of travel literature, cosmographical theory and inner conviction. Da Gama was selected to command an expedition long under royal consideration; Columbus's proposals were his own; he secured the backing of the Spanish monarchs and his own appointment to command by persistent and persuasive importunity. Da Gama's ships were specially built and equipped for the service in which they were to be employed; Columbus was given the ships that happened to be available. Da Gama's objects were as precise as available intelligence allowed them to be: the Cape of Good Hope, the Christians of the Barbarian Gulf, India, and Calicut, source of spices. Columbus's agreement was in vague and general terms: he was to "discover and acquire islands and mainland in the Ocean Sea."

Columbus was a self-taught man, of little formal education but of vigorous and active mind, possessed by the conviction that he was destined for high adventure. If he had been a prince, instead of the son of a Genoese weaver, his inner conviction might have been fortified, as we are told Prince Henry's was, by a formal horoscope; as it was, he strengthened it by

eclectic reading. He was much addicted to prophecies. A postil written by his son Hernando associates him with a prophetic passage in Seneca's *Medea:* "An age will come after many years when the Ocean will loose the chain of things, and a huge land lie revealed; when Tiphys will disclose new worlds and Thule no more be the Ultimate." Nothing illustrates better than this famous passage the spirit in which Columbus approached possible patrons in the ten years or so before 1492. He was painfully sensitive to ridicule, and conscious of the difficulty of explaining his conviction to skeptical men who were more highly placed, better educated and in general better informed than he was. With such men, he probably thought it safest to stick to generalities and avoid specific detail. On generalities he could be—he was, all witnesses agree—extraordinarily persuasive. On details he could be challenged. His geographical ideas were muddled and vague, the product of hearsay and extensive, but selective and uncritical, reading; probably he was unable to produce convincing detail.

Possibly the clever men he dealt with believed his vagueness to be deliberate; if he really possessed secret and valuable information, he might well, with peasant cunning, refuse to divulge it to possible competitors. We cannot tell; but eventually, through persuasiveness and persistence, he got what he wanted— backing for an expedition—and got it without committing himself to a specific discovery. No document dated before Columbus's departure defines the islands and mainland he was to seek.

We do not know, therefore, exactly what Columbus hoped to find, and possibly he did not know himself. The standard phrase "islands and mainland" could obviously include Antilla of the seven cities, and any of the other islands with which report and legend dotted the Atlantic. It is possible that Columbus's object was to establish a personal fief in Antilla; it is possible that, sailing much farther west than he expected before sighting land, he concluded that he had missed his destination, and identified the islands he actually discovered with those believed to lie off the southeast coast of Asia. The idea of a western route to Asia, in other words, first occurred to him after his arrival in the West Indies, not before his departure from Spain; it formed no part of his agreement. This theory has been argued persuasively by at least one modern scholar; it has its attractions; it can be used to explain some apparent oddities and inconsistencies in Columbus's conduct on the voyage; but it is not really convincing. It raises more problems than it solves. The high price which Columbus consistently set upon his services, and the serious consideration given to his proposals both in Portugal and in Spain, suggest that something much bigger than Atlantic islands was in question. John II of Portugal was notoriously hardheaded and tightfisted; Isabella of Castile, though a fanatic in some respects, was certainly no fool. They both knew the current price of island-finding; they and their predecessors had granted many patents for the purpose. Neither would have been likely to advance money and promise extravagant rewards to a penniless adventurer for a service which many of their subjects were willing to undertake without cost to the Crown. Yet Isabella supported Columbus with—for her—considerable generosity, and even John seems to have taken

him seriously. What did he offer them? More significant, perhaps, what did they think he was offering?

A western route to some part of Asia is the most generally accepted, the traditional answer, and the answer which most nearly fits the known facts. It was the answer given, explicitly or implicitly, by all the major writers who described Columbus's achievements in the first fifty years or so after his return in 1493: by Peter Martyr, the sophisticated Italian diplomat and cleric who was in Spain at the time of the discovery and who wrote the first history of the New World, the Decades *De Orbe Novo;* by Hernando, Columbus's son, whose *Historie* is a pious, illuminating, though not always reliable biography of a famous father; by Bartolomé de las Casas, missionary, polemicist and historian, who knew the Columbus family and whose voluminous *Historia de las Indias* is the richest of all the narrative sources; by Gonzalo Fernández de Oviedo, adventurer and administrator, author of the *Historia General y Natural de las Indias,* the first

A dugout canoe, from Oviedo's *Historia General,* 1535

official history, a masterpiece of precise observation and description. None of these men had any interest in associating Columbus with an eccentric geographical theory. They all, in differing degrees, admired him and acknowledged him as the first discoverer of the West Indies, the New World; but they all believed that he had proposed a voyage to "India"; that is, to Asia. Barros, in his account of Columbus's application to the Portuguese government, made the same assumption. No one in the sixteenth century suggested that Columbus's identification of the West Indies with eastern Asia was an afterthought.

Some of Columbus's books can still be seen, with many marginal annotations in his hand. They were inherited by Hernando Colón, his illegitimate son, who in turn bequeathed them with his own extensive library to the Cathedral Chapter of Seville. The canons, over the centuries, neglected the collection and lost many of the books, but about two thousand survive today in the Colombina Library, including four which belonged to Christopher Columbus. These are: Marco Polo's *Description of the World,* in Latin, in an edition of 1485; Pliny's *Natural History,* in Italian, 1489; the *Imago Mundi* of Cardinal Pierre d'Ailly, with sundry minor

treatises by the same author, all in Latin, 1480–83; and the *Historia Rerum Ubique Gestarum* of Aeneas Silvius (Pope Pius II), 1477. The annotations show the eagerness with which Columbus seized on every statement, in these revered authorities, about the geographical length of a degree of longitude, the proportion of land to water on the earth's surface, the east–west length of Asia, and the width of the ocean between eastern Asia and western Europe. The dates of the publications do not, in themselves, prove that Columbus read the books before 1492; but some of the postils are themselves dated, the earliest in 1481. They suggest that Columbus was interested in the western passage from Europe to Asia long before he began making practical plans about it. His startling proposal—however muddled, however wrapped in mystification—was the product of years of thought and study.

This is not to say, of course, that the idea of a western route to Asia originated with Columbus. As a theoretical possibility, it had been familiar for a very long time. Strabo, in the first century A.D., asserted that it was possible to sail clear round the world in open water. A similar dictum was attributed to Aristotle. In the fourteenth century "Sir John" Mandeville was saying much the same thing on a more popular level. If one could sail round the world, one should be able to sail to any part of it; discover the sea, and any land could be discovered. The spread of Ptolemaic theory in fifteenth-century Europe upset some of this reasoning, but not all fifteenth-century scholars accepted Ptolemy whole; and against Ptolemy could be set the positive encouragement of Seneca in the *Quaestiones Naturales:* "A ship may sail in a few

An Antillean stone axe, from Oviedo's *Historia General,* 1535 days with a fair wind from the coast of Spain to that of India."

There were theorists in Columbus's own day who maintained that a western route to Asia might be easier to follow than an eastern route—might, indeed, be the only sea route, if Ptolemy was right about the enclosed Indian Ocean. The most eminent of these was Paolo dal Pozzo Toscanelli, whom we have seen in 1459 passing on to his Portuguese friends information about the East, obtained from Conti. When in 1474 Portuguese explorers made the dismaying discovery of the southerly trend of the Gabon coast, one of these friends consulted Toscanelli informally, but on behalf of the King. Toscanelli replied confidently to the effect that the city of Quinsay (Hangchow), capital of Mangi (the southern Chinese province, south of Cathay) was the equivalent of five thousand nautical miles west of Lisbon; and that a ship following that course would encounter no great difficulty, because it could put into island harbors on the way: Antilla ("known to you") and Cipangu—Japan. Toscanelli based his information on his reading of Marco Polo; he was one of the few fifteenth-century scholars who took Marco seriously. The Portuguese paid no attention to his advice, and went on patiently exploring the African coast; but Columbus, who desperately wanted Marco Polo to be taken seriously, somehow heard of the correspondence. He wrote to Toscanelli in his turn, probably in 1480 or 1481, and received an encouraging answer, with a copy of the original letter, and a chart which is now lost. Doubts have been cast on the authenticity of these exchanges, as on that of almost every document in the Columbus story; they are probably unfounded. The Toscanelli

letter, so far as it went, was one of the strongest supports of the case Columbus was to present; but it did not go far enough.

Columbus was not concerned with theory for its own sake, but with promoting a practical proposal. He did not study the available authorities in order to draw conclusions; he began with the conviction—how formed, we cannot tell—that an expedition to Asia by a westward route was practicable and that he was the man destined to lead it. He then combed the authorities known to him, and selected from them any assertion which supported his case. The practicability of the voyage—assuming that no major land mass barred the way—depended partly on the pattern of winds and currents likely to be encountered, but mainly on the distance to be covered. Columbus had to show that the westward distance from Europe to Asia was within the operating range of the available ships. We can trace, from what is known of his reading, from his own later writings, and from the biography written by his son Hernando, how he set about it.

First Ptolemy in an important respect had to be rejected. According to Ptolemy, the land area of the world covered about 180 degrees of longitude, measured eastward from the meridian of Cape St. Vincent to that of "Catigara" at the extremity of Asia. For Columbus, the remaining 180 degrees of water were too much. He found a more acceptable figure in the *Cosmographiae Tractatus* of Pierre d'Ailly, the author of the *Imago Mundi,* who in this second treatise, following Marinus of Tyre in preference to Ptolemy, allotted 225 degrees of longitude to the land and only 135 degrees to the water. Cardinal d'Ailly, however, had known nothing of Marco

Polo, who had revealed to Europeans the enormous east–west length of Asia. Columbus therefore added 28 degrees of land for Marco Polo's discoveries, and a further 30 degrees to allow for the reported distance from the Cathay coast to the island of Cipangu. This left only 77 degrees of longitude between western Europe and Cipangu, from which a further 9 degrees could be subtracted, since Columbus proposed to embark on his ocean passage from the western Canary Islands, leaving 68 degrees. By a final arbitrary correction, almost breathtaking in its illogic, on the assumption that Marinus had overestimated the length of a degree, Columbus succeeded, to his own satisfaction, in reducing this 68 degrees to 60 degrees.

The next problem was to translate longitude into linear distance. There had been many estimates, from which Columbus could choose, of the length of a degree of latitude, and thus of a degree of longitude at the equator. The correct figure, for a modern navigator, is 60 nautical miles. Eratosthenes in 250 B.C. had come very near that figure. Translated into nautical miles for convenient comparison, his estimate was 59.5.

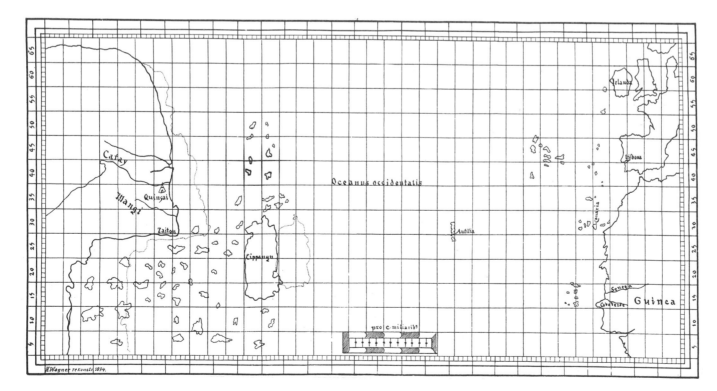

Reconstruction of the Toscanelli chart of c. 1474

Ptolemy made it about 50. Casting about for a smaller figure, Columbus found one, or thought he found one, in the *Imago Mundi:* the estimate commonly attributed to Al Farghani (Alfraganus), the medieval Arab cosmographer. This was 56⅔ "miles"; but a "mile" could have many different values, and Columbus assumed, wrongly, that Alfraganus's mile had been the short Italian mile of 1480 meters. On that basis, Alfraganus's degree would have been only 45 nautical miles at the equator, or about 40 nautical miles in the latitude where Columbus proposed to make his crossing—probably the shortest estimate of a degree ever made. Columbus claimed, with what truth we cannot tell, to have verified this figure by his own calculations. His world, in other words, had a circumference 10 per cent smaller than Ptolemy's and 25 per cent smaller than the real world. The result of his calculations was to place Japan 2400 nautical miles west of the Canary Islands; a long voyage, but feasible, especially if a stop could be made at Antilla. It placed Japan in approximately the true position of the Virgin Islands, not very far from the first land which Columbus was to sight on his actual voyage. This coincidence must have seemed conclusive; it gave a crazy consistency to the whole calculation. In fact, the airline distance from the Canaries westward to Japan is 10,600 nautical miles.

Such was the case which Columbus had to present, to secure the backing of a government or a private investor. His first approach was made, naturally enough, to the Portuguese government. Columbus had arrived in Portugal in 1476, a victim of piracy, swimming ashore from a sinking ship. He had been kindly received, probably by the Genoese community in Lisbon; he had prospered, and for eight years made Portugal his home. In Portugal he learned most of what he knew of navigation. He made several voyages—in what capacity we do not know—in Portuguese ships: to Madeira, to Elmina, probably one to Iceland. He married into a family with Madeira interests, spent some time in the island, and acquired information about Atlantic islands in general, including the fact that flotsam sometimes drifted to their beaches, apparently from the west. All this, together with his reading, encouraged his design. In 1484 he succeeded in getting the attention of the royal council and laid before it his proposal for sailing to Japan.

The proposal was rejected; yet it seems to have been taken seriously, and the possibility of reconsideration was held open. We can only guess at the grounds for rejection. Possibly Columbus's demands, both for ships and equipment, and for reward in the event of success, were thought excessive. This was the explanation suggested by Hernando Colón and by las Casas; but it is not likely that Columbus would have stated his precise terms until his proposal had been approved in principle, and the negotiations apparently never reached that point. More probably las Casas, writing years later, simply assumed that Columbus demanded from Portugal the same terms that he subsequently obtained from Castile.

Possibly the proposal was rejected as impracticable. This was the explanation given by Barros, who wrote that it was submitted to a committee of experts—that same *junta* of mathematicians who were already considering the problem of solar altitude—and that the experts pronounced it "vain." Master Rodrigo, Master

José Vizinho and the Bishop of Ceuta may well have had doubts about Cipangu; the only evidence that such a place existed was in a hearsay report by Marco Polo. Almost certainly, also, they must have challenged Columbus's geographical calculations. They could only state an opinion, however; no answer could be final. In the state of geographical knowledge at the time, the circumference of the earth, the proportion of land to water on its surface, the size of Asia, were all open questions; the answers depended on which "authorities" one chose to quote. If Cipangu were imaginary, there was no denying the existence of Cathay; if the breadth of the western ocean turned out to be double the figure suggested by Columbus, it might still be within the range of a well-found fleet; and if neither Cipangu nor Cathay were within reach, Antilla might be. Moreover, Columbus's case did not rest only on cold figures; the prophecies, the inner conviction, the hints of secret information, Columbus's own air of confident certainty, may each have made an impression. Such matters lay outside the field of mathematical expertise. The King and his advisers were not immune to the superstitions of their day, and Columbus was a persuasive advocate; they could not be sure.

Probably the most cogent reason for rejecting Columbus's proposal was that, even if practicable, it was inopportune. The Portuguese government was already involved in a series of exploratory voyages along the west coast of central Africa, with the purpose of finding a passage to the Indian Ocean and entering the spice trade. Columbus proposed a voyage to the other extremity of Asia. Cipangu and Cathay were not known to produce spices. They were said to be attractive in other ways, civilized and powerful

kingdoms, rich in gold; but the Portuguese were already developing a promising source of gold, in west Africa. In 1484, the year of Columbus's application, Diogo Cão returned from his first Congo voyage with deceptive reports of success. With the Indian Ocean and the spice routes apparently within reach, it might well have seemed a rash dispersal of resources to invest government funds in a westward expedition to Cathay.

This did not mean that the western route was ruled out; in 1485 the King issued a patent to one Fernão Dulmo of Terceira "to seek and find a great island or islands or mainland by its coast, which is presumed to be the Isle of the Seven Cities." Dulmo was to make the voyage in 1487, at his own expense, and was to have the lordship of anything he might discover. This looks like part, at least, of Columbus's plan. Nothing came of it; if Dulmo ever sailed, the prevailing westerly winds in the latitudes of the Azores would have prevented his getting very far, and he would have returned empty-handed. Diogo Cão's people, however, also returned empty-handed from the second Congo voyage; India was not, after all, within easy reach. When Columbus, writing from Seville early in 1488, indicated a wish to renew his application to the Portuguese government, the King responded with a warm, almost a pressing invitation to return; but Columbus delayed, and arrived in Portugal towards the end of the year, to witness Dias's triumphant return. This, naturally, put an end to negotiations about the westward route to the Indies, so far as Portugal was concerned.

In 1485, after the initial rejection of his proposal, Columbus had removed to Castile. He knew the language, having learned it in Portugal

—Castilian, indeed, is the language of all his surviving writings—but he had no friends there. He had to begin again the long disheartening business of explaining himself and his project, scraping acquaintance, securing introductions from modestly influential people to others more influential, beginning with the prior of the Franciscan convent of La Rábida, on the Río Tinto, where he first sought hospitality after landing at Palos; ending with the Andalusian grandee, the Duke of Medina Celi, and eventually the Queen herself. Columbus's ability to thrust himself into the circles of the great was one of the most remarkable things about him. Grandees, it is true, were more accessible then than they are now, and monarchs saw suitors in person; but still we must marvel at the confidence, the persistence, the persuasiveness of the man. His proposal, again, was seriously considered. The Duke—a considerable shipowner —was tempted to back the enterprise himself, but stood down when the Queen showed interest. The Queen, like the King of Portugal, sought the opinion of a committee which, according to one contemporary, consulted "wise and learned men and mariners." We do not know who the mariners were; the members of the committee were not mathematicians and cosmographers, but scholars and theologians. The "authority" which they opposed to Columbus's arguments was not Ptolemy, but Saint Augustine; a writer with whose works Columbus, so far as we know, was not familiar. He must have found the whole discussion baffling and infuriating; though he would have done well in later life to have paid more attention to one, at least, of Saint Augustine's maxims: *Melius est dubitare de ocultis, quam litigare de incertis.*

The Queen's committee took more than four years to reach a definite conclusion. When they finally reported, probably in 1490, they recommended the rejection of Columbus's proposal, on grounds (according to las Casas) which do little credit to the state of cosmographical science in Spain at the time. In general, the members thought the project impracticable. They did not say, though they might have done, that it was also inopportune. Columbus did not have to compete, it is true, with a rival project for reaching the "Indies," as he had done in Portugal. He had the field to himself. The Castilians in 1480 had accepted their exclusion from Guinea, and except for the piecemeal conquest of the Canary Islands they had no plans for discovery, trade or settlement overseas. They were engaged, however, in a more immediate, more demanding enterprise nearer home: the conquest of Granada, the last surviving Muslim kingdom in the Iberian peninsula. There was no likelihood that the Queen would invest heavily in a project of discovery, however attractive, while the holy war was in progress. Yet the Queen was interested in the man and his project. Financial gratuities, letters of recommendation to local officials, commands to appear at court, came Columbus's way from time to time. Even after the adverse report in 1490, Columbus continued to hope that the end of the war might bring a change in his fortunes. He had no other recourse. The Portuguese government had lost interest; tentative approaches in England and France evoked no response; Castile was the only hope.

The capital city of Granada capitulated early in 1492; but shortly afterwards Columbus received another and apparently definite "no." Possibly, on this last occasion, it had come to bargaining, and Columbus's grasping demands became the sticking point. The circumstances of Isabella's final, dramatic change of mind suggest this explanation. One of Columbus's most enthusiastic supporters was Luis de Santángel, a trusted official in Ferdinand's—not Isabella's—household. Santángel persuaded the Queen to back Columbus, partly by engaging to find at least half of the necessary money. The investment was to be borrowed from the funds of the Santa Hermandad, the powerful self-help police force of which Santángel was treasurer. Santángel also seems to have invested some of his own money, and Columbus himself produced some, probably borrowed from Italian friends and supporters. With a major obstacle removed, the Queen gave way; presumably the project appealed to her imagination, and Columbus's own personality may have impressed her. She agreed to all Columbus's demands, including the titles and rewards he was to receive in the event of success, not foreseeing the immense range of the concessions she was making, and the trouble they were to cause later. The King, with misgiving, consented because it was the Queen's wish. Columbus, still without any precise definition of the destination he was to seek, got the fleet and the command he asked for.

The fleet was relatively modest, a small *nao* and two caravels. It was based on the little port of Palos, on the Río Tinto, where Columbus had first landed in Castile. Among the many harbors of western Andalusia, Cádiz might have seemed a more obvious choice; but Cádiz harbor was then crowded with shipping, preparing to take Castilian Jews into exile. Palos had committed some municipal misdemeanor, for which it was

fined the use of two caravels for a year: an important economy; but it was a good choice on other grounds. The Palos people had long experience in trade to the Canaries, and probably in Guinea smuggling. The two caravels, though small, were eminently seaworthy. The ship *Santa María,* built in the north of Spain, was found in nearby Puerto de Santa María, and chartered for the voyage. Columbus later complained that she was unhandy; compared with the caravels, she probably was, but she performed reliably on the outward passage. The ships, like Vasco da Gama's, carried a modest supply of small truck for trading; unlike da Gama's, they had no provision for ceremonial display and were almost unarmed.

We know much more about Columbus's company than about da Gama's. There were about ninety men in all, about forty of whom sailed in the *Santa María.* The Crown paid their wages, and fairly complete nominal rolls have survived. Columbus had some acquaintance in Palos, from his time at La Rábida; members of local seafaring and shipowning families—the Pinzón of Palos and the Niño of Moguer—supported the enterprise, and sailed in the fleet. Martín Alonso Pinzón commanded the *Pinta,* Vicente Yáñez Pinzón the *Niña.* Juan Niño, owner of the *Niña,* sailed in her as master; Peralonso Niño went navigator in the *Santa María,* and a younger Niño brother shipped as an apprentice. They were all capable seamen, familiar with the type of ship they were called upon to handle. Probably these respected citizens recruited, from their own home ports, the crews of the two caravels. The crew of the *Santa María* seems to have been more heterogeneous; some came from the north of Spain; not all were professional seamen. Significantly, perhaps, it was only in this ship that mutterings of mutiny were heard on the outward passage. Her master was the Biscayan Juan de la Cosa; there is some doubt about the identity of this man, but most scholars agree that he was the cartographer, who made several subsequent voyages to the West Indies, and who produced, early in the sixteenth century, a celebrated world chart, probably the earliest surviving chart to show the American continents.

Columbus, then, commanded well-found ships, competent, experienced officers, and on the whole reliable men. Of his own qualifications for command, he is himself the principal witness; he was not a man to belittle his own achievements, and balanced judgment is difficult. He suffered from three disadvantages: foreign birth, humble origin, lack of experience in command; there is no evidence that he had ever commanded a ship, much less a fleet. Many captains of discovery had one or other of these disadvantages, but few had all three. Disaffection in various forms, from insubordinate muttering to open mutiny, threatened his authority on many occasions. Columbus seems rarely to have taken his officers into his full confidence; some of them may have resented his secretiveness and distrusted his vague, muddled exuberance. On the other hand, he had immense strength of character and tenacity of purpose, and was capable of inspiring loyalty. He had the Queen's backing; and the 1492 voyage, from its first inception as an idea to its deceptively triumphant end, was his own.

Technically Columbus, though he knew something of seamanship before he left Palos, was probably less qualified than some of his officers. He learned a great deal, naturally, as he went along. He did his own navigating from the start, and did not depend on Peralonso Niño to tell him where he was. As a navigator, he used the standard dead-reckoning techniques of the time; he was not in the forefront of new developments, or even abreast of them. He knew very little about celestial navigation; nothing, apparently, of the new Portuguese method of measuring latitude by solar altitude. He understood the principle of latitude sailing, but some of his Polaris observations, which he recorded, were badly out. Even his dead reckoning, on the outward passage, left something to be desired, probably because he was unfamiliar with his ship and overestimated her speed. Peralonso Niño's reckoning was more accurate at first; but Columbus's improved, and indeed developed an uncanny precision. Columbus had a flair for it, a compass rose in his head. He made astonishingly accurate landfalls, too often for them to be attributed to good luck; once he had been to a place, he could always find it again.

The voyage was a Spanish enterprise and nearly all those who sailed on it were Spaniards. Columbus, as we have seen, turned to Spain only after disappointment in Portugal; but by doing so he secured a vital advantage: access to a harbor in the Canary Islands, from which to take his final departure. This in large measure determined the outcome of the voyage, and may even to some extent have affected its plan. Contemporary maps of the world showed the Canary Islands, Antilla, Cipangu and Quinsay in approximately the same latitude. They are all so drawn on Martin Behaim's celebrated globe—the earliest globe which survived to modern times—which was made at Nürnberg in 1492. Columbus

ABOVE: A lateen-rigged caravel. Columbus's *Niña* originally looked something like this.

BELOW: A square-rigged caravel. *Pinta* looked something like this, and so did *Niña* when re-rigged at the Canaries.

OPPOSITE: Columbus's *Santa María*, a conjectural model

cannot have seen the Behaim globe before he sailed, but he probably saw—and may have drawn himself—*mappae-mundi* which made similar assumptions. The advantage of departing from the Canary Islands must have seemed obvious. There were real practical advantages. If Columbus had sailed under Portuguese colors, he would have had a choice between the Azores, Madeira and the Cape Verde Islands. Sailing west from the Azores, he would probably have met head winds and, like Dulmo, accomplished nothing; he might have done better from Madeira, though, except in the height of summer, he would probably have run into calms and variables not far out; from the Cape Verde Islands, he might have reached the coast of South America, but after a passage much more troublesome than he actually experienced. Sailing west from the Canaries, however, he could be reasonably sure of the northeast trade wind, for the first few days at least. The wind patterns in the neighborhood of these various island groups must have been well known to experienced Portuguese and Andalusian navigators, and Columbus could have got the necessary information, if not from his own experience, then from his Madeira connections. So he made for the Canary Islands, put into harbor at Gomera, refitted his ships, took in meat, wood and water, and from there sailed out due west.

Columbus's expedition of 1492 is the first major voyage of discovery of which we have an account by the commanding officer in his own words; or more or less his own words. The original *Journal* was no doubt a confidential document, and it has disappeared. What we have is an abstract made by las Casas from an imperfect copy of the original some years after the event. It contains long extracts from the original, in the first person, with intervening passages, which the editor presumably thought less interesting, summarized in the third person; and with comments and asides interpolated by las Casas himself. Las Casas was a capable historian and a well-informed commentator. There is no reason, in this matter, to doubt his honesty and reliability. In all probability the *Journal* represents, as closely as a summary by another hand could do, Columbus's own experiences and thoughts.

It is a highly personal document. In the circumstances, it would be unreasonable to expect in Columbus the professional detachment of a Cook. The voyage was his personal enterprise. It was not surprising that he should tend to represent all ideas and initiatives as his own, and to deny credit to his companions; few commanding officers are exempt from this temptation, and Columbus had more excuse for it than most. His judgment, his interpretation of everything he saw and heard, was colored by his own preconception concerning Asia. He was credulous, over-ready to accept half-understood gestures and statements of native informants: indications, for example, of busy harbors and cities to the west, or tales of the Amazons of "Matinino." Amazon islands had been mentioned by Marco Polo; though both these stories could conceivably also have had some basis in New World fact, in the cities of Yucatán, and in the Carib practice of kidnapping Arawak women and slaughtering the men.

In describing what he had actually seen, Columbus was usually accurate. He might exaggerate, but he did not invent. He saw no giants or dog-headed men. He was sensitive to natural beauty, unlike most Iberian explorers, and sometimes lapsed into excited hyperbole in describing it, but with reason: some of the West Indian islands were, and are, surpassingly beautiful. When he wrote that flocks of parrots "obscured the sun," he was making a point—parrots were Asiatic birds, described by Pliny—but he was not exaggerating wildly, as anyone knows who has seen West Indian parrots raiding an orange grove. His careful observation in such matters is most admirably illustrated by the story of the mermaids. Mermaids were a familiar property of nautical legend. Their existence had been confirmed in the fifteenth century by reports from west Africa of an aquatic mammal, the dugong. This creature has an articulated head, arm-like flippers and, in the female, protuberant breasts. Its habit of rearing up in the water gives it, from a little distance, a vaguely human appearance. A similar animal, the manatee or sea-cow, occurs in the Caribbean. Columbus saw manatees off Hispaniola. The entry in the *Journal* reads: "He saw three mermaids, who rose very high from the sea, but they were not as beautiful as they are painted, though to some extent they have a human appearance about the face. He said he had seen some in Guinea on the coast of Malagueta." This was the account of a good observer, not of a plausible storyteller. In general, the *Journal* is not an exercise in fantasy, deception or self-advertisement; it is a detailed, revealing and sometimes moving narrative of a notable voyage.

The outward passage was remarkably prosperous. The trade wind is not always reliable so far north. Gomera is in 28 degrees north, and well within its influence; but the northern limit of the trade winds, at the season when Columbus

sailed, dips south to 25 or 26 degrees in mid-Atlantic. Later navigators, including Columbus on subsequent voyages, profited by his experience and made their passages farther south. Columbus on his 1492 voyage was lucky to have a fair wind nearly all the way, with only a few days of variables, accompanied by a heavy swell from some distant disturbance. Even those days were useful, in calming the fears of those who worried about their return. There were no long periods of calm, and no sickness. The first sight of continuous sheets of gulf weed in the Sargasso caused temporary alarm; sightings of birds and false sightings of land, occasional excitement; but most of the time the ships drove on west at a good speed, sometimes 180 miles in the day, in clear fresh trade-wind weather, with boredom the only serious danger.

After the temporary loss of the trade wind, between about 41 and 48 degrees west, the course fell off slightly to the south. In 69 degrees west or thereabouts a deliberate alteration was made to west-southwest, apparently because flocks of land birds were observed flying in approximately that direction. This was part of the regular autumn migration of North American birds to the West Indies via Bermuda; a good omen, and crucial for the outcome of the voyage. If the fleet had continued due west, the first landfall would have been at the northwestern extremity of the chain of the Bahamas, on Eleuthera or Grand Abaco; the route west would have led between these two islands, through the Northeast Providence Channel; and that would have taken them into the Gulf Stream. Once in that broad and powerful current, they would have been carried away to the northeast; if they avoided the dangers of the Florida coast, they

would have returned to Spain without sighting the Greater Antilles and without finding gold, or any sign of gold. That, probably, for some years at least, would have been the end of western ocean exploring.

In the event, on a course west-southwest, thirty-three days out, with the *Santa María*'s company grumbling, demanding return and threatening mutiny, they sighted land at an island much farther to the southeast, in the middle of the Bahama chain. This was probably Watlings Island. Its appearance from the sea has not changed greatly. The tall trees have gone, replaced by sun-bleached scrub, but the low cliffs, the sandy beaches and the dangerous ring of reefs are much as Columbus found them. The island was inhabited. Its people were primitive and naked, "poor in everything" as Columbus put it, but they possessed canoes and were skilled in using them. Once more European ships had entered a new area—new to them—of maritime communication. During the next three months of exploring among the islands, Columbus—insofar as he could understand their signs—could obtain from the inhabitants of each island a course for the next, and some indication of what other islands had to offer. These indications he could interpret in the light of what he himself hoped to find.

One might expect the untilled sandy islands of the Bahamas and their simple Arawak inhabitants to have been a grievous disappointment to Columbus and his companions; but the impression conveyed by the *Journal* is less of disappointment than of delight in having made a discovery, the expectation of more and better discoveries, and an anxious determination to represent everything in the best possible light.

Primitive the natives might be, wrote Columbus, but they were also friendly, ingenuous, docile; they would be—both thoughts automatically entered the fifteenth-century European mind—willing converts and tractable servants; and Columbus proposed to entice or kidnap a few, as samples. A similar determination and delight filled his descriptions of the natural scene, the trees, the most beautiful he had ever seen, "as green and leafy as those of Castile in the months of April and May," the land "the best and most fertile and temperate and goodly land that there is in the world." We need not accuse Columbus of deliberate exaggeration; any land looks attractive to a man who has been long at sea, and no doubt the islands were then greener, more forested, than they are now. Everywhere he went Columbus picked twigs and leaves of aromatic trees—of which there are many in the West Indies—as samples of "spices."

Slaves and wild spices, however, were not among the principal objects of the expedition; and clearly neither Watlings Island, nor Long Island, nor Rum Cay, was Cipangu. Columbus had, of course, no precise notion of where he was. He believed himself to be somewhere in an extensive archipelago, which included Cipangu among many other, smaller islands, all lying off the east coast of Cathay or Mangi. The mainland coast lay to the west, but at a considerable distance. Not knowing where in the archipelago he was, Columbus could not know the bearing of Cipangu, except that, obviously, it could not lie between east and northeast; but it was probably nearer than the mainland. The plan, therefore, which Columbus set out in his *Journal* on October 21—being then at anchor, probably off Fortune Island—was first to find Cipangu, and

OPPOSITE: Marine life in the Tropics, from de Bry's *Voyages*

later, if possible, sail on to Quinsay on the mainland.

Columbus's wanderings among the islands show an apparent aimlessness, in sharp contrast with the steady determination of his westward course across the ocean; they had, nevertheless, a perverse consistency. The one characteristic of Cipangu on which all reports agreed was the abundance of gold. Here and there in most of the islands, natives were seen wearing small scraps of gold as ornaments. The obvious procedure was to ask the owners, by signs, where the gold came from. In interpreting their answering gestures, two general propositions were to be applied: gold came chiefly from hot countries, and hot countries lay south, not north. Everywhere he went, Columbus showed these two preoccupations: an obsession with gold, and a preference—other things being equal—for a southerly over a northerly course of exploration.

With its pressed Indian guides, the fleet steered south-southwest to the north coast of Cuba. Here, "The Admiral says that he never beheld so fair a thing; trees all along the river [where he anchored—probably Bahía Bariay], beautiful and green and different from ours, with flowers and fruits each according to their kind, and little birds which sing very sweetly"; but this, however beautiful, was not Cipangu. The coast ran on north-northwest, so continuously that Columbus began to think that he was off the mainland; but he found no cities, no indication of Quinsay, and after a few days sailing he encountered a "norther" which made further progress impossible. The ships put about and ran southeast down the coast, to shelter in the inlet now known as Puerto Gibara. There the people spent some days exploring and trading ashore.

First of all Europeans, they ate cassava, maize and sweet potatoes (which "tasted like chestnuts") and saw tobacco smoked. They found a variety of spurious spices, but no gold worth mentioning. Then on eastward along the coast. Off Tánamo Bay the ships became separated; Columbus followed the Cuban coast to Cape Maisi and thence sailed southeast by east across the Windward Passage to Port Saint Nicolas on the northwest coast of Hispaniola. Martín Alonso Pinzón, who by this time was on bad terms with Columbus, went off in the *Pinta* (without permission, according to the *Journal*) on a gold search of his own to the east, following a native indication. He found the island of Gran Inagua, but no gold, and eventually, six weeks later, rejoined Columbus on the north coast of Hispaniola.

Cuba had been a heavy disappointment. The initial excitement of discovery had worn off, and though Columbus himself remained in high spirits, the shores they visited must all have seemed much alike to his companions. In Hispaniola prospects brightened; the population was denser, the local economy more developed and varied than any so far encountered, and hammered gold ornaments more plentiful, or at least less rare. The country was fertile and pleasant—the northern plain of Haiti, which in French hands two centuries later was to become briefly the most productive colony in all the Americas. The two ships sailed on east along the coast, beat through the Tortuga Channel, and in Acul Bay made contact, through messengers, with Guacanagarí, the first chief they had encountered of more than merely local influence. Natives in great numbers came on board to trade, with food, including wood ducks—the first

European mention of that beautiful and all-too-edible creature—scraps of gold and skeins of cotton. Wild cotton was extensively used by the Arawaks, who spun it and netted it into hammocks—an important gift of the West Indies to the ships of the world. From Guacanagarí's people the Spaniards got their first firm information about the source of gold. It came from streams in the mountainous area inland, known to the Arawaks as Cibao; and Columbus, presumably from the similarity of the names, formed the conclusion that the great island he was coasting was indeed Cipangu.

In response to invitations from Guacanagarí the ships pressed on, past the rocky headland now called Cap Haitien. A few miles past the cape, they met their first major accident. During the night of Christmas Eve the *Santa María* went on a reef in Caracol Bay. Almost everyone, apparently, was asleep; a state of discipline for which Juan de la Cosa must bear responsibility. The night was fine and the ship might have been kedged off; Columbus blamed la Cosa's disloyalty or cowardice for the ensuing confusion and failure. She broke up and had to be abandoned. Guacanagarí's people in their canoes throughout the next day helped to transfer her stores and gear to a dump ashore. Guacanagarí himself proved friendly and helpful, and his hospitality encouraged Columbus to establish the first—and until then unintended—European settlement in the New World. Columbus had, indeed, no choice; the forty-odd men who had manned the *Santa María* could not have been crowded into the *Niña* for a trans-Atlantic passage. A rude blockhouse was built from the *Santa María*'s timbers, on the open bay which Columbus named Navidad, and about forty men were left behind to man the place, to plant crops and search for gold. None of them was to survive the year.

While all this was going forward, news arrived through native reports that the *Pinta* had been sighted off the coast, and early in January Columbus in *Niña* sailed east to join her, in fear, apparently, that Martín Alonso Pinzón might precede him back to Spain with the news. Pinzón had news indeed. He had sailed south from Inagua and made the north coast of Hispaniola somewhere near Monte Cristi. According to his own story, recorded later, he had been struck by the relative abundance of gold trinkets, had explored inland about fifty miles, and had actually found some of the gold-bearing streams of the Cibao. Columbus himself, not to be outdone, reported finding gold grains in the gravel of the Río Yaque del Norte, near Monte Cristi, where he watered his ships. It is true that the Río Yaque drains the Cibao, and the Cibao streams certainly held gold—they still do, in very small quantities; but no gold was subsequently found in the river. Probably Columbus was deceived—as las Casas suggested—by "fool's gold," pyrite.

It is curious that these promising clues were not more thoroughly investigated; but the expedition was in poor condition for further exploring, with the flagship lost, forty men left behind, and the senior officers at loggerheads. The caravels were riddled with shipworm, and some time had to be spent at Monte Cristi in scraping, caulking and plugging holes. Everyone, including Columbus, apparently wanted to get home. They ran out the north coast as far east as Samaná Bay; there they had another unpleasant experience, their first serious brush with natives.

These Ciguayos, according to las Casas, were all too familiar with Carib raiders. The place is called Las Flechas, The Arrows, to this day. From Samaná Bay, the fleet set sail for Spain.

Columbus's winter passage back to Spain presented far more difficult problems of navigation and seamanship than the outward voyage had done. The trade wind, which had served him well westbound, now became the enemy. He can have had only a rough idea of where he was. During his wanderings among the islands he had made several Polaris observations, which produced impossible results—42 degrees north, on one occasion, the latitude of Cape Cod; a modern study plausibly suggests that he mistook the star Alfirk, which then bore due

The earliest known drawing of a hammock, from Oviedo's *Historia General*, 1535

north, for Polaris. Wisely, he discarded these results and relied on dead reckoning. He must have known that he was in a latitude well to the south of the Canary Islands—Samaná Bay is in fact in 19 degrees north—and in a latitude where easterly winds blew steadily across the Atlantic. He knew that in the eastern Atlantic westerly winds could be expected in the winter months in the latitudes of Portugal. It was reasonable to hope that these westerly winds, like the trade winds, prevailed clear across the ocean. The obvious strategy was to work to the north, close-hauled on the trade wind, making as much easting as possible in the process, until in roughly the latitude of Cape St. Vincent, and then, if the wind allowed, run east. Whether this was obvious to Columbus may be doubted. In the *Journal* for January 16, the day he left Samaná Bay, he wrote of "the direct course for Spain, N.E. by E." If he really meant to follow a rhumb-line course northeast by east for the whole passage, it would have put him somewhere off North Cape; but with the trade wind blowing, northeast by east was impossible. In the event, whether by luck or judgment, he sailed nearly the best possible course throughout most of the passage.

For about three weeks the caravels made northing steadily, on a course first north by east, then north-northeast, then northeast. Their weatherly qualities had never been so well demonstrated as in this part of the passage; sea-worn as they were, their performance was remarkably good. When at last the wind hauled west, Columbus estimated from the altitude of Polaris (by naked eye, because the ship was rolling too much for the quadrant) that he was in the latitude of Cape St. Vincent, *i.e.* 37 degrees

north; so he altered course due east. According to a careful modern reconstruction of his track, from his dead reckoning, he was actually in about 34 degrees north. A course due east would have taken him to the coast of Morocco; but his course made good was somewhat north of east, because—not knowing its value—he made no allowance for westerly compass variation. The two errors more or less canceled one another. If the weather had held, he would probably have sighted land somewhere near Cape St. Vincent. His estimates of his position on this passage, though out by several hundred miles, were nearer the truth than those of his navigating officers, who also differed considerably among themselves. As they were passing south of the Azores, however, all calculations were brushed aside by a heavy storm. The ships became separated, and Columbus in the *Niña* found himself unexpectedly off Santa María, the southernmost island of the group, and one of the smallest.

Columbus had not intended to approach any Portuguese harbor, for obvious reasons; but at that juncture any shelter was welcome. His reception there was grudging and suspicious; attempts were made to arrest him and his people, and he had some difficulty in getting away when the wind abated; but at least he knew where he was. His course for Cape St. Vincent was due east; but again he was forced off it by a storm of unusual violence; sighted land, uncomfortably close, at Cape Roca; and was obliged to enter the Tagus for shelter and refit. Lisbon was the last place Columbus would have chosen for the end of his ocean passage. John II and his advisers were not likely to be pleased with him; if they seriously suspected him of trespassing in

Portuguese preserves, they would probably arrest his ship. According to Rui de Pina's chronicle, Columbus himself was in some personal danger; there were those about the King who wanted him quietly murdered. In the event, however, he was received in audience; his story was heard with close but courteous interest; the needs of his ship were supplied in the royal yards; and he was allowed to proceed.

What passed in the King's mind can only be guessed. Probably he accepted Columbus's story but made generous allowance for Italian exaggeration. The discoverer's account of Hispaniola and Cuba, his party of naked "Indians," even his gold trinkets, did not suggest the silken East. If Columbus had indeed discovered part of the "Indies," it was a part in which Portugal was not immediately interested; if, as was more likely, he had found an extensive but remote group of oceanic islands, Portuguese plans need not be seriously endangered. Probably the legend of Antilla came to Columbus's help; it was the Portuguese, not the Spaniards, who first applied the name "As Antilhas" to the new discoveries. In any event, the arrest or murder of Columbus might lead to serious trouble with Castile, and might not even be effective in suppressing knowledge of his discovery. Nothing had been heard of Martín Alonso Pinzón, who might already have arrived with the news. (In fact, he had made the land at Bayona, near Vigo in Galicia, and was on his way south.) Nothing, in short, was to be gained by quarreling with Castile over islands which appeared to be of no outstanding value. Portuguese diplomacy thereafter worked not to assert a serious Portuguese claim to the Antilles, but to ensure that the discovery should not lead

to Castilian voyages in the south Atlantic.

Columbus returned to the port from which he had sailed, Palos, in mid-March 1493. The entire voyage had taken thirty-two weeks. It is tempting to imagine that his thoughts, as the *Niña* rounded Cape St. Vincent, turned to Prince Henry, and to the great strides which discovery had made since Gil Eannes reached Cape Bojador. Probably, however, he had other matters on his mind. The *Pinta* was close behind him, and by ironic coincidence the two ships came up the river on the same tide. Whether they spoke, we do not know; Martín Alonso Pinzón was dying. He gave Columbus no more trouble, though his descendants contended with Columbus's heirs in the courts for many years. Columbus himself—who had already sent a brief report overland from Lisbon—despatched a messenger on the eight-hundred-mile ride to Barcelona, where the sovereigns were residing. Within three weeks their answer came back: an order to proceed at once to court, addressed to "Don Cristóbal Colón, their Admiral of the Ocean Sea, Viceroy and Governor of the Islands that he hath discovered in the Indies." Thus promptly, his success was recognized, and all the rewards he had been promised confirmed.

In Spain Columbus was dealing with a government much less informed in geographical matters than that of Portugal, much more willing to share his own enthusiasm. Ferdinand and Isabella, unlike John II, seem initially to have accepted without question not only the fact of Columbus's success, but broadly his own interpretation of it; and their minds turned promptly to the problems of exploitation and development. Columbus had discovered in their name a westward short cut and a series of stepping stones to Asia, to the "Indies"; what were they to do with it? The voyage, though successful, had been expensive; it was essential to follow up the discovery and produce a return on the investment; essential also to assert possession before foreign competitors could move in. Immediately on receipt of Columbus's first report, and even before his arrival in their presence, the sovereigns commanded him to begin preparations for a second voyage.

The big fleet—seventeen sail—which Columbus took out to the West Indies in the autumn of 1493 was got ready in the short space of five months. There was no lack of volunteers to man it. Its composition, no less than the instructions which the admiral carried, indicated the purpose for which it was sent. It contained no heavily armed fighting ships; it carried no trade goods, other than small truck for barter. Its chief cargo was men: twelve hundred people, priests, officials, artisans, farmers; and agricultural stock: tools, seed and animals; a whole society in miniature. The immediate object of the voyage, clearly, was not to open a new trade or conquer oriental kingdoms, but to settle the island of Hispaniola, to found a mining and farming colony which should produce its own food, pay the cost of the voyage by remitting gold to Spain, and serve at the same time as a base for further exploration in the direction of Cipangu and Cathay.

While these preparations were going forward, the sovereigns took steps to protect their legal and diplomatic position and to forestall Portuguese objections. They began by seeking papal support for a monopoly of navigation and settlement in the seas and lands which Columbus had discovered. The Pope had the right and the duty to provide for the instruction and conversion of pagan peoples; this no Catholic could deny. By extension, in the opinion of some canonists at least, he might grant corresponding temporal sovereignty in territory not claimed by Christian princes. The Portuguese Crown had invoked these doctrines in the past; now it was the turn of Castile. The Pope of the time, Alexander VI, was a Spaniard, already under heavy obligations to the Spanish monarchs, and looking to them for support in his endeavor to create a principality for his son in Italy. He issued a series of Bulls, each successively strengthening and extending the provisions of the preceding ones, in accordance with successive demands made by Ferdinand and Isabella, upon Columbus's advice.

The first two Bulls granted to the sovereigns of Castile all lands discovered, or to be discovered, in the regions explored by Columbus; but this was too limiting. The Portuguese already claimed, under the Bull *Aeterni Regis* of 1481, a monopoly of navigation south of the Canary Islands and west of Guinea; Columbus wished to sail in latitudes south of that of the Canaries. The third Bull, accordingly, the famous *Inter caetera,* drew an imaginary boundary line from north to south a hundred leagues west of the Azores and Cape Verde Islands, and provided that the land and sea beyond the line should be reserved for Spanish exploration. The fourth, *Dudum siquidem,* extended the previous grants to include "all islands and mainlands whatever, found or to be found . . . in sailing or travelling towards the west and south, whether they be in regions occidental or meridional and oriental and of India."

Dudum siquidem, with its specific reference to

India, caused serious alarm in Portugal, and all the resources of Portuguese diplomacy were used to limit its effect. Unable to move the Pope, John II opened direct negotiations with Ferdinand and Isabella. Dropping any possible claim to Columbus's islands, he accepted the Bull of Demarcation, *Inter caetera,* as a basis for discussion, but asked that the boundary line be moved 270 leagues farther west, to protect his African interests. The Spanish monarchs, secure in the delusion which Columbus had fostered concerning the western route to Asia, agreed. Both sides must have known that so vague a boundary could not be accurately fixed. The longitudes of the Azores and the Cape Verde Islands are, in fact, different; neither was accurately known; distances could be measured only approximately; and no one could mark the sea. Both sides, however, were anxious to avoid an open quarrel; and since their immediate objects did not conflict, a rough formula sufficed. The treaty of Tordesillas was duly signed in 1494: a notable diplomatic success for Portugal, excluding Spaniards from the route to India and —as shortly afterwards appeared—from Brazil.

What was Columbus's contribution to the discovery of the sea? Chiefly, that he set bounds to the Atlantic. The Ocean Sea, except at its narrow, island-studded Arctic extremity, had seemed for practical purposes limitless. After Columbus it became finite: five weeks' trade-wind sailing took one to the other side. Columbus in fact crossed the Atlantic at almost its widest point, if the great indentation of the Caribbean be excluded. His first voyage, it is true, revealed only islands, though islands bigger and more numerous than in any of the Atlantic groups then occupied by Iberians, and far more attractive

than any in the Arctic. His later voyages, however, found stretches of mainland coast. Younger contemporaries—Cabot, Cabral, Vespucci, Ojeda—added longer stretches, which quickly appeared on a series of early sixteenth-century maps. Within little more than a generation, the Atlantic was revealed in roughly its true shape: an immense canal running north and south between two continuous continental coasts.

Columbus was directly responsible for the colossal error of identification which made the western shore of the Atlantic part of Asia. We have traced the arguments by which he deceived himself and others. Probably the deception was essential not only to the initial enterprise, but also to the further progress of discovery. It is unlikely that the Caribbean, for example, would have been so promptly and eagerly explored, had the explorers not been given reason to hope for a short cut to Cathay. Shrewd geographers, to be sure, soon decided that Hispaniola was not Japan, that Cuba was a long way from China and farther still from India; but for many years many of them continued to believe that the new discoveries were connected with Asia in some way. Traces of their belief lingered in language long after the geographical facts became known. For three hundred years after Columbus's landfall, the lands he discovered were known as the Indies of the Crown of Castile; their native inhabitants—those who survive—are known as Indians to this day.

Columbus and his companions were the first Europeans to set foot in the tropical New World; the first to make contact with a great branch of the human race which for many millennia had been almost entirely isolated from the rest of

OPPOSITE: Columbus discovering the New World; allegorical engraving from de Bry's *Voyages*

mankind. Columbus was the first to make systematic proposals for European settlement; and Columbus was responsible initially for carrying the proposals into practice. Unlike the brief Norse encampments in Newfoundland, Columbus's precarious colony in Hispaniola managed somehow to survive and grow. Columbus is commonly said to have "discovered America"; but America, in the sense in which the word is used today, is a European invention. It was created by Europeans who, as time went on, crossed the Atlantic in thousands, eventually millions, taking European culture with them in simplified, diluted form, and spreading it on a vastly expanded scale all over the New World. It would be more accurate to say that Columbus found the materials of which an America could be constructed. The New World which he discovered has all but disappeared.

A New World?

olumbus's Journal *disappeared into the Spanish archives,* and in its original, complete form was probably never read except by a few officials. On the return voyage, however, probably at the Azores, Columbus composed a summary or preliminary letter, which he apparently sent on ahead to Barcelona, keeping the *Journal* manuscript with him to be presented to the sovereigns in person. This letter was copied and distributed to various officials, including Luis de Santángel, who had played so vital a part in mounting the expedition. Whatever the precise channel of transmission, it quickly got into the printers' hands, and was published in pamphlet or newsletter form in a number of editions in Spanish, in Latin and in Italian. It circulated widely, in some parts of Europe at least, and aroused considerable interest. The news of Columbus's exploit, therefore, was announced to the reading public more or less in Columbus's own words, with Columbus's own interpretation of the geographical significance of his discovery.

European reactions to the announcement were very diverse. No comment came from Portugal. The official Portuguese view of the matter was that Columbus had found yet another group of Atlantic islands; as far as Portugal was concerned, the Spaniards were welcome to occupy and exploit those islands, provided that they kept away from

Guinea and out of the south Atlantic. After the conclusion of the Tordesillas negotiations, the Portuguese lost interest in Columbus. In northern Europe the news traveled slowly and was received at first with comparative indifference. Latin editions of Columbus's *Letter* were printed in Basel and Antwerp in 1494, but no German translation appeared until 1497. The *Nürnberg Chronicle,* which was printed four months after Columbus's return, makes no mention of him.

The most complete and enthusiastic acceptance of Columbus's news, as might be expected, was in Spain. Well before Columbus's appearance at court the Duke of Medina Celi—who had probably received intelligence overland—wrote in a private letter that Columbus had arrived in Lisbon, having found all that he went to seek. Both in Barcelona and in Seville, the Indies, the negotiations with the Papacy, and the assembly of the second fleet must have been topics of common gossip; Spanish opinion, for what it was worth, seems to have followed the royal lead and accepted Columbus's claims at his own valuation.

The great clearing-houses of geographical information, however, were in Italy, and Italy provided the most sensitive and the most interesting reactions. The news traveled rapidly, not only through printings of Columbus's *Letter* but also through private letters written by Italian diplomats and businessmen in Spain to correspondents at home. The lively interest revealed in these letters, and subsequent comment on them, was chiefly literary and scientific. All the writers mention gold; gold strikes are always interesting and the fact that the gold of Hispaniola was found in river beds recalled, for the well-read, the legend of King

Midas and the River Pactolus. Another favorite topic was the prelapsarian innocence of the natives of Columbus's islands, their peaceable disposition, their lack of weapons, above all their nakedness. Animals and plants, particularly crocodiles (presumably iguanas), parrots, and naturally, spice-bearing trees, provoked some comment. Few of the early newsmongers, on the other hand, showed much interest in the precise geographical location of the new discoveries. Phrases such as "islands in the Indian Ocean," "islands of India," "islands towards the Orient" occur in most of the surviving letters; but Asia, as everyone who had read Marco Polo knew, covered an immense area and its peoples were extremely diverse. This knowledge, perhaps, explains the initial Italian indifference to the commercial implications of Columbus's voyage. Even in Venetian comment there was no hint of alarm, no indication of fear that the westward passage to the Indies might undercut and damage the oriental trade which brought such profits to Venice. Informed Italian opinion seems to have accepted, at first, that Columbus's islands lay in, or near, some region of Asia, but a remote and primitive region, far from any of the places in which Europeans were commercially interested.

The question of geographical location had to be faced sooner or later. Gold in Hispaniola might be a sufficient reason for settlement there; but was the settlement to be an end in itself, or a stage in commercial contact with richer, more civilized oriental countries? Funds for investment were not unlimited; should the main emphasis be upon settlers and their stock, miners and their tools? or upon explorers and their ships, merchants and their goods? There was always the nagging possibility that the Portuguese were right and Columbus wildly wrong; that the new discoveries lay out in the Ocean Sea, nowhere near Asia. And even if Columbus were right, even if his "islands and mainland" were really part of Asia, how far were they from the Spicery? Were they "the Indies"? Were they a "New World"?

The first writer to address himself systematically to these questions was the worldly and cultivated cleric and humanist, Peter Martyr, an Italian by birth and upbringing but a Spaniard by choice, resident for most of his life at the Castilian court. Peter Martyr was a prodigious letter writer, who supplied news and gossip in voluble Latin to many eminent correspondents, mostly in Italy. His official duties—he was chaplain to Isabella and an apostolic protonotary —kept him about the court and gave him opportunities to question returned explorers; but they also left him plenty of time for writing. He was with the court at Barcelona when Columbus arrived there in April 1493. He did not immediately jump to the conclusion that something important had happened. His first allusion to the event was a perfunctory remark, seven weeks after Columbus's return, that a certain Colonus had returned from the western antipodes with samples of gold; but as time went on he became more and more interested and concentrated his letter-writing more and more upon western discovery. Eventually he compiled from his conversations and letters a connected history, *De Orbe Novo*. His work is marred in places by haste, by the wish to get the latest news out quickly; and by heavy reliance on the personal reports of explorers, who were not always objective interpreters of their own achievements. It remains, nevertheless, the earliest and one of the best connected accounts of the discovery of the New World, and of the intellectual reactions to discovery in European learned circles. Peter Martyr never went to the New World, but he became titular bishop of Jamaica and ended his life as a respected councillor of the Indies.

Peter Martyr's detailed and critical accounts began in the autumn of 1493. "A certain Colonus," he wrote in October, "has sailed to the western antipodes, even to the Indian coast, as he believes. He has discovered many islands which are thought to be those of which mention is made by cosmographers, beyond the eastern ocean and adjacent to India. I do not wholly deny this, although the size of the globe seems to suggest otherwise, for there are not wanting those who think the Indian coast to be a short distance from the end of Spain. . . . Enough for us that the hidden half of the globe is brought to light, and the Portuguese daily go farther and farther beyond the equator. Thus shores unknown will soon become accessible; for one in emulation of another sets forth on labours and mighty perils." Here, in a few pointed words, was the whole question. Castile, a late-comer to ocean exploration, had challenged Portugal in a maritime race to Asia, sailing west while the Portuguese sailed east. The Spaniards, relying on Columbus, believed themselves to be in the lead. From Portugal came only an impenetrable silence; the keels of Vasco da Gama's ships were not yet laid. Like most people in Spain who thought of the matter, Peter Martyr wanted to believe Columbus; but he was conscious of intellectual difficulties, among which the most serious was the Admiral's procrustean treatment of Ptolemy.

The dilemma persisted. In November (writing to Cardinal Sforza) Peter Martyr wrote of *Colonus ille Novi Orbis repertor,* "that discoverer of a New World." This looks like a change of mind; but too much should not be made of a conventional phrase. Columbus himself sometimes spoke of *otro mundo,* "another world." Peter Martyr on other occasions used the words in direct connection with Asian names. Late in 1494, after the first news had arrived of Columbus's doings on his second voyage, "Daily more and more marvels from the New World are reported through that Genoese Colonus the Admiral. . . . He says that he has run over the globe so far from Hispaniola that he has reached the Golden Chersonese, which is the furthest extremity of the known globe in the east." A little later, "When treating of this country one must speak of a New World, so distant is it and so devoid of civilization and religion"; but at the same time "The Admiral despatched some thirty of his men to explore the district of Cipangu which is still called Cibao." The Golden Chersonese was the Ptolemaic name for the Malay peninsula; Cipangu was Japan. It was not necessarily inconsistent to describe as a New World places which were believed to be remote parts of Asia; they were new to Europeans. Nor did the simplicity of the New World natives necessarily prove that they were not Asian; Nicolò de' Conti had reported some very primitive people in Asia. If the Caribs ate their neighbors, so, according to Conti, did the Bataks of Sumatra. On the whole, Peter Martyr for some years inclined to give Columbus the benefit of the doubt and to bring up in his support Pliny, the crocodiles and the parrots.

The relation of Columbus's primitive islands to more desirable, more civilized parts of Asia could be established only by further exploration. Columbus took the lead, in his voyage of 1493–96. Profiting by the experience of the first voyage, he followed the best possible route across the Atlantic, somewhat to the south of his original course. The fleet made a prosperous passage, with the trade wind all the way, and a good landfall at Dominica, the wild Carib island whose sharp volcanic spires were to be, for thousands of travelers, their first glimpse of the New World; though for many years none settled there. They sailed on along the beautiful arc of the Lesser Antilles, through the Virgin Islands, along the south coast of Puerto Rico and so, guided by their returning "Indians," across the Mona Passage to the north coast of Hispaniola.

Here Columbus's good fortune ended. The original settlement had been wiped out; Columbus ordered the site to be searched for buried gold, but there was none. A new colony had to be started on a new site; the local natives neither could nor would support it. The undisciplined mob which landed from the second fleet gave constant trouble and suffered great hardship. The available food was unfamiliar, unpalatable and scanty. Exposure—not, indeed, to cold, but to frequent rain—took its toll. Search in the Cibao produced gold, but not enough to justify an early return to Spain. Exploration by sea revealed only the south coast of Cuba, with its harsh xerophytic vegetation, its eastern rocks and mountains, its western shoals and mangroves, as far west as Bahía Cortés, fifty miles short of its western extremity; and Jamaica. Columbus was much impressed—as well he might be—by the beauty of Jamaica, and noticed the great size and good workmanship of the

dugout canoes in use there (a skill which modern Jamaicans have to some extent inherited); but what did all this amount to? Jamaica was profitless. No one in Spain was much impressed by Columbus's insistence that Cuba was a mainland coast. He had simply found more islands, all much alike. Where was the mainland?

Columbus actually found mainland on his third transatlantic voyage. This was a much more modest expedition than the second; three vessels for Hispaniola direct, with supplies, and three for discovery. Disquieting news had trickled back from Hispaniola, and Columbus had difficulty in manning his ships; jails were opened and pardons offered for the purpose. The route for discovery was much farther south than on either of the previous voyages. According to las Casas, who made an abstract of the *Journal* of this voyage, as he had done of the first, Columbus had heard in conversation with the King of Portugal (presumably in 1493) of a continental extent of land in the Atlantic west of Guinea. There is no good ground for identifying this with any particular land—Brazil, for example—discovered or to be discovered; it may equally well have been a hypothetical antipodean continent suggested by one or other of the academic geographers; Vincent of Beauvais, perhaps. Apparently Columbus proposed to look for this continent, among other objectives. His own predilection for exploring to the south of his original landfall in the West Indies has already been noted; south was the direction for "gold and things of value." So he proposed to cross the Atlantic in the latitude of Sierra Leone as far as the meridian of Hispaniola and then, if no land had been found, turn south.

With this intention, Columbus sailed in 1498 by way of Madeira and Gomera to the Cape Verde Islands. Castile and Portugal were then on friendly terms, and the captain of Boavista offered the facilities of his island, which did not amount to much. Columbus, apparently, had never been in the Cape Verdes before, and was surprised to find them so parched and sterile. From there, he steered southwest for a week, until the Doldrum calms brought the fleet to a standstill. They drifted for eight days; eventually they caught the northern edge of the southeast trade wind, approximately in the latitude of Sierra Leone; steered west, and made their landfall at Galeota Point, at the southeastern extremity of the island of Trinidad. Columbus made no doubt that it was an island, for he sailed through the dangerous channel which he named the Serpent's Mouth, along the south and west coast, and out to the open sea through the Dragon's Mouth. He seems to have thought initially that the Paría peninsula was also an island; curiously, since he had noticed the great volume of fresh muddy water in the Gulf of Paría flowing from the mouths of the Orinoco. The Orinoco, however, like many of the world's biggest rivers, is unimpressive from the sea. It is so big that it does not look like a river, and its vast muddy delta stretches flat and low-lying for many miles. Not until he had cruised for a considerable distance along the north coast of the Paría peninsula, did the Admiral grasp that he had found a continent. He chose then to identify Paría with the Garden of Eden, the terrestrial Paradise which lay, according to Isidore of Seville and many others, at the farthest extremity of the East.

Columbus had found pearls in Paría, worn by native women. He did not find their source, which was Margarita Island off the Venezuelan coast, because he was in a hurry to get back to strife-torn Hispaniola. Over and over again it was Columbus's fate to be diverted at the brink of a major discovery. The news of pearls attracted a series of lesser adventurers, many of whom had sailed with Columbus on the earlier voyages: Alonso de Ojeda, Juan de la Cosa, Cristóbal Guerra, Diego de Lepe, Peralonso Niño, Vicente Yáñez Pinzón. The Spanish government, eager for profit, anxious to have the identity of its New World established, conscious of the Admiral's failing powers, allowed these men to make voyages in infringement of what Columbus considered to be his monopoly. This was the time of Columbus's supersession as governor of Hispaniola, and his temporary disgrace. Some of the interlopers—Niño and Guerra—made fortunes from Margarita pearls; others, notably Pinzón, lost men, ships and investment; all made their contributions to geographical knowledge, though probably this was not their primary concern.

Ojeda in 1499 made the coast of Guiana and sailed west as far as the Gulf of Maracaibo. Pinzón in the same year found a great river which may have been the Amazon (as he later claimed) or as probably the eastern mouth of the Orinoco. In 1500 Rodrigo de Bastidas and Juan de la Cosa made a more leisurely examination of the Venezuela coast, with frequent stops for trade with the natives, and sailed west beyond Cape de la Vela, across the mouth of the Gulf of Urabá and a short distance along the Isthmus coast. These were all Spanish expeditions, which began their exploration west of the line of demarcation and dutifully sailed west.

The first recorded Portuguese landfall on what later came to be called South America occurred in the same year, 1500, as an incident in a voyage to India. After Vasco da Gama's return, a second and larger fleet had been despatched from Portugal under the command of Pero Alvares Cabral. Cabral had left Lisbon earlier in the year than da Gama had done, in March, and had sailed farther south before he found the southeast trade wind. On da Gama's advice, he had taken his departure from the Cape Verde Islands in a southwesterly instead of a southeasterly direction. More fortunate than Columbus, who had done the same thing two years before, he was not seriously delayed by Doldrum calms, but made his passage through the central Atlantic somewhat farther west than da Gama. He sighted the coast of Brazil in about 17 degrees south: the commanding height of Monte Pascoal, about two hundred miles south of modern Bahia.

So far as we know, the sighting was unexpected. There is no suggestion in contemporary accounts, it is true, of a deviation from the course to the Cape, such as might have been caused by storm or navigational error. It is possible that Cabral had been instructed to look for a coast whose existence was already known or suspected; but there is no evidence of such an instruction, and the normal trade wind—which, within a general pattern, is capable of wide variation—could easily have put him over to the Brazil coast. Being by then near the southern limit of the southeast trade wind, Cabral could probably have worked off without much difficulty; but he decided, very naturally, to close the land and investigate. He spent only a few days at anchor, in the harbor which he called Porto Seguro, before sailing on to India; but he

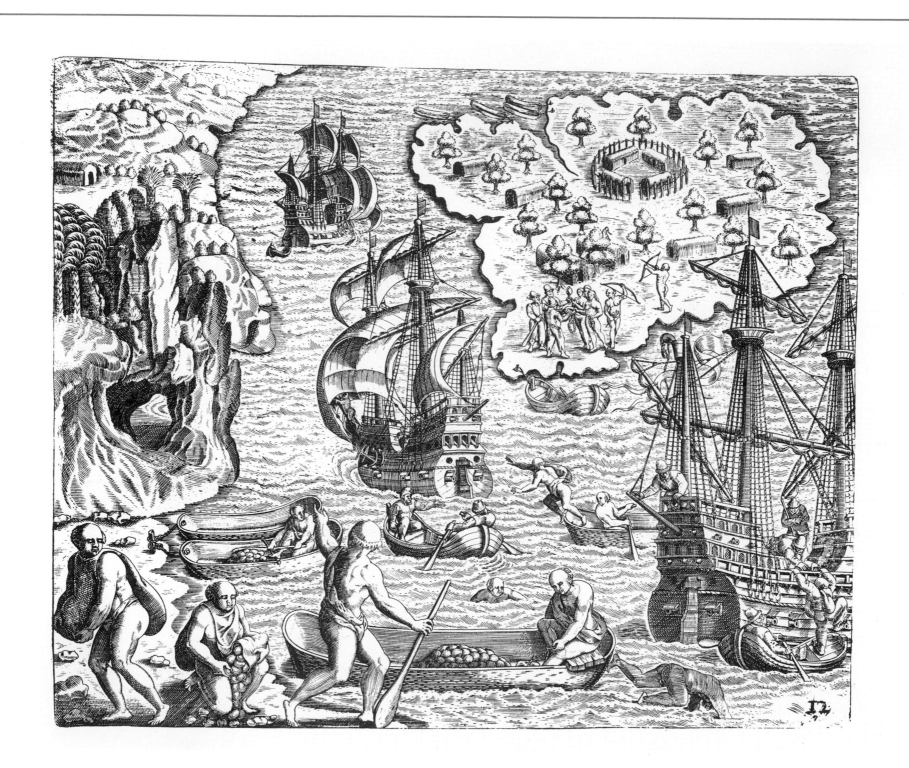

was sufficiently impressed by the importance of the discovery to give it a name—Santa Cruz—and to send a ship back to Portugal to report.

Cabral's Porto Seguro was at least two thousand miles from the nearest point the Spaniards were known to have touched, and the question naturally arose of whether a continuous coastline connected the two areas, or whether Monte Pascoal and its surroundings were merely another large island. They were assumed, correctly, to lie on the Portuguese side of the Tordesillas line; a continuous continental coastline would have the effect—if the treaty were strictly interpreted—of barring the south Atlantic to Spanish shipping. An answer to this, and to several other questions about what is now called South America, was provided by that enigmatic personage, Amerigo Vespucci.

Vespucci's place in the story of the discovery of the sea has always been difficult to assess; accusations and counter-accusations of fraud and charlatanism have surrounded his name from his own time to the present. The controversies have usually concentrated on the justice, or otherwise, of attaching Vespucci's name, rather than that of Columbus, to the continent of America; a question of mainly academic interest today, and one on which there is plenty of room for difference of opinion. The basic facts of his career, by contrast, are relatively clear. Vespucci was a businessman, a man of substance, and indeed of some eminence in his native Florence. He first went to Spain in 1492 as a representative of the Medici, engaged, among other duties, in the supervision of marine supply contracts. His study of geography and navigation was a pastime, though one which, to judge from his letters, he pursued systematically and seriously. His residence in Seville gave him the opportunity to apply his theoretical knowledge to practical ends, and in early middle age he left his business concerns and joined the procession of explorers engaged in following up Columbus's discoveries. He took a prominent part in two major voyages of discovery, one in Spanish ships in 1499, the other in 1501 under Portuguese auspices. Other voyages attributed to him are probably apocryphal. His reports, and garbled versions of those reports which appeared in print, earned for him a reputation as a geographical expert, highly respected both in Portugal and in Spain. In 1505 he settled permanently in Spain and became naturalized there. In 1508 he was appointed *Piloto mayor,* in charge of the training and licensing of navigators and the preparation and revision of charts for the Indies navigation. He served in that important and responsible office until his death in 1512.

The two Vespucci voyages generally accepted as authentic are described in three manuscript letters addressed to Vespucci's Medici patron, dated respectively in 1500, 1501 and 1502. They are personal rather than official communications, containing detailed descriptions of places and peoples but relatively few navigational data. They are enough, however, in conjunction with contemporary maps, to trace roughly the course of the voyages. On the first, in 1499, Vespucci accompanied Alonso de Ojeda, apparently in the capacity of cosmographer and commercial adviser. They sailed from Cádiz via the Canaries and probably made land somewhere on the coast of what became French Guiana. Here they parted company; Ojeda, who was chiefly interested in pearls, made for París; Vespucci sailed south and east on an extended coastal

OPPOSITE: The Venezuela pearl fishery, from de Bry's *Voyages*

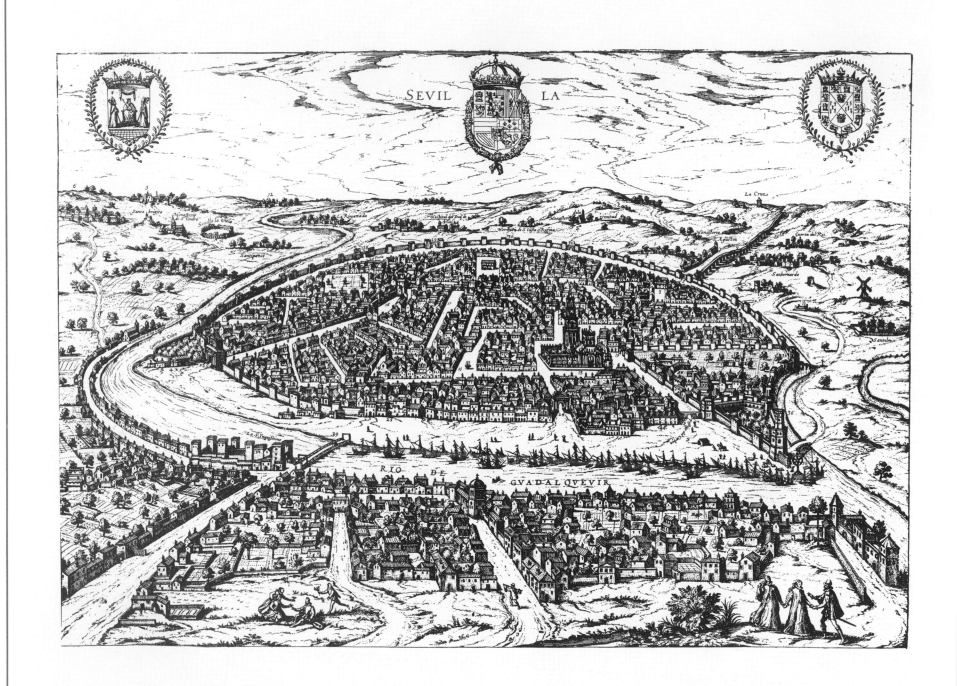

SEVIL LA

reconnaissance. He reported an immense muddy estuary full of islands, the delta of the Amazon and the Pará, and spent twelve days exploring it before continuing to the southeast. Headed by wind and current, he put about somewhere west of Cape São Roque, and sailed northwest in Ojeda's wake. His description of the Guiana coast, with its mud and its mangroves, is recognizably accurate. He visited two of the islands off the Venezuela coast, probably Curaçao and Aruba, and made a disappointing probe into the Gulf of Maracaibo. Like other dedicated explorers, Vespucci might have gone on indefinitely in fascinated curiosity. He was compelled to give up, somewhere in the neighborhood of Cape de la Vela, by shortage of provisions, the ravages of shipworm and the mutinous complainings of his crew. The ships returned to Spain by way of Hispaniola and the Azores, arriving in June 1500; about the time the news of Cabral's landfall reached Lisbon.

Vespucci came back, then, with few pearls but a good deal of valuable information; nor were his inquiries only geographical. While off the Venezuelan coast, he made some interesting and apparently original attempts to calculate longitude from the angular distance, at a precisely fixed moment, between the moon and a star. Before the introduction of chronometers, lunar distance seemed to many astronomers to offer the most promising possibility for longitude determination, and in Cook's day a practicable method was in fact devised. In the sixteenth century, with crude instruments, and without lunar tables, it was impossible for Vespucci or anyone else to make much progress; but the idea was sound, and as far as is known Vespucci was the first seagoing navigator to experiment with it.

In describing this voyage, Vespucci alluded to the area he was exploring as "the Indies," and stated that his intention had been to sail south in the hope of finding the "Cape of Catigara" and rounding it, if a seaway existed, into the "Sinus Magnus" (the Great Gulf which separated "Mangi" from the "Golden Chersonese"). Catigara and Sinus Magnus were, of course, familiar names to students of Ptolemaic maps; and in general, Vespucci's picture of the world, and his estimate of its size, seems to have been derived from Ptolemy. The voyage must have been in this respect a severe disappointment; the great easterly "bulge" of Brazil, the trade wind and the Brazil current together prevented him from sailing south as he wished. Even if he had been able to reach the eastern extremity of the "bulge," moreover, there would still have been a political difficulty; he must have known, or at least suspected, that this great extent of coastline to the east stretched on to the Portuguese side of the Tordesillas line. If he wanted to pursue the search for Catigara, he must begin his coasting farther south and must make his voyage under Portuguese auspices. Like most Italian explorers, Vespucci had no very strong national attachment either to Spain or to Portugal. At some time late in 1500 or early in 1501 he declined a Spanish offer of ships for a second expedition and removed to Lisbon.

Whether Vespucci knew at that time of Cabral's landfall in Brazil is uncertain. That information arrived in Lisbon in the summer of 1500, and for about a year was kept officially secret; but probably sailors gossiped and the word got about. In any event, the Portuguese government wanted a more thorough examination of the "Santa Cruz" coast, and a

OPPOSITE: Seville, from *Civitates Orbis Terrarum,* 1576

more precise estimate of the point at which the Tordesillas line crossed the coast. They found it convenient to employ Vespucci for this purpose, and in May 1501 he sailed from Lisbon in a fleet of three caravels, commanded by Gonzalo Coelho. The expedition made first for Cape Verde, where they met by chance two of Cabral's ships returning from India, and among their company the much-traveled Gaspar da Gama. According to his own account, Vespucci had difficulty in reconciling Gaspar's account of the Indian Ocean with his own interpretation of Ptolemy. He inclined to distrust Gaspar's information and to trust Ptolemy; certainly he was not deterred from the search for Catigara. The ships sailed on across the Atlantic, made their landfall near Cape São Roque, and coasted south.

It is impossible to discover, from Vespucci's surviving manuscript letters, how far he coasted. The figures he gave were eight hundred leagues from the first landfall, to a latitude of 50 degrees south. That would be approximately the latitude of Port Saint Julian on the Patagonian coast, where Magellan later found shelter. Galvão, the only early Portuguese historian even to mention the voyage, says 32 degrees south; and Vespucci's own descriptions of land and people are all of tropical areas. It is uncertain whether the expedition even reached the Río de la Plata. The Canerio map of *c.* 1502–4 marks a Rio Giordan in the correct latitude of the Río de la Plata, and so far as we know this information could only have come from the Vespucci expedition. Unless he passed far out of sight of land, Vespucci could hardly have missed a river which drives muddy water eighty miles out to sea; but the manuscript letters make no mention of it.

Similar mystery surrounds Vespucci's own interpretation of his discoveries. He wrote, of the 1501 voyage, "we came to a new land, which we perceived to be a continent"; but other explorers, including Columbus, who firmly believed their discoveries to be part of Asia, used similar phrases. Vespucci's words do not prove that he considered the coast he was exploring to be a distinct continent, separate from Asia. Equally probably, he thought that he was sailing down the great tongue of land which, in the Ptolemaic maps, stretched from Cathay and Mangi south to the unknown *Terra Australis;* and that Catigara and the strait to the Great Gulf, if any such·existed, lay still farther south. The main, the certain result of Vespucci's two voyages was the knowledge that a great continent existed, with a continuous coastline running thousands of miles from the western extremity of the Caribbean to a point, still to be found, far south of the Tropic of Capricorn.

The surviving letters of Vespucci, we must presume, represent only a fragment of what he must have written, both in official reports and in private correspondence; and no doubt some, at least, of the questions which have puzzled historians were answered in the "little work" which he promised to send to Lorenzo di Pier Francesco de' Medici, when the King of Portugal had finished with it. But Vespucci's friend died in 1503, and the work is lost. In any event, Vespucci's great popular reputation in his own day derived not from his own writings, but from tracts printed in Florence in 1504 and 1505, purporting to be written by him. The first, *Mundus Novus,* is a highly exaggerated account of the 1501 voyage. The second, the so-called Letter to Soderini, attributes four voyages to

Vespucci, apparently by simple analogy with Columbus. Both pamphlets are now generally, though not universally, considered to be forgeries, pirated accounts partly based on Vespucci's reports and letters, partly invented. Both were widely read and went through many editions. Both came to be incorporated in magisterial collections and treatises; from *Mundus Novus* in particular, the idea became general in the mind of the reading public that a new continent had been found and that Amerigo Vespucci had discovered it.

While Columbus, his successors and his imitators were revealing a new continent in the south Atlantic, John Cabot and his successors and imitators were making an analogous but separate series of discoveries much farther north. Cabot was the Columbus of the north Atlantic. We know far less about him than about Columbus himself, but the analogy between them is so close as to suggest conscious imitation. Like Columbus, Cabot—Cabotto, "the coaster"—was a Genoese, though naturalized in Venice. Like Columbus, he peddled an ambitious proposal for western discovery round to several European governments until he found a ruler willing, up to a point, to support him. "Up to a point," because Cabot was expected to raise the necessary money himself; the King merely gave his royal approval, and promised rewards in the event of success. Henry VII of England had not hitherto shown much interest in such projects; he had earlier turned down Columbus's own proposal; possibly he saw in Cabot's offer the chance of retrieving a missed opportunity. Like Columbus, Cabot secured an agreement in general terms; his letters-patent of 1496 authorized him to sail to "all parts, countries and seas . . . unknown to Christians."

Bristol, the base of Cabot's enterprise, like Columbus's Palos, was a small but busy harbor, home port of ships and seamen long interested in Atlantic trade, and to a modest extent in Atlantic exploration. Bristol ships were said to have been engaged for some years past in a search for the island of "Brasill," and according to one report had even sighted it. What exactly the anonymous explorers were looking for, can only be guessed; possibly no more than a new base for an Atlantic fishery, less contentious than Iceland and less dominated by the Hanse Germans. The formality of Cabot's letters-patent, however, and his own subsequent claims, indicate that he himself had something much more ambitious in mind. In any event, he could find in Bristol men and ships apt for long-range discovery. His resources were limited; Bristol investors, perhaps, were skeptical of Italian advertisement; he made his first recorded voyage in 1497 in a single vessel, a small ship, *navicula,* probably about the size of Columbus's *Niña.* According to plausible Bristol tradition, her name was *Mathew.*

Like Columbus, Cabot made an Atlantic crossing on the familiar principle of latitude sailing. He took his final departure from Dursey Head, the northern cape of Bantry Bay in southwestern Ireland, and sailed due west. He sailed in May, usually a good time of year for easterly winds, though probably April would have been better. The outward passage, coast to coast, took thirty-three days, the same time as Columbus's. The distance—1720 nautical miles—was much less than Columbus had covered, but for that latitude it was a good passage. The landfall, most probably, was at the northeastern tip of Newfoundland, not far from where the

Greenlanders, five hundred years before, had tried to make a settlement, though it is unlikely that Cabot knew of that. We have no log, journal or other direct record of his proceedings. According to the most plausible modern reconstruction of his voyage, he sailed down the east coast of Newfoundland, with only one brief landing, rounded Cape Race, probably reached Placentia Bay, and then returned to his original landfall. No contemporary record mentions ice or fog; though surely, off that forbidding iron-bound coast, Cabot must have encountered both. He was back in Bristol in August, having made the whole voyage out and back in the remarkably short time of seventy-seven days.

Cabot, like Columbus, believed that he had found a part—whether islands or a peninsula—of eastern Asia. He thought, apparently, that by following his new-found coast to the southwest, he would come eventually to the inhabited and civilized regions of Cipangu and Cathay. In England his discoveries were called, then and thereafter, simply the New Found Land or New Found Isle; but his own interpretation seems initially to have been accepted. New investment came in, new letters-patent were issued—despite Spanish protests—still in very general terms; and in 1498 Cabot sailed with five ships on a follow-up voyage. Of these five ships, one put into an Irish port in distress when outward bound. No one knows what happened to the others. Juan de la Cosa's map has a long stretch of mainland coast described as "coast discovered by the English," with English names and banners, which might conceivably represent information gleaned from survivors of the 1498 voyage. Equally conceivably, it might represent misinterpretation of the 1497 discoveries; or the results of a later and otherwise unrecorded English voyage; or even simply the cartographer's own imagination and desire to fill up the blanks on his map. The map itself is not certainly known to be an original; it may be a copy; the date, 1500, marked on it, is not beyond question. No independent evidence connects la Cosa's "English coast" with Cabot. So far as surviving record reveals, Cabot's ships disappeared without trace, and Cabot with them.

English interest in northwestern exploration persisted for a few years after Cabot's death. It was stimulated by the arrival in England from the Azores, in 1501, of João Fernandes "the farmer," who claimed knowledge of those waters, and whose nickname is attached, in contemporary maps, either to the territory now called Labrador, or to Greenland; an indication of how completely Norse Greenland had been forgotten. Bristol seamen, usually with Azorean partners, made several voyages into the western Atlantic between 1501 and 1506. These were more than mere fishing voyages, but no surviving record states where the explorers went or what they found. A series of Portuguese expeditions sailing directly from the Azores had more identifiable results. In the first years of the new century the brothers Gaspar and Miguel Corte-Real made between them three, possibly four voyages in the general area of southern Greenland, Labrador and Newfoundland. Like Cabot, they found no spices; but they appreciated the value of Newfoundland as a fishing station and as a source of mast timber, and before their deaths—both were lost at sea—they claimed the whole coast for Portugal. The Cantino chart of 1502, which was made in Portugal, records their discoveries. This is the earliest surviving map to

OPPOSITE: Vespucci; allegorical engraving from de Bry's *Voyages.* He holds a quadrant in his left hand.

FOLLOWING PAGES: The "Cantino" world map, Portuguese, anonymous, 1502

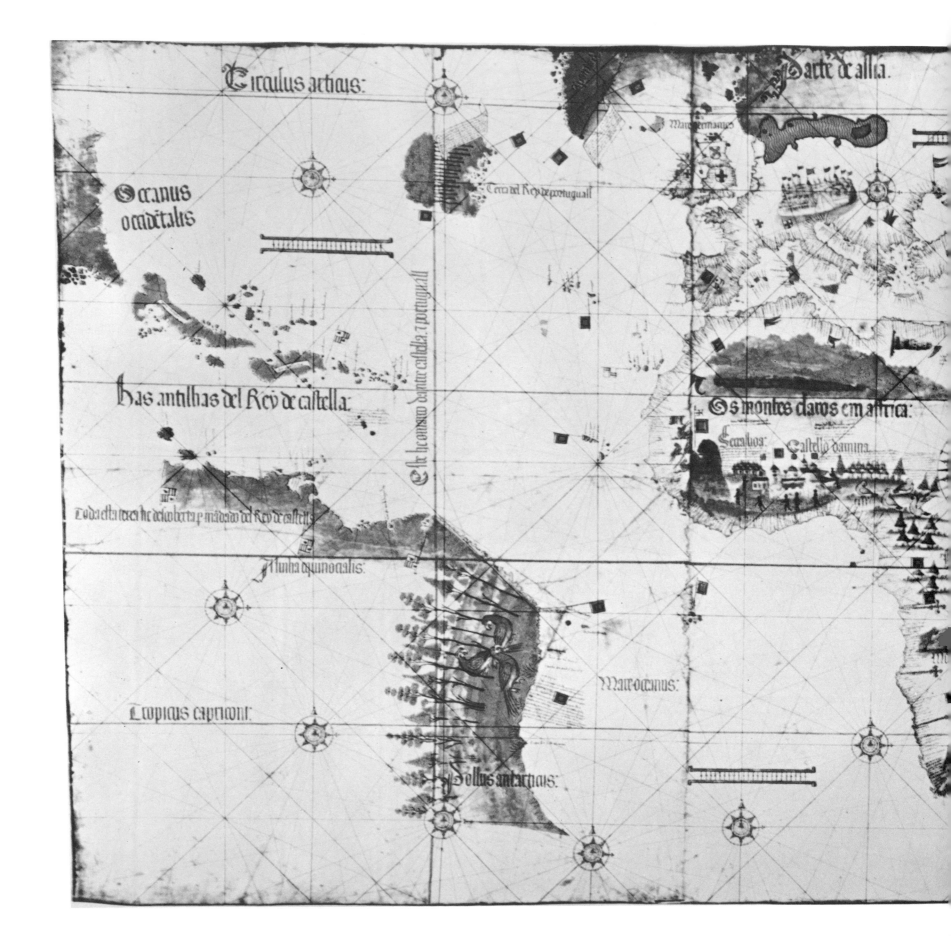

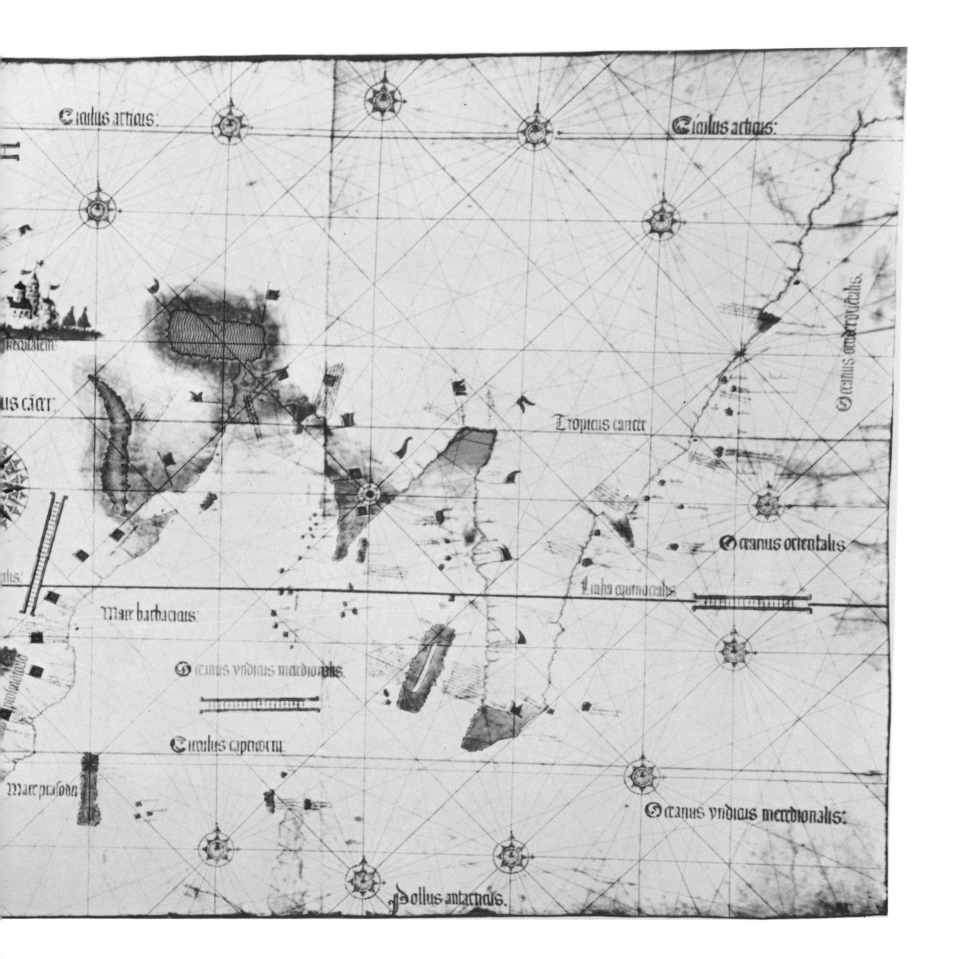

Circulus articus. Circulus articus.

Oceanus ocaeroutalis.

Jerusalem.

us cācer.

Tropicus cancer

Oceanus orientalis

Linha equinocialis

Mare barbaricus.

Oceanus yndicus meridionalis.

Circulus capricorni.

Mare prasodi.

Oceanus yndicus meridionalis:

Pollus antarcticus.

mark the Tordesillas line of demarcation. Just east of the line is a heavily forested land, presumably Newfoundland, firmly labeled *Terra del Rey de Portuguall.* There is no reference to Cabot or to English discoveries. The chief practical result of all this activity—economically a very important result—was the development of the Banks cod fishery, which Cabot had been the first to notice, but which Portuguese fishermen were the first to exploit.

While Cabot and the Corte-Reais were seeking, in the northwest Atlantic, a sea route to Cathay, Vasco da Gama had shown to an envious Europe, and opened for Portugal, the real sea route to India. To Spaniards, the desirable parts of Asia seemed farther away than ever. The first ten years of new-world exploration had revealed a number of sizeable lumps of land; in the southern hemisphere, indeed, a continuous continental mass. A suspicion was growing in some quarters that even the northern lumps might be continuously connected. Juan de la Cosa's map shows two continuous coastlines, one running from an exaggerated Brazil northwest, the other from the Newfoundland region roughly southwest, the two converging towards an indeterminate area lying to the southwest of Hispaniola and a contorted insular Cuba. This unknown area is coyly hidden, in la Cosa's map, by a decorative drawing of St. Christopher. In another respect also, la Cosa apparently "hedged his bets." There is no indication in the map of whether the northern coast represents part of Asia, or part of a separate continent. Its continuity was probably an imaginative conjecture; no existing evidence connects it with actual exploration. Not until Verrazzano's day, a generation later, was la

Cosa's general conception proved correct.

A few of la Cosa's contemporaries followed his lead, but most were more cautious. The Cantino map shows widely scattered land areas: in the south, the great continental mass, decorated by vermilion parrots and bisected by the Line; in the north, Greenland, which appears to be a peninsula, connected with the old world rather than the new; Cape Farewell is "believed to be the point of Asia." Southwest of Greenland is Newfoundland–Labrador, "Terra del Rey de Portuguall." Much farther west are the islands, "Las Antilhas del Rey de Castella." Northwest of Cuba is a large triangular peninsula, its landward boundary indeterminate: possibly Yucatán, more probably Florida. There is no firm surviving record of a discovery of Florida before 1513 or of Yucatán before 1517; but this peninsula looks too circumstantial for guesswork. It is perfectly possible that some Spanish expedition, beating north from the islands on its way back to Spain, had sighted the coast of Florida.

Cartographers were influenced by political as well as by geographical considerations; they were always tempted to depict what their employers wished to see. The last thing la Cosa's Spanish masters wanted was an expanse of open water between Newfoundland and Florida, through which Englishmen or others—not parties to the treaty of Tordesillas nor respectful of papal donations—might venture to Cathay. The unknown Portuguese compiler of the Cantino map, similarly, was almost certainly moved by a desire to put as much land as possible on the Portuguese side of the Tordesillas line; hence his enormous eastward misplacement of Newfoundland. Wherever the line might be drawn, however, one thing was certain: nearly all the discoveries since 1492 had been well to the east of Columbus's original landfall, farther and farther away from the long-sought Spicery to the west. There had been no systematic exploration west of the points on the Cuban coast where Columbus had turned back in 1492 and 1494. Columbus himself had been deflected by his own preconceptions, by the chances of the weather, and by the eagerness of his search for gold. The Portuguese had been inhibited by the treaty of Tordesillas, and after da Gama's return had lost interest, except in the practical matters of dye-wood from Brazil and codfish from the Newfoundland banks. As for the lesser Spanish adventurers—la Cosa among them—who followed in Columbus's wake, they had been more interested in pearling and slaving than in serious exploration. Even the insularity of Cuba, which la Cosa accepted and Columbus indignantly denied, was probably no more than hearsay.

Clearly the desirable parts of Asia could be opened to Spain only by finding a seaway between the various blocks of land with which the cartographers were dotting their maps; and once again it was Columbus who took the lead. Without ever explicitly departing from his belief that the Antilles were part of Asia, he undertook a fourth voyage, a last desperate cast, into the mysterious region which lay beneath the picture of St. Christopher on Juan de la Cosa's map. He had noted, on his third voyage, the strong current setting east to west along the Main coast, and argued, reasonably enough, that this great volume of water must find an outlet. He would sail via the islands to a point beyond where Ojeda and Vespucci had turned back, and follow the current to the west. As before, Genoese

backers seem to have provided some of the money, and a Genoese patrician, Bartolommeo Fieschi, later to become distinguished in other ways, went captain of one of the ships. Another captain, Pedro de Terreros, had been on all three earlier voyages, initially as Columbus's servant; and two other officers, Juan Quintero and Pero Fernandes Coronel, had sailed twice before with Columbus. Difficult character though he was in some ways, Columbus could inspire loyalty. Two devotedly loyal relatives, his brother Bartolomeo and his young son Hernando, accompanied him also. The Crown once again provided the ships; probably the sovereigns were weary of financial importunities and glad to get Columbus out of Spain. It is interesting that they also provided a letter of introduction to Vasco da Gama, in case they should meet in the East.

We know a good deal about this voyage, chiefly from Hernando's *History,* written many years later. Columbus's own account, in the so-called *Lettera Rarissima,* is incoherent, at times hysterical; he was worn out, querulous, becoming prematurely old. Yet sick man though he was, this was to be in many ways a distinguished voyage. The Atlantic crossing may well have been a record for the sixteenth century: twenty-one days from Grand Canary to Martinique. Columbus called at Santo Domingo, contrary to his instructions; was refused permission to land; and rode out a hurricane which wrecked a whole fleet bound for Spain. At Santo Domingo he met survivors of the Bastidas-la Cosa expedition returning from the Main coast, and may have got from them encouraging reports. From Santo Domingo, when the hurricane damage was repaired, the fleet steered west to the "Queen's Gardens" off the south coast of Cuba, and thence southwest. They sighted land at Guanaja, one of the Bay Islands off the north coast of Honduras, and here a familiar dilemma presented itself: could they best circumvent the newly discovered land by turning east, or west?

There were strong arguments for sailing west. One was the prevailing wind, blowing strongly along the coast from the east, with frequent drenching rain. Another argument came in sight as they lay among the islands: an exceptionally large and well-made canoe, "as long as a galley," fitted with an enclosed cabin, "like a gondola," carrying twenty-five men with some women and children, all wearing well-made cotton clothes. The cargo was even more interesting than the people: dyed woven textiles, both in made garments and in the piece; a quantity of small, unfamiliar beans; copper tools and utensils; and weapons—stout staves set along either side with sharp obsidian blades. Columbus's people had intercepted a route of sophisticated trade; they were the first Europeans to handle cacao beans, the common currency of Meso-America, and to examine the *maquauhuitl,* the formidable battle-axe which later, at the conquest of Mexico, was to inflict terrible wounds on Spanish men and horses. The people in the canoe had apparently come from the west: they were either Mayas or, more probably, local coastal traders; but if Columbus had followed their indications he might have found Yucatán with its Maya cities; might even have anticipated, by fifteen years and more, the soldiers of fortune— Hernández, Grijalba, Cortés—who sailed through the Yucatán channel and discovered Aztec Mexico. As well, perhaps, that he did not; Columbus was no Cortés, and his people were

not equipped for serious fighting. He seized the best of the merchandise, detained one of the Indians as a guide, and sailed east.

The reasons for this decision are not difficult to guess. Columbus's plan required him to make more southing. He believed Cuba to be a mainland peninsula. He probably suspected that if he turned west he would find himself sailing along a continuous coast, which would eventually lead him back to Cuba. The fleet beat painfully to the east, taking a month to make less than two hundred miles, until they could round the cape which Columbus named Gracias a Dios. They then sailed south, and spent nine months exploring the coasts of what are now Nicaragua, Costa Rica and the isthmus of Panama—the coast which Columbus named Veragua. Near the site of the modern Panama Canal, the coast trending uncompromisingly east, they turned back.

Veragua showed some promise: settled cultivations, and considerable quantities of alluvial gold; but the natives were fiercely hostile, attempts to establish a settlement failed, men were killed in shoreside fighting when they tried to take on water or buy or steal food, the weather was bad. Eventually Columbus, his ships riddled with worm and opening at the seams, decided, or was persuaded, to return to Hispaniola. By this time he was no longer physically, nor perhaps even mentally, capable of command. Two ships had to be abandoned. The remaining two got no farther than Jamaica where, in a sinking condition, they were run ashore in shallow water in St. Anne's Bay. One of the company, Diego Méndez, succeeded in crossing to Hispaniola in a paddling canoe, to seek help: more than a hundred miles against wind and current from Northeast Cape of

Jamaica to Cape Tiburón, and a further 350 along the coast to Santo Domingo. In later years, Méndez directed in his will that a canoe be carved upon his tombstone. The rest—quarrelsome, demoralized and mutinous—endured a year of waiting for tardy, grudging rescue. When Columbus eventually got back to Spain in 1504, he found the Queen dying, the King indifferent and evasive. He died himself in 1506, unhappy, ignored, though still moderately rich from his share of the Indies revenue and still—when people remembered him—respected.

Columbus's fourth voyage, then, was a failure in its principal purpose. He had explored the eastern end of the Caribbean and found no outlet, no seaway to the civilized parts of Asia. It is impossible to say how many other, unrecorded voyages were made in the same general area in the first few years of the sixteenth century. The maps of the time show many coastal features which bear a recognizable resemblance to reality, but which cannot be associated with any voyage of which record now remains; the Florida of the Cantino map is only one such example. Whether as a result of actual exploration, or of geographical guessing, the maps show the New World growing more solid and detailed year by year; the possibilities of a seaway between its land masses correspondingly more limited. If the New World were not a string of islands but a continuous land mass, or several land masses separated by channels, what connection, if any, had it with Asia? Some cartographers in the first decade of the sixteenth century were already suggesting that it had no connection, that it was a continent, a grand division of the earth separate alike from Europe, Africa and Asia.

In the Cantino map, the east coast of Asia borders on open water; the new-world land masses (except Newfoundland) have no west coast; they are bounded only by the edge of the map. The map, however, covers only 257 degrees of longitude, leaving 103 degrees unaccounted for; and obviously the compiler thought that some of this unknown area was open sea. The somewhat similar manuscript map drawn about 1504 by the Genoese Nicolay Canerio or Caverio, is more specific: it gives the central land mass a western coast line, and a long peninsula or isthmus stretching towards the southern land mass, *Terra Crucis*. On the eastern side of this peninsula or isthmus, it has a large island-studded bay, apparently representing the Gulf of Mexico. Between the central land mass and an insular Newfoundland-Labrador, is open sea. None of the land masses has any connection with Asia.

The tentative suggestions of the Cantino and Canerio maps and many reports of voyages were combined in a splendid synthesis: the huge woodcut world map produced by Martin Waldseemüller at Saint Dié in Lorraine, in 1507. Only one copy of this map now survives; but according to its maker, a thousand copies of the original edition were printed, and its influence on geographical thought was great and lasting. It shows the new world as northern and southern continents, of which the southern is much the larger. In the main map, the two continents are separated by a narrow strait, but in an inset map on the same sheet they are connected by a continuous isthmus. East of the continent or continents is the Atlantic, with Newfoundland-Labrador as an island far off-shore; to the west is another great sea, with the island "Zipangri" in the middle, and its western shore marked "Chatay." The west coast of the New World is conventional, *terra ultra incognita;* but though its configuration is vague, it is undoubtedly a coastline. There is open-water access between the two oceans at both ends of the continent, north-about and south-about, as well as through the problematical strait.

Waldseemüller not only made the New

World unequivocally a separate continent; he also gave it a name which complimented Amerigo Vespucci as its discoverer. Vespucci's fame had spread widely since the first publication of *Mundus Novus* in 1504. The pamphlet got even wider publicity through its inclusion in the collection of accounts of voyages published by Fracanzano da Montalboddo at Vicenza in 1507, under the title *Paesi novamente retrovati.* This work

The New World inset from Waldseemüller's world map, 1507

included Cadamosto's account of his voyages to Guinea; the letters of Girolamo Sernigi describing da Gama's voyage; a narrative of Cabral's voyage; accounts of Columbus, Pinzón and the Corte-Reais; and the Vespucci pamphlet. It was the first great source book of the discoveries, enormously popular and widely influential. It went through six Italian editions, six French and two German.

In the year of the first appearance of the *Paesi,* 1507, Waldseemüller published as a companion to his map his own geographical treatise, *Cosmographiae introductio,* a book which rivaled the *Paesi* in popularity, though not in merit; in it, he also included the Soderini letter, in a Latin version entitled *Quattuor navigationes.* Vespucci's name, through these various channels, became familiar to readers all over Europe. The suggestion, in Waldseemüller's book, that the new continent should be named America, and his use of the name on his map, caught the popular fancy in northern Europe, though not in Spain or Portugal. America meant initially South America; it was extended to include North America only in the later sixteenth century, through Mercator's use of it. Waldseemüller himself soon discarded it; in the map of the New World which he drew for the Strasburg Ptolemy, in 1513, South America is labeled simply *Terra incognita;* but the name America stuck.

Waldseemüller's 1507 map, and even more its new-world inset, provided so neat a solution, and in general conception came so near to the truth, that it might have been expected, with its derivatives, to dominate geographical thought thereafter. Rival geographical theories, however, were still very much alive. The Contarini-Rosselli map of 1506, the first printed map to show any

part of the New World, has the Antilles surrounded by open sea on all sides; to the south is continental South America, *Terra crucis;* to the west, out in the ocean, Cipangu; far to the north, a great peninsula of Asia—*Tanguti provincia magna*—stretches across the map from west to east, terminating in "land found by the King of Portugal's ships," presumably compounded of Greenland, Labrador and Newfoundland. The Ruysch map of 1508 and the manuscript Maggiolo map of 1511 follow, with variants, approximately the same tradition. These "open-water" maps, representing what might loosely be called the Cabot theory of the New World, were already out of date when they were drawn; but they were not without influence. A much more serious obstacle to the general acceptance of Waldseemüller's ideas was the persistence of Ptolemy. It was difficult for academic cosmographers, trained in the tradition of deference to the ancients and familiar with a world-picture based on Ptolemy, to accept a totally new, totally separate continent. They accepted, perforce, the existence of continental land north, west and south of the Antilles, as more and more such land was revealed by exploration; but they felt—rather than reasoned—that this land could, and must, somehow be fitted into the Ptolemaic pattern; must at some point be connected with the continent of Asia. Waldseemüller himself was not immune to doubts, and in 1516 he retreated significantly from his 1507 position. His *Carta marina* of that year shows the central American land mass abutting on the western edge of the map and labeled *Terra de Cuba Asie partis.*

The America of 1507, then, was an inspired guess. It was deservedly influential—

Chart of the Atlantic, MS.,
by Vesconte Maggiolo, 1511

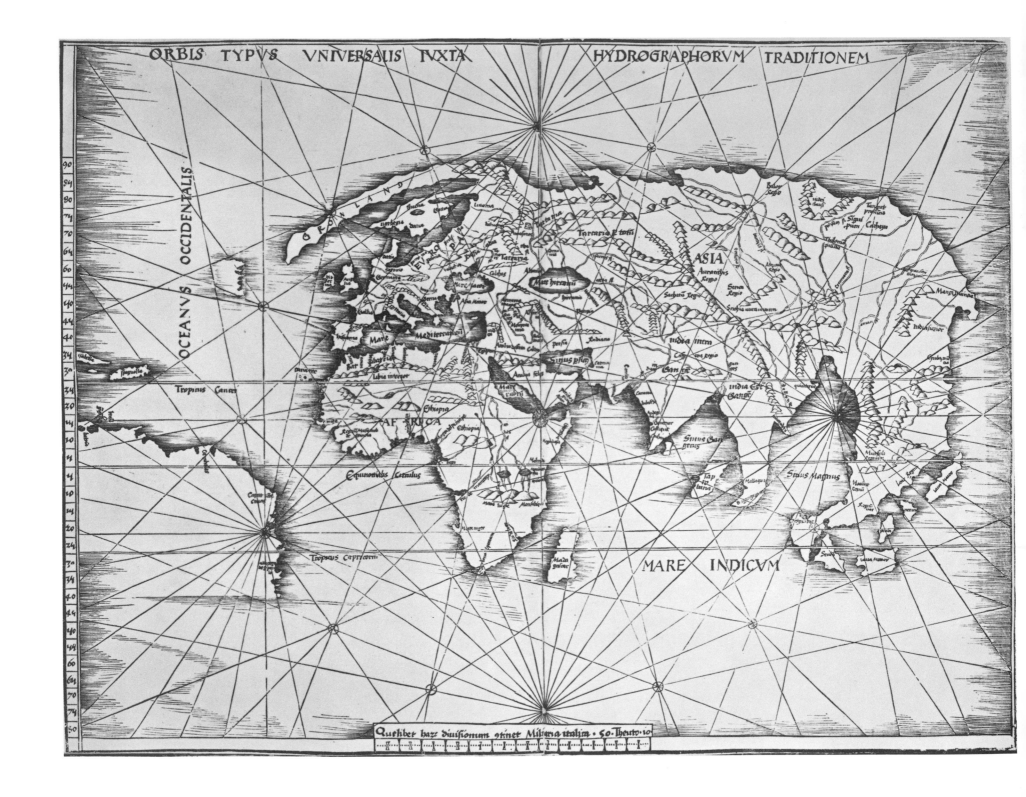

Waldseemüller had many imitators—but it was not immediately or universally accepted. It contradicted a great body of accepted theory, and was inadequately supported by eyewitness knowledge. No European explorer had actually seen the west coast of continental America. No one could be *sure* whether or not America was separated from Asia; whether or not another ocean lay to the west; whether or not the other ocean, if it existed, was accessible to Atlantic ships.

Meanwhile for Spain there was the gold of Columbus's Veragua to be exploited. Spaniards had their choice, to settle and develop the new world they had already found, for its own sake, or to pursue, in competition with Portugal, the search for the Spicery. The ideal, obviously, was to combine the two projects; but with the resources available, this was difficult. They called for different types of men and different kinds of skill and effort. It was easy enough, with prospects of immediate plunder, gold, free land and labor, to attract conquerors and settlers, and such men would finance themselves; but only a few of the most imaginative among them—Balboa for example, and later Cortés—were to show much constructive interest in the search for the Spicery. Voyages to Asia required well-armed, well-manned fleets, carrying trade goods and specie for making purchases. Heavy capital investment would be required and this—as the Portuguese discovered in organizing their trade to India—involved the participation of the great German and Italian commercial and banking houses. These shrewd investors would not risk their money in Spanish expeditions merely on vague assurances that the Spice Islands lay just round the corner. More precise

information would be needed about the extent of the New World and its position in relation to Asia. The Crown would have to provide the ships and employ the navigators. Competent ocean navigators were few; and even those of them who might—a little anachronistically—be called professional explorers were apt to be diverted by the prospect of immediate profits.

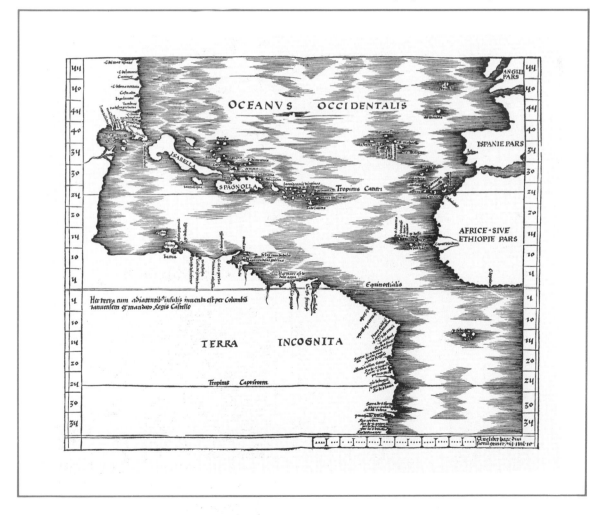

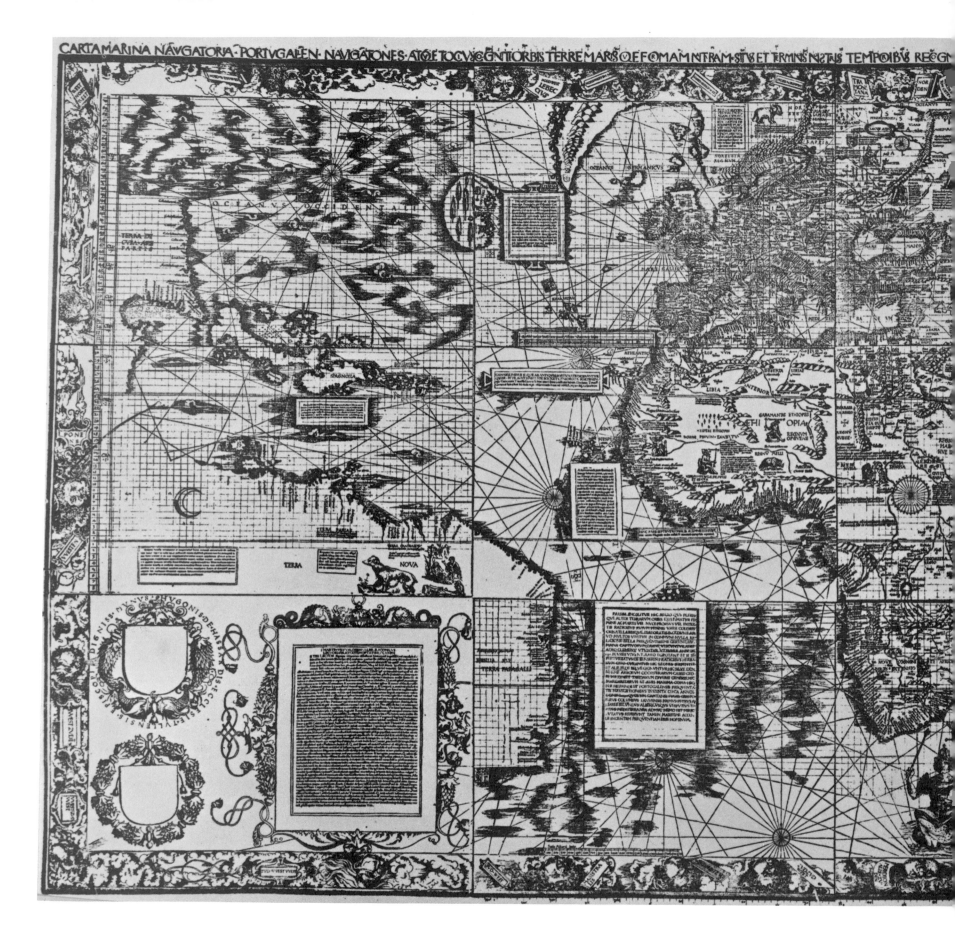

Carta marina by
M. Waldseemüller, 1516

Columbus had turned aside from Quinsay to look for gold; Juan de la Cosa took to slaving, and died of a poisoned arrow in Urabá.

The Crown inclined this way and that as fresh reports came in and as successive monarchs or their ministers were moved, either by the need for immediate revenue or by the hope of long-range commercial profit. In 1505 a conference convened at Toro to discuss, among other matters, prospects in the Indies, had recommended that Vespucci and Vicente Yáñez Pinzón should take out a fleet to search for the Spice Islands; but the disturbed political situation following Isabella's death had prevented its despatch. A second *junta,* called together at Burgos in 1508, with Vespucci as principal technical adviser, made two separate proposals, one for maritime discovery, the other for territorial conquest. The first proposal led to a fleet being equipped at royal expense and sent off under the joint command of Pinzón and Juan Díaz de Solís to look for a strait in central America. It sailed through the northern Caribbean, calling at Santo Domingo on the way out, and probably coasted northern Honduras and eastern Yucatán. Solís and Pinzón found no strait. They may have entered the Gulf of Mexico; if they did so, they would soon have realized their search was hopeless. One glimpse of the wall of high mountains behind the Vera Cruz coast would have put an end to any hope of a strait in that region.

The second proposal was to authorize the first formal occupation of mainland territory; it resulted in the expeditions of Ojeda and Nicuesa, in 1509, to the coast immediately east and west of the Gulf of Urabá. These expeditions were privately financed. The leaders were not

interested in the route to Asia—the coast where they operated was already known to be continuous—nor in the spice trade, nor even in any systematic way with settlement. They were concerned with taking possession, with prospecting for gold, and (though this was not explicitly stated) with slaving. Both expeditions were disasters; most of the participants died or were killed by Indians. Ironically, however, whereas the royally sponsored exploring expedition, led by able captains, achieved nothing, the private expeditions of conquest, led by careless soldiers of fortune, had a sequel significant for the progress of discovery.

A small band of survivors from the Ojeda expedition succeeded in establishing themselves on the Darién coast. Vasco Núñez de Balboa, a forceful but penniless adventurer from Hispaniola, became their unofficial leader, and eliminated or evicted his competitors, some of whom held royal commissions. Under his vigorous leadership, the settlement took root. The local Indians possessed worked gold, raised abundant crops, and proved amenable to a mixture of diplomacy and force. From them, Balboa learned of the further coast, only a few days' march away. In 1513, with about a hundred followers, he forced his way through the mountain forests of the Isthmus, and reached the shore of the Pacific. Oviedo, who knew Balboa personally, gives a convincing account of the discovery: the sighting from a distant hilltop, the long march down to the foreshore, the anti-climax of low water and miles of exposed flats between the shore and the edge of the sea. As the explorers rested by the shore, the tide came rushing in over the flats; and this tide—which has a range of eighteen feet in the Gulf of

OPPOSITE: Shipbuilding in the New World, from de Bry's *Voyages.* This engraving, by J. Sadeler, did duty on several occasions. Stradanus used it to illustrate Noah building the Ark. De Bry adapted it and provided a new background, to show a shipwreck in Veragua and emergency shipbuilding by the survivors.

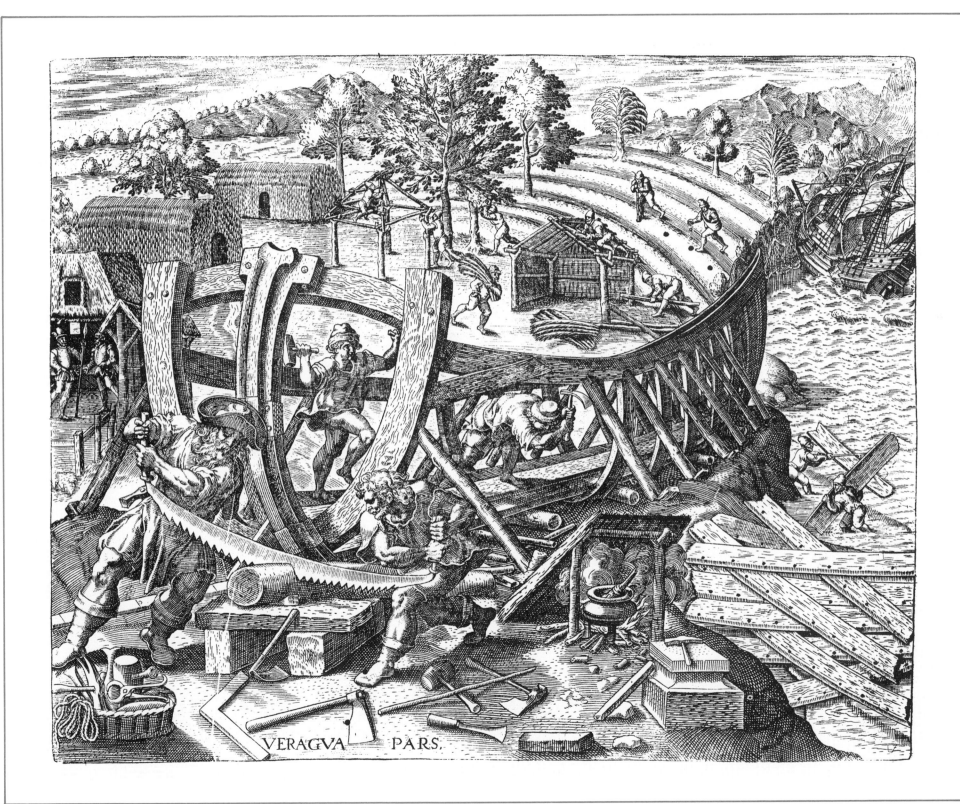

VERAGVA PARS.

San Miguel—settled the matter. This was the salt water of an extensive ocean, distinct from the Atlantic, though separated at that point only by a narrow neck of land.

Balboa's discovery received wide and early publicity. Within a year of the event Peter Martyr was informing his correspondents that Balboa had "scaled the mountains and saluted the ocean." The discovery posed questions to the academic geographers analogous with those raised some years earlier by Vespucci. How were Vespucci's land and Balboa's sea to be fitted into the orthodox Ptolemaic picture of the world? Vespucci had called South America a new country and had shown it to be a continental land mass; but it might still prove to be an immense southerly peninsula of Asia. Balboa called his ocean the South Sea, because the Panama coast runs locally east and west; but might it not turn out to be identical with Ptolemy's Great Gulf?

It was obvious that those who hoped to reach the Spicery by sailing west must cross, or coast round, the South Sea; and must reach that sea either by surmounting or by circumventing America. Surmounting America meant building ships on the further coast. Balboa tried this, but he got little encouragement. The ruthless manner in which he asserted his leadership in Darién had affronted the King. Ferdinand was interested in Darién chiefly for its gold, and so was Pedrarias Dávila, the officer appointed in 1513 to take over the government from Balboa. The instructions issued to Pedrarias summarize clearly the official rules of the time on conquest,

settlement and civil administration; on native policy, the distribution of *encomiendas,* and the circumstances in which resistant natives might be enslaved; on trade, the collection of gold and the sharing of profit. On Balboa's dream of Pacific exploration they are silent. Pedrarias, in any event, was not the man for it. Cunning, brutal and lazy, he cared for little save plunder. He soon fell out with Balboa, placed obstacles in the way of his shipbuilding projects, and eventually had him beheaded.

Balboa's proposal to surmount America by Pacific shipbuilding was not abandoned. Later *conquistadores,* including Cortés, were to take it up, with active royal encouragement; but some years were to elapse before the little bush harbors of Panama and Tehuántepec could build ships good enough for long ocean passages. Meanwhile there remained the possibility of circumventing America by finding a sea passage through or round it. If—as it appeared—the Caribbean was landlocked on the west; and if—as many believed—America was joined, somewhere in the northern hemisphere, to Asia; then the strait, if it existed, could be found only by sailing south-about in the direction indicated by Vespucci, and passing between America and Ptolemy's *Terra Australis—* if *that* existed—into the Great Gulf. The discovery of such a passage would be extremely unwelcome to the Portuguese, who were heavily committed to the Cape route; but if it could be reconciled with the provisions of the treaty of Tordesillas, it would be much in the interest of Spain.

12

The Pacific Crossing and the World Encompassed

asco da Gama returned from India at an auspicious time, from the point of view of a government wishing to enter the international spice trade. Spice prices were abnormally high throughout western Europe. The price of pepper on the Rialto at Venice almost doubled between 1495 and 1499, and some of the rarer spices were unobtainable. At Genoa, Medina del Campo and Antwerp the story was much the same. The shortages and the abrupt increases in price were not attributable simply to the ordinary causes—to the steady endeavors of middlemen and intermediary governments to push up their profits and their imposts; they arose from a series of political interruptions, occurring coincidentally in different parts of the Mediterranean.

Italy from 1494 suffered a series of French invasions. The resulting disturbances and exactions drove several big banking and trading houses into bankruptcy, and disorganized the distribution of spices. At the same time, supplies were interrupted. Fighting broke out in Egypt in 1496 over a succession dispute. The government was unable to protect the trade routes and for considerable periods the Cairo bazaars dealing in spices suspended business. In 1498, communication between the Adriatic and the Levant was interrupted by war between Venice and the Turks over control of the Dalmatian coast. The Venetians imported no spices from Alexandria or Beirut in 1499–1500; nor did the Genoese, Catalan and French merchants, who moved in to take advantage of Venetian preoccupation, do much better. Vasco da Gama returned to a Europe starved even of its normal supply of spices. The Venetians, however, were so preoccupied by their war that they failed, for a year or eighteen months, to grasp the full implications of what da Gama had done. A Venetian embassy visited Lisbon in 1500, but its main purpose was to seek Portuguese help against the Turks. Portuguese monarchs had long prided themselves on being always ready to fight the infidel; King Manoel promised modest naval support, and in 1501 he kept his promise; but he also suggested to the Signory that in future they might find it convenient to purchase their spice requirements at Lisbon.

The quantity of spices brought back by da Gama, though welcome and valuable, was very small, and the Venetians had some excuse for underestimating its importance. Da Gama also brought back, however, the information that a hundredweight of pepper, which in 1499 fetched eighty ducats on the Rialto, could be bought in Calicut for three ducats. If the Portuguese seriously intended a regular trade in spices by the Cape route, they would do well to move quickly, to get themselves established as suppliers while the shortage and the abnormal prices lasted, before the Venetians could find a way out of their own difficulties and resume shipments from Alexandria. Hence the eager haste and the indifference to expense with which a second fleet was prepared in 1500: thirteen ships, of which ten belonged to the Crown and three to private partnerships, part Portuguese, part Florentine.

The voyage of Pero Alvares Cabral, like da Gama's, was a costly success. He ran into a succession of storms in the south Atlantic, and lost six ships, including one commanded by the veteran Dias. Like da Gama, he passed well south of the Cape; picked up pilots and refitted his remaining ships at Malindi; and anchored at Calicut after a six-month passage. Feeling had hardened against the Portuguese since da Gama's visit; it came to street fighting between Portuguese and "Moors," and an open breach with the Zamorin. Cabral seized and looted some of the ships lying in the harbor, bombarded the town, and sailed on south to Cochin, where the local ruler—who was on bad terms with Calicut and welcomed a possible ally—granted the Portuguese a site for a factory and permission to buy spices. He left hastily after two weeks' trading, to avoid a fleet which the Zamorin had sent in pursuit of him; but completed his lading at Cannanore, about a hundred miles north of Calicut. He got back to Lisbon in the summer of 1501 with only four ships of his original thirteen, but with full cargoes of spices.

Cabral's voyage, despite its losses, demonstrated the feasibility and the profitability of a trade in spices by the Cape route. It revealed also the unrelenting hostility which the Portuguese must expect from almost all groups already engaged in maritime trade in the western Indian Ocean. Force would clearly be needed to protect their factories and shipping; naval force could be employed also in reprisal against injuries done to Portuguese interests at Mombasa, at Calicut and elsewhere; and possibly, if enough force were provided, it could serve to prolong the exceptionally favorable trade conditions prevailing in Europe, by hindering the supply of spices to the ports of the Red Sea and Persian Gulf. By the middle of 1501 the Venetians, in high alarm, had awakened to these possibilities. Giovanni Camerino, *Il Cretico,* their learned and very intelligent agent in Lisbon, wrote home that Manoel "felt that he had India at his command" and that soon the Portuguese King "would forbid the Sultan to go for spices." There was very little that the Signory could do to counter this possibility. They brought pressure on Egypt in the only way open to them—by threatening to desert Alexandria and buy their spices in Lisbon—in order to induce the Sultan to mount a serious naval offensive against the Portuguese in the Indian Ocean. The Sultan had no fleet adequate for the purpose; he began to build one, but meanwhile he threatened to destroy the Holy Places if the Portuguese persisted. The Portuguese, knowing the financial importance of the pilgrim traffic to the Sultan's government, remained unmoved; as the threats flew back and forth, they hastened to forestall the eventual Egyptian counterattack.

Vasco da Gama sailed for India for the second time in 1502, with twenty-five heavily armed ships, of which twelve belonged to the Crown. This was the beginning of commercial war in earnest. In east Africa da Gama secured, by threats of bombardment, the submission of Kilwa and Mombasa. From Kilwa he extorted the tribute in gold, of which the great monstrance in the Jeronymite monastery at Belém was later made. One of his squadrons even made a minatory cruise into the Red Sea. In Malabar, he carried out a punitive bombardment of Calicut; defeated in a pitched battle a fleet sent out against him by the Malabar Arabs; concluded commercial agreements with Cochin, Cannanore and Quilon and established factories in all three places; and captured and looted every Arab ship he could find. He left a squadron, based on Cochin, to cruise against Arab shipping, and sent back to Lisbon the extraordinary quantity of 35,000 hundredweight—over 1900 metric tons—of spices, mostly pepper. As a result of these massive imports, the price of pepper at Lisbon dropped to little more than a tenth of the Alexandria price; though still, in view of cheapness of supplies in Malabar, a good price. Portuguese dealers developed an agency at Antwerp, whence they could sell their spices throughout northern Europe, and where they could buy copper, silver and other goods for export to India in payment for still more spices. Merchant bankers, Florentine and German, rushed to invest, on terms laid down by the Portuguese Crown, in successive India fleets.

Da Gama's tactic of terror thus achieved a striking initial success. In 1507 came the expected counterattack: a large combined fleet, Egyptian and Gujerati. It was defeated off Diu by a smaller but stronger fleet commanded by Almeida, the first Portuguese governor-general on the coast. The solid construction of the Portuguese ships, and their relatively heavy armament, decided the encounter. The Egyptians made no further naval move; in 1517 Egypt itself was overrun by the Turks. Meanwhile, however, it began to appear that piracy, however ruthless, however systematic, was not enough in itself to inhibit competition. Portuguese commerce raiders could not be everywhere, and Arab traders soon learned to avoid the Malabar harbors which the Portuguese frequented. There were many alternative ports, in Ceylon and on the Konkan coast. In Malabar itself, Calicut remained open until 1513. Many of the spices sold in Malabar, moreover, were shipped there from Malacca. It was possible for Arab traders to buy cargoes in Malacca and carry them to the Red Sea or the Persian Gulf, bypassing Malabar altogether. The privileged position of the Portuguese could be maintained only by the increasing use of force over an ever wider area.

From about 1507 the Portuguese in the Indian Ocean, commanded by Almeida and subsequently by Affonso d'Alboquerque, embarked on a plan of strategic control much more comprehensive than that originally contemplated by Vasco da Gama. Trading factories were not enough; the plan called for territorial acquisition of harbor bases, where squadrons could be stationed permanently to cruise against competitors. The principal bases were to be Ormuz, at the entrance to the Persian Gulf; Aden, at the entrance to the Red Sea; Goa, on the west coast of India north of Malabar; and Malacca, commanding the strait of the same name, through which shipping between India and the Malay archipelago had to pass. Operations against these key places were not uniformly successful. Ormuz, the ancient and famous island bazaar, was taken by Alboquerque with only six ships, by a combination of seamanship, gunnery and bluff, in 1507. It was to remain in Portuguese hands for more than a century. Aden was better defended; Alboquerque's attack there was beaten off. As an alternative the Portuguese occupied the island of Socotra; but this proved an unsatisfactory base, rocky, waterless, and too far from the mainland to be effective. Socotra was abandoned after a few years, and the Red Sea route remained open.

Goa was a city of some size, built on an island,

with a reasonable harbor, one of the centres of the shipbuilding industry of the west coast of India. In order to take the place, Alboquerque formed a temporary alliance with a Hindu adventurer named Timoja, ambitious to found a territorial dynasty as many of his kind had done. He also demanded, and received, military help from the Raja of Cochin; and selected for the attack a moment when the Muslim suzerain was occupied with a rebellion inland. Even so, the capture of Goa was a bold and difficult operation, and its defense against the armies of the Sultan of Bijapur a lesson in the effects of sea power. The channels which separate Goa from the mainland are shallow and could be forced— were in fact forced several times—by Indian cavalry. Horses will not breed satisfactorily in south India; they had to be imported. The Portuguese themselves never developed an effective cavalry arm in India, but their ships cruising off Goa could deny to their enemies this essential weapon, and could confine the supply of horses to friendly states. Goa was taken in 1510 and was retained until modern times.

Malacca was known to Europeans already, at least by report. Ludovico di Varthema of Bologna, who traveled extensively in the East between 1502 and 1508, passing himself off as a Muslim as Conti had done, claimed to have visited Malacca, and included a description of it in his *Itinerary,* which he published in Rome in 1510. Portuguese ships made an exploratory voyage there in 1509 and a more serious commercial reconnaissance, with Florentine agents on board, in 1510. Their reception, owing probably to the influence of Arab or Gujerati traders in the harbor, was unfriendly. In 1511, almost immediately after the taking of Goa,

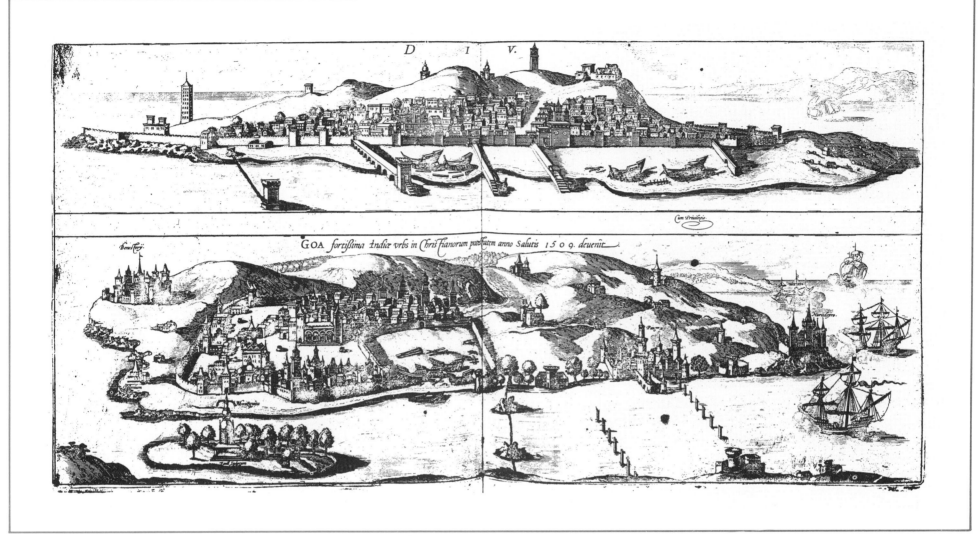

Alboquerque himself sailed with nineteen ships to attack Malacca, risking his hold upon Goa in order to do so. The monsoon which took him to Malacca made it impossible to return until five months later. The siege strained his resources in men and ships to the utmost and Goa all but fell in his absence; but the gamble succeeded. The Sultan of Malacca fled down the coast, to establish himself in the marshes of Johore, whence he sent petitions for redress to his remote suzerain, the Chinese Emperor. These petitions later caused the Portuguese, in their efforts to gain admission to trade at Canton, a great deal of trouble; but for the time, the route to the Far East seemed to lie open.

These rapid, successive operations throughout the Indian Ocean were carried through with breathtaking boldness and with extraordinary savagery. On many occasions, Portuguese victory was followed by the systematic butchery or

Diu and Goa, from *Civitates Orbis Terrarum*, 1576

mutilation of prisoners and the massacre of civil populations. To some extent, this cruelty reflected traditional religious hatred; to some extent, particularly with Almeida, the pitiless ferocity of the man's own nature. With Alboquerque, the ferocity was calculated. The Portuguese were engaged in a desperate gamble for very big stakes. They employed a policy of terror in order to make themselves dreaded, and to demonstrate the value of their alliance. Naturally they made themselves hated also; but in regions of petty rulers, such as the Malabar coast, or east Africa, or the archipelago, they never lacked allies. Even more important, more significant in their eastward progress, they had no difficulty in finding local navigators to take them wherever they wanted to go.

This dependence on local skill and knowledge became more marked than ever after the taking of Malacca. Malacca was one of the major ports of trans-shipment in the international spice trade. Tomé Pires, the apothecary's son who served from 1512 to 1515 as accountant of the Portuguese factory there, wrote in his *Suma Oriental* an excited description of its harbor and godowns, its shipping, its busy polyglot trade. "Malacca is a city made for merchandise, fitter than any other in the world, the end of monsoons and the beginning of others." East of Malacca lay a vast, mysterious region of shallow seas and beautiful, productive islands, including the Moluccas which produced the cloves, the mace and the nutmeg the Portuguese had come to find. Northwest lay the south coast of China, source of silk and porcelain and itself an eager market for island spices. So much Pires and his compatriots could learn in Malacca, if they did not know it already. "Whoever is lord of

Malacca has his hand on the throat of Venice. As far as from Malacca, and from Malacca to China, and from China to the Moluccas, and from the Moluccas to Java, and from Java to Malacca and Sumatra, all is in our power."

This was an exaggeration; from Malacca to the Moluccas is more than two thousand miles of intricate navigation; to the nearest Chinese ports, about the same distance, across the stormy China Sea; and certainly none of these places, except Malacca itself, was in Pires's day in Portuguese power. They were, however, accessible through a dense and efficient network of local shipping, Chinese and, even more, Javanese. It was relatively easy for the Portuguese to open business in places farther east by consigning their goods in local ships. Their initial contacts with China were made in this way, at minor harbors in Lin-tin Bay, downriver from Canton. The first recorded Portuguese visit was that of Jorge Alvarez in 1514; Alvarez purchased, besides silk and porcelain, a quantity of tung oil, which the Chinese used for varnishing ships' planks. When the Portuguese tried to penetrate, in their own ships, to Canton itself, their reception by the Chinese authorities—understandably, in view of their reputation at Malacca—was unwelcoming, and several decades elapsed before they secured a tolerated toehold at Macao.

Cloves, however, interested the Portuguese more than silk, and the Moluccas rather than China were the principal goal of their search. The only independent account of these islands available in Europe at that time came from Varthema, who may or may not have visited them himself. Varthema's *Itinerary,* in any event, was not published until 1510 and was not known to the Portuguese officers who took Malacca, though some of them may have met Varthema in India. These officers picked up most of their knowledge of the islands in Malacca itself. For the navigation between Malacca and the Moluccas they depended on Javanese information and guidance; and this, apparently, was readily available. Many Javanese lived in Malacca; besides the usual floating population of seafarers, they included a big mercantile colony and many craftsmen, including shipwrights. Alboquerque was so impressed by the skill of the shipwrights that he recruited some of them to work at Goa. The Javanese trading community, at first, was not wholly hostile. The Sultan had been a grasping ruler; some of them were probably glad to see him go, and possibly they thought the Portuguese too inept in business to be serious competitors. At least one Javanese prince, who had had commercial differences with the Sultan, initially welcomed the Portuguese victory. Although other Javanese rulers were less friendly, and although the Portuguese were discouraged from visiting Javanese ports, they were able to recruit Javanese pilots for their early expeditions to the Moluccas.

The term Maluco, as used by Europeans in the early sixteenth century, covered a much smaller area than the Moluccas as they are marked on maps today. It included the five spice islands, Ternate, Tidore, Motir, Makian and Bachan, together with the larger island of Halmahera on which the others depended for much of their food supply. The Amboina and Banda groups were regarded usually as separate archipelagos, though included with the Moluccas in the general term, the Spiceries. This compendious name was often used loosely, also, to describe a much larger area, including Celebes, the Sunda Islands and even Sumatra. Borneo was usually considered separately from the Spiceries, and grouped with China, Japan and the Philippines under the general head of "countries to the East." All the islands of the Spiceries produced pepper, or could produce it; only the small islands of the Molucca group produced cloves, only the Banda Islands nutmeg, with mace its derivative. Politically, the islands were divided among hundreds of small sultanates. Their only unity derived from seaborne trade.

Immediately after the capture of Malacca the Portuguese set about investigating this complex geographical puzzle, with a view to making their own contacts with the sources of cloves and nutmeg. António de Abreu left Malacca for this purpose late in 1511, with three ships, carrying Javanese pilots. The fleet sailed along the northern side of the Sunda Islands as far as Flores, then northeast to Amboina, the south coast of Ceram, and the Banda Islands. In the Bandas, they loaded nutmeg, and with this cargo Abreu decided to return to Malacca. He had lost one of his ships among the islands, but as captain and crew were picked up, he bought a local ship to replace it. On the return passage this vessel became separated from the others in rough weather, and was wrecked in its turn. Its captain, Francisco Serrão, with a few companions, made his way to Amboina and eventually to Ternate. Ternate is a small island, only about eight miles across: a single volcanic cone, surrounded by a narrow but extremely fertile coastal plain. Its population, though dense, was small. There was only one town. The clove trees which grew on the coastal ring, however, made the people of the island commercially rich, and its Sultan a ruler of consequence, the dominant ruler of the

Javanese native craft,
from de Bry's *Voyages*

island group. Serrão settled down to a
comfortable beachcombing life as mercenary
captain and adviser to the Sultan. This was the
first Portuguese contact with the Moluccas. It was
followed up, in the next few years, by trading
voyages from Malacca; but the results of these
voyages were not made public and no detailed
record of them survives.

In the five or six years after Abreu's return to
Malacca in 1513, there were two channels
through which information about the Spiceries

reached Europe. One was the normal channel of
official report. One of Abreu's navigating officers,
Francisco Rodrigues, compiled in 1514 a brief
set of sailing directions for the route the fleet
had followed, and supplemented it with a series
of cartographic sketches, based on Javanese
originals, in which the position of the Moluccas
was vaguely indicated. Rodrigues's work was sent
to Portugal, and has, in part at least, survived.
Traces of it appear in charts of the East Indies
made by the cartographers Pedro and Jorge

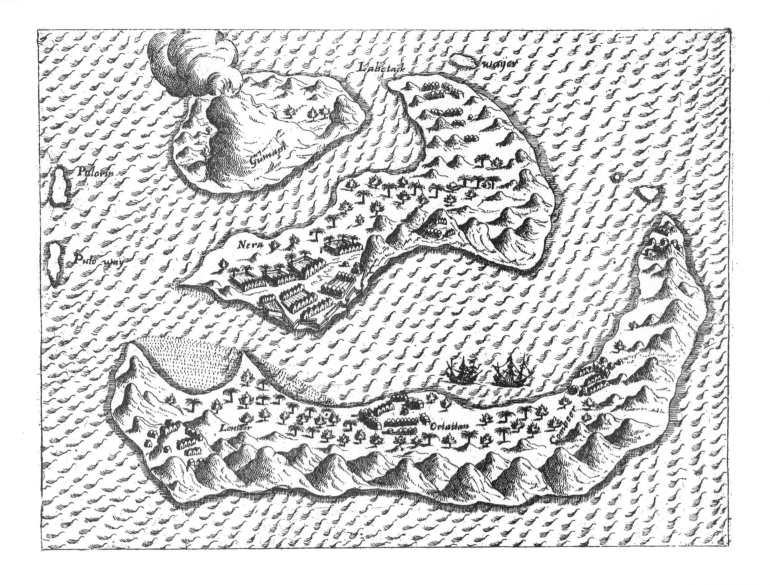

The Banda Islands, from
de Bry's *Voyages*

Reinel between 1517 and 1519, and by Lopo
Homem in 1519. These charts, naturally, were
treated as confidential, and were not made
public. The other channel of communication was
the intermittent correspondence which Serrão at
Ternate kept up with Portuguese friends,
conveying somewhat unreliable information
about island affairs. This private correspondence
eluded the official net. Among other pieces of
misinformation, it conveyed a greatly
exaggerated estimate of the eastward distance

from Malacca to the Spice Islands.

This became a matter of diplomatic
consequence. Portuguese officials had good
reason for wishing to minimize the distance.
Spanish expeditions were known to be searching
for a westward route to the Spiceries. If they
should find one, awkward questions would arise
over the interpretation of the treaty of
Tordesillas. That treaty had established in the
Atlantic a meridian of departure for Spanish and
Portuguese exploration, respectively. By a simple

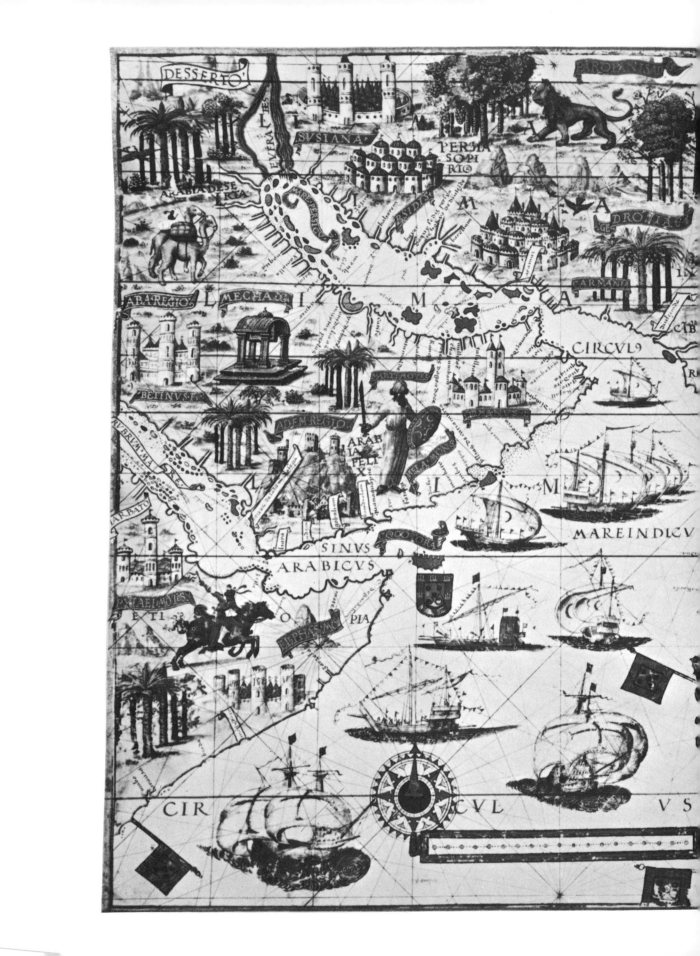

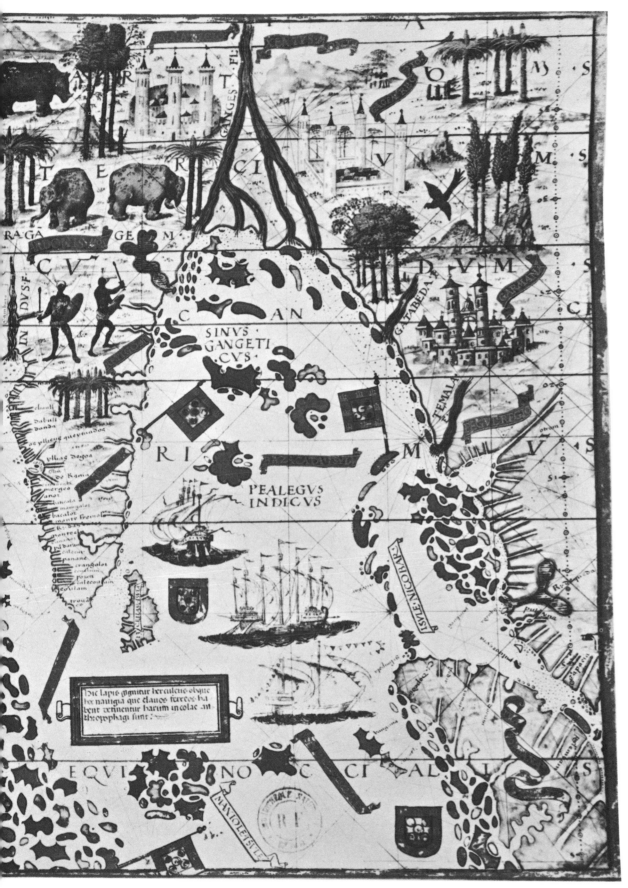

Map of the Indian Ocean,
by Lopo Homem/Reinéis,
1519

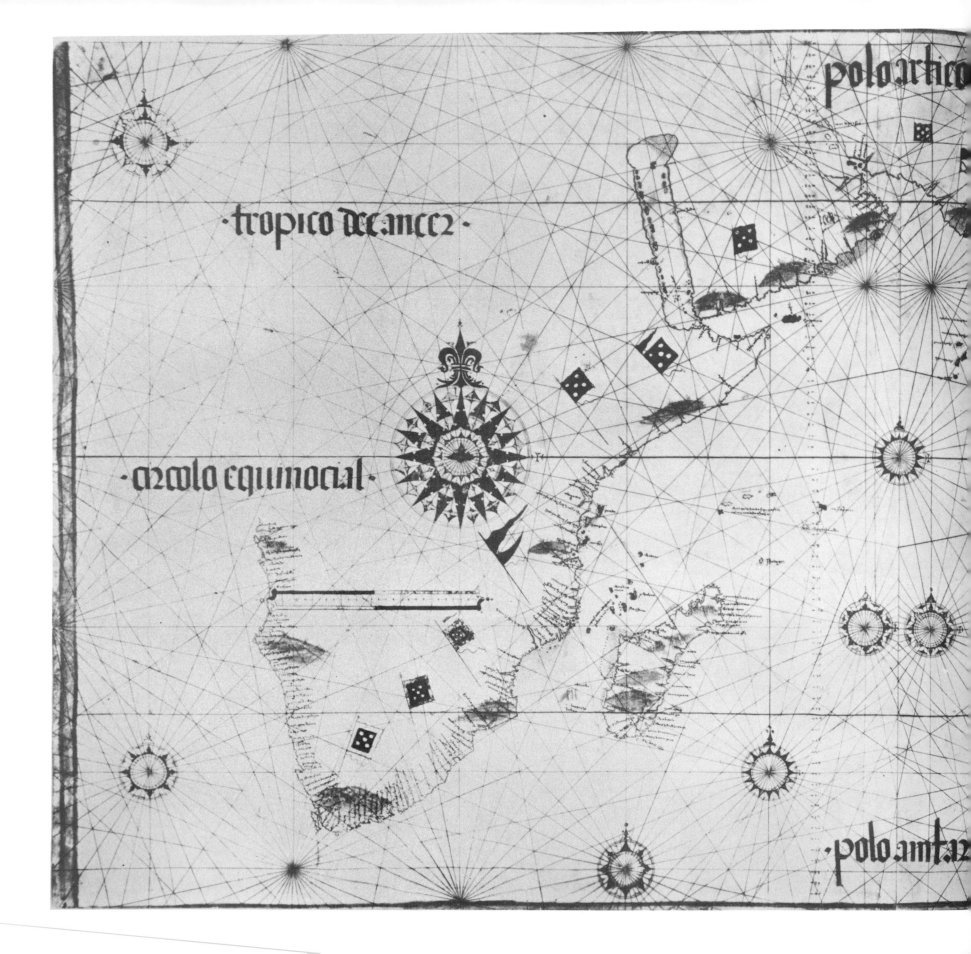

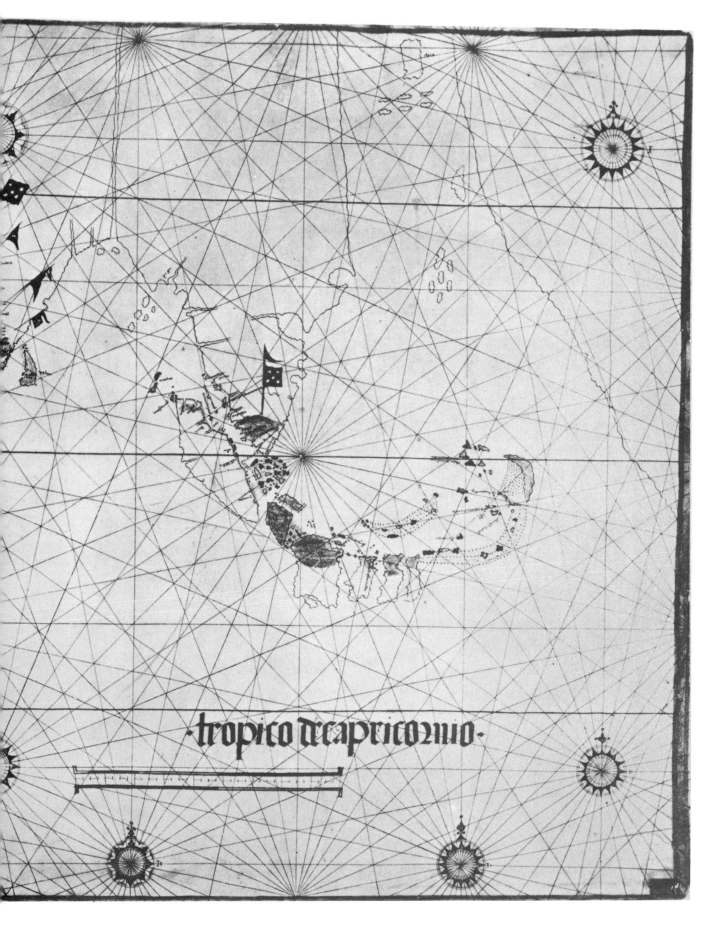

·tropico ɒecapricoꝛnio·

Marine chart of the Indian
Ocean, by Pedro Reinel,
c. 1517

construction, the line could be interpreted as passing through the poles and round the world, so dividing the globe into two hemispheres of exploratory opportunity. If this interpretation were accepted, a limit would be set to Portuguese expansion eastward. Moreover, if Ptolemy's estimate of the circumference of the earth was correct, parts of eastern Asia, including the Moluccas, might well turn out to be in the Spanish hemisphere. Spanish policy, accordingly, favored the extended Tordesillas line, Portuguese policy rejected it. In 1514 the Portuguese Crown secured from Leo X a Bull, *Praecelsae devotionis,* which granted to Portugal all lands which might be seized from heathen people in *any* region reached by sailing east. The force of such a Bull, however, was disputable; the Spaniards certainly would not be prevented by it from establishing themselves in the Spice Islands, if they could get there. The Portuguese, therefore, wished to ensure that, if they were forced to accept a line of demarcation in the East, the Moluccas would lie on their side of it. All official Portuguese maps of the area at that time were drawn with this consideration in mind.

In fact the Portuguese cartographers were right; but in the existing state of geographical knowledge no one could be sure, and the Spaniards persevered. As hope of a strait through central America faded, their attention was concentrated more and more upon the southwestern Atlantic. The much-publicized results of Vespucci's 1501 voyage suggested, correctly, that the coast of South America, trending southwest, extended well to the west of the Tordesillas line. The use of this route by Spaniards in itself involved a stretch of the terms of the treaty, which the Portuguese resented but

could not prevent. In 1515 Juan Díaz de Solís—who in 1512 had succeeded Vespucci as pilot-major—was sent off to look for a strait in that direction. He entered the Río de la Plata, explored for some distance upstream, and died there, killed by Indians; the river for some years afterward was called by Spaniards the Río de Solís. Clearly this great flow of fresh water was a river and not a strait. The strait, if it existed, was farther south.

The Spanish government, unlike the Portuguese, regularly employed foreigners in long-distance voyages of discovery. It had, indeed, little choice, partly because relatively few Spaniards had the necessary knowledge and training, partly because those who had were often drawn away by the counter-attraction of gold, pearls and slaves in the West Indies. Columbus was a Genoese, Vespucci a Florentine, Solís a Portuguese; they were all, in a sense, international mercenaries, *condottieri* of the sea. The Spanish authorities never wholly trusted these foreigners, and usually insisted on their being accompanied by Spanish officers who shared in the command; but they valued their services, and particularly welcomed, in the search for the Spiceries, skilled and informed defectors from Portugal. In 1516–17 a fortuitous combination of such defectors produced the plan which led to the discovery of the long-sought strait.

The Portuguese gamble in the East made many fortunes, and ruined many; and in the process created many malcontents. Manoel I was notoriously capricious in rewarding service overseas. Power and influence in the East was the object of vicious, sometimes literally cut-throat competition; the long struggle between Almeida and Alboquerque for supreme command in India was only the most famous among many. Many a captain with long service in the East—often finding himself on the losing side of some such contest—returned to Portugal expecting recognition and promotion, and was rewarded with obscure neglect. Nor were the soldiers and sailors who actually went to the East the only malcontents; the merchants and bankers who helped to finance the expeditions also had their grievances. There were two principal foreign groups or cartels involved in the business, one Florentine, with some Genoese participants, the other south German. Both groups had reason to be dissatisfied with royal regulation of eastern trade, which fixed prices and controlled sales in order to protect Crown profits against private competition. After 1505 foreign investors in general were prohibited from sending their own factors to the East, and were required to purchase spices through the royal factors. The German group, however, had the greater grievance. The King could not do without the Germans, but he did not like them. On several occasions between 1505 and 1515 ships belonging to German houses had their cargoes confiscated on one pretext or another, and in many smaller ways officials discriminated against Germans in favor of the more pliant Italians.

The most vigorous spokesman of German discontent was Cristóbal de Haro, merchant, financier and promoter of oversea enterprise. Haro was Spanish born, probably of *converso* background, but had lived since 1486 in Portugal, where he represented the Fuggers as their Lisbon agent. He was a European personage, like many of the explorers, without any strong national allegiance. He made a great fortune by dealing in Portuguese spices, and financed many ships sailing to the East, but was interested also in the possibility of a westward route to Asia. He may have had something to do with the Cabot enterprise. In 1514 he was involved in a project for southwestern exploration, by the route of Vespucci and Solís. Probably these interests, highly suspect in Portugal, together with his ostentatious wealth and his outspoken opposition to the royal spice monopoly, brought upon him the royal displeasure. In 1516 he removed himself—fled, indeed—to Spain.

Haro presented himself in Seville to the Bishop of Burgos, Juan Rodríguez de Fonseca, the politician-prelate who had been responsible in 1493 for fitting out Columbus's fleet (and had incurred Columbus's dislike) and who since then had become, in effect, royal minister for the affairs of the Spanish Indies. Fonseca's character in some ways resembled Haro's: bold, intelligent, vigorous, acquisitive. Like Haro, Fonseca was interested in the southwestern route to Asia and had been instrumental in mounting the Solís expedition. The two men at once, apparently, began planning a bigger expedition, and looked around for a suitable man to command it. They found one in Fernão Magalhães, Ferdinand Magellan.

Magellan was a Portuguese *fidalgo* and soldier of fortune who had gone out to India in 1505 and served eight years in the East. He had been at Goa and at the taking of Malacca; whether he had been farther east is uncertain; but he was a friend of Francisco Serrão the beachcomber, and corresponded with Serrão, after the latter's establishment at Ternate and Magellan's own return to Europe. In this correspondence he

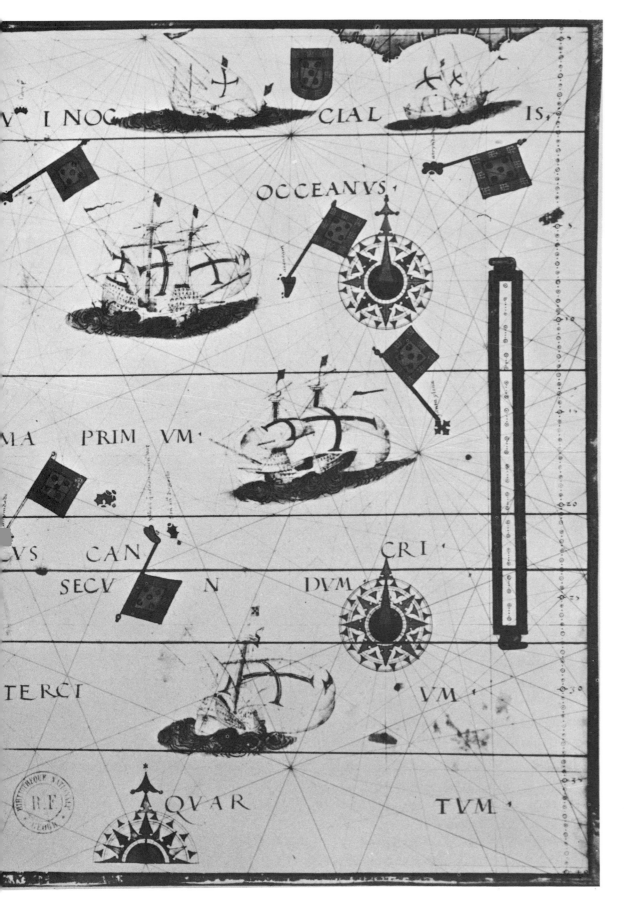

Map of the south Atlantic,
by Lopo Homem/Reinéis,
c. 1519

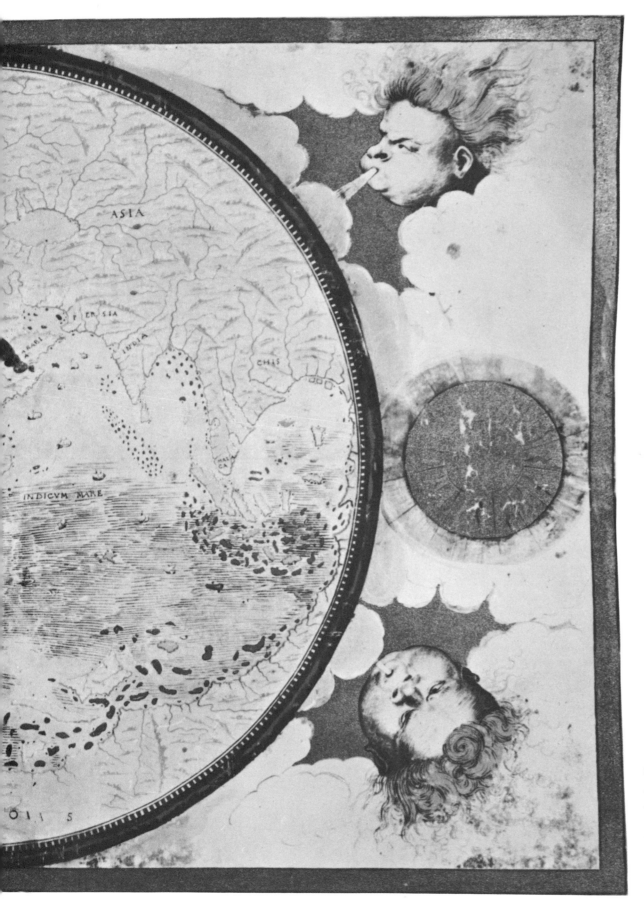

Circular world map by Lopo
Homem, c. 1519. The
southern continent, a
Ptolemaic survival, blocks
Spanish access to the East.

presumably received information about the Moluccas, including their latitude—roughly on the equator—and an exaggerated estimate of their east longitude. In India, he had somehow incurred the dislike of Alboquerque, which had blocked his prospects of promotion. He returned to Portugal in 1513, failed there to secure what he considered adequate recognition or employment, and decided in 1517 to offer his services and his very valuable information in Spain. With him went another friend, Rui Faleiro, mathematician and astrologer, who had acquired a great—though not altogether deserved —reputation for cosmographical learning, including, most appropriately but most deceptively, knowledge of the problem of determining longitude. Faleiro was a strenuous advocate of the southwestern route to Asia.

Each of the four men in this fortuitous combination had an important contribution to make: Faleiro, plausible geographical theory; Magellan, knowledge and experience of the East; Haro, commercial acumen and Fugger money; Fonseca, official support. The combination coincided with the accession of an impressionable, glory-seeking youth to the Spanish throne. Fonseca arranged for Magellan's presentation to the young Charles I. Magellan is said to have used, among his arguments, Varthema's *Itinerary;* probably he did not reveal that his countrymen were already trading to the Moluccas—may not even have mentioned the Moluccas by name at all. He was to sail by a Spanish route, west of the Tordesillas line; find a seaway round or through the continental mass of South America; and reach a group of spice-producing islands believed to lie in what was beginning to be regarded as the Spanish

hemisphere. The plan was agreed; angry diplomatic protests by the Portuguese ambassador were rejected; and in 1519 the fleet set sail.

Magellan sailed with five ships, all small or medium-sized merchantmen, purchased for the expedition by the royal purveyors on the open market at Cádiz. No details are known of their build, rig or dimensions. Apparently there was nothing unusual about them: no special preparation, such as had gone into Vasco da Gama's first fleet. The Portuguese ambassador, indeed, reported to his master that they were so rotten as to be unsafe; but in view of their subsequent performance this seems to have been an exaggeration; the wish, no doubt, was father to the thought. The navigational equipment was adequate, without new or experimental devices, though it included twenty-three charts, some of which were drawn with the help of Magellan's countrymen, the Reinels, father and son, who were persuaded to visit Seville for the purpose. The armament was relatively heavy; it included eighty-two mounted guns, some of which may have been cast pieces; and the supply of small arms, crossbows, pikes and body armor was correspondingly generous. Evidently fighting was expected; but trade goods also were generously provided by the investors, in good variety. Besides the usual truck for primitive barter, such as hawks' bells—twenty thousand of them—and brass bracelets, there were more sophisticated articles for trade on arrival in the East: looking-glasses (five hundred), a quantity of velvets, and over two thousand pounds of quicksilver. These were good selling lines; they reflected the investment and the experience of Haro and his Fugger friends. The company numbered about 250, mostly Spaniards, though

Holbein's ship, c. 1532.
Apart from the general air
of carousal, Magellan's
ships probably looked
something like this.

many other nationalities were represented, including one Englishman (a gunner), and two Malays. The polyglot character of the force probably reflected difficulty in recruiting men locally for a dangerous expedition commanded by an unpopular foreigner.

Some of the officers, including all the navigators, were Portuguese, presumably selected by Magellan himself; but Fonseca thought it prudent to limit the number of Portuguese in the fleet, and one of the senior Spaniards, Juan de Cartagena, who commanded one of the ships, was also appointed *conjunta persona;* whether this vague title was intended to mean second-in-command or something more, was not, apparently, made clear, though it clearly implied a right to be consulted. Uncertainty about the precise chain of command in this, as in some other sixteenth-century fleets, was to cause a great deal of trouble, especially since Magellan never took his officers into his entire confidence. It was customary, on long and dangerous voyages, to submit major decisions to a council of officers, sometimes even to a whole ship's company; but Magellan kept his own counsel, and the Spaniards were inclined from the start to distrust him.

The first instance of this mutual diffidence occurred after passing the Cape Verde Islands, when Magellan, presumably wishing to make more southing before striking across the Atlantic, made a board to the southeast parallel to the African coast. This was recognized practice among Portuguese pilots, particularly in the summer months, but probably unknown to Spaniards. Cartagena objected to the deviation from the direct course; possibly he suspected that Magellan, despite strict orders to keep clear of Portuguese stations, planned some act of piracy off Guinea. He was given no explanation; merely told to mind his own business and follow the flagship. Subsequent events appeared to justify his complaint, for the fleet ran into protracted calms and torrential rain. A second quarrel broke out off the coast of Brazil, arising from Cartagena's demand to be consulted, Magellan's insistence on being obeyed, and an obscure dispute about formal salutes. On this occasion Magellan relieved Cartagena of his command, and was with difficulty dissuaded from putting him ashore. It was an unhappy fleet that sailed on south, made a cursory examination of the Plata estuary, and found a wintering harbor on the Patagonian coast; a cold, desolate place, inhabited only by a handful of the most primitive people in the world. Here Magellan was faced with full-scale mutiny, in which most of his Spanish officers were involved. He regained control by a combination of stratagem and force. Several of the leaders were executed; Juan de Cartagena was marooned ashore and was never heard of again.

The major task of exploration began in Patagonia. From there on, for many months the fleet was in waters totally unknown; unknown not only to Europeans, but to anyone. This terrifying passage, fortunately for history, was well described by a participant in its horrors. Antonio Pigafetta of Vicenza, Knight of Rhodes, had shipped with Magellan as a gentleman volunteer, apparently for the adventure. He was one of the eighteen men who completed the voyage. He had a remarkable capacity for survival; he probably spent more time ashore during the voyage than any other member of the company; but when his companions were trapped into a murderous shoreside battle, he was on board nursing a previous wound; when he slipped while fishing at night, and fell into the sea, there happened to be a rope hanging over the side; when most of the company were prostrate with scurvy, he kept his health (perhaps his assiduous fishing had something to do with this). He had boundless, somewhat naïve curiosity, a capacity for keen observation, a remarkable ear for languages, and a genial manner which made him an excellent emissary in dealing with strange people ashore. As a supernumerary and a foreigner, he was a fresh and independent observer. He kept a regular journal and careful notes of everything he saw, and after his return compiled a narrative of the voyage entitled *Primo viaggio intorno al Mondo,* which survives in four early manuscripts, besides many subsequent printed versions. It is perhaps the best, the most detailed, the most moving of all the eyewitness accounts of the great voyages of reconnaissance.

It has its defects. Pigafetta wrote very little about the mutinies. He certainly had no sympathy for the (not entirely groundless) complaints of the mutineers. As a member of a disciplined military Order, with an ingrained belief in the virtue of loyalty, he must have found the whole affair abhorrent. He developed, also, an admiration for Magellan amounting almost to hero-worship, and probably did not wish to record events which reflected on Magellan's powers of leadership. Pigafetta, moreover, was not a seaman. He had only a sketchy knowledge of navigation, presumably picked up in conversation on the voyage, and apparently was not interested in mastering the subject. It would be impossible, from his fragmentary and often garbled references, to follow the course of the fleet in detail on a chart.

These defects can be supplied to some extent from other sources. Several navigators' logs have survived; most are fragments, but one, that of Francisco Albo, covers most of the voyage. It is a workmanlike record of courses, distances and observations. Latitudes which can be checked are in general—considering the coarseness of the instruments used—remarkably accurate. In the Pacific, Albo's work must have been helped by the remarkably good weather and calm sea which the fleet encountered, though observations ashore were naturally more accurate than those taken afloat. He made some surprisingly good estimates of longitude. Like most working logs, the Albo record makes dry reading, and has never been published in full. As for the mutinies, Sebastián del Cano, who latterly commanded the *Victoria,* the only ship to complete the voyage, and two of his shipmates, were interrogated after their return, and their depositions have survived. Del Cano had been among the Spanish mutineers, and his testimony, though terse and factual, was naturally self-justificatory and sharply critical of Magellan.

There are a number of early printed accounts, though these, too, all have their defects. Magellan's delicate position as a Portuguese in Spanish service raised difficulties for sixteenth-century chroniclers in both countries. Except for royal succession disputes, no question between them roused more angry feelings than that of the Spiceries. Among major Portuguese historians, Barros, Castanheda, Correa, Galvão and Góis all included accounts of the voyage in their chronicles. The Barros account is particularly valuable because of the use its author made of sources now lost. Of the five, only two, Correa and Galvão, made any serious attempts at objectivity; the others emphasized Magellan's defection rather than his achievement. They were not, of course, entirely free agents; Galvão was the only one who had no official position to maintain. As for Spain, the manuscript of Peter Martyr's full account, written shortly after the event, was lost in the sack of Rome in 1527. *De Orbe Novo* contains only a brief abstract of it. The best independent summary which early appeared in print was also the nearest in time: the essay *De*

Moluccis Insulis, written in 1522 by Maximilian of Transylvania, and printed in 1523. Maximilian was a natural son of the Archbishop of Salzburg, a pupil of Peter Martyr and a relative by marriage of Cristóbal de Haro. As might be expected from one of his courtly training, he tried intelligently to relate the events of the voyage to their diplomatic and political background in Europe. For the events themselves, he relied on Peter Martyr's method, questioning survivors immediately after their return. His account, though brief and secondhand, supplements Pigafetta's in several significant details.

All these printed narratives were written after the event; Pigafetta's, in effect, was written while the events were taking place. It gives valuable clues, not only to what Magellan found, but to what he expected to find. The first reference to Port St. Julian, the Patagonian harbor where the mutiny occurred, is so casual as to suggest that the place was already known, that some other European explorer—Vespucci presumably—had been there before, though this, as we have seen, is questionable. Farther south, the strait proved difficult to find. They found the entrance "by a miracle"; yet they clearly expected to find it, sooner or later. The captain-general, wrote Pigafetta, "knew where to sail to find a well-hidden strait, which he saw depicted on a map in the treasury of the King of Portugal, which was made by that excellent man, Martin de Boemia." Martin Behaim, the maker of the 1492 Nürnberg globe, had died in Lisbon in 1507. Magellan might have met him. His globe does indeed mark a strait, between the extremity of the most easterly peninsula of Asia and a large island labelled Seilan; but it shows Java Major and Minor and many other islands east, not west of the strait. It is unlikely that Magellan ever saw the Behaim globe which, so far as we know, never left Nürnberg; more unlikely still, after his years in the East, that he could have taken this muddled, archaic picture of Asia seriously. Behaim, however, may have made later, better maps. Another Nürnberg globe, that of Johan Schöner of 1515, shows an America completely separate from Asia and divided by two straits, one in central America, the other in about 45 degrees south running between "America" and "Brazilie Regio." The southern strait may, perhaps, have originated in garbled reports of the Río de la Plata. There is no evidence that Schöner's globe, any more than Behaim's, came to Magellan's attention; but clearly the notion of a passage through South America was familiar to some cartographers before Magellan sailed. As to what lay beyond the strait, to judge from his subsequent movements, and from a later reference in Pigafetta's narrative to "Catigara," Magellan's ideas were probably derived from neo-Ptolemaic maps; he expected the strait, when found, to lead him into Ptolemy's Great Gulf, lying between the Cape of Catigara and the Golden Chersonese. Within the confines of the Great Gulf he would find the islands he was supposed to be looking for.

Magellan's Strait has never been used regularly by deep-sea shipping, though nowadays it carries a considerable traffic of coastwise steamers. For sailing ships it is a difficult and dangerous passage; a tortuous, labyrinthine navigation with strong and variable tidal currents and frequent thick weather. Coming from the east, its aspect is deceptive. The entrance is unobtrusive. The eastern part of the strait, from Cape Virgins to

Cape Froward, runs between relatively low, grassy banks; the country is habitable, pleasant even, as Pigafetta noted. The western part is a narrow fjord between abrupt ice-capped mountains, a funnel through which the prevailing west wind drives in savage, unpredictable gusts. The whole distance from Cape Virgins to Cape Pillar on the Pacific is 310 nautical miles; the width of the strait in some places is less than two miles; there are few reliable anchorages; the bottom in many places is of sharp rock ridges, which chafed through hempen cables and caused the loss of anchors. Safe passage of the narrows, for a sailing ship, depends on a lucky conjunction of favoring spring tides with rare and brief periods of easterly wind. The record passage for the sixteenth century was Drake's: sixteen days; but some later navigators took three months and more; some gave up the attempt in despair.

Magellan's fleet came near to giving up. They had had poor refreshment at Port St. Julian. There is no wood there, and water is poor, the upper end of the bay being a salt marsh. The only food supply came from fish, sea birds and a few wild guanacos. The Tehuelche Indians were not helpful. (The thing about them which most impressed Pigafetta was their stature, compared with the wiry little Mediterranean sailors; the myth of Patagonian "giants" persisted for centuries.) Though not unfriendly, they were primitive nomads. They had no seagoing canoes, and as guides were useless. The fleet arrived off Cape Virgins short of provisions, and short of one ship; the *Santiago* had gone ashore just north of the cape, and her people were rescued with difficulty. One at least of the surviving captains advised Magellan, having found the strait, either to return home to report, or else to bear away

for the Cape of Good Hope. Magellan was adamant, and his captains, with misgivings, obeyed; but inside the strait the biggest ship, the *San Antonio,* which had been Cartagena's, became separated. Her company mutinied, overpowered their Portuguese captain, and sailed the ship back to Spain. The rest, giving the *San Antonio* up for lost, stood on through the narrows, anchoring or making fast to rocks at night, sending boats ahead to reconnoiter promising openings. It was a relatively prosperous passage: thirty-eight days from Cape Virgins they cleared Cape Pillar— Cape Deseado, the longed-for cape—entered open water, and fired a *feu de joi* to salute the South Sea.

The Pacific Ocean—pacific, at least, at the time —in fact covers one third of the total area of the globe; an area equal to all the land masses of the world combined. Magellan's people can have had no notion of these dimensions. In every map available to them, the Great Gulf was of manageable size. They probably expected a passage of, at most, a few weeks; in fact they were at sea for nearly four months, reduced to scraping the barrels for powdered wormy biscuit, eating rats, chewing sawdust, gnawing leather, suffering all the torments of hunger, thirst and scurvy. Eventually they came to Guam in the Marianas. During the whole terrible passage from Cape Pillar to Guam, their only sightings of land were two small uninhabited islands.

Magellan's course across the Pacific has been the subject of much discussion. From Cape Pillar he sailed north or north by west up the Chilean coast, probably lying-to at night, for eighteen days; he would have had initially no choice, since the prevailing wind would have prevented him from steering farther west. Between 20 and 25 degrees south, however, he would have entered the zone of southeast trade winds; these winds are less constant in the Pacific than in the Atlantic, but they are reliable enough, and would have allowed him to decide when to make his westing. According to the Albo log, he altered course to northwest somewhere in the neighborhood of Juan Fernández; to west in about 15 degrees south; and subsequently northwest again, to cross the equator in about 154 degrees west. If this record is correct, the first of the barren "Isles of Misfortune" was somewhere in the northern Tuamotus. There are hundreds of islands in this scattered archipelago, many mere rocks, bird-haunted, steep-to, inaccessible, but also some substantial inhabited islands. Magellan might have been expected to sight some of these, and the fact that he did not do so has raised doubts about the reliability of the log and the courses it records. North of the Tuamotus, however, separating them from their nearest neighbors the Marquesas, is a wide channel of open water. Magellan probably passed through this channel. If so, his second barren island would be one of the small southern outliers of the Line Islands, lying athwart the open channel at its western end. The islands, in any event, are crumbs of land in an immensity of sea; they are easily missed; birds give no certain indication of their presence; the whole south Pacific is alive with pelagic birds. The absence of sightings does not seem, in itself, a good enough reason for rejecting the Albo record.

An alternative interpretation would have Magellan steering north or north-northwest much longer, crossing the equator in about 105 degrees west and reaching almost to 20 degrees north before turning west. If this were correct,

the Isles of Misfortune would be Clipperton Island and Clarion Island, the second of which is only a few hundred miles off the coast of Mexico. There is no land between Clarion and the Marianas. Clipperton and Clarion answer Pigafetta's descriptions, more or less, but so do hundreds of other islands. The only possible explanation of such a course is that Magellan hoped to find the head of the Great Gulf and sail coastwise to the Spicery. This idea, it is true, was in the air. During Magellan's absence, in 1519, a Spanish explorer, Gil González Dávila, actually tried it, sailing west and north from Panama in the ships Balboa had built, though he did not get very far. There is no evidence that Magellan entertained any such idea. The Clipperton-Clarion theory flatly contradicts Albo's usually careful account. It is much more probable that Albo was substantially accurate; that of the two Isles of Misfortune the first was Puka-puka in the northern Tuamotus, the second ("Shark Island") one of the Line Islands, possibly Caroline.

It is certain that Magellan made the last, westward leg of his passage well north of the equator, probably in about 12 degrees north, and this too calls for explanation. He knew the Moluccas were on the equator; why did he not turn west on the equator and follow the latitude? He could have done so; the usual northern limit of the southeast trade wind in those waters is between 3 and 8 degrees north. One can only guess; but probably, knowing that Portuguese ships had reached the Moluccas, he thought those particular islands might best be avoided, and decided to try some other group farther north. From waterfront talk at Malacca, or from correspondence, he must have known of the existence of such islands—the Philippines, Formosa, the Ryukyus. He might reasonably—though wrongly—have assumed that these islands produced spices similar to those which grew in the Moluccas. He sailed through the western Pacific in roughly the latitude of Samar in the Philippines, and lighted on Guam on the way.

In the Marianas Magellan's people found themselves, for the first time for many months, among seafaring people. Pigafetta described, with accurate interest, the single-outrigger canoes with triangular matting sails, and the skill and enjoyment with which the owners handled them. He also described, like many later explorers, the magpie kleptomania of the Micronesians, who snatched every item of loose gear they could lay their hands on. The Europeans resented this, and there was fighting, so that the fleet had poor and grudging refreshment. Dubbing the islands the Ladrones, the Thieves' Islands, they sailed on west, and a week later sighted Samar.

In the Philippines the Spaniards were on the edge of an extensive region of sophisticated maritime communication, in which the dominant commercial seafarers were Chinese, though many other peoples participated. If Magellan had been more adroit, and if he had so wished, he could have recruited navigators to take him on to the Spice Islands; but he proved himself less able as politician and diplomat than as a sea commander. At first all went well. They had a friendly reception on Limasawa, watered and victualed the ships, and spent an agreeable time trading and carousing ashore. They were then escorted to the larger island of Cebu and presented to the local ruler, who was so impressed by Spanish weapons and the evidences of Spanish power that he consented to an alliance and went through the motions of baptism. As a result, Magellan became involved in a local power struggle, and went in person with forty men to support an attack on the smaller neighboring island of Mactan. Del Cano later explained sourly that Magellan "went to fight and burn the houses of the town of Mactan to make the King of Mactan kiss the hands of the King of Cebu, and because he did not send him a bushel of rice and a goat as tribute"; Magellan apparently proposed to build up the power of his "Christian" ally as paramount chief of the neighboring islands and as a centre of Spanish influence. He underestimated local resistance; the attack was driven off and Magellan himself killed on the beach.

This defeat naturally caused the ruler of Cebu to have second thoughts about his alliance. A few days later, twenty-seven Europeans, invited ashore for a banquet, were massacred. Those left on board, helpless, weighed anchor and left the harbor. They had no pilots, no clear idea of where they were, no established command. One of the ships had to be burned, for lack of men; the other two wandered about the islands for many weeks, demoralized, confining their landings to minor harbors, committing random piracies as they went. They sailed down the northwest coast of Borneo as far as Brunei, then back to Palawan. Eventually, somewhere in the Sulu Sea, they captured a local ship whose navigator was able to guide them to the Moluccas, which most of them had assumed to be their destination from the beginning. In November 1521 they anchored off Tidore, one of the few islands in the world where cloves grew.

They found an uneasy political situation in the

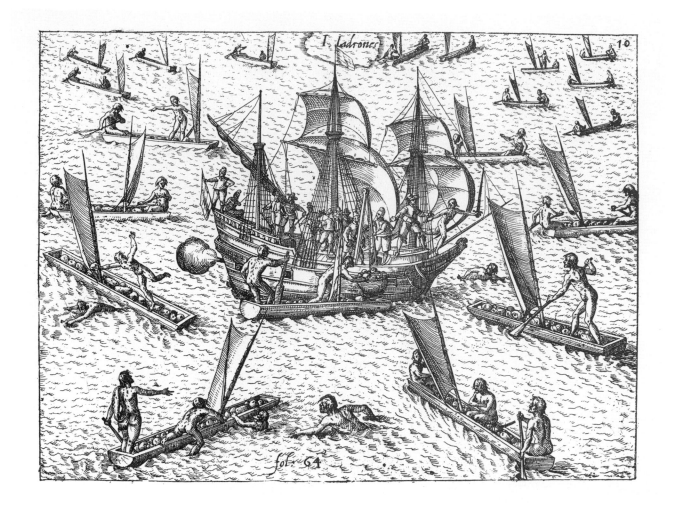

Canoes surrounding a European ship in the Marianas, from de Bry's *Voyages*. The design of the canoes is fanciful.

Moluccas. The ruler of Ternate had recently died by poison and a succession struggle had ensued between his sons. At the time of the poisoning, Magellan's friend Serrão had been away on a trading mission to Tidore, and while there he too had been poisoned. The Sultan of Tidore wished to take advantage of the situation in Ternate, but feared that the Portuguese at Malacca, when they heard of Serrão's death, might hold him responsible and make reprisals; on both grounds he was delighted to see the Spaniards and to place himself under the Emperor's protection. A Portuguese fleet was in fact fitting out at Malacca for the Moluccas; not,

however, to avenge Serrão—they knew of his correspondence with Magellan and were glad to be rid of him—but to establish a fort and factory at Ternate and to forestall the Spaniards. News of Magellan's departure from Seville had long since reached Goa and Malacca and the governor-general had been instructed to intercept and if possible destroy his fleet.

The Spaniards, for their part, were in no state to fight the Portuguese or anyone else; their only thought was to load with cloves and get away as quickly as possible; and this—by a remarkably adroit diplomacy, we must suppose—one ship at least succeeded in doing. The other, the

Trinidad, was badly in need of repair and could not leave until April 1522. Her captain decided to make for Darién, as the nearest land under Spanish control; he worked his way back to the Marianas, set out across the Pacific, ran into heavy weather, and returned in distress to the Moluccas, where his ship was taken by the Portuguese. Her people were set to work building the new fort at Ternate, and few of them saw Spain again.

The *Victoria* left Tidore in December 1521, commanded by Sebastián del Cano. We know very little about this taciturn Basque. Pigafetta had a profound admiration for Magellan; he neither admired nor liked del Cano, and in his narrative never mentioned him by name. Del Cano was a sailor, not a soldier; a man of humble origin, elevated to command by an obscure process of acclamation; he had been involved in mutiny; nothing in his record claimed Pigafetta's respect. He must have been a consummate seaman; perhaps something less than that as a navigator. He decided to return to Spain by way of the Cape of Good Hope. Nobody in the ship wanted to face Magellan's Strait again, and the season—the early southern summer—was right for the passage through the Indian Ocean. Piloted by a Moluccan navigator, the *Victoria* sailed south through the Banda Sea to Timor, where she watered and provisioned; then out to the open ocean.

In the Indian Ocean her people were once more on their own, with no local experience to help them. Del Cano did not know those waters, and in the latter part of the crossing seems to have taken his ship too far south. This probably accounted for the head winds they met, which forced them north again. They made their

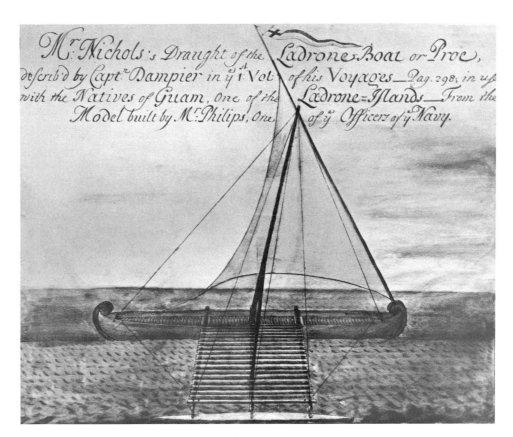

African landfall near the Keiskama river. Food was running short; but del Cano refused the suggestion that they should make for Mozambique—which would have meant certain arrest—and sailed on to the Cape of Good Hope. The season by then was too far advanced for favoring conditions, and once again del Cano made the mistake of sailing too far south, to 42 degrees south according to Pigafetta. They beat for weeks off southern Africa, but finally rounded the Cape in early May. From there on they had no more navigational difficulties, but hunger and scurvy accompanied them all the way to the Cape Verde Islands. They bartered spices

A seventeenth-century impression of an outrigger dugout from the Marianas

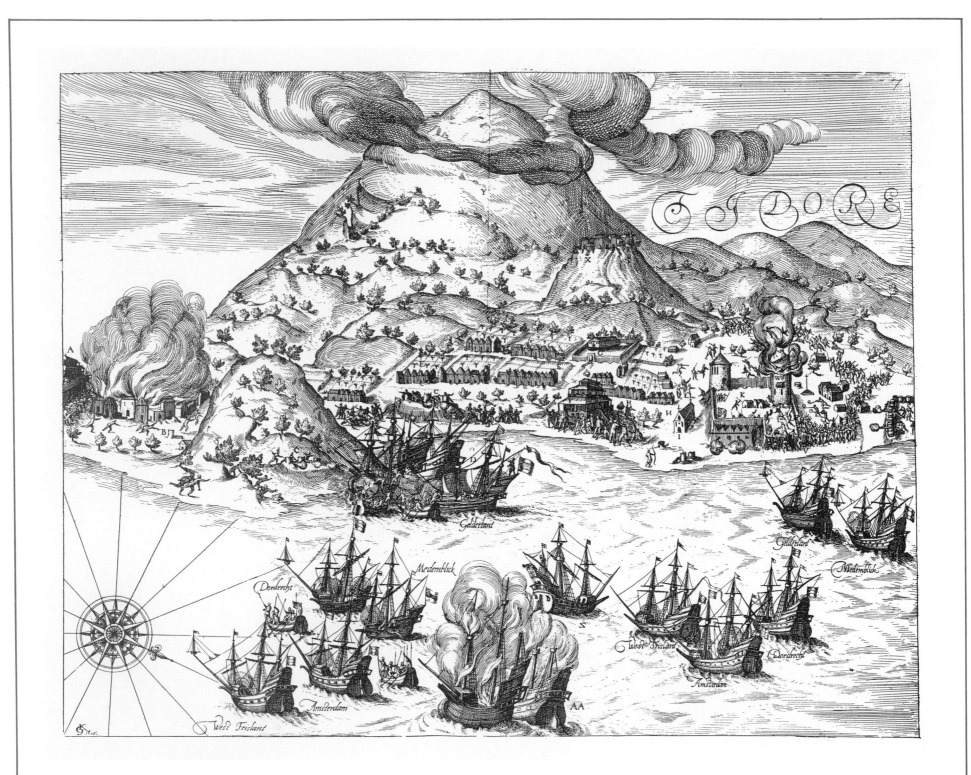

for rice, but had to weigh hurriedly to escape arrest, leaving thirteen of their people behind. They made the customary *volta do mar* by way of the Azores, and crossed the bar at San Lúcar in early September. Eighteen enfeebled survivors staggered ashore at Seville, and the following day went barefoot in their shirts to the shrine of Santa María de la Victoria, to give thanks for their deliverance.

So ended the first circumnavigation of the world. In human terms it had been a disaster: three ships lost out of five, and near two hundred men. Commercially its results were trifling. True, the *Victoria* brought back about 500 hundredweight of cloves, but the proceeds of their sale barely covered the cost of the expedition. The Emperor and Cristóbal de Haro naturally had first claim on the returns. Other investors got nothing. Nor did the survivors become rich; del Cano was allowed to sell his own parcel of cloves privately, free of tax, and was given a coat-of-arms in which cloves, nutmeg and cinnamon were depicted; the crest a globe, with the resounding motto *primus circumdedisti me.* He was also awarded a pension; but as this was to be paid out of duties chargeable on a spice trade which failed to develop, it yielded him no income. In 1522, however, the Spanish attitude towards this future spice trade was one of excited optimism. The voyage was counted a success; the losses were explained away by blaming Magellan; the delay in despatching another fleet by Magellan's route was caused by financial stringency, not by official hesitation.

Politically, del Cano's return to Spain produced two parallel sets of consequences. The first was a state of open war between Spaniards and Portuguese in the islands; the handful of men left behind by del Cano as storekeepers at Tidore lived for eight years in a state of intermittent siege. The second was a series of outwardly amicable negotiations between Spain and Portugal in Europe. A conference of experts was convened at Badajoz-Elvas to determine the position of the Moluccas; the respective claims of Spain and Portugal to trade and settle there, in accordance with the treaty of Tordesillas; and the state of actual possession. No agreement was reached on any of these questions. The only practical result of the conference was the opportunity it afforded to the Spanish Crown to buy Portuguese cartographers into its service.

Meanwhile, the slow preparation of Spanish fleets went forward. García Jofré de Loaisa sailed from Coruña in 1525, with seven ships, to follow Magellan's route. Del Cano went second in command. The fleet lost three ships, one by shipwreck and two by desertion, before entering the Pacific. Loaisa and del Cano both died at sea. Only one ship reached Tidore. Another fleet under the specious Sebastian Cabot got no farther than the Río de la Plata. In 1527 Hernán Cortés, established as conqueror and effective ruler in Mexico, himself despatched a small fleet of Pacific-built ships from Tehuántepec for the Moluccas. Again, one ship arrived, none returned. This was a serious setback; in view of the length and the dangers of Magellan's route, the only serious hope of establishing Spanish Asian trade depended on regular communication between the western Pacific and Spanish America. This in time came to be recognized; but it was not until 1565 that Urdaneta discovered the only practicable return route, in the forties of north latitude.

By 1527 it was clear that whatever happened

OPPOSITE: The island of Tidore, from de Bry's *Voyages*

in Europe, the value of the Spanish claim to the Moluccas was beginning to depreciate; the Emperor, at war with France and on the verge of insolvency, decided to sell or pawn it before it should depreciate further. In 1529, despite the opposition of the Cortes of Castile, the treaty of Saragossa was duly signed. By this treaty, Charles V pledged all his rights in the Moluccas to Portugal for 350,000 ducats. Spanish and Portuguese spheres of exploration were divided by an arbitrary line seventeen degrees west of the islands; a demarcation which the Spaniards, in occupying the Philippines, subsequently chose to ignore. The little garrison at Tidore, which had held out so stubbornly and so long, was instructed to hand over to the Portuguese, and the survivors took passage home in Portuguese ships.

It was a small return for so great an expenditure of lives, of persistence, of courage and of skill; a Pyrrhic victory over the sea. Yet the most important cargo the *Victoria* brought back was not cloves, nor delusive commercial hopes, but information. The world, everyone knew, was round; in theory it was circumnavigable. Now it had been circumnavigated. The sea and the wind, in the southern hemisphere at least, flowed continuously round it. Pigafetta, not usually a man given to general reflection, was struck by this awe-inspiring fact: "When we left that strait, if we had sailed continuously westward we would have circumnavigated the world without finding other land than the cape of the XI thousand virgins." In the course of circumnavigation, some well-entrenched beliefs, mostly associated with Ptolemy, had to be abandoned, and major new facts had to be accepted. The world turned out

to be considerably larger than most people had supposed; and a third great ocean, bigger than either of the others, stretched between Asia and the Americas. These terrifying dimensions sobered the optimism of people who had supposed the riches of the Orient to lie within their grasp. The central fact, however, could not now be disputed: the oceans of the world were all connected. Given skill and courage, adequate stores and a reliable ship, a man could sail to any part of the world he wished.

Many major questions, of course, still remained unanswered. Magellan's Strait and the Cape of Good Hope were not necessarily the only sea passages leading out of the Atlantic into other oceans. The range of possibilities, however, was narrowing. While Magellan was at sea, in 1519, Alonso de Pineda sailed along the whole north coast of the Gulf of Mexico, and closed that possibility. In the fifteen-twenties a series of expeditions coasted north from Florida or south from Nova Scotia. The leaders were the Spaniard Vázquez de Ayllón, who tried to settle on Chesapeake Bay; Estevão Gomes, Portuguese in Spanish service—the same man who had been navigator in the *San Antonio* and who engineered the mutiny and desertion; and most thorough and conclusive, Giovanni da Verrazzano, Italian in French service, who discovered New York harbor. Between them these men closed another possibility, the broad seaway to China which John Cabot had hoped to find. North America was a continent. If a seaway existed, it was farther north, beyond the codfish coast.

Whole continents, whole oceans, might still await discovery. What of Ptolemy's *Terra Australis?* There is an intriguing statement in Maximilian of Transylvania's essay, to the effect that Magellan's people while in the strait heard the roaring of the sea beyond the land on their port side, suggesting that Tierra del Fuego was an archipelago and not a continent. This observation did not receive the attention it deserved; many sixteenth-century cartographers continued to draw a continental land mass across the southern ocean, because Ptolemy had it so. Similarly in the north: many geographers found difficulty in accepting America as a wholly separate continent and continued to join it to Asia. They were not very far wrong; the Bering Strait is in fact very narrow; but sixteenth-century delineations of the north Pacific owed nothing to factual report. The continuous coastline was an intellectual bridge between the world of Magellan and the world of Ptolemy.

Ptolemaic geography, in modified forms, enjoyed an extensive revival in the middle of the sixteenth century. The beautiful world map drawn by Giacomo Gastaldi about 1550, for example, has a southern continent, *Tierra de Fuego Incognita,* and a continuous continental coast north of the tropic, linking Mexico to China. For Gastaldi, the Pacific, though of immense size, was an enlarged Great Gulf. Gastaldi was one of the ablest of sixteenth-century cartographers, and many of his best maps were drawn for a series of elegant editions of Ptolemy which appeared in Venice between 1548 and 1574. Ptolemy was not discarded as a cartographical authority until after 1570, when Ortelius's *Theatrum Orbis Terrarum* set new standards of independence and empirical accuracy, though even Ortelius has a southern continent.

The dead hand of Ptolemy lay heaviest on printed maps drawn by academic geographers. It had little or no influence on manuscript charts drawn for practical use. The *Casa de la Contratación* at Seville maintained a master chart of the world, the *padrón real,* embodying the latest reports, with which all charts issued to ships in the *Carrera de Indias* were required to conform. The original is lost, but its quality can be judged from the fine world charts drawn by Diogo Ribeiro in the fifteen-twenties. Ribeiro was a Portuguese cartographer in Spanish service who himself worked on the *padrón real.* His charts reflect the prompt assiduity with which the *padrón* was revised as reports came in. That of 1525, the "Castiglione map" is the earliest surviving chart to include the information brought back by del Cano about Magellan's Strait. It also shows Yucatán as an island; but even as the chart was being drawn Cortés was setting out in his ill-fated expedition to Honduras, to march across the neck of the Yucatán peninsula and to return to Mexico by sea. The *padrón* was changed accordingly, and Ribeiro's 1529 chart, now in the Vatican, shows Yucatán in peninsular outline. This chart has been called the most beautiful example of the map-maker's art. At its head is the title "All the world which has been discovered up to this time." It has its mistakes, to be sure: Africa is too broad in proportion to its length, India too narrow, for longitude was still a matter of guesswork; the Isthmus of Suez is much too wide; and the east–west extent of Asia is exaggerated, doubtless for political reasons. In its delineation of coastlines, however, the chart is wholly empirical, beautifully drawn, meticulously careful. It includes no information which had not been confirmed by actual exploration. It cites its sources. It owes nothing to hearsay or traditional authority. Areas where the facts were unknown—

World chart by Diogo Ribeiro,
MS., 1529 (CONTINUED ON
FOLLOWING PAGE)

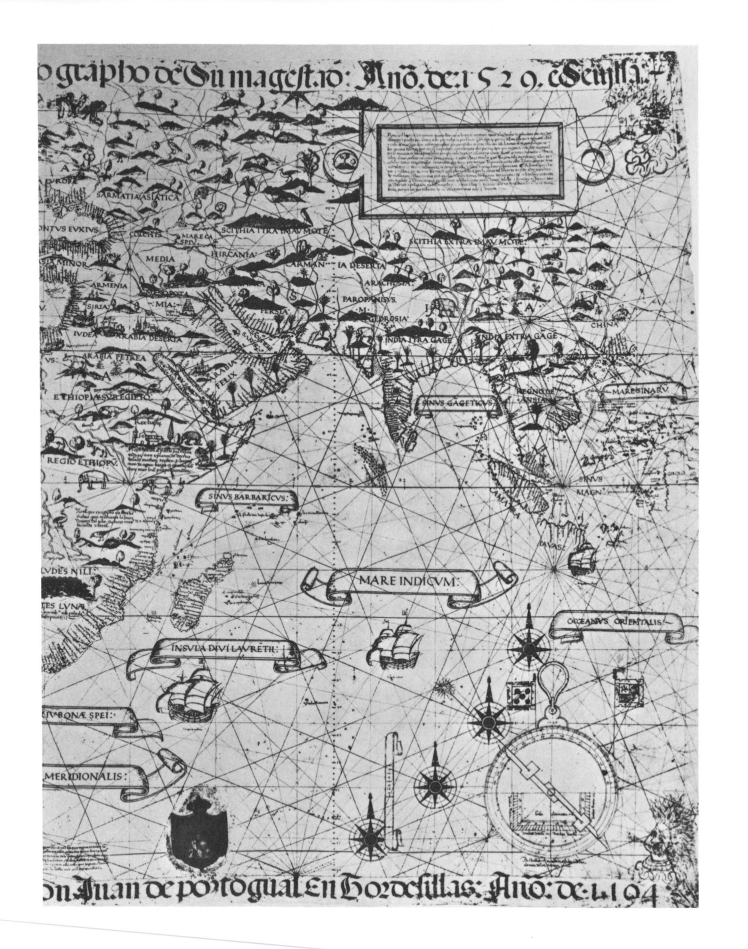

the north Pacific, much of the west coast of America, the Arctic, and the great circuit of the southern ocean—are left blank.

These blank areas of ocean and coastline were to engage the attention of explorers for three hundred years and more; yet compared with the rush of new knowledge from Prince Henry's time to Magellan's, the progress of discovery was slow. It was not until the seventeenth century that Dutch ships found open water south of Cape Horn and blundered on the continental mass of Australia; not till the eighteenth that Bering discovered a Pacific passage to the Arctic Ocean, that Cook charted an insular New Zealand and removed *Terra Australis* from the map. As for the northern passages, which were to raise such high hopes and claim so many lives, they were dead ends, in effect, long, tortuous, choked with ice. They exist, but they have only been penetrated in our own day; they are passable only by ice-breakers or nuclear submarines.

Despite its blank spaces, the impression given by the Ribeiro chart is one of completeness. The oceans are all there, in roughly their true shape and proportion, and they are all connected. One has only to compare it with, say, the Behaim globe; yet little more than a generation separated them. The Ribeiro chart is the finest of all memorials to the discoverers of the sea: to Dias, Columbus, Vespucci, Vasco da Gama, Magellan; to their forerunners whom Prince Henry sent in search of Guinea gold; and, it should be added, to the Arab, Indian, Chinese, Malay and Arawak seafarers who—once the connecting passages had been found—told the European navigators where to go. The central task of the discovery of the sea took less than a century. In essentials it was completed when the *Victoria* berthed at Seville.

Epilogue

he little Victoria *was not broken up,* or preserved as a national monument. She was patched up and sent back to sea. She made two passages to Hispaniola, and on the second return passage sank with all hands in mid-Atlantic.

Magellan's Strait never became a route of regular trade. The Cape Horn route, though difficult and dangerous enough, was surer and safer than the strait; but not until the eighteenth century did shipping develop sufficiently to make regular commercial use of it. For two hundred years most trade to Pacific South America was carried on the backs of mules across the Isthmus of Panama; or, later, up the Río de la Plata and across Tucumán to Potosí in the Andes. The portages were troublesome and expensive, but less dangerous, less costly in ships, money and time, than the all-sea route, in sixteenth-century conditions. Similarly, for more than two hundred years, a flourishing trade to China plied between Acapulco and Manila, making a long portage across Mexico.

The passage round the Cape of Good Hope was safer and easier than that round Cape Horn or through Magellan's Strait, but it was not necessarily cheaper or more convenient than the older routes to the East, which involved carriage overland. In the first few years of the sixteenth century the Portuguese succeeded in interrupting the regular Arab sailings which supplied the ports of the Red Sea and the Persian Gulf; but their monopoly proved short-lived. Formidable though they were at sea, the Portuguese could not hope, with a few warships operating from widely scattered bases, to suppress permanently a whole flourishing commerce which supplied Egypt and the Turkish empire as well as European customers. The Indian Ocean spice trade—or a large part of it—soon re-entered its old channels; with it revived the Mediterranean trade in Venetian ships. In the middle decades of the sixteenth century immense quantities of pepper entered the Mediterranean by the Red Sea route.

In straight commercial competition over price and quality, the advantages were by no means all on the side of the Portuguese oceanic trade. The costs and risks of the Cape route were great, and tended to increase. For small ships carrying small quantities of valuable goods, trans-shipment mattered less, sheer distance mattered much more, than they do to modern bulk carriers; and besides the cost of carrying the goods, there was the cost of protecting them *en route*. When there was war in the Levant, the Venetians suffered and the Portuguese profited by it; but the Portuguese often found themselves at war too, either with the Turks in the Indian Ocean or with the English or the Dutch in the Atlantic; their shipping losses, and the expense they were put to in providing armed escort, brought

advantage to Venice and the Levant trade.

Many years, sometimes centuries, can elapse between a major discovery and its practical application. The discovery of the sea was among the most significant events in the history of the world, but it was a precocious development, and its full results were long delayed. The Portuguese discovered the sea route to the East, and in the sixteenth century began to exploit it; but it was the Dutch, the French and the English, in the seventeenth and eighteenth centuries, who destroyed the older Arab and Venetian trade between the East and Europe. The Spaniards, with Portuguese guidance, discovered the sea route between Atlantic and Pacific, and tried in the sixteenth century to exploit it; but it was the Dutch, the French and the English who, in the seventeenth and eighteenth centuries, learned to use it profitably.

The discovery of the sea inaugurated a new age, in which control of the world's trade, and to a considerable extent also political control, fell gradually into the hands of a small group of states, mostly in western Europe, which could build enough reliable ships to operate in all the oceans at once, and move at will from ocean to ocean. They created maritime empires, networks of trade, influence and power, on a scale formerly undreamt of. It is not, perhaps, entirely accidental that the decline and disappearance of these maritime empires has coincided with a relative decline in the effectiveness of power exercised on the surface of the sea.

Bibliographical Note

*he basis of our knowledge* of the discovery of the sea is in the eyewitness accounts of the men who did the discovering. There are several societies devoted to the publication of critical editions or translations of such accounts; of these, the most important are the Hakluyt Society in England, the Linschoten Vereeniging in the Netherlands and the Cortés Society in the United States. The publications of the Hakluyt Society, which now number several hundred volumes, include English versions of nearly all the narratives mentioned in this book.

The most convenient select bibliography of the subject as a whole is in Boies Penrose, *Travel and Discovery in the Renaissance, 1420–1620,* Cambridge, Mass., 1955, to which the reader is referred. This useful book contains also a good chapter on the geographical literature of the period. The few titles listed here are of books which proved particularly useful in the preparation of the present work and which, for the most part, are not mentioned in the Penrose bibliography, either because they lie outside its scope or because they appeared after the publication of Mr. Penrose's book.

Among many recent books on ships and shipping, one of the most notable is the admirably illustrated Björn Landstrom, *The Ship,* London, 1961. There is a good chapter on shipbuilding by G.P.B. Naish in *A*

History of Technology, vol. III, edited by C. Singer and others, Oxford, 1957. On fifteenth-century European shipping there are two long articles on "The Ship of the Renaissance" by R. Morton Nance in *The Mariner's Mirror*, vol. XLI (1955) and a third by G. la Röerie, "More about the Ship of the Renaissance," in the same journal, vol. XLIII (1957). *The Mariner's Mirror* is the leading journal in English devoted to nautical history, and contains many articles bearing on the subject of this book. On the early development of ships and boats in general the standard work is still J. Hornell, *Water Transport, Origins and Early Evolution*, Cambridge, 1946. There are relatively few reliable works on early Indian Ocean shipping; among them may be mentioned G.F. Hourani, *Arab Seafaring in the Indian Ocean in Ancient and Early Mediaeval Times*, Princeton, 1951; W.H. Moreland, "The Ships of the Arabian Sea about 1500," in *Journal of the Royal Asiatic Society* (1939); and J. Poujade, *La route des Indes et ses navires*, Paris, 1946. An important recent publication is A. Prins, *Sailing from Lamu*, Assen, 1965. Chinese shipping has been more widely studied, notably by G.R.G. Worcester in a series of works, the most recent of which is *Sail and Sweep in China*, London, 1966; and by Joseph Needham in his magisterial *Science and Civilisation in China*, vol. IV, part 3, Cambridge, 1971.

The best introduction to the history of navigation in Europe is E.G.R. Taylor, *The Haven-Finding Art*, London, 1956. Chinese navigation is dealt with in vol. IV of Needham's *Science and Civilisation*. An impression of the quality of Arab navigation in the fifteenth century can be gained from T.A. Shumovskii, trans. M. Malkiel-Jirmounsky, *Tres roteiros*

desconhecidos de Ahmād ibn-Mādjid, o piloto arabe de Vasco da Gama, Lisbon, 1960; and from G.R. Tibbetts, *Arab Navigation in the Indian Ocean Before the Coming of the Portuguese . . .*, London, 1971. Outstanding recent studies of the skills and limitations of primitive navigation—in this instance in the Pacific—are T. Gladwyn, *East Is a Big Bird*, Cambridge, Mass., 1970; and D. Lewis, *We the Navigators*, Canberra, 1972. Among journals, *Imago Mundi* is for the history of early navigation and cartography what *The Mariner's Mirror* is for the history of shipping, and contains many articles bearing on the subject of this book.

The extensive literature on geographical knowledge before the great discoveries is very well summarized by Penrose, but a few recent additions may be noted: on the Norse voyages, Gwyn Jones, *The Norse Atlantic Saga*, London, 1964; on the attraction of the East for late medieval Europeans, F.M. Rogers, *The Quest for Eastern Christians*, Minneapolis, 1962; on early travelers to the East, D. Lach, *Asia in the Making of Europe*, vol. I, Chicago, 1965. A number of major non-European works on travel and oceanic geography have recently been translated into European languages. They include: Ma Huan, *The Overall Survey of the Ocean's Shores* (1433), edited by J.V.G. Mills, Cambridge, 1970; and *The Travels of Ibn Battuta*, edited by H.A.R. Gibb, 3 vols., Cambridge, 1958–71.

A definitive book in English on Prince Henry and his activities in connection with discovery is eagerly awaited. Meanwhile the Portuguese government has published a huge mass of source materials, in connection with the five hundredth anniversary of the Prince's death: A. J. Dias Dinis, ed., *Monumenta Henricina*, Coimbra, 1960–, 8 volumes to date, in progress. In the same year appeared the definitive edition of Zurara's chronicle: Léon Bourdon, ed. and trans., *Gomes Eanes de Zurara, Chronique de Guinée*, Ifan-Dakar, 1960. The settlement of the Atlantic islands is discussed in C. Verlinden, *The Beginnings of Modern Colonization*, Ithaca, 1970. Other recent major works include: V. Magalhães Godinho, *A economia dos descobrimentos Henriquinos*, Lisbon, 1962; R. Mauny, *Les navigations médiévales sur les côtes sahariennes antérieures à la découverte portugaise*, Lisbon, 1960; and C-M. de Witte, *Les bulles pontificales et l'expansion portugaise au XVe siècle*, Louvain, 1958. E.W. Bovill's *Golden Trade of the Moors*, London, 1958, is a revised version of his earlier fascinating book, *Caravans of the Old Sahara*, London, 1933. An excellent account of the African voyages of Cão and Dias is E. Axelson, *Congo to Cape*, London, 1973. Mr. Axelson has investigated the sites of many of the *padrões*.

On the purposes, progress and results of the Portuguese move to the East as a whole, a number of important works have appeared in recent years. They include: V. Magalhães Godinho, *Os descobrimentos e a economia mundial*, 2 vols., Lisbon 1965–68, and *L'Economie de l'empire portugais aux XVe et XVIe siècles*, Paris, 1969; M. Mollat and P. Adam, eds., *Les aspects internationaux de la découverte océanique aux XVe et XVIe siècles*, Paris, 1966; M.A.P. Meilink-Roelofsz, *Asian Trade and European Influence in the Indonesian Archipelago between 1500 and 1630*, The Hague, 1962; D. Lach, *Asia in the Making of Europe*, vol. I, Chicago, 1965. An excellent rapid survey is given in the first few chapters of C.R. Boxer, *The Portuguese Seaborne Empire*, London and New York, 1969.

On the Atlantic crossing and the discovery of the Americas, S.E. Morison—whose *Admiral of the Ocean Sea* (2 vols., Boston, 1942) remains the standard work on Columbus as a maritime discoverer—has added *The European Discovery of America, the Northern Voyages*, New York, 1971. The best English version of the Columbus journal is *The Journal of Christopher Columbus*, edited by L.A. Vigneras, Cambridge, 1960. An English version of Hernando Colón's *History* appeared in 1959: B. Keen, ed. and trans., *The Life of the Admiral Christopher Columbus by His Son Ferdinand*, New Brunswick, N.J., 1959. J.A. Williamson, in *The Cabot Voyages and Bristol Discovery under Henry VII*, Cambridge, 1962, sets out the little that is known about John Cabot. On the English north Atlantic voyages in general, the present state of knowledge and conjecture is summarized in D.B. Quinn, *England and the Discovery of America, 1481–1620*, New York, 1973. Controversy about Vespucci—whether he made two voyages or four, how far south he sailed in 1501, and so forth—continues. Recent contributions are R. Levillier, *Américo Vespucio*, Madrid, 1966 (four voyages and 50 degrees south); V.D. Sierra, *Amérigo Vespucci; el enigma de la historia de América*, Madrid, 1968; and most authoritative, a series of articles by G. Caraci, in *Imago Mundi* and elsewhere, all strongly critical of the Levillier thesis. Caraci's own interpretation, which seems convincing, is stated succinctly in "The Vespucian problems—what point have they reached?", *Imago Mundi* 18, 1964. On Verrazzano, whose 1524 voyage ended the first phase of North American exploration, the last word, probably, is in L.C. Wroth, *The Voyages of Giovanni da Verrazzano*, New Haven, 1970. On the exploration of the Caribbean an excellent recent work, full of geographical insight and controversial *obiter dicta,* is C.O. Sauer, *The Early Spanish Main,* Berkeley, 1966.

Magellan's exploits have provoked considerably less scholarly controversy than those of Columbus or Vespucci, though many questions about them remain unanswered. C. McKew Parr, *Ferdinand Magellan, Circumnavigator,* New York, 1964, is essentially a reprint of his earlier book, *So Noble a Captain,* New York, 1953 (which, curiously, is not included in Penrose's bibliography). It supersedes neither the much older biography in English, F.H.H. Guillemard, *The Life of Ferdinand Magellan and the First Circumnavigation of the Globe,* London and New York, 1890, nor the excellent J. Denucé, *Magellan, La question des Moluques et la première circumnavigation du globe,* Brussels, 1911. Two important recent publications on Magellan are: C. E. Nowell, ed., *Magellan's Voyage around the World: Three Contemporary Accounts,* Evanston, 1962, which reprints the Robertson (1906) translation of Pigafetta's narrative, without Robertson's apparatus, but with a very good introduction; and Antonio Pigafetta, *Magellan's Voyage: A Narrative Account of the First Circumnavigation,* translated and edited by R.A. Skelton, 2 vols., New Haven, 1969. This contains a facsimile of the early French MS. of Pigafetta in the possession of Yale University; a highly decorative as well as a thoroughly scholarly edition. A very useful bibliography of works on Magellan has appeared recently: M. Torodash, "Magellan Historiography," *Hispanic American Historical Review,* LI, May 1971.

It is difficult to follow voyages of discovery without the use of maps; but it is impossible, in a modest volume such as this, to reproduce maps in sufficient number or on a large enough scale, to illustrate the voyages in intelligible detail. To follow the story closely, the reader must have an atlas at hand. As for contemporary maps—maps which give clues not only to where the explorers went, but to where they thought they had been —these are even more difficult to reproduce on a scale large enough to be of any use. Most of the maps and charts mentioned in this book are manuscripts, preserved for the most part in libraries in Europe; and even of printed early maps, few copies survive. A good general introduction to the cartography of discovery is R.A. Skelton, *Explorers' Maps,* London, 1958. Of the various facsimile collections, the following are the most valuable: A.E. Nordenskiöld, *Facsimilé-Atlas to the Early History of Cartography,* Stockholm, 1889; R. Almagia, *Monumenta cartographica Vaticana,* 2 vols., Rome, 1944; *Mapas españoles de América, siglos XV–XVII,* Madrid, 1951; A. Cortesão and A. Teixeira de Mota, eds., *Portugaliae Monumenta Cartographica,* 6 vols., Lisbon, 1960–62. This last, the most lavish of all, has detailed descriptions in Portuguese and in English. It was issued in connection with the 1960 celebrations in honor of Prince Henry, and is the most splendid of all monuments to his memory.

Index

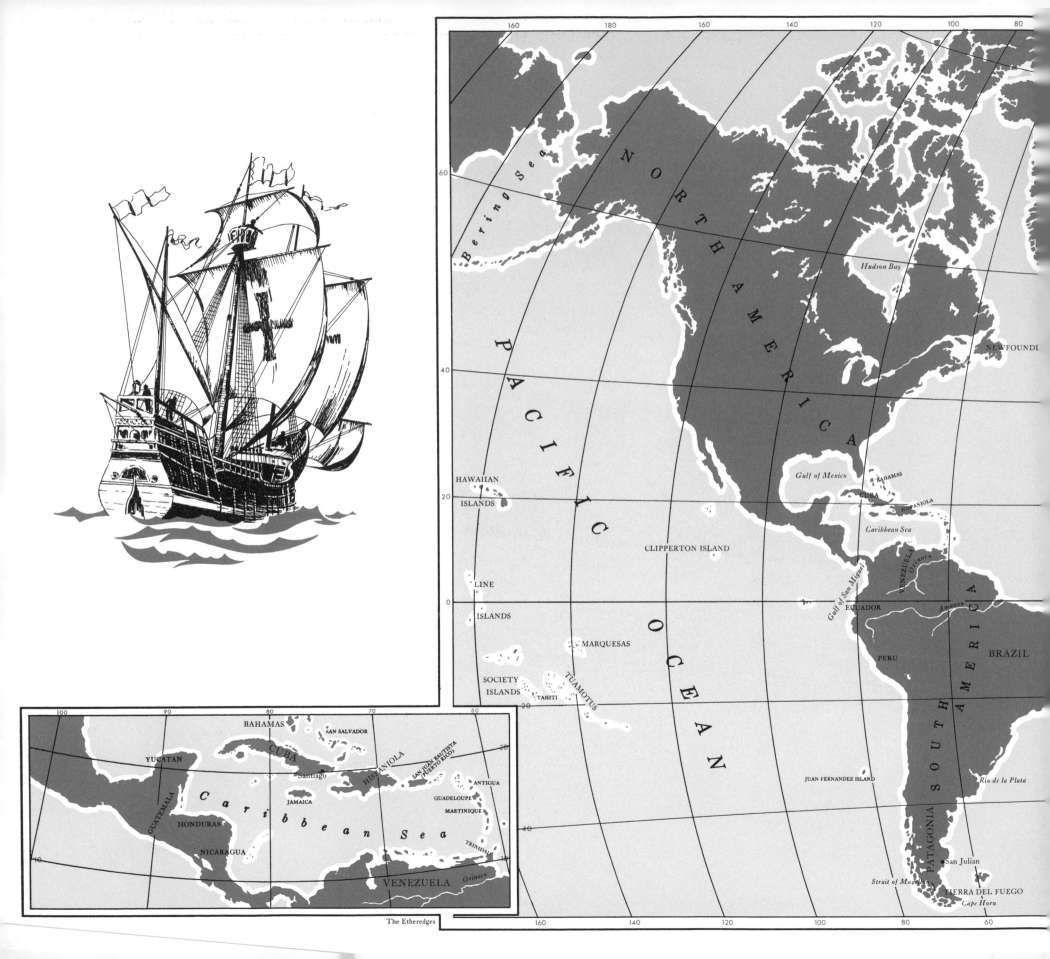

160   180   160   140   120   100   80

60

Bering Sea

NORTH AMERICA

Hudson Bay

40

NEWFOUNDL

P A C I F I C

HAWAIIAN
ISLANDS

Gulf of Mexico   BAHAMAS
CUBA
HISPANIOLA

Caribbean Sea

CLIPPERTON ISLAND

VENEZUELA   Orinoco

LINE

0

ISLANDS

Gulf of San Miguel   ECUADOR   Amazon

MARQUESAS

O C E A N

PERU   BRAZIL

SOCIETY
ISLANDS   TAHITI   TUAMOTUS

S O U T H   A M E R I C A

20

JUAN FERNANDEZ ISLAND   Rio de la Plata

40

PATAGONIA

San Julian

Strait of Magellan   TIERRA DEL FUEGO
Cape Horn

160   140   120   100   80   60

100   90   80   70   60

BAHAMAS   SAN SALVADOR

YUCATAN   CUBA   HISPANIOLA   SAN JUAN BAUTISTA
(PUERTO RICO)   20

Santiago   ANTIGUA

GUATEMALA   C a r i b b e a n   S e a   GUADELOUPE

JAMAICA   MARTINIQUE

HONDURAS

NICARAGUA   TRINIDAD

10

VENEZUELA   Orinoco